INTRODUCTION
TO
EDUCATIONAL
ADMINISTRATION

Roald F. Campbell
The University of Chicago

John E. Corbally, Jr.
The Ohio State University

John A. Ramseyer
The Ohio State University

Allyn and Bacon, Inc., Boston, 1966

Introduction

to

Educational

Administration

Third Edition

Library of Congress Catalog Card Number: 66-11453

Printed in the United States of America

To Della, Betty, and Zoa

Foreword

The Third Edition of this book, like the editions that went before it, has two major purposes. Primarily, we have prepared the volume to assist in the orientation of the prospective educational administrator. We have thought it necessary that such a person get a view of the field and also of himself as a possible worker in it. We believe the student or beginning administrator with this information will be in a better position to decide whether or not such a profession is the one for him. Should he decide in the affirmative, the book can be useful in helping him plan his initial preparation for the job and for his continued professional development.

A second purpose of this book is to give teachers an understanding of the role of administrative personnel in the schools. The book will help them, as teachers, to participate more effectively in administration. For those teachers who may be interested in becoming administrators, it will suggest ways of getting into the field.

Certain sections of the book may also be useful to many practicing administrators. For instance, the academic study of some administrators has included little material on the administrative process, leadership behavior, social systems, or policy formation. This book may be helpful to school board members and interested lay citizens who wish to know more about educational administration. By acquainting such people with the field, with its purposes and its problems, the book will give them a better understanding of administration in their own schools and school districts. Finally, the book may provide useful information for those administrators and educators who are working to improve programs for the selection and training of administrative personnel for the schools.

In the preparation of this book, we have taken certain positions. We believe that the field of educational administration is now too comprehensive to be adequately surveyed; thus a first book should be an *introduction to,* not a *survey of,* the field. Such a book, we believe, should be concerned as much with helping a prospective administrator to understand himself as with helping him to understand the job. We are convinced that educational administration covers a wide range of positions, of which the school superintendency, although very important, is but one. In order to provide a more adequate concept of educational administration, we deal with the purpose of educational administration and then present four ways of viewing the field. In addition to considering the internal operation of schools, we also examine the external forces in society that impinge upon school operation. Finally, we take the position that competent administrative leadership is crucial to the perpetuation of the democratic way of life in America.

This volume is organized into three parts. In the first part we deal with the actual job, the tasks that comprise it, the steps of the administrative process, leadership in administration, and administration of the school as a social system. In the second part we examine the administrator as an individual, in terms of the demands made on him by the job and the qualifications necessary to meet these demands. We also suggest methods of determining one's potential for the job and ways of preparing oneself for an administrative position. In the last part we discuss the field of educational administration as a whole, its opportunities and challenges as a profession, and emphasize the role of administrative leadership in a democratic society.

This book is built upon the conviction that an understanding of educational administration is developed as one examines concepts and relates them to actual experiences. This posits a partnership between the campus and the field. Each chapter of the book should be seen as a part of the whole rather than as a separate entity. Thus the reader will obtain maximum meaning from the book if he sees the content of these chapters as aspects of a developmental process of concept building.

How may this book be used? As we see it, the book can be useful as a text in the beginning course in educational administration. In many institutions such a course is available to students early in the graduate program. Actually, the material in the book has been used with many groups of graduate students beginning their study of educational administration. The questions, concerns, and reactions of these people have helped shape the book into its present form. We are grateful for their help.

We are also grateful to those contributors to the profession of educational administration who have helped create the changes that have necessitated this Third Edition. Society itself, as well as the technological advancements of our world, has been responsible for much of this change. But, to be more specific, the role of the school as an instrument of social policy is clearer than it was when we last revised this volume. The issues of desegregation and cultural deprivation have been faced more squarely in recent years than ever before. The critical nature of relationships between teachers, both as individuals and within organized groups, and boards of education and administrators has come into sharp focus. The role of the federal government in education is now firmly established; the pertinent question is no longer *whether,* but *how?* All of these and other changes since the appearance of the Second Edition have been considered as much as it is possible to do so in an introductory treatment of educational administration.

We have tried here to give frank expression to our convictions about the book and our aspirations for it. We want it to make a contribution to the growing professionalism of an important calling. We know that the extent to which this proves to be the case now rests in the hands of those who use the book.

R.F.C.

J.E.C., Jr.

J.A.R.

Contents

    The Development of Administration   66
    The Development of Educational Administration   75
    An Overview of Educational Administration   83
    Unique Aspects of Educational Administration   87
    Theory in Administration   92
        Suggested Activities   94
        Selected Readings   95

4. THE ADMINISTRATIVE TASKS   96

    School-Community Relationships   97
    Curriculum and Instruction   102
    Pupil Personnel   108
    Staff Personnel   112
    Physical Facilities   120
    Finance and Business Management   124
    Organizing to Achieve the Tasks   129
        Suggested Activities   136
        Selected Readings   137

5. THE ADMINISTRATIVE PROCESS   138

    The General Concept   138
    Steps in the Process   144
    A Case Report   151
        Suggested Activities   161
        Selected Readings   161

6. LEADERSHIP BEHAVIOR AND EDUCATIONAL ADMINISTRATION   163

    Some Preliminary Considerations   164
    Leadership Behavior   171
    Implications for Educational Administrators   178
    Deterrents to Educational Leadership   184
    Status Is Not Enough   187
        Suggested Activities   187
        Selected Readings   188

7. THE SCHOOL AS A SOCIAL SYSTEM   189

    The Conceptual Work   189
    Some Empirical Studies   196
    Limitations and Extensions of the Theory   203

Part Two *The Man* 283

INTRODUCTION
TO
EDUCATIONAL
ADMINISTRATION

Part One:

The Job

PART ONE DISCUSSES THE JOB OF EDUCATIONAL ADMINISTRATION. To introduce the subject, we have presented in Chapter 1 a number of incidents that have actually occurred in schools, and in Chapter 2 a survey of the historical background of the development of the American school system and the relationship of that development to administration. Chapter 3 treats the meaning and purpose of administration. Chapters 4 through 7 present a four-way view of administration: its tasks, the administrative process, leadership behavior, and the school as a social system. An understanding of these four views, the authors believe, is imperative to an understanding of the job of educational administration. Too often in the past, failure to recognize their importance has resulted in administration by recipe in place of organizational problem-solving. This part concludes, in Chapters 8 and 9, with a discussion of the important roles of school personnel in administration and of policy formation in education.

1

1

A Preliminary Look

at Administration

WHAT IS THE FUNCTION OF ADMINISTRATION IN THE MODERN SCHOOL? Does it have a counterpart in business, government, the military, and other established organizations? How does educational administration differ from, and in what ways is it similar to, administration in these other organizations? What are the best modern theories and expert opinions with regard to the art or science of administration? What contributions do administrators make to help organizations become more efficient and effective? What should the role and responsibility of the educational administrator be in working with civic and other leaders to solve the many complex problems that confront communities and people in today's rapidly changing, high-pressure, pluralistic society? What are the duties of the principal, the supervisor, and the superintendent of schools? If I were to be employed in one of these positions, what would be expected of me? Could I live up to those expectations? These are a few of the questions asked by those who are anticipating educational administration as a career.

Teachers, too, are concerned about the roles of administrators in the schools in which they work. The beginning teacher, for example, wants to know what the principal of the school "will be like." How much will he help? Will he understand that I may have certain difficulties in getting started? May I go to him with my questions? How much administrative support can I expect if parents and others are somewhat critical of my beginning efforts? Experienced teachers may have similar questions, but they know that teachers have a part in decision-making. They have worked with parent-teacher organizations, and some of them have participated actively with lay groups in educational planning. These teachers are asking for a clarification of their roles, and the roles to be played by others, in the important decisions that are to be made about school matters.

This book is designed to help both the prospective administrator and the teacher answer the basic questions: Why is administration necessary? What is it? How does it affect me? What role do I play in the administration of schools today? The student's problem is to answer these questions and others that come to mind as facts, issues, and propositions are presented in this and following chapters.

Chapter 1 describes some interesting incidents that have occurred in certain schools and school districts. Similar happenings could certainly be cited by the readers. It is suggested that these incidents be read largely for the purpose of identifying the problems that require solution. The reader should attempt to play the role of the administrator of the school in which the incident took place and think about the means he would use to solve these problems. The reader should understand that there is probably no "right" solution to the problems presented in the incidents. Even experts in administration and the social sciences have conflicting opinions about how some of these matters should be handled.

SOME INCIDENTS

JIMMY IS PROMOTED

Jimmy was in the eighth grade. He had been a good citizen of the Midland schools since the time he enrolled as a pupil in the fourth grade. Although slow to learn, he was co-operative with his teachers and liked by his classmates. When the boys chose sides to play ball, Jimmy was always among the first selected. His friends admitted that he was "a little dumb, but a nice guy."

When Jimmy transferred to the Midland schools in the fourth grade, his report cards showed that he had received failing marks in reading and arithmetic several times. Because these failures persisted, his teachers thought it best that he repeat the fourth grade. In the two ensuing years his progress was fair; it appeared that he had found about the right level of learning for him. After all, he had an I.Q. of only about 90 and, with considerable help from his teachers, he had managed to pass the fifth and sixth grades. In the seventh grade he failed arithmetic and history. Again he was required to repeat the grade. Now in the spring of the year he was one of six eighth-graders whose promotion was a subject of deep concern among the faculty members.

A faculty meeting was called by Superintendent Jones. The teachers of both the elementary and secondary divisions of the school were present, since the business of this meeting seemed to concern both groups. The first item on the agenda, "Promotions," had been discussed many times in the lunch room, the halls, and any place where a few teachers chanced to meet.

"This year, as has been true in years past, we have a number of pupils who, the elementary school teachers think, should be admitted to high school even though their work in the elementary grades has not been too satisfactory. According to board policy these teachers have the authority to promote them, but knowing that some of you would be displeased, I thought that we should discuss the matter together," was Superintendent Jones's opening remark.

Mr. DeMuth, the high school mathematics teacher, asked, "Who are the kids being passed this time?"

Mrs. Wirth, the head teacher for the elementary school, read off the list of names.

"Well, take Jimmy Keith, for example. We all like him and all of that, but from what I've heard of him he just can't do high school work," said DeMuth.

A number of teachers joined in the discussion. Most of the elementary school teachers took the position that these pupils were working almost to the limit of their individual capacities. High school teachers, on the other hand, reflected the feeling that grade school teachers "were not tough enough."

DeMuth, the most outspoken member of the high school staff, said, "I don't suppose that there is anything we can do about it now, but I'm warning you, if he comes into my algebra class, he's a dead duck."

After a few minutes of this kind of talk, Superintendent Jones broke into the conversation with, "Now that Jim has been pointed out as our example, I guess we would have to admit that he might not get as much out of high school as most of our students. Let's keep in mind, though, that he is only one of six pupils that we are talking about."

One of the high school teachers expressed his point of view this way: "It isn't Jim. I like him. But you know what people are saying. 'High school graduation doesn't mean anything any more.' How can we make it mean something if we keep graduating these morons all the time? The elementary teachers don't have to take the rap for this, but we do. I'm against it."

Miss King, a teacher in the elementary school, said, "Isn't the policy on matters of promotion clear? I thought we settled all of this two years ago. Now, here we go again."

Sensing that this was the time to channel the meeting into a more objective course, Superintendent Jones agreed that a policy had been adopted by the board of education two years ago. He then read from the Teacher's Handbook this statement of board policy on promotions:

1. When the work of any child has been below the minimum level of achievement commonly accepted for promotion, the case may, upon recommendation of the grade teacher, be referred to the appropriate faculty to be acted upon in terms of their judgment as to what is best for the child and the school.

2. No child shall be retained in any grade more than one year, or in either the elementary or secondary school more than two years beyond the normal number of years for pupils to complete this work.

"Although I was not superintendent at the time this policy was adopted," he continued, "I would interpret this last statement to mean that when a child has been retained in any grade for one year or in either division of the school for the two years, the faculty has no choice in the matter. Promotion is automat . . ."

"That's just it. You said it!" shouted DeMuth. "Promotion is automatic. What do the teachers have to say about it? The kids know that. Do you think that makes them respect us any more? They know they'll pass. What should they care. . . ."

Superintendent Jones interrupted to say, "I wasn't finished with my statement, Mr. DeMuth. The policy statement does give the faculty the right to decide at least four times in a pupil's career—twice in the elementary grades and twice in high school—whether or not to promote him.

"I'm not saying that I agree with the policy. I'm merely stating that according to the policies we inherited—those statements in your handbook—the elementary teachers have acted within their rights as nearly as I can determine. The high school teachers have a similar privilege—or responsibility—for the pupils in that division."

Another high school teacher, seemingly resigned to accepting the decision in part, commented, "O.K., we get Jim! But I thought we were going to consider. . . ."

What do you suppose the last teacher had in mind? Is there some alternative to the present policy that might be considered? Whose responsibility is it to mention alternatives? What should the superintendent do now? Given the action of the teachers of the elementary school, the dissatisfaction of the high school teachers, and the board policy, what course of action would you recommend?

MERIT PAY AND THE NOVILLE TEACHERS' UNION

The large suburban school district of the City of Noville enjoyed a record of amicable teacher-administrator-board relations for a number of years. But recently there have been difficulties in this area. Two events appear to be related to the present problem: one, the introduction of a merit salary schedule; and two, the organization and growth of the Noville chapter of the American Federation of Teachers.

In 1959 a large automobile subassembly plant was built in the area between Noville and the nearby metropolis of New Troy. This new industry not only swelled school enrollment generally, it also changed the composition of the Noville Board of Education. Less than eighteen months after the plant opened, two of its executives were elected to the five-man board. The new board members were sincerely interested in better education for the children of Noville. Largely because of their efforts, several changes were made to provide greater diversity in the curricula of the schools and to increase teachers' salaries.

The desire to attract better teachers to Noville led the board to consider the adoption of a merit salary plan. The board studied the problem for a few months and became convinced that the idea was sound. In December 1961, the teachers were notified that their 1962–63 salaries would be based in part on merit. The plan was fairly complex. It involved 19 salary steps, a detailed evaluative process to be carried out by principals, and four possible ratings.

Teachers rated "highly competent" were to be given double increments on the salary schedule; "competent" teachers would receive single increments up to Step 14; "satisfactory" teachers would receive single jumps up to Step 10. "Unsatisfactory" teachers were to be placed on probation for one year without any increment, and, if they did not attain a "satisfactory" rating after the probationary year, they were to be released. Salary levels for beginning teachers were not increased, but top salaries for teachers with masters' degrees were increased $800. A list of the criteria to be used in the evaluation process was distributed to each teacher.

While these events were taking place, the teachers were changing their professional organization alignments. Before 1959, over 85 percent of the teaching corps belonged to the Noville Teachers' Association (NTA), about 5 percent belonged to the local AFT, and 10 percent were unaffiliated. After 1959, the Noville AFT, spurred by the success of the teachers' union in the New Troy system, began to pick up membership. Just before the merit pay plan was announced, the AFT membership was about 35 percent of the total staff, while NTA membership had dropped to some 55 percent. By the second month after the new pay plan was announced, the AFT membership had increased to over 65 percent of the total staff. According to one union member, about 85 percent of the teaching staff were opposed to the merit plan, and 100 percent were "burned up" because the board had not included teachers in devising or considering the plan. The AFT made its big gains in membership mainly because it promised to "do something" about the merit pay plan.

And do something it did! Copying the procedures of its brother union in New Troy, the Noville AFT was able to become recognized, in strict accordance with state legal procedures and rulings, as the exclusive bargaining agent for all classroom teachers in the system. Although the union was officially recognized as the exclusive bargaining agency for all Noville teachers on April 23, 1962, no contract was entered into with the board of education for the 1962–1963 school year. The merit plan went into effect as scheduled. No teachers were rated below "satisfactory" during the year, but even so the majority of teachers remained violently opposed to the plan.

At the May meeting of the Noville Board of Education, the teachers' union made its first contract proposal to the board. The proposal contained seven "articles" and sixty-three different "items" covering matters of working conditions, grievance procedures, dues check-off, union-superintendent consultations, and teachers' salaries. The teachers' union specifically demanded that the merit salary system be abandoned, and that a new salary schedule with "general salary increases" be adopted. Major points made by the teachers' union against the merit plan included:

1. Merit increases are unfair and destroy morale.

2. There is no good system for measuring merit, and therefore the idea is not workable.

3. Politics and favoritism will inevitably enter into evaluation.

4. Merit plans will ultimately destroy the professionalism of teachers.[1]

The board received the union's proposal and stated that it would require at least one month to study it before a decision could be made. Since that time the board and union officials have been unsuccessful in their attempts to reach a contract agreement. There are no provisions in the laws of the state with regard to arbitration in cases of board-union impasse. The board refuses to accept the union's demands, and the union has threatened to take the teachers out on strike. Strikes by public employees are illegal under state law, but teacher alienation and discontent is so great in Noville that a majority of the staff appears to be willing to violate the law.

---

[1] From "A Proposed Agreement Between The Board of Education of the City of Noville and Local 23, American Federation of Teachers, AFL-CIO for the Period July 1, 1963—June 30, 1964," p. 4. Submitted to the board on May 16, 1963.

This case points up some important questions about the scope, limitations, and domain of negotiations. What is properly negotiable? Are there certain aspects of educational administration that are reserved for the board and the superintendent? Should teachers' unions have a voice in the determination of the school program or should they be limited to salaries and working conditions of certificated personnel? To what degree, if at all, does the teachers' union have a responsibility to exercise its power to affect policy development?

MOTIVATING STUDENTS IN NORTHTON:
A STUDY IN FRUSTRATION

Northton is the capital of an important industrial and agricultural state in the Midwest. The population of the Northton metropolitan area is slightly over 1,000,000 persons. This population is largely middle-class, native-born, and politically conservative. About 4 percent of the core city population of 600,000 persons has recently immigrated to Northton from the Appalachian area, and about 14 percent is Negro.

The Northton City School System has a total enrollment of just over 100,000 pupils. There are 9 senior high schools (grades 10–12), 24 junior high schools (grades 7–9), and 132 elementary schools (grades K–6) in the system.

Much of the southeastern section of Northton is comprised of low-value slum or slum clearance dwellings. A large percentage of the city's Negro, chronically unemployed, and "on-relief" citizens live in this section. Most of the teen-age children living within this part of the city are sent to the four junior high schools and the one high school (Tower Park) which are found in the eight-square-mile area.

A recent survey of the Tower Park enrollment area revealed that most of the homes are either in low-cost public housing projects or in somewhat higher cost (in terms of rent) crowded, semislum apartments. Less than 10 percent of the residents of the area own their own homes.

Over 12 percent of the family units in this area have no male head of family present in the home. A large percentage of the female heads of family are unwed mothers, others have been deserted by their husbands, or the husbands are in prison. Of the family units with male heads of family present, 27 percent of the men are unemployed. In 11 percent of these families, *both* parents are unemployed. Over 40 percent of all family units are dependent upon some form of welfare or unemployment payments. A rough breakdown of the welfare picture is as follows: 24 percent of all family units receive Aid to Dependent Children, 9 percent receive Poor Relief, 7 percent are drawing Unemployment Compensation, and less than 1 percent receive Aid for the Blind and Aged.

No matter what instruments are used for evaluation, there is little question that Tower Park High School and its feeder junior high schools qualify as depressed or underprivileged area schools.

The crux of this case involves the frustrations experienced by Mrs. Beck, a teacher of commercial subjects at Tower Park, as she attempted to help some of her students help themselves to overcome some of the disadvantages and deprivations under which they lived.

Mrs. Beck was in her eighth year as a teacher at Tower Park during the months when the incidents described took place. She invariably had a warm relationship with her students; she was understanding, firm, and fair. Her students recognized that Mrs. Beck was a teacher who respected them, was interested in them, and wanted to help them.

As a result of her experience over the years at Tower Park, Mrs. Beck was convinced that one of her pupils' most important needs was that of "gaining a feeling that they have a chance in life," a feeling that "they are not destined to spend their lives living on the relief roles as most of their parents have." In short, despite her occasional feelings of hopelessness about the school, she believed that the students needed personal accomplishments and success experiences in order to demonstrate to themselves that there was some opportunity to move out of the environment in which they lived.

Mrs. Beck spent a great deal of her off-duty time trying to find ways to provide these experiences for her pupils. She had learned long ago that success in class work and activities was not enough for these children—this kind of success motivated them for a very short time. The culture from which her students came recognized only more tangible gains, such as success in athletics or making money. She could not, of course, do much to help her students become star athletes, so she attempted to provide for achievement through teaching wage-earning skills.

For the past five years Mrs. Beck had been helping students in her advanced typing, bookkeeping, and general office practice courses obtain part-time employment in business offices throughout the city. She had been able to develop many contacts with employers in Northton, most of whom were sympathetic to the problems her students faced. Students recommended by Mrs. Beck were, in almost every case, found to be dependable, honest, and, for their age and experience levels, competent. Thus the relationship between Mrs. Beck, the employers, and the student-workers gradually but steadily improved over the years. Most of the students enrolled at Tower Park were aware of the opportunity to "prove that they could do something" and to "earn some money" which Mrs. Beck tried to provide. Consequently, her classes were always full to capacity, and motivation was high. Mrs. Beck felt that, although her efforts fell far short of solving all the problems of all her students, her work was a promising step in the right direction.

During the previous four years, increasing numbers of students had been placed annually in part-time positions. The program seemed to be developing very well; student morale and motivation, while still not high enough, were definitely improving. But far from being content with her efforts, Mrs. Beck's constant concern was to find more jobs—and better jobs, if possible —for more of her students.

On Thursday, November 12, Mrs. Beck was asked to stop in at the principal's office after school. The principal, Mr. Gordon, was aware of and appreciated Mrs. Beck's efforts to help her students. He had offered her constant support and encouragement and had tried to see that she received all the teaching materials and supplies that she requisitioned. Many times Mr. Gordon had helped Mrs. Beck find positions for her students, and he felt a personal concern for the progress of her program. After her last class, Mrs. Beck stepped into Mr. Gordon's office. After they exchanged greetings and some small talk, the following conversation took place:

GORDON: Mrs. Beck, I feel badly about having to tell you, but it looks like we may be in trouble with your job program.

MRS. BECK: Oh, Mr. Gordon, what do you mean! The children are all old enough to work, they all have work permits, their parents approve, and I've had no complaints from any of the employers. Do you mean that the people downtown at the central office don't think that I should be getting jobs for the students?

GORDON: No, that's not it at all. I wish it were that simple. You see, this afternoon I had a call from Mr. Bartholemew of the County Welfare Department. He told me that he had received a complaint from an 'interested citizen' with regard to 'chiseling' by relief recipients. The 'chiselers' involve the families of the children in your program, or so he said.

MRS. BECK: But Mr. Gordon, I just don't understand! What have welfare and 'chiseling' to do with the work of my students? What are they trying to do?

GORDON: Well, Bartholemew said that he probably shouldn't have called at all, but that he wanted to let us know that because of this complaint he would be *forced* to make an investigation of the incomes of some of the relief recipients who have children in Tower Park. I don't quite understand it myself, but it seems that there is a standard allotment set by the state and county for the monthly amount to which a family receiving Aid to Dependent Children or other welfare funds is entitled. Bartholemew said that if *any* family receiving welfare funds has any income at all from any member, this income *must* be reported to the Welfare Department and it *must be deducted* from the amount of aid to which the family is entitled.

MRS. BECK: Do you mean to tell me that the tiny bit of income that these children make must be reported? The *kids* aren't on relief!

GORDON: That's exactly what I said to him. But his answer was that the law is clear—the income must be reported, and no matter how little it is, or who makes it, it has to be deducted from the sum the family usually gets from the Welfare Department. Bartholemew said that it was a state law and that if anyone pushed the matter further the parties involved could lose their welfare benefits entirely. They could even be prosecuted for fraud.

MRS. BECK: But it's not fair! Isn't there anything we can do? How can I face the children when they find out about this? How can I explain to them why they can't get anything for their work? Think of all the work in school that they've done so that they could get these jobs, and that doesn't include all the work I've done to get this thing going. I don't care if it is the law, how can we be expected to help these children become self-respecting, productive members of the community if this is what the community is going to do to them as soon as they begin to try to help themselves? Actually, it's forcing them *not* to try. What sort of person would do such a thing? Who could have complained?

GORDON: I know how you must feel, I feel the same way. I think it's one of the most unjust situations I've heard of in a long time. Mr. Bartholemew couldn't tell me who lodged the complaint, but from the way he talked I got the impression that it was someone from a family in our area; someone who is envious because his child does not have a job. He didn't say that the kids would have to quit their jobs, only that they would have to declare their earnings so that they could be deducted. I pointed out to him that this was rather a poor way to help these kids—the families' total income would be the same whether the kids worked or not. They would be, in effect, working just for the sake of working. These children aren't stupid. They can see that they will be just as well off to stay home and watch T.V. I'm sure their parents won't be able to see any reason for them to continue working for nothing when they could be home to help around the house. Bartholemew said that he recognized the problem that we face, but that his hands were tied—he must see to it that the law is followed. He pointed out that any students from families not receiving welfare aid would not be affected by the law. I felt like saying, 'Thanks a lot,' but he was only doing what he had to do, and I don't think he likes doing this at all.

MRS. BECK: Well, about one-third of the children we have on jobs will not be affected, but the ones that will be hurt are the very ones who need the jobs and the self-respect that goes with them most. Isn't there anything we can do? I mean, after all, if we can't get any more help and cooperation than this, then what's the use?

GORDON: Well, I've tried to think of what we might do. We can try to talk Bartholemew into looking the other way on this. I'm willing to go with you to speak with him. We know that what we're trying to do for these children is right, but we have to consider what might happen if looking the other way backfires and these families lose all their welfare aid because of us. If this happens the parents are going to blame us, the schools, and their children for the loss of the little money they get—and rightly so, since we have been warned of how the law reads. I don't know if we have the right to risk the parents' much-needed income in spite of the need we see for continuing our program.

MRS. BECK: No, you're right, we can't risk other people's money or take the chance of being the agency that involves them in legal difficulties. But isn't there anything we can do . . . what am I going to say to the children? I've been trying for years to instill in them the belief that effort will pay off for rich man, poor man, white man, or colored man. Now this happens and makes a lie of all that I've said as far as they're concerned.

GORDON: The only other thing that I can think of is to take this problem to the superintendent and to the board of education. Perhaps we can get support from the public if our case is presented to them. The Urban League and the NAACP should be willing to help us. The newspapers may help, but you know how the city is 'down' on relief recipients. The newspapers are continuously crying about 'chiselers' and reliefers who drive in cabs or Cadillacs to pick up their money—some of those reporters should spend a week with us just seeing how these people really live. The problem of explaining to the students is going to be a tough one. I'll try to help you. We're going to have to do some fancy talking to keep this from destroying their morale completely.

In this case, an interpretation of parents' legal rights seems to thwart the efforts of the teacher and principal, who are attempting to help their disadvantaged students. What might have been done to resolve problems resulting from such restrictions? Should the principal take the problem to the superintendent? What might the superintendent do? How far should schools be expected to go in solving this kind of problem? What other community agencies should schools be working with on problems of this kind? How would you explain what had happened to the students involved in this situation? What are some other factors that tend to limit the schools' efforts to help such children?

THE CHRISTMAS ASSEMBLY IN P. S. 42[2]

Late in October, the mother of a Jewish child attending school in Central City's P. S. 42 called the Central City Jewish Community Relations Council (the CRC) and reported that a Nativity scene was planned for the school

[2] This case has been adapted from "Conflict in Central City: The Christmas Assembly in P. S. 42," case number 19 in the University Council for Educational Administration's *Case Series in Educational Administration*. Written by Glenn Immegart.

Christmas program. Her child had been asked to take part in the Nativity scene, which was, according to tradition, a short two-minute scene at the close of the assembly program. Essentially a tableau, the scene was a live posed Nativity representation that was accompanied by Christmas carols. Reportedly, the parent contacting the CRC was sensitive to this Christologically centered part of the program.

The Director of the CRC and a local Rabbi, who was the Chairman of the CRC Church-State Committee, decided to approach the problem in a most direct manner. The Director called the principal of P. S. 42 and asked for an appointment to discuss the Christmas program with him. Principal Evans was informed at the time that the CRC Director would be bringing the Rabbi along to the informal meeting. Admittedly somewhat worried, Principal Evans decided that it might be best to include a teacher in the meeting to represent the interests of the school staff.

The main concern voiced by the CRC representatives was that the Nativity scene per se was objectionable to many Jewish parents and children. It was suggested that, due to the sensitivity to this part of the program, it might be possible to substitute something in its place. The CRC indicated specifically that they hoped the Nativity scene might be removed from the current Christmas program. Especially, the Christological nature of the Nativity scene was viewed by the CRC representatives as confusing to the thinking of young Jewish and other non-Christian children. Too, the CRC representatives felt that such an observance tended to inculcate a particular kind of religion.

According to all concerned, rapport at this meeting was very good, although relationships were somewhat tense; further, all agreed that Principal Evans understood clearly just what the complaint was. Evans concluded the discussion by stating that he would take the matter under advisement and would consult with the Central City Superintendent of Schools. He indicated that his decision would be communicated to the CRC Director.

Evans felt he needed more advice before making a decision on the Nativity scene. He discussed the matter with the teachers in P. S. 42. No attempt was made to conceal what had happened, and the P. S. 42 teaching staff was not, as a body, perturbed by the possibility of losing the traditional Nativity scene from the Christmas assembly. Evans also called the Central City Superintendent of Schools, Mr. Henry Overholt, and discovered that there was no policy or rule covering this situation and, therefore, the decision was up to Evans himself. Principal Evans was also informed at this time that it was customary to yield to pressures from community groups. He was advised by the superintendent not to "crusade" or "stir up difficulties."

In light of the general reaction of the teaching staff and Superintendent Overholt, Evans was left to make the decision on the Nativity scene. Having appealed for assistance and received little direct help, he was on his own.

Personally, Evans had feelings that Christmas was not as theologically significant as Easter. Thus, he decided to remove the Nativity scene from the Christmas program. Immediately after he reached the decision, Evans notified the CRC director, and the five or six P. S. 42 teachers working on the program, of his ruling.

Shortly after announcing his decision, Principal Evans began to receive numerous telephone calls and letters criticizing him for his decision. A phone campaign had even been initiated to enlist support for the "cause." Not only was Evans besieged at school by phone calls and letters, but he also received numerous phone calls at his home, some of them quite inflammatory.

Once again Evans called the superintendent of schools to ask for direction. And he was once more assured that this was *his* problem. In light of the wave of opposition, Evans indicated to the superintendent that he might possibly have to change his decision.

On Thursday morning, December 13, one citizen residing in the attendance area of P. S. 42 called Evans' office at 8:30 A.M. and demanded that the principal reverse his decision. The man had already talked to Superintendent Overholt and had been informed that this was a local school problem and that the decision was in the hands of the principal.

The citizen, dissatisfied with the results of his overtures, gave the story to a local newspaper. In the home edition of that paper on Thursday, December 13, there appeared the following news release:

SOME OBJECT: SCHOOL PUTS NATIVITY SCENE AWAY

The principal of School 42 said today a Nativity scene at the school had been removed after some parents of pupils asked him to do so.

Thomas Evans told The News he ordered the scene dismantled in response to the request. The school is located at 3100 E. 39th.

This action prompted one parent to go to the superintendent of city schools and demand the Nativity scene be put back in the school's Christmas program.

Henry Overholt, the superintendent, said he told the man the decision was in the principal's jurisdiction since there is no city-wide policy on Christmas scenery or programs.

Original objections to the Nativity scene were made by parents who disliked having the school use what they regarded as religious scenery.

The decision regarding school programs and activities, including those relating to what might be pointed to as having religious significance, is left to the principal.

"A principal must get to know his community and fit in school activities to the sentiment of his community," Overholt pointed out.

The only policy regarding school activity and its association with religion is in the Central City school principal's manual. It states that no child shall be forced to participate in any activity that could be considered to be "against his religion."

By the time the initial news report had circulated throughout Central City, the principal had already informed the superintendent (actually early the same morning) that he had changed his mind and was going to put the Nativity scene back in the pageant because of the weight of opinion against his earlier decision. In addition, Mr. Evans authorized the following news release for the evening editions of the local newspapers:

NATIVITY SCENE OUT, BACK IN PAGEANT

The principal of School 42 said today a Nativity scene—deleted from his school's Christmas pageant—has been reinstated "because of overwhelming public pressure" and the visit of one pupil's father to the superintendent of schools.

Thomas Evans said a two-minute Nativity scene had been part of the pageant "since the first gravel was hauled to construct this building."

After that day's news releases, there was an intense reaction. Violent opposition was voiced against the original home edition story. Letters and phone calls were directed toward Evans and the paper, both in praise and in opposition to his stand.

Principal Evans' decision was made; to all intents and purposes, the die was cast. But his "administrative sixth sense" conveyed to him the relative certainty that the problem was far from being resolved.

Who should have made the decision about the Nativity scene—the principal, the superintendent, the board, or some other group? Should a principal reverse a decision he has made because of public pressure? Should teachers be involved in making decisions on matters such as the one presented in this case? How might a written policy on Christmas programs have helped in this case? What should the policy be? How would you, as principal or as superintendent, have handled this problem?

CIVIL RIGHTS AND NEIGHBORHOOD SCHOOLS IN CLEVELAND

The public schools have been focal in the civil rights movement in America during the Negro struggle for equal opportunity and full citizenship. Problems associated with segregation and the public schools are complex and emotion-packed. One issue that has continued to confront educators is the question of the neighborhood school and its effect on segregation in the public schools. Some of the dynamics involved are pointed up in a Cleveland, Ohio, incident reported by the National Committee on

Professional Rights and Responsibilities of the National Education Association. The facts reported in this case are not too unlike those found in other school districts of the United States which have faced the same issue. The following is a direct quote from the Cleveland report:

Civil Rights Strife

Negro pupils comprise approximately 52 percent of the city's public school enrollment. According to the PACE report, neighborhood residential patterns have created many all-Negro schools in the East Side area of the city. The Cleveland School Board's policy of promoting the neighborhood school concept has constituted an endorsement of de facto segregation.

Several years ago, the severe overcrowding of some of the East Side schools made it necessary to place these schools on half-day sessions. The growth of parochial schools during this period was resulting in declining enrollments in some of the city's predominantly white schools. To relieve the overcrowding of the East Side schools, the system in 1961 began transporting Negro pupils by bus to empty classrooms in the predominantly white schools of the East Side fringe areas. This was regarded by school officials as a temporary measure, to be continued only until new schools and additions could be constructed to accommodate in their own neighborhoods the transported pupils. These pupils were moved as administrative units and were not integrated into the classrooms of the receiving schools. In the view of many people, however, the policy of "separate but equal" educational opportunity was no more workable in racially segregated classrooms than the Supreme Court had ruled it to be in racially segregated schools. The protests of civil rights leaders influenced the Board to agree to a gradual diffusion of transported pupils into the classrooms of receiving schools, the process of diffusion to be complete by September 1964.

The passage of a $55 million bond issue in November 1962 opened the way to a five-year program of school construction. Included in the projected building program were a number of new schools and additions planned for certain areas in the East Side. Upon completion of these facilities, according to the Board, the transporting of Negro pupils would be discontinued. As East Side school sites were chosen, and as diffusion of transported pupils progressed, perhaps with more deliberation than speed, civil rights activity accelerated. At the same time, many parents in the areas of the receiving schools became increasingly militant against the diffusion process.

UFM Proposals

In September 1963, the United Freedom Movement (UFM), a confederation of approximately 50 civil rights groups in Cleveland, had submitted a number of proposals to the Board of Education, including a demand for immediate integration of transported classes into the receiving schools' programs, and a request for the establishment of a bureau of integration and human relations with a permanent director and staff. Further pressured by UFM picketing of School Board headquarters, the Board of Education agreed to integrate transported classes into receiving schools by early 1964.

Appointment of Human Relations Committee

At a meeting in November 1963, the Board appointed seven persons to form the nucleus committee of a citizens council on human relations, to "foster meaningful integration." At the same meeting, the Board unanimously endorsed a resolution by the president, affirming the principle of neighborhood schools. In a statement to the press, the superintendent of schools said, "Students now transported will be reassigned to their neighborhood schools when possible, probably by the end of 1964 or February 1965."

School Construction Dispute

January and February 1964 brought further racial upheaval in Cleveland, as civil rights groups protested the School Board's choice of East Side school sites by picketing and sit-in demonstrations.

According to one UFM spokesman, the building of new schools in Negro areas of the city "would only resegregate schools—not desegregate them." Three elementary schools have been the target of recent civil rights protests.

East Side residents have also objected because school sites have been poorly chosen, with little regard to the safety and well-being of the children and to future redevelopment plans of the city. The Board of Education has ignored the objections expressed by the City Planning Commission to its choice of school sites. One site is deemed unsafe because it fronts a road that will be widened to six lanes, taking some of the school property. The only means of access to this school will be from the front. A second school will be located on a site that, according to a press report, "is a house lot deep, and 13 house lots wide." The total area of the site, 1.7 acres, is considered too small by the City Planning Commission. Parents further object to the fact that in order to fit a 30-room school on this lot, the Board has approved a three-story construction plan. The third disputed school site is also considered too small, and objections have been made to its proximity to another school.

The Integration Policy Resolution

On February 10, 1964, the Board of Education adopted a resolution pledging full integration of transported pupils into receiving school classes "forthwith," but at the same time ordering an end to the transportation program as soon as new school construction would permit accommodation of pupils in their own neighborhoods.

The Letter of "Instructions"

On the day following the Board's resolution on integration of transported pupils, the president of the Board wrote a lengthy letter to the school superintendent, instructing him to "prepare a written plan in detail concerning the procedures to be followed . . . in carrying out the policies of this Board as they relate to the transportation of students, bearing in mind that it is not to be disruptive to the education program or routine of the students and that any changes be for the improvement of educational opportunities for all pupils involved only." After outlining specific instructions as to how the plan should be developed and what considerations it should include, the president of the Board concluded his letter with the following paragraphs:

I firmly believe that much of the unpreparedness of this Board for the recent episodes was due to the fact that we have not been kept thoroughly informed of plans of the administration as they relate to the objects of the recent demonstrations, and indeed that no firm, written details were available to this Board.

We intend that this situation be corrected immediately, and that this Board be completely apprised of all planning in detail, and also of communications or contacts with groups or individuals seeking to pressure this Board in any direction.

According to testimony received by the NEA Committee, this letter was received by the superintendent and published by the Board president in the Cleveland newspapers on the same date.

The day after this letter appeared in the newspapers, the superintendent submitted his resignation to the Cleveland Board of Education.

According to press accounts during this period, public reaction to the president's letter and to the superintendent's decision to retire was explosive. Citizens and teachers groups and individuals urged the Board not to accept the superintendent's resignation.

Request for Moratorium on School Construction

On February 28, 1964, the UFM requested the Cleveland School Board to declare a school-building moratorium and asked to meet with the Board to discuss the disputed buildings and to review new proposals for ending segregation. The Board rejected these requests, the president describing the UFM as "not a responsible group."

Two Months of Turmoil

During March and April 1964, the Cleveland Board of Education proceeded with the awarding of contracts for construction of the three controversial elementary schools; its integration policy for transported pupils went into effect; demonstrations, sit-ins, and school boycotts continued amidst growing protests against integration by white citizens groups. Also, during this period, the Board received the report and recommendations of its Council on Human Relations, and it received and rejected a request for a meeting on school integration policy with the Greater Cleveland Conference on Race and Religion. The public statement of the tri-faith council called upon the Board to "suspend its building program pending full consideration of the report of the Citizens Council on Human Relations and pending a re-evaluation of proposed neighborhood school construction in the light of population movement, the need for adequate facilities, techniques and site locations, and pending the results of the investigations of the National Education Association."

The Board president's response to this request was to describe the conference group as "the same old crowd we have been dealing with all along, except now they are using the Catholic Church to give themselves a presentable quality."

The week preceding the Special Committee's investigation in Cleveland brought about a series of stormy climaxes to the months of turmoil within the school system. A school boycott on April 20 kept an estimated 60,000 Negro pupils away from regular classrooms. Describing the boycott as the "ultimate repudiation" of the Board, the Emergency Clergy Committee for Civil Rights, composed of 200 Protestant and Jewish clergymen, called for the resignation of all members of the Cleveland Board of Education.

On April 24, 1964, a taxpayers suit was filed against the Board of Education, asking a halt to construction of the disputed schools and seeking $1 million in damages, charging that the Board's hasty construction of these schools was an effort to perpetuate de facto segregation.[3]

Numerous socio-economic factors helped to create Cleveland's civil rights difficulties, but actions by the school board appear to have compounded the problem. Which of these actions do you consider to be the most damaging? Did the school board behave in an appropriate manner? What alternative actions might have been taken? What is your reaction to the resignation of the superintendent? Can long-range planning by educational leaders in a community help in easing integration problems? What sort of plans might have helped in Cleveland?

The neighborhood concept is considered by many educators to be educationally sound. How, then, might a school system provide neighborhood schools and, at the same time, avoid de facto segregation?

SOME UNDERSTANDINGS

All administrative situations have a past history. Even when an entirely new district has been formed and new schools are built, there remain from the former districts certain perceptions of what schools should do and how they should be operated. Often there remain, also, certain habits or ways of making decisions that are characteristic of the people who live there. Some of the teachers who are selected for the new school have built their expectations of an administrator out of past experiences. However much the administrator would like to start anew, these remnants of past situations are real and must be reckoned with. Even the administrator is a product of his past experience and cannot escape some influence from it. So the usual administrative problem is to "move from where we are," not to "start from scratch."

PROBLEM-MAKER OR PROBLEM-SOLVER

Each of the administrative incidents described above has been lifted from context. There are additional factors and circumstances affecting all of them. It could scarcely be said that these factors are unrelated to other circumstances of the same situation. Undoubtedly the causes for incidents such as these are more complex than they appear on the surface. Occurrences of this kind represent problem situations that require solutions. To ignore them is an abdication of leadership responsibility which often allows an already serious problem in school affairs to grow worse.

[3] National Commission on Professional Rights and Responsibilities, *Cleveland, Ohio: When a Board of Education Fails to Fulfill its Proper Responsibilities* (Washington: The NEA, June 1964), pp. 19–23.

It would be naïve of any administrator to expect to find a position devoid of problems. But situations do differ in the kinds of problems they present. Often problems differ in complexity and ease of solution. The questions of concern here are: What are the causes for problems that arise? Are these causes inherent in the situation itself? Is a climate being created which is conducive to problem-making or to problem-solving?

WHAT LABEL IS APPROPRIATE?

The manner in which problems are solved often determines the label with which people characterize the administrator of their schools. Pupils might call him a *dictator* because of their perception of his rigidity in solving problems that concern them. Yet the same behavior might cause parents to speak of this administrator as a *good disciplinarian*.

Sometimes teachers refer to the principal or the superintendent as *the boss*. The term may connote a feeling of warmth and kindliness toward a person whom they fondly call the boss, or it may be a sign of disrespect for one who treats his teachers as underlings rather than as professional equals. Usually the latter interpretation results from the feeling on the part of teachers that the administrator does not consider their opinions, that he tells them what to do and does not seek their co-operation. He has to have the final answer, regardless of the time and energy which the teachers have given to the solution of the problem.

A *good manager* is a label that often goes along with efficiency. An administrator who is economical in the use of funds, who organizes his time wisely, or who manages to have appropriate facilities ready and handy is said to solve management problems effectively. Good equipment, clean school buildings, well-organized services, accounts in good condition, buses running on time and in good order, funds available when needed, and smoothly running schedules represent some of the more apparent evidence of effective management.

The *co-ordinator* is one who sees relationships and organizes events so that they appear to work in harmony. He is contrasted with the person who solves each problem as though it were unrelated to any others, for whom activity is a series of separate acts. Management problems are solved without reference to their relation to program development; public relations is the strategy employed for passing bond issues or special levies. The co-ordinator, however, relates these activities so that all administrative tasks are linked together in a meaningful chain of events that promote the instruction of boys and girls. Activity interrelated in a meaningful way is his objective.

Two abilities, at least, characterize *the leader*. He has a goal for the future and a plan for achieving it. In addition to this, he understands that effective planning for the achievement of goals involves the people who are affected by those goals. The leader marshals the intelligence of these people to get a job done. The leader is expected to furnish ideas. He in turn expects to receive ideas from his associates. He inspires people to co-operate in dealing with these ideas, so that the purposes of education are served.

In all problem situations, administrators face the decision of when to suggest, when to urge, and when to require people to act. A leader must make up his mind about who should help make a decision—the lay public, the board of education, the teachers, the pupils. What will the circumstances permit in this case? Is this the appropriate time? What are we waiting for? How will this decision affect the educational program? Will this answer make it easier or more difficult to answer questions or solve problems in the future?

Pondering such questions may render some people inactive altogether. These people are not the administrative type. An administrator must act with the full knowledge that the manner in which he acts, the way in which he involves other people in action, and the way people perceive the results of the action will determine the label that people place upon him.

DEVELOPING A CONCEPT OF ADMINISTRATION

To look at administration in terms of the problems that arise and the manner in which the administrator goes about the solution of problems, as we have done in this chapter, is just one of many ways of beginning to think about the subject. Certainly administration has a problem-solving dimension. For some people this may be the most challenging aspect of administration as a profession. Others may find it tiresome to be forever facing the prospect of solving problems created by people and the circumstances that surround them. Can administration be defined as the process of solving problems such as those presented in the incidents above? Or is it more than that? Perhaps a consideration of the following questions will be helpful in building a concept of administration.

What Is the Purpose of Administration?

Nations, states, and municipalities have their executive officers and branches of government. The armed forces, business, the church, and social, governmental, and professional organizations, like schools, have some administrative arrangement with an executive officer at the head. The duties and functions of an administrative officer and the staff which assists him must be determined by the organization to be served. A major task before the prospective administrator is that of determining how to serve the functions for which the group is organized in the way in which the group intended. This question is treated in some detail in Chapter 3.

What Is Educational Administration?

In recent years we have become increasingly conscious of the problems of human relations in all sorts of organizations. Public administration, business administration, church administration, social welfare administration, and educational administration have many common elements. Some studies have been made of military organization, procedure, and strategy in the search for clues to improve administrative behavior in other areas. Undoubtedly there is much to be learned by a transfer of knowledge from one field of administration to another. But in an attempt to get help from research in a related field, one could make a grave error by incorporating practices designed to accomplish a mission different from that of the public schools.

Big business deals in production of goods. It is prompted by the profit motive. Although it is the aim of our country and others to limit war to a protective measure to permit freedom to flourish, this is not the usual military motive. In waging war a nation must be prepared to kill and destroy if necessary. Education, on the other hand, promotes the enrichment of living. The strategies employed for the accomplishment of these various objectives may be quite different. Later we shall consider the elements which educational administration may have in common with other kinds of administration. It is sufficient for our purposes at this time to point out that in some respects educational administration is unique.

What Do People Expect of the Educational Administrator?

Research findings indicate that expectations differ. Recent studies have shown that the board of education, the faculty, and the citizens of a town differ in what they expect of their school administrators. Differences of opinion exist even within each group. Sometimes individuals hold two or more expectations, which are opposed and cannot be fulfilled, as a realization of one would deny the achievement of the other. The problem of the administrator is to determine how to deal with various expectations, however different or similar they may be.

Do I Have an Adequate Concept of the Job?

Probably not. Most prospective administrators in education come to the job through teaching. They view the administrator's job from the viewpoint of the teacher; their sympathies are with the teacher. In many respects this is good, because administrators may often be accused of failure to appreciate the teacher's point of view. But that is only one of the points of view to be considered. The pupils, the parents, the board of education, other patrons of the school, the state as a whole, and even the nation have a stake in the school. Administrative decisions must be made with due consideration for all parties concerned. To broaden one's own outlook to encompass all viewpoints, and yet not lose the vividness of each, is indeed a task of high order.

How Can I Gain a More Adequate Understanding of Educational Administration?

This book is the beginning. It is designed, first, to provide the student with some *perspective* from which to view administration. In this chapter, one's own experience furnished the setting in which to think about problem situations similar to those encountered in many public schools.

It is our intention that as students build their own concepts of educational administration, moving progressively from one consideration to the next, they will continue to draw upon their own experience, the experience of their associates, and that of other writers in this field. Hence, at the close of each chapter, the suggested activities and selected readings provide guides for obtaining greater depth and breadth of meaning. Our purpose will have been served if this book alerts the student to the need for a more critical analysis of the nature of administration, the competencies required for it, and the professional obligations and challenges which it provides, and if it helps him make his own decision about administration as a career.

SUGGESTED ACTIVITIES

1. For one of the incidents reported in this chapter:
   a. Identify the problem or problems confronted by the administrator.
   b. List the facts in the case which might be useful in solving the problems.
   c. State the unknowns in the incident that complicate the solution to the problem.
   d. State your idea of some next steps to be taken. Upon what do you base your projected solution?
2. Write an incident that occurred in a school in which you were a member of the professional staff. Give your analysis of the problem presented in the incident and the procedure you would employ in its solution.
3. Read one of the cases presented in Sargent and Belisle or in Culbertson, *et al.* (see Selected Readings). How does this case differ from the incidents presented in this chapter? Identify the administrative problems in the case you selected.
4. Attend a meeting of a board of education. Briefly describe what happens at the meeting. List your criteria for the effectiveness of such a meeting, and evaluate this meeting in terms of them.

SELECTED READINGS

ANDERSON, LESTER W., and VAN DYKE, LAUREN A. *Secondary School Administration.* Boston: Houghton Mifflin Co., 1963. Chapter 2.

BURR, JAMES B., COFFIELD, WILLIAM, JENSON, THEODORE J., and NEAGLEY, ROSS L. *Elementary School Administration.* Boston: Allyn and Bacon, Inc., 1963. Chapter I.

CORBALLY, JOHN E., JR., JENSEN, T. J., and STAUB, W. FREDERICK. *Educational Administration: The Secondary School.* Boston: Allyn and Bacon, Inc., 2d ed., 1965. Chapter I.

CULBERTSON, JACK A., JACOBSON, PAUL B., and RELLER, THEODORE L. *Administrative Relationships: A Casebook.* Englewood Cliffs, N.J.: Prentice-Hall, Inc., 1960. Chapter 1.

HACK, WALTER G., RAMSEYER, JOHN A., GEPHART, WILLIAM J., and HECK, JAMES B. *Educational Administration: Selected Readings.* Boston: Allyn and Bacon, Inc., 1965. Chapter I.

HODGKINSON, HAROLD L. *Educational Decisions: A Casebook.* Englewood Cliffs, N.J.: Prentice-Hall, Inc., 1963.

JENSON, T. J., and CLARK, D. L. *Educational Administration.* New York: The Center for Applied Research in Education, Inc., 1964. Chapters I–III.

MILLER, VAN. *The Public Administration of American School Systems.* New York: The Macmillan Company, 1965. Chapter III.

MORPHET, EDGAR L., JOHNS, ROE L., and RELLER, THEODORE L. *Educational Administration: Concepts, Practices, and Issues.* Englewood Cliffs, N.J.: Prentice-Hall, Inc., 1959. Part I.

SARGENT, CYRIL G., and BELISLE, EUGENE L. *Educational Administration: Cases and Concepts.* Boston: Houghton Mifflin Co., 1955.

2

The Evolving

American School System

IT IS IMPORTANT FOR EVERY SCHOOL ADMINISTRATOR to realize that he is the appointed leader of a segment of America's school system, a system in a constant state of growth and change. The present chapter is designed to acquaint the administrator with the broad dimensions of this evolutionary process. It has often been said that what makes American schools different from other educational systems is the extent of local autonomy in their operation. Perhaps it is this same characteristic of American education that accounts for what many critics call "lack of system." But on one point protagonists and antagonists of American schools agree: These schools have a quality of uniqueness that distinguishes them from schools in countries with a national system of education. Americans generally believe that this quality is something to be maintained.

While the dynamics of the evolutionary process tend to push for better organization and a more effective system of education, the American people would be reluctant to give up a large measure of the local control of education which they have cherished so long. Yet the interdependence of our several communities and states is irrevocable, and the mobility of our population is a trend that is seemingly irreversible. Not only is this interdependence evident among our communities and states, but it increasingly permeates international relationships as well. Although educational planning and school operation restricted to local school districts have their place, they are not adequate for our day or for the future.

School districts throughout the nation are now in the position of having to face up to several questions: What can and should they do alone? What can and should they do in co-operation with other districts? What must they do as parts of a larger educational unit—that is, the state and the nation? The fact that in recent times the number of basic school districts has been greatly reduced suggests that people find that the school districts which were in existence in the first half of the twentieth century are no longer adequate for the educational program needed in the second half of the century.

To gain perspective for the leadership task ahead, let us briefly review some of the steps through which the American school system has passed. Notice that throughout much of the development of American education, the lay people, through town councils, directors, and boards of education, along with much state legislation and litigation over various disputes, provided the basic control for the American system of education. This tremendous expression of lay interest in education is without precedent anywhere else in the world. It is incumbent upon the school administrator to build upon this lay interest and to supply the element of professional guidance necessary to wise decision-making in the future.

GROWTH OF EDUCATION IN AMERICA

DECISIONS MADE IN COLONIAL AMERICA

Even while the early American settlers, lacking the conveniences of the homes and towns from which they came, struggled for existence amidst the hardships of remaking a wilderness into a fit place to live and raise their children, their faith in education was manifested by the steps which they took to develop an educational system as an essential part of their program of living. When we remember that the Boston Latin Grammar School, the first secondary school in America, was established in 1635, and that Harvard University was founded in 1636, we realize that education was recognized as important to the future development of the country, even at that early date in American history.

The New England Common School

Attitudes toward education differed throughout the colonies. In New England people began to teach their children in the home. At the elementary level the objective of this instruction was to help children understand and participate in religious ceremonies at home and at church. This proved to be inadequate, however, and by 1642 Massachusetts passed a law requiring all children to be taught to read and write and to know the principles of religion.[1]

This was the beginning of compulsory education in America. The law did not require that children attend a school, but it did place pressure on each town or community to see that parents provided for instruction in the home. Enforcement was difficult because of different interpretations of the meaning and effect of the law. A notable consequence, however, seemed to be that, although the law did not require instruction *other than* by parents, there was an increase in the amount of teaching done by masters of apprentices, by private tutors, and by town school masters. Latin grammar schools were established in the larger towns to prepare boys for colleges. This educational plan, of course, was dominated by the church. In the law of 1642, the people of the Massachusetts Colony had merely recognized the state as servant of the church. In this case, the civic body became the legislative and enforcement agency of the church. Thus, the New England educational pattern began as part of the program of the religious state—a pattern much like that of England.

Colonial America, however, was not entirely like the mother country. Colonial towns and communities were made up of people who had to carve out their own way of life in a land where precedents were lacking. Ideas about many things, including education and schools, differed. By 1647, the enforcement of compulsory education in the home had proved to be inadequate; but faith in education persisted, and a new law was written in Massachusetts ordering:

1. That every town having fifty householders should at once appoint a teacher of reading and writing, and provide for wages in such manner as the town might determine; and

2. That every town having one hundred householders must provide a grammar school to fit youths for the university, under a penalty of five pounds (afterward increased to twenty pounds) for failure to do so.[2]

While these laws did not enforce attendance, they clearly established the precedent for compulsory schools. The Massachusetts Colony, by passing the laws of 1642 and 1647, had pioneered the common-school concept in America.

Parochial School Concept

In the middle colonies, particularly New York, Pennsylvania, and Maryland, where Baptists, Catholics, German Lutherans, German Reformed,

---

[1] Ellwood P. Cubberley, *The History of Education* (Boston: Houghton Mifflin Co., 1920), p. 363.

[2] *Ibid.*, p. 365.

Mennonites, Moravians, Presbyterians, Quakers, and other religious denominations were represented, the concept of the parochial school developed. In these colonies each church wanted to teach the children of its
denomination according to its own beliefs and doctrines. Instruction carried
on in the homes was under the direction of clergymen. Private schools,
which developed in the larger centers of population, wère church schools,
supported by church funds and by the tuition paid by families who could
afford the cost of this kind of education.

Even though such a program of education obviously favored families of
means, the churches stubbornly resisted any move toward the establishment
of a state system of education. They wanted to preserve at all costs the
right of each church to educate its children and youth. Representing many
different denominations, the churches of these colonies supported each other
in this position and thus established the private school. Even today these
schools are recognized as essential elements of our total educational system.

This is not to say, of course, that the right of attendance at private schools
has never been questioned. In 1922, the people of the state of Oregon
passed an initiative measure that, in effect, required that children attend the
public schools. The law was to become effective in 1926, but two private
corporations—the Sisters of the Holy Names of Jesus and Mary, and the
Hill Military Academy—sought a restraining injunction against the enforcement of the law and received favorable action from the District Court. In
1925, the state of Oregon appealed to the Supreme Court of the United
States, which ruled in favor of the two corporations. The *Oregon Case* stated
in part:

We think it entirely plain that the Act of 1922 unreasonably interferes with the
liberty of parents and guardians to direct the upbringing and education of children under their control. . . . The fundamental theory of liberty upon which
all governments of this Union repose excludes any general power of the state
to standardize its children by forcing them to accept instruction from public
teachers only. The child is not the mere creature of the State; those who nurture
him and direct his destiny have the right, coupled with the high duty, to recognize and prepare him for additional obligations.[3]

This seems to make it clear that parents have the right to educate their
children in private schools as long as these schools meet the state's educational requirements.

The Pauper School

One of the problems that disturbed the consciences of people who developed these early concepts of education was that of making adequate

---

[3] *Pierce v. Society of Sisters of the Holy Names of Jesus and Mary* (and *Pierce v.
Hill Military Academy*), 268 U.S. 510, 45 Sup. Ct. 571 (1925).

provision for orphans and children of the poorer classes. This problem plagued the people of the middle colonies more than it did their neighbors to the north, due partly to the fact that the private-school pattern established in the middle colonies definitely favored people of some means. Then too, the poorer classes immigrated in greater numbers to the middle colonies than to the New England colonies.

The Southern colonies had an even larger number of poor immigrants. While the church and state made some provisions for schooling the paupers and orphans, these were temporary measures. People of means resisted proposals to extend such provisions into some kind of permanent remedy for the lack of educational opportunity for all. Some historians believe that the need to extend education to the many who were being denied the opportunity during colonial days was a powerful force in promoting legislation leading to the tax-supported educational program now existing in all of the states.

A Dual Program Emerges

To students of American education it is quite apparent that by the time the colonies were ready to declare their independence, two patterns of education had emerged—*public schools,* having their beginnings in Massachusetts and the other New England colonies, and *private schools,* still largely under the direction of church groups.

Throughout our history as a nation we have witnessed the separation of church and state. From the laws which have been enacted and the court decisions that have been made in reference to this principle as it affects education, it appears that the people have reserved the right to educate their children in either a public or a private school, but that they have conceded to the state the right to enforce a minimum standard in private and in public schools. The Oregon Case, to which reference has just been made, and the Hawaiian Cases, which established the right of parents to send children to foreign-language schools,[4] give ample evidence that the courts agree that the interest of the state in an education for all children can be served in both private and public schools.

EDUCATION AS A STATE RESPONSIBILITY

The time between the Declaration of Independence and the War of 1812 is generally regarded as a period in which American education deteriorated. As a matter of fact, because of the impoverished condition of the nation at that time, schools and colleges did suffer severe setbacks. People could not

[4] *Farrington v. Tokushige,* 273 U.S. 284, 47 Sup. Ct. 406 (1927) and *Stainback v. Mo Hock Lok Po,* 336 U.S. 368, 69 Sup. Ct. 606 (1949).

afford the advantages of private education and they were reluctant to increase their tax burdens to support public education. Nevertheless, this period is important in the development of our schools because it was the time when the first state constitutions were written.

State Responsibility Grew Out of Colonial Action

By 1800, sixteen states had joined the new Union. Of these, seven had incorporated in their state constitutions certain provisions concerning the state's responsibilty for education. The New England states, having gone through a long colonial period during which state responsibility for education was being developed, incorporated in their constitutions the most comprehensive provisions for public education. The middle states, which had espoused the parochial-school concept, were less emphatic in placing state responsibility. The Southern colonies and the new states of Kentucky and Tennessee ignored the matter entirely.

Federal Recognition of State Control

By the time the ordinance for the organization of the Northwest Territory had been adopted (1787), the theory of education as a state function had been quite generally accepted. Article 3 of the Ordinance of 1787 is significant in this regard as it provides that:

Religion, morality, and knowledge being necessary to good government and the happiness of mankind, schools and the means of education shall be forever encouraged (in the states to be formed from this territory).[5]

When Ohio was admitted to the Union, Congress gave the new state land to establish and maintain a state system of schools, a practice continued by the federal government as states were admitted to the Union. General state school laws began to be adopted by the older states in the Union. In 1784 the University of the State of New York, an administrative organization similar to present-day state departments of education, was formed to supervise secondary and higher education in New York.

No provision was made in the Constitution of the United States for federal support or control of education. Article X of the Bill of Rights, passed by Congress in 1789 and ratified by three-fourths of the states in 1791, stated that "The powers not delegated to the United States by the Constitution, nor prohibited by it to the States, are reserved to the States respectively, or to the people." This clause clearly indicated that the growth of state control of education was entirely acceptable to the founders of our federal government.

[5] Quoted in Ellwood P. Cubberley, *Public Education in the United States* (Boston: Houghton Mifflin Co., 1934), p. 92.

Article X is often cited by advocates of a "states rights" point of view in federal-state relations. Paradoxically, those who would like to see the federal government take a more active role in certain affairs that have traditionally been the responsibility of the states use the same Article to defend their position. Those who advocate increasing federal responsibility point to the last four words of the clause—the "or to the people" phrase— as a Constitutional justification for federal intervention *if* such intervention is the will of the people.

General Acceptance of State Regulation

Many of the early state laws on education were permissive. Such laws provided that people had a right to establish schools in their own communities if they so desired. The people were also permitted to tax themselves for school purposes if they wished. The fact that legislation was permissive left many communities without adequate provision for education, and it can be readily understood that in time of stress the school program deteriorated. Gradually, however, permissive legislation gave way to mandatory provisions. The adoption of state financial aid for public schools completed a series of actions and regulations which now made it mandatory that the powers of the state be defined. Thus, in each state we witness the adoption of a *school code* that provides a framework by which the school districts of the state are regulated.

All state constitutions now have sections devoted to education. It should be noted that the states reserve to themselves the authority and power over education. The school district is a subordinate creation of the state and is established for purposes of local administration. The districts—towns, townships, villages, cities, or counties—derive their powers from the state legislature. Thus, the people of the state, acting through their state legislature and not in small competing groups representing individual communities, have given their sanction to such a system. The courts have upheld this action and have repeatedly ruled that the state may establish standards below which the district programs of education may not fall.

Delegation to Local Districts

An examination of the educational programs of the several states reveals, however, that much power is delegated by the state to the local district. In the beginning, such a practice was necessary just to get schools started, and all of the states find it necessary for efficient administration of the schools. The states differ, however, in the degree of delegation of powers and in the size and number of districts to which such power is delegated. The tendency in recent years has been to provide a greater amount of state aid, to enforce minimum standards more rigidly, and to increase the size of school districts.

The current movement to reduce the number of administrative units has been encouraged by state governments not only to take better advantage of the taxable wealth, but also to provide an educational program to meet more adequately the needs of children growing up in our expanding communities. Some people have interpreted this movement as a gradual revocation of delegated powers. They would argue that there is not only an increasing amount of state control, but also a tendency toward centralization of administration of schools at the district level; and these schools are becoming more and more remote from the people. Even so, the school district reorganization movement has gained momentum in recent years. In New York the number of school districts has been reduced from 9,500 in 1925 to 1,932 in 1955. In Illinois the major reorganization took place in a period of 10 years, 1945 to 1955, and reduced the number of school districts from approximately 12,000 to 2,349. In the United States the number of districts reached a peak of about 127,000 in the 1930's, was reduced to approximately 80,000 by 1950, and by the middle 1960's the number of operating districts was only about 25,000.

The writers of the 1954 Yearbook of the Department of Rural Education take this position:

The size of the administrative unit best suited to provide all the educational services which would be included in a comprehensive program has not yet been determined. . . . Distance, topography, climate, density of population, patterns of communication, occupational diversity, social responsiveness, and social unity are among the factors which influence the operation of an educational program.[6]

Thus, the size of the school and of the school district, which at one time was the major criterion in determining the number of schools and districts, is now just one of many criteria that need to be considered in organizing our schools to meet the needs of children who are growing up in rapidly changing communities.

BASIC PRINCIPLES AFFECTING THE EVOLUTION OF OUR SCHOOL SYSTEM

As we review the evolution of the American school system, it is apparent that certain basic principles are emerging to guide us in the further development of our schools. Some of these principles have withstood and continue to withstand severe tests of both public and legal opinion. All educational

---

[6] Department of Rural Education, *The Community School and the Intermediate Unit* (Washington: National Education Association, 1954), p. 15.

leaders have the obligation to acquaint themselves with the manner in which these principles have been established, to weigh the evidence for or against them, and to provide leadership to help the people of the school district in which they work to establish for themselves sound principles of action and the means of implementing those principles. With this in mind, let us turn our attention to the eight principles that seem to have become firmly established by the American people as guides for the continuing development of our schools.

Universal Education Is Essential

One of the basic struggles in the history of America has been the determination of whether or not education should be universal. That is, should it be required of all? Is education basic to our way of life? America's answer to these questions has been an emphatic *Yes!* Sometimes we wonder if the American people have always been aware of the responsibility that has devolved upon them as they have given their answer.

The early settlers of America had great faith in education. They proceeded earnestly and quickly to provide educational opportunity. Although at first the purpose was largely to create understanding of religious doctrine, secular concerns and interests soon modified this purpose. The fact that some educational provisions were made for paupers and orphans suggests a feeling that all children had a right to receive some education. The unwillingness to develop an adequate tax base to help make education generally available may suggest, on the other hand, that education did not receive top priority on the colonists' list of essentials. Or it may suggest that the purposes of education differed so much from community to community, church to church, and colony to colony that no uniform practice could be developed.

Later, however, these purposes did become clearer. Some of the founders of America eloquently expressed their belief that ignorance and freedom are incompatible. Thomas Jefferson expressed it well when he said, "If a nation expects to be ignorant and free, in a state of civilization, it expects what never was and never will be." To develop a nation of free people—free to think, to express their thoughts, to remold these thoughts in the melting pot of ideas, and finally to put them to work for the betterment of society—that was the purpose of the founders of America and the purpose for which we struggle today.

The elimination of the pauper school was a big step in the movement to provide education for all because of the prospect which it holds for the betterment of society. The chief battle was waged in Pennsylvania and New Jersey, two of the states in which the idea of the pauper school had developed. Political statesmen approved the new plan for free schools on the principle that "all men are created equal, and endowed by their Creator with certain inalienable rights." People caught the spirit of this concept and saw the obvious implication: The continuation of private schools for those able to pay, and of public schools at state expense for the poor, could lead only to the development of class distinction, a condition unacceptable to our democratic way of life.

The separation of the population into upper and lower classes was to have no place in American education. The Pennsylvania Free School Act of 1834, together with subsequent legislation in that state and in New Jersey, eliminated the pauper school from the Northern states. The West had never tolerated it. Although the idea lingered somewhat longer in a number of the middle and Southern states, it was almost entirely eliminated in the reorganization that took place in these states following the Civil War.

With the decision that schools are a responsibility of the state and that class distinction should be eliminated from the educational program, much of the battle for universal education had been won. However, education was still considered a privilege, not an obligation. It was not until 1852 that the first compulsory school-attendance law was passed. Here again, it was the state of Massachusetts that led the way. More than 200 years had elapsed since the passage in Massachusetts of the school law of 1647.

We know, of course, that prior to this time some of the states could not have supported an educational program that would have been adequate to meet the requirements of compulsory school-attendance laws. This is one of the reasons why such laws appeared so late in our educational development. Without doubt, the reluctance to force education upon those who did not wish it was also a deterring factor. Here was a problem in democracy that required some real thinking. In a freedom-loving country, do we have the right to force people to do something against their will? Or, in reality, is the education of all essential to the freedom that people desire to achieve and maintain? The history of legislation from 1852 to the present time indicates that the American people have answered the latter question in the affirmative because, by 1918, all forty-eight states had enacted some form of compulsory education law. Alaska and Hawaii have, of course, enacted like statutory provisions.

Current compulsory education laws vary considerably. The most common practice is to require children to attend school between the ages of seven and sixteen years. In some states the age range is eight to sixteen years and in others eight to eighteen. Most of the states have regulations that deal both with school attendance and with employment of children between the ages of fourteen and sixteen, or fourteen and eighteen. Under these regulations, permission to accept employment may be granted a pupil when it is believed that the child can profit more from employment than from attendance at school.

Parents are held responsible for the attendance of their children in school during the age range for compulsory education adopted by the state in which they live. The recent tendency, however, has been to place some responsibility on the school for meeting the wider range of needs of the children and youth as growing numbers of them crowd our schools. Increased provisions for vocational education, education for children with special problems, programs to meet individual differences of the so-called normal children, cooperative work and school arrangements, and many pupil personnel services are incorporated into our educational program to meet this obligation.

Education Should Be Free

Despite the many reforms made in the educational system throughout the first half of the nineteenth century, many states were unable to raise sufficient money to support the system. Thus was prolonged the undesirable practice, held over from colonial days, of adjusting costs above those paid by taxation on a pro rata basis according to the number of children per family. This so-called *rate-bill* had an effect similar to that created by the pauper school. Wealthy districts voted local taxes, which together with state funds were sufficient to provide free schools for their children. Poor districts, unable to do so, struggled along with shorter school terms and inferior programs of education.

By the middle of the century, however, the fight for free schools was being waged. Cities led in the battle by securing legislation to form school systems operated apart from city governments under the administration of local boards of education. Boards of education were given power to levy taxes at the local level for educational purposes. Pennsylvania was the first of the Northern states to eliminate the rate-bill (1834).

After a stormy battle and much agitation over this subject in New York State, the legislature, in 1849, submitted the problem to the people who overwhelmingly voted in favor of "making the property of the state educate the children of the state." Immediately, opponents of the action organized in sufficient strength to convince the legislature to turn again to the people for their voice in the matter. The action of the previous year was sustained, and the battle for free schools in this state was won. Indiana, Ohio, and Illinois passed similar legislation in the years immediately following that in which New York made its decision. Other Northern states were going through similar struggles at about the same time; in a five-year period they too had won the battle for free schools. In the Southern states free education was provided in the reorganization that took place following the Civil War.

The story just related is a very brief description of the struggles which the people of America have undergone to provide free schools. This statement should not be mistaken to mean that we now have free education. The problem that remains with us is, how much education should be free? For the most part, we seem agreed that it should include the elementary and the secondary school, with college education at nominal cost. Kindergarten and junior colleges represent extensions in public educational opportunity provided in some parts of the country.

How much instructional material is to be included in "free" education? Should laboratory fees be charged? What special services are to be provided? Do the schools that are free to the children provide them equal educational opportunity? Should schools attempt to provide extensive vocational-technical training, perhaps including thirteenth and fourteenth years for pupils who do not intend to work for a college degree? Might the schools provide free programs for school drop-outs who wish to resume their education? Should free education be provided for adults who are unemployed or underemployed simply because their particular skills are no longer needed in our highly automated society? Is free education for adult avocational and leisure time activity a proper function of the schools? Finally, should the schools provide free preschool programs, of a compensatory nature, for culturally disadvantaged children? Inferior programs, programs inadequate to the special needs of some children, and the hidden costs imposed by activities sponsored by the school are just a few of the problems that remain to be solved in providing free education.

The State Has the Responsibility

The obvious consequence of the actions related so far has been to place the state in control of education. The process of extending education to all children and youth, and providing public funds to support an adequate educational system required that the issue of state versus local control be settled over and over again throughout the entire nation. The previous discussion indicates that many problems remained unsolved until state legislation was provided.

Authority for education, then, was left to the people of the several states when our national Constitution was formed. The people, in turn, in attempting to solve their problems, found the state to be the logical agency for the final resolution of issues. Along with this recognition of the authority of the state came its obligation to control the educational program. Towns, cities, villages, and rural areas were organized into school districts and were asked to meet state requirements in providing schools. In the early days this problem was even greater than it is today.

One way to meet the problem was to appoint a state officer to supervise the schools of the state. New York was the first state to create such a position, and in 1812 it enacted legislation providing for the appointment of the first State Superintendent of the Common Schools. Gideon Hawley, the first superintendent, apparently was so vigorous in his enforcement of state law that local pressures on the legislators caused the position to be abolished for a period of time. However, the secretary of state acted ex officio in this capacity for some time. Some states, fearing that they might have similiar difficulties with a chief state school officer, used the ex officio arrangement as a temporary solution to their problem.

Another means of exercising state control was through the formation of a state board of education, with a secretary who performed the same functions as a state superintendent of schools. Horace Mann, as secretary of the Massachusetts Board of Education, became a vigorous leader in school organization. Mann and Henry Barnard, secretary of the Connecticut State Board of Commissioners for the Common School, and later State Commissioner of Public Schools in Rhode Island, became the nation's outstanding campaigners for educational reform. They were not merely officers who controlled schools through the enforcement of legislation. These were men of vision who helped the people define their problems, visualize new prospects for their schools, and develop new interest and enthusiasm for public education and its support.

Now all states in the United States have chief state school officers, and virtually all of them have state boards of education in each of which the chief state school officer is the executive officer of the board. State control is not always as enlightened as was that exemplified by Horace Mann and Henry Barnard. Nevertheless, all states recognize an obligation to enforce state school regulations and have state departments of public instruction with extensive staffs consisting of personnel who carry out specialized regulatory, research, or leadership functions to improve schools throughout the state. Adjustments are constantly being made concerning the relative amount of state and local tax funds to be used for school purposes. The functions of state departments of education are redefined periodically. What state control exists and how it functions changes from time to time and from state to state. It is significant that the people, through their representatives in the legislatures, exercise their authority and responsibility for regulating education at the state level.

There seems to be little controversy over the states' right to fix minimum standards for the schools. Questions do arise concerning the nature of the standards and the means that shall be used for enforcing them. Likewise, the use of public monies for schools is a privilege of the state which has general acceptance, but considerable controversy ensues when these monies are used for purposes of regulation. School administrators and local boards of education usually display an active interest in these matters and often are responsible for the initiation of legislation that will determine what the state does toward improving education at the local district level.

It is generally agreed that the state is most successful in assuming its obligation for school improvement when it emphasizes a leadership rather than a regulatory function. What the state department of education can accomplish through state-wide planning and co-ordination, and through advice, assistance, and encouragement to local districts far outweighs the results obtained from mere enforcement of regulations. Unless a large percentage of the schools can exceed the minimum standards which the state can enforce, public education is not meeting the challenge of our time. Dynamic, forward-looking school programs thrive under the stimulation of appropriate leadership, as was demonstrated by Mann and Barnard. The need is equally great today.

Local Districts Operate the Schools

The recognition that the state has an obligation for the education of its children and youth by no means implies that the state is the appropriate agency to administer the schools. In fact, the history of the reorganization of school districts within states indicates that the people hold very zealously to their local schools and to their right as citizens to participate in decisions about what the schools shall do.

In the United States the development of the school system has never been from the top down. State governments, early in our history, accepted from the people the obligation to regulate the formation, support, and standards of the school program so as to equalize educational opportunity. These are still the functions which the people exercise through their state governments. It seems probable that the people will never permit the regulatory framework that is established by the state to become so rigid that some local initiative in educational program development is eliminated.

The number, size, and types of school districts vary from state to state. In some states the town or township is the basic unit. For twelve states the basic unit is the county. One state (Hawaii) is organized as a single state-wide district. In most states, whatever the classification of basic units may be, there are exceptions by which certain towns or cities have been constituted as independent or separate districts. The current movement for district reorganization is an effort on the part of the states to perform their function of improving local schools and equalizing educational opportunity for all of the children of the state.

For purposes of operation, the state delegates most of its powers to the local district. A district board of education is elected by the people of the district to represent their wishes in formulating the policy by which their local school is to operate within the framework established by the state. Sometimes members of these boards of education find themselves in a quandary because they are officers of the state and at the same time elected officials of the local district. Where local interests conflict with state regulations, the course of action to follow may become complicated. If the regulation in question is a state law, the most common course of action is to submit to it. But, as we have seen from the previous discussion, there may be times when state regulations should be challenged. Many court actions have actually clarified the regulatory powers of the state, because someone had the courage to test the interpretation of a regulation as it was being enforced.

The control problem that confronts educators and citizens today is that of deciding upon an optimum level of local control. The current nationalizing influences upon public education in the United States tend to reduce the efficacy of a policy of strict local control. And it seems certain that these forces and influences from outside the local community will increase, rather than decrease, in the future. Among them are federally-sponsored programs aimed at the equalization of educational opportunities throughout the United States; their purpose is to provide better training for potential contributors to the national defense program, as well as vocational-technical training for unemployed adults. There are also nongovernment nationalizing influences upon education today, such as the various national curriculum programs in physics and mathematics, and the national testing programs.

It is no longer a simple task, as it may once have been, to decide just what matters are properly and solely the concern of the local school district. Certainly, some matters are of such universal concern and importance that the state and federal governments should assume some control. Most people would agree that complete autonomy at any one level,—federal, state, or local,—is not in the best interest of public education. But even with this agreement, the problem of deciding "what should be rendered unto Caesar" remains. There are a few people who sincerely believe that good education is predicated upon substantial local control of public education. There are others who contend that local control of education is an anachronism which Americans can no longer afford. Campbell points out some of the issues involved:

It is quite clear that the public schools of this country have always operated within a framework established by the various states and that federal influences of some kind have always been prevalent. In recent decades, state controls over schools have been strengthened and federal activities in education, widely dispersed among many agencies, have multiplied. Federal influence has been piecemeal, haphazard, perhaps even surreptitious and often clothed in pious affirmation of state and local control. But inevitably the national stake in education and the growing social and economic interdependence of the nation have required congressional action and United States Supreme Court interpretation on educational questions. The time seems ripe for a realistic view of circumstances as they are and the forging of an honest local-state-federal partnership in education.[7]

[7] Roald F. Campbell, "The Folklore of Local School Control," *The School Review,* LXVIII (Spring 1959), p. 15.

The terms "control" and "operation" do not mean exactly the same thing, however. Reasonable controls from the state and federal levels could be imposed upon the local schools, while at the same time provisions for local operation would allow latitude and flexibility for adapting school programs to local needs and conditions.

The main reason that it seems appropriate to keep the operation of schools at the local level is that this is the way they remain the people's schools. The rank and file of the citizenry should give regular attention to the kind of education that is required to promote the way of life in which we believe. When the operation of the school becomes so remote that few people have an opportunity to participate in decision-making as to its nature, interest in education withers and the co-operative relationship between the school and other educating agencies of the community diminishes.

Several of our larger cities have been concerned with this problem for some time. New York and Chicago, for instance, have developed at least the first stage of regional administrative areas under the jurisdiction of the general administrative organization of the city school system. This decentralization may permit the people to share in making the decisions that concern their local schools.

We find ourselves at a stage in our history where we are seeking an optimum size of local operating school districts. Undoubtedly the size will vary with many conditions; but we can be fairly certain that the principle of local initiative has been so firmly established in the minds of both the educator and the layman that more adequate means will be found to make it effective in determining the role of the school in the community.

The school administrator must be aware of the influences that, rightfully or wrongfully, tend to reduce local control over public school operation. For most assuredly there will be continued and increased pressure from outside to reduce local control, while at the same time local communities will continue to struggle to retain some control of the schools.

Federal Participation Is Desirable

An issue of current importance to people throughout the nation is whether or not the federal government should give further financial support to the public schools. Most advocates of additional support for schools base their case essentially on two arguments: (1) that there is great need for equalization of educational opportunity among the states; and (2) that since almost 75 percent of the tax dollar now goes into the federal coffers, there is little chance that an appropriate part of our total wealth will be spent for educational purposes unless this source of revenue is used.

The basic arguments against additional federal aid at this time are that federal control would be the inevitable result and that the states can meet their school needs if they so desire. Some of the opponents of federal support claim that a recognition of the possibility of federal control was the reason why the framers of the Constitution made no mention of education, and also the reason for the Tenth Amendment, which reserves to the states and to the people all powers not expressly delegated to the United States. It is difficult, of course, to document the motives that prompted the founders of our government to leave education to the states and to the people. Whatever the reasons may have been at that time, the Congress representing the people of the United States has not interpreted the Tenth Amendment to mean that the federal government cannot participate in the improvement of educational opportunity.

As mentioned earlier, the people, referred to in the Tenth Amendment, have many ways of making decisions in this country. At the neighborhood level, these decisions may be made quite informally. At the village, town, city, state, and national levels we have duly constituted legal procedure. Nevertheless, these are the processes through which *the people* act. Hence, in matters of education the people may act through their district organization, their state government, or even their federal government.

As a matter of fact, the people have been using all of the levels of government for the support of their schools for a long time. The participation of the federal government began immediately after the ratification of the Tenth Amendment, when the government made land grants to aid the states in the establishment of public schools and colleges. Additional ways in which the educational program of the country has been assisted by the federal government include: grants for special education, particularly in the field of vocational education; maintenance of certain types of schools for special purposes, notably the military schools and military programs in our colleges and universities; financial support of schools in the District of Columbia, in the territories, and for the Indians; authorization and maintenance of welfare programs having certain educational benefits, such as the Civilian Conservation Corps, the National Youth Administration, and the Works Progress Administration; aid to school districts affected by war-incurred federal activities; support for the education of veterans of World War II and of the Korean War; support for special programs thought to be in the interest of national defense under the National Defense Education Act; support of the United States Office of Education; the Vocational Education Act of 1963; the Economic Opportunity Act of 1964; and the Elementary and Secondary Education Act of 1965. A more complete discussion of the extent and impact of federal participation in education may be found elsewhere.[8]

[8] F. J. Munger and R. F. Fenno, Jr., *National Politics and Federal Aid to Education* (Syracuse, N.Y.: Syracuse University Press, 1962).

In all of these instances, it seems fair to say that the fear of undue federal coercion is not borne out by the facts. The great bulk of the activity that affects the program of general education is carried on with a minimum of federal control and with much of the responsibility delegated to the states. It seems unreasonable to expect the federal government to supply funds for school building construction and further equalization of educational opportunity among the states without certain controls. The states supplying the great amount of the wealth to make such equalization possible would insist that federal legislation contain provisions for the appropriate use of these funds. Neither is it likely that the wealthier states will be completely altruistic in this matter. When such legislation is passed, the problem that our legislators in Washington will need to solve is not how to eliminate federal control, but how to provide that federal control which insures to each of the states its fair share of federal funds.

The mobility of our population being what it is, inequities in educational opportunity become increasingly apparent. Economists tell us that the trend toward the collection of the large bulk of our taxes at the national level will not be reversed. If schools are to receive a greater portion of the tax dollar, and if these monies are to be used to provide our children and youth with comparable opportunities for education, it seems imperative that we move toward even greater federal participation in education, especially in the form of financial support.

The School System Should Be Extended

The recent trend toward continuing education beyond the high school raises once again the old question of how far the public school program should go. Many school districts now provide for kindergarten. Some people have raised the question of whether or not there should be any limiting age. Adult education is serving a useful purpose and will be more and more necessary. Should the state make some provision for education at all age levels?

The answer lies squarely within our system of values. How much do we value education and where do we place it on our scale of wants? While it is impossible to compare meaningfully the relative expenditure for education in Russia and the United States, we do know that by edict from the Kremlin Russia can spend for education that portion of its national income that its leaders deem necessary to meet the desired ends. In the United States, on the other hand, the decision to increase expenditures for education depends in large part upon the intelligence, the insight, and the understanding of need on the part of the citizenry. Only history can tell how far we shall go in extending and improving our educational program. If the behavior exhibited by the American people in the past is to be taken as a clue to what will happen in the future, with effective leadership we shall continue to extend our effort to meet adequately the challenges which face us.

The common school, our first division of publicly supported education, provided the rudiments of the 3 R's. The extension of this school into the primary age brackets permitted extensions of the curriculum. The next problem to be faced was the addition of high schools. Up to about 1850, most of what we now call high school education was taught in the Latin Grammar School. Later, the academy, a semi-private school depending largely upon tuition and grants of money from churches and other benevolent organizations and groups, became the popular "high" school.

The academy was not simply a college preparatory school like the Latin Grammar School. It was open to both girls and boys, and its curriculum contained a variety of subjects not unlike those found in many of our secondary schools today. Although the Boston Latin Grammar School admitted boys at the secondary school level, its single aim of college preparation rules it out as the real forerunner of the modern secondary school. Perhaps the Massachusetts Law of 1827 really marks the beginning of the high school movement as we know it.

The Latin Grammar School movement was not widespread. Very few schools were established, and most of them died out when the academy grew in popularity. This new kind of secondary school spread throughout the eastern half of the United States and reached its peak of popularity about 1850. Its decline in number after 1850, however, was almost as spectacular as its rise in the preceding fifty years.

Massachusetts and New York were leaders in the development of the high schools as an upward extension of the common school system. Legislation permitting districts to tax themselves for this purpose was passed in a number of states, but progress came slowly because many schools had to be supported solely by local taxation.

The enactment of permissive legislation is an illustration of a device that has been used by the states over and over again, one which gives the people a chance to try out the idea. Where the legislation is seriously questioned, it is tested in the courts. The famous Kalamazoo Case,[9] in which the Supreme Court of the state of Michigan upheld the right of the state to enact such legislation, is an illustration of the impetus given by such legislation to extend public education to include the secondary school. The speed with which the states incorporated the high school as a part of the common school system was greatly accelerated after the settlement of this case.

The Vocational Education Act of 1963 (Public Law 88–210) is an ex-

[9] *Stuart v. School District No. 1 of Kalamazoo* (1874) 30, Mich. 69.

ample of permissive legislation which may serve to extend the public school system beyond the traditional twelve-year program of instruction. Authorizations for federal grants to the states under this Act were intended, among other things, to allow the extension of vocational programs of the public schools beyond the twelfth-grade level. One of the purposes of the Act is:

> To provide instruction so that persons of *all* ages in *all* communities will have *ready access* to vocational training or retraining which is of high quality, realistic in relation to employment, and suited to the needs, interests, and ability of the persons concerned. Such persons were identified: (a) those in high school, (b) those who have completed or discontinued formal education and are preparing to enter the labor market, (c) those who have already entered the labor market and who need to upgrade their skills or learn new ones, and (d) those with educational handicaps.[10]

The growth of the state university is still another chapter in the history of the upward extension of our school system. The earlier colleges and universities were private institutions, supported by tuition, church, and endowment funds. By 1800 there were about two dozen of these institutions, with not over a hundred professors and no more than two thousand students in all. By 1860, the total number of colleges and universities had grown to 246, of which 17 were state universities. In this case, as well as at the lower levels of the school program, great effort was made to change church-dominated colleges into state schools. The idea did not work out in practice, but the movement to establish state universities persisted. Weak at first because of inadequate state support, state universities have grown in strength and have now become the institutions of higher learning in which the great majority of our youth receive their college education. The basic theory upon which this gradual development is founded is that the welfare of the democratic society can best be achieved by raising the educational level of the people.

Religion and the Public Schools.

There can be little doubt that religion played a large part in the early development of American education. In New England, it was the concept of the Calvinistic religious state, the state as servant of the church, which gave the state the power to regulate the schools. All churches throughout the several colonies continued many of their European habits, one of which was education for the furtherance of the church. They could not break

---

[10] M. D. Mobley and M. L. Barlow, "Impact of Federal Legislation and Policies Upon Vocational Education," Chapter VIII in *Vocational Education,* 64th Yearbook of the National Society of the Study of Education, Part I (Chicago: University of Chicago Press, 1965), p. 200.

away from this idea, even though a strong motive for many of the early settlers to come to America had been to break away from religious oppression.

When we recall that, in the beginning, schools were controlled by the church and maintained largely to promote religious purposes, we recognize how much the public schools as we know them now have changed. History supports the conclusion that this change has not been easy, but that people gradually have come to recognize the wisdom of the principle of separation of church and state. Religious instruction became a private concern and a right which the state has always protected on that basis.

The parochial school of the middle colonies has withstood the test of time and has established itself along with the public school as a recognized agency in which children and youth may receive the education prescribed by the state. Many of the court cases cited below indicate that the principle of separation of church and state gets much of its support from church groups. Hence, even today, the protection of the minority from religious domination and the right of different denominations to provide religious instruction as they see fit influences the kind, the place, the time, and the responsibility for instruction in the community.

The public school, however, became an educational agency that reached many different church groups; hence the parochial interests of each could not be protected. Public monies, collected as they were by different forms of taxation and paid by individuals and groups with vastly different concepts of religion, could not be spent in such manner that each of these interests was appropriately served. Cubberley points out two factors that he says served to bring about the secularization of the public schools. They were:

1. The conviction that the life of the Republic demanded an educated and intelligent citizenship, and hence the general education of all in common schools controlled by the State; and

2. The great diversity of religious beliefs among the people, which forced tolerance and religious freedom through a consideration of the rights of minorities.[11]

Not only did this principle of secularization of the public schools serve to shift the control from the church to the state, it also eliminated the practice of using state funds to support church and other private schools. There was a bitter battle in most of the Eastern states because such a principle required almost a complete reversal in policy and practice. Horace Mann was a leader in the struggle in Massachusetts while he served as secretary of the Board of Education. Pennsylvania, New Jersey, and New York were the states where the problem seemed to be unusually difficult to solve. New

[11] Cubberley, *The History of Education*, p. 692.

Hampshire, as early as 1792, was the first state to settle the issue by a constitutional amendment. The matter was resolved generally throughout the country by the adoption of constitutional amendments forbidding a division or a diversion of public funds for the support of parochial or private schools. Most of the states joining the Union after 1850 had this provision in the original constitutions. Butts reminds us that

from 1876 onward all new states added to the Union were required by Congress to include in their basic laws an irrevocable ordinance guaranteeing religious freedom in line with the principles of the First Amendment. . . .[12]

and that

the principle of separation of church and state in education was almost completely accepted through the United States by 1900.[13]

There is still another aspect of the problem that plagues us. This is the use of the school for religious instruction. "Released time" programs of religious education, a practice whereby a portion of the school day is set aside for religious instruction, have been ruled by the courts to be unconstitutional. The case of *McCollum v. Board of Education of School District No. 71, Champaign, Illinois*[14] is just one example of many such cases where released time was seen as a violation of the principle of separation of the church and state. In this case, the interpretation of the court was that the use of school buildings for religious instruction resulted in making the school "an establishment of religion." Thus, the practice of providing religious instruction within the school building, even on time released from public school responsibilities, was ruled illegal.

On the other hand, in 1952, the Supreme Court of the United States in *Zorach v. Clauson,*[15] upheld the school board of the city of New York in providing that children may be released from school for religious instruction off the school premises.[16] The combined effect of these two actions seems to be that children may be excused from regular classroom activities for religious instruction that is conducted off the school premises. It would appear from the comments of the judges that in such cases the released

---

[12] R. Freeman Butts, *The American Tradition in Religion and Education* (Boston: Beacon Press, 1950), pp. 103–4.

[13] *Ibid.,* pp. 137–38.

[14] *McCollum v. Board of Education,* 333 U.S. 203, 68 Sup. Ct. 461 (1948).

[15] *Zorach v. Clauson,* 343 U.S. 306, 72 Sup. Ct. 679 (1952).

[16] Clark Spurlock, *Education and the Supreme Court* (Urbana, Ill.: University of Illinois Press, 1955), pp. 126–33.

time would need to be kept to a minimum, and administration on the part of the school would be improper. Presumably, a case could arise to test the extent of time, money, and effort that could go into such an enterprise without jeopardizing the public school function.

It is interesting to note in this connection that in 1961 when federal participation in the financial support of public education was proposed by President Kennedy, the religious issue again reached a peak in the intensity of heat generated. The President saw public support of non-public schools as unconstitutional, a violation of our time-honored principle of the separation of church and state. One of the arguments used in the defeat of his program for federal financial aid to the public schools was that aid to the public schools without aid to private schools was in violation of the principle of equal educational opportunity for all.

In 1963 the United States Supreme Court disposed of two cases in a single opinion expressed by Justice Clark. These cases, *Abington Township v. Schempp*[17] and *Murray v. Curlett*,[18] are considered of major significance because they appear to indicate a basic shift in the Court's interpretation of the First Amendment. While previous decisions of the Court placed great stress on the concept of the "wall of separation between church and state" the *Abington* decision set forth a "neutrality" concept. This concept means that the state (and the schools) must be neutral in its impact upon religion. In effect, the opinion makes the "wall of separation" illegal, for if the schools erect a wall they are not being neutral in their impact upon religion.

The Court has not dealt with every issue that may arise or every public school practice involving religion. The school administrator still has a responsibility for guiding the development of local policies and practices.[19]

The chief administrative problem in communities where the issue of religious instruction is raised is to help people understand that the principle of separation or of neutrality is intended not to prohibit religious instruction in the community by a church or private enterprise, but to protect the right of all by restricting the use of public school funds and property to that which is a public and not a private concern.

In fact, this issue caused the Congress much concern as they were debating the enactment of the *Elementary and Secondary Education Act of 1965* (Public Law 89-10).

[17] *Abington Township v. Schempp,* 374 U.S. 203 (1963).

[18] *Murray v. Curlett,* 374 U.S. 203 (1963).

[19] Help in guiding policy development is offered by the many suggestions to be found in: American Association of School Administrators, *Religion in the Public Schools* (Washington, D.C.: The Association, 1964).

Title II proposes a five-year program to assist states in the purchase of books for school libraries and for student use, including instructional materials and textbooks, to be made available to children in public and private nonprofit elementary and secondary schools.

Title III proposes a five-year program to provide supplementary educational centers and services within the community and to develop exemplary elementary and secondary school programs to serve as models for regular school programs.

. . . .

Children attending nonpublic, as well as public schools, and out-of-school youth and adults would be able to receive services and participate in these educational and cultural activities.[20]

The Melting-pot Influence

In a very real sense, the growth of public education in America reflects the development of a pattern of values which we like to think of as distinctively American. Gunnar Myrdal, a Swedish student of the American way of life, has observed that "America, compared to every other country in Western Civilization, large or small, has the *most explicitly expressed* system of general values in reference to human relationships." He goes on to say that "this body of ideals is more widely understood and appreciated than similar ideals are anywhere else." [21] He refers, of course, not only to the Bill of Rights and other formal documents in which these ideals have been expressed, but also to the struggles through which we have gone as a nation to realize them.

While the majority of the people who first settled America were of Anglo-Saxon origin, coming from England, Wales, and Scotland, these settlers were soon joined by Dutch, Swedish, French, Spanish, Irish, and German nationals and people of other races and nationalities. By and large, these were common people—people of the middle or lower classes. The Beards tell us "it seems probable that at least one-half the immigrants into America before the Revolution, certainly outside New England, were either indentured servants or Negro slaves." [22] Religious and political dissenters, a few English adventurers and French aristocrats, some people who sought wealth and power, others who withstood the misery of illness and poverty to be free, carved out their fortunes together. To them, coming to America meant the hardships of frontier life; but it also meant freedom to shape their way of life as they saw fit.

[20] *Elementary and Secondary Education Act of 1965* (Public Law 89-10).

[21] Gunnar Myrdal, *An American Dilemma* (New York: Harper & Brothers, 1944), Vol. 1, p. 3. (Italics in original.)

[22] Charles A. Beard and Mary R. Beard, *The Rise of American Civilization* (New York: Macmillan Company, 1927), Vol. I, p. 103.

These were the people who settled America—different in beliefs, values, customs, stations in life, homeland, and culture. It is largely people like them who have continued to come to America. Counts describes them as the "common people" of the world, but common people who "were beyond or outside the ordinary in some way." [23] In an extraordinary sense, these people have built a new kind of common school—a school to which all children may go, and a school through which children may, by their own efforts, rise above their own stations in life.

The equality of all men, the worth and dignity of the individual, the faith that problems can be solved and society advanced through the application of intelligent thinking ("the method of intelligence"), and a belief in the co-operative process of decision-making are ideals and values that urge us constantly to re-examine our practices. So it is even in the last half of the twentieth century. The careful student of American history realizes that the decision of the United States Supreme Court on May 17, 1954, though truly a memorable event, was not a precipitous one. [24] It marked the climax of a long series of events and decisions through which the American people have been developing a workable plan of racial equality and relationships.

Throughout this entire chapter, we have described the struggle that was necessary to solve problems similar in kind to the problem of desegregation of the races in the public schools. The elimination of the pauper school and the events leading up to the achievement of free common schools were battles against forms of discrimination among people. The persistence of our democratic values, the insistence on the rights of the minority, and a faith that the people can work out their differences are all reflected in the many decisions, from early Colonial days to the present, that make our school system what it is today.

The Cleveland, Ohio, incident reported in Chapter 1 took place in a northern state. Thus we are reminded that the problems of discrimination against minority groups, including racial segregation in the schools, are not confined to one section of our country. They are more dramatically illustrated, perhaps, in the Southern states because of the long history of segregated education and the delay on the part of a number of these states in enforcing the Supreme Court ruling.

Introduced to this country as a mere chattel, the American Negro has won many freedoms but has, nevertheless, endured a long and bitter struggle to achieve the rights and privileges of citizenship. The Thirteenth, Fourteenth, and Fifteenth Amendments to the Constitution of the United States specify the privileges and status afforded him as a result of the

[23] George S. Counts, *Education and American Civilization* (New York: Teachers College, Bureau of Publications, 1952), Chapter 5.

[24] *Brown et al. v. Board of Education of Topeka,* 347 U.S. 483.

Civil War. At the beginning, Negroes did not have many educational privileges. In the Northern states some of them attended the pauper schools of
Colonial times. As free schools were provided, Negroes were gradually accepted in them. But in the South Negro education began to be accepted
much later. Philanthropic interests and agencies assisted in its development
until the separate public schools were established.

After the Civil War, the principle of *separate but equal* was established
to meet the standards for racial relationships which had been set forth by
the newer amendments to the Constitution. Although the principle was
contested in the courts, the case of *Plessy v. Ferguson* in 1896, in which the
Supreme Court ruled that "separation did not necessarily mean inferiority,"[25]
gave it support sufficient to establish the principle as the legal basis for the
development of a dual school system in the South. It was not until the
mid-thirties of the present century that this principle was challenged successfully. At this time there were a number of court cases in which Negroes
were granted the privilege of attending graduate schools in certain Southern
colleges and universities.

The following excerpts from the Supreme Court decision of 1954 clarify,
for our purposes, the position of the court:

The doctrine of "separate but equal" did not make its appearance in this Court
until 1896 in the case of *Plessy v. Ferguson, supra,* involving not education
but transportation. American courts have since labored with the doctrine for
over half a century. In this Court, there have been six cases involving the
"separate but equal" doctrine in the field of public education. In *Cumming v.
County Board of Education,* 175 US 528, and *Gong Lum v. Rice,* 275 US 78,
the validity of the doctrine itself was not challenged. In more recent cases, all
on the graduate-school level, inequality was found in that specific benefits enjoyed by white students were denied to Negro students of the same educational
qualifications. *Missouri ex rel. Gaines v. Canada,* 305 US 337; *Sipuel v. Oklahoma,* 332 US 631; *Sweatt v. Painter,* 339 US 629; *McLaurin v. Oklahoma State
Regents,* 339 US 637. In none of these cases was it necessary to re-examine the
doctrine to grant relief to the Negro plaintiff. . . .

Segregation of white and colored children in public schools has a detrimental
effect upon the colored children. The impact is greater when it has the sanction
of the law; for the policy of separating the races is usually interpreted as denoting the inferiority of the Negro group. A sense of inferiority affects the
motivation of a child to learn. . . .

We conclude that in the field of public education the doctrine of "separate but
equal" has no place. Separate educational facilities are inherently unequal.[26]

There seems to be little doubt that the American public in general agrees
that racial segregation should be eliminated from our schools. The un-
resolved issue, however, centers about the urgency of enforcement which in

[25] *Plessy v. Ferguson,* 163 U.S. 537 (1896).

[26] *Brown et al. v. Board of Education of Topeka, op. cit.*

some states is looked upon as unfortunate and unnecessary. The Supreme Court decision, coming at a time when progress was being made toward giving Negroes equal treatment with regard to voting privileges, jury duty, eligibility for employment, and equivalent pay for equivalent work, as well as when a real effort was being made to provide Negro schools equal in quality to those for whites, has led some of the people of the South to conclude that these honest efforts to improve the status of the Negro have not been appreciated.

A number of attempts have been made to set aside or to ignore the decision of the Supreme Court. Probably the most notable among these was the incident in Little Rock, Arkansas, in which the state government opposed the federal government in the desegregation of the public high schools on the basis that public education is a state, not a federal, function. Nevertheless, the basic rights of all people of the nation, the principle upon which the Supreme Court decision was rendered, have held firm. Desegregation of the schools is far from universal, but states are gradually moving toward compliance with Supreme Court decisions in this area. As the states proceed toward the implementation of desegregation in the schools, we can hope that they will consider their actions in terms of the system of values to which we ascribe.

The segregation that exists in the South is essentially de jure segregation; schools in the North are experiencing difficulties because of de facto segregation. A first step in understanding the factors contributing to this form of segregation is to note what has been happening in the past two decades to Negro-white relationships in the North.

One significant change that has implications for the schools is the massive migration of southern Negroes into northern cities. The Negro population in some of these cities has more than doubled as the result of this migration. The influx of Negroes into the near central core of the northern cities has precipitated an out-migration of many whites to the suburbs. The net result of this in- and out-migration has been to create a stable or even an increasing amount of residential segregation for Negroes, while other ethnic groups have continued a pattern of desegregation. In addition, national economic growth has outpaced the Negroes' economic advance. High unemployment among Negroes, particularly the Negro youth, has aggravated the problems associated with inability to provide for one's economic needs.

These factors have led to de facto segregation in a number of school districts in the North. Such districts usually have schools in which the enrollment is largely, if not totally, Negro, while in the same districts there are schools in which the enrollment is largely, or totally, white. While the schools may be innocent victims of larger social problems and conditions which have created segregation, the adverse effects and racial antagonisms are no different than those encountered in de jure segregation.

Havighurst suggests that educators who are disturbed by the existence of racially segregated schools (he also includes economically segregated or lower-class schools) must choose one or both of these policies for action:

1. Accept the existence of such schools and work to improve them within these limits. Many people in effect resign themselves to the fact of economic segregation, and say that we must make the best of it. In particular, they say that the schools should not be used to influence the structure of the city; what the structure of the city presents to the schools is a reality with which the schools must live, they believe.

2. Work through the schools as well as in other ways to reduce economic segregation. That is, work for mixed-class schools by working for mixed-class communities. The group of people who want to reduce economic segregation see a chance to do so through the enormous material resources now going into physical urban renewal programs.[27]

The choice presented by Havighurst involves either accepting society as it is and working within the schools to improve the lot of economically and racially segregated children, or using the schools and school leaders to effect a basic change in society which will automatically improve the lot of these children. Perhaps, as Havighurst suggests, a combination of both policies is most desirable.

Thus we see that the American people have not been afraid to come to grips with issues caused by differences among the people in beliefs, values, and circumstances. As a result, equal educational opportunity is being extended to meet the needs of all at public expense as long as public funds are used to serve a public rather than a private interest. In so doing, the rights of special interest groups to serve their special needs is protected. The people of each school district are faced with the problem of how they, by joining the efforts of neighboring districts and states, can extend the privileges of public education on an equitable basis to ever-increasing numbers.

OTHER INFLUENCES ON THE EVOLUTION OF OUR SCHOOL SYSTEM

The struggles through which the American people have gone, and in which they are yet engaged to establish the American school system, represent democracy in action. Despite our borrowing from other countries and

[27] R. J. Havighurst, "Urban Development and the Educational System," in A. H. Passow, ed., *Schools in Depressed Areas* (New York: Teachers College, Bureau of Publications, 1963), p. 36.

cultures, the school system that has evolved in the United States has been greatly influenced by a number of factors which may be characterized as truly American.

THE FREEDOM MOTIVE

Historians tell us that great migrations seldom involve people who are satisfied with their stations in life. There is no need to re-emphasize here the need to be free which our immigrants felt, for the historical documentation of this point is clear. The freedom motive is equally evident in the development of the schools. The tenacity of the American people to decide for themselves is reflected in the overthrow of church domination, the struggle to make schools free to everyone, and the enforcement of equal educational opportunity to all.

Moreover, the schools have been called upon to keep the freedom motive alive. To learn what America stands for is one of the accepted objectives of our schools. It has been said in many ways that people must be informed to be free. Does the struggle for freedom that has been characteristic of America make us better able than other nations to understand the nature of freedom and pass this understanding on to later generations? It seems to the American people that this is true, and they express the hope and faith that through education this freedom can be kept alive in the world.

CIVIC AND OCCUPATIONAL RESPONSIBILITIES AND NEEDS

The needs to make a living and to participate intelligently in decision-making at all government levels have always had their influence on the schools. Even though in early days the major purpose for the instruction of the children was to make it possible for them to participate in the affairs of the church, it was not long before these other needs also had to be served.

It is not uncommon to hear adults inquire of children in school, "What are you studying?" From their common experiences with the question, children know that it has reference to their future occupation and that a correct answer is "Oh, I'm going to be a nurse," "a doctor," "a lawyer," "an engineer," "a teacher," or "a bricklayer." Going to school to develop the competence required for a job has become an important objective of the school.

Civic competence, meaning the knowledge, interest, and understanding needed to vote and participate intelligently in community, state, national, and international affairs, has broadened in significance throughout the years. In Colonial times it often referred to a special kind of occupational competence, such as preparation to become a local official in the town meeting, a lawyer, a mayor, or a higher government official. Today it is even more important for all citizens to participate in civic affairs. It has become a duty of the schools to play a major role in helping to make people competent for this responsibility. These civic and occupational influences have been important factors in the secularization of the schools.

GROWTH IN PROFESSIONALISM

The first institution in America that provided some instruction for prospective teachers was established in Concord, Vermont, in 1823 by Reverend Samuel R. Hall. This was a three-year program including instruction in the common-school subjects and a series of lectures during the latter part of the third year on the "Art of Teaching." In 1839 Horace Mann established the first state normal school in the United States at Lexington, Massachusetts. The normal school had a much more complete teacher education program than that started by Hall. By 1870, the state normal school had grown greatly in popularity. Today the teachers college, often a part of a state university, is an essential portion of the educational system.

With the coming of the normal school there was a renewed emphasis on influences from the European schools. In addition to the ideas that continued to come from England, the thinking of such educators as Pestalozzi, Froebel, Rousseau, and Herbart began to have an effect upon practices in American schools. A new profession seemed to be in the making and, with its development, there grew up a great body of educational literature.

Professional Knowledge About Teaching and Learning

The rise of the normal school and the teachers college brought about a great interest in investigating the nature of the learning process and, hence, the determining of appropriate methods of teaching. Soon American educators were carrying on their own investigations and adding to the professional literature contributions that were equally as important to teaching as the knowledge which they had gained from their colleagues in other parts of the world.

During the latter part of the nineteenth century, G. Stanley Hall led a movement which became identified as Child Study. As a part of this movement, educators sought to ascertain how the personality of the child develops. Children were observed, weighed, and measured to determine aspects of physical growth. Detailed records were kept on these phases of growth and on achievement in school. By the turn of the century, the scientific movement, so important in the development of our technology, had begun to have a real impact on the field of education. Thus were developed such courses as "The Physical Development of the Child," "Educational Psychology," "Intelligence Testing," "General Methods of Teaching," and "Special Methods" (for the teaching of special subjects). Thorndike and Terman are familiar to students of education as men who made tremendous contributions to testing and measurement.

Such studies led investigators into further examination of teaching procedures, the grade placement of children, promotions, individual differences, the social development of the child, curriculum reorganization, the methods of adjusting to individual differences, and many other such topics. One need but glance at a recent volume of the *Encyclopedia of Educational Research* to be impressed by the great body of knowledge about education and the educative process that is accumulating year by year.[28]

The interest in the social development of the child has caused the educator to realize that education is perhaps both an art and a science. Hence, in recent years considerable attention has been given to a combination of these approaches. Philosophical considerations have made it necessary to raise again the question of purposes. New knowledge about child development and evaluation of the "total growth" of the child has led to a consideration of new procedures, new methods of classifying pupils, new curricular interests, and new concepts of the role of the school in modern society.

Articulation of Purposes

Throughout the development of the schools, the American people have shown a profound faith in knowledge. A prime responsibility of the school was to pass on to each generation the heritage of the past. Fact-gathering was essential. The acquisition of course content in the several subject-matter fields became very important.

The disciplinary concept of learning, now discredited because it was based upon a faulty psychological theory, had a tremendous influence on our schools. According to this concept, the training of the mind, which disciplined the child in the learning process, was a major value to be derived from schooling. Proponents of the concept believed that mastery of the more difficult subjects had a greater disciplinary effect than that of learning the content of easy subjects.

In recent years, the schools have been guided in a further clarification of their role by a careful examination of the unique function of the school in a democratic society. In 1918, the Commission on the Reorganization of Secondary Education emphasized the fact that in a democracy education "should develop in each individual the knowledge, interests, ideals, habits, and powers whereby he will find his place and use that place to shape both himself and society toward nobler ideals." The Commission then went on

[28] Chester W. Harris, ed., *Encyclopedia of Educational Research* (New York: Macmillan Company, 1960).

to name the major objectives of education in a democracy, the seven "cardinal principles" of secondary education, which, in brief, are:

1. Health knowledge and habits.
2. Command of the fundamental processes.
3. Worthy home membership.
4. Education for a vocation.
5. Education for citizenship.
6. Worthy use of leisure time.
7. Ethical character.[29]

Practically all basic textbooks in elementary and secondary education, as well as those on the special aspects of these programs, summarize professional thinking about the purposes of education. Usually such statements point out the unique purposes of education in a democracy, especially as we view them in America. Among the statements of purposes that have made a deep impression upon school people are those issued by the Educational Policies Commission.

In 1938, this Commission grouped the objectives of American education under the four headings, Self-Realization, Human Relationship, Economic Efficiency, and Civic Responsibility.[30] Two more recent reports, *Education for All American Children*[31] and *Education for All American Youth,*[32] outlined ways in which elementary and secondary school programs can be extended to reach the basic "needs" of *all* children and youth. In 1959, the Commission, on behalf of the profession, took up the challenge of lay critics and issued *An Essay on Quality in Public Education* in which many of the aspects of program, organization, administration, and commitment to education are spelled out for the American people.[33] This same Commission, in 1961, issued a statement on *The Central Purpose of American Education.* In this publication, the "freedom of the mind" achieved by the development of one's "rational powers," or ability to think, was conceived as being central to the accomplishment of the full range of objectives that had been

[29] Quoted in Ellwood P. Cubberley, *An Introduction to the Study of Education and Teaching* (Boston: Houghton Mifflin, 1925), p. 160.

[30] Educational Policies Commission, *The Purposes of Education in American Democracy* (Washington: National Education Association, 1938).

[31] Educational Policies Commission, *Education for All American Children* (Washington: National Education Association, 1948).

[32] Educational Policies Commission, *Education for All American Youth: A Forward Look* (Washington: National Education Association, 1952).

[33] Educational Policies Commission, *An Essay on Quality in Public Education* (Washington: National Education Association, 1959).

stated previously. Thus these professional spokesmen reiterate in succinct and forceful language the overarching purpose of American education. Their concluding statement presents the challenge in these words:

Man has before him the possibility of a new level of greatness, a new realization of human dignity and effectiveness. The instrument which will realize this possibility is that kind of education which frees the mind and enables it to contribute to a full and worthy life. To achieve this goal is the high hope of the nation and the central challenge to its schools.[34]

Professional Organizations

From the preceding discussion it is obvious that professional organizations tend to become the official representatives of the school workers. The National Education Association, with its many departments, serves as a clearing house for the expression of ideas about education which come from its large membership throughout the country. State and local teachers' associations, too, are organizations created to give expression to the leadership that is growing up among members of the emerging teaching profession. The American Federation of Teachers, a teachers' union affiliated with the A.F.L.-C.I.O., has been active particularly in improving the welfare of the teacher.

The three major professional organizations for school administrators are the Department of Elementary School Principals, The National Association of Secondary School Principals, and the American Association of School Administrators. These organizations have auxiliaries at the state level in most states.

Administrators' professional organizations, especially the A.A.S.A., have been active in attempting to upgrade their standards for admission and continued membership. This, of course, tends to upgrade the standards for admission and membership in the profession itself. These organizations set standards not only to create minimum qualifications for entry into the organization, but also to provide rules for ethical behavior of their membership. Many educators see control of entry into and regulation of standards for continued membership in professional education organizations as an important step toward the total professionalization of all educators. For education cannot become a "true" profession until its members are able to control both the minimum qualifications for entry into the profession and minimum standards of competency and ethical behavior for continued membership.

[34] Educational Policies Commission, *The Central Purpose of American Education* (Washington: National Education Association, 1961), p. 21.

SPECIAL INTEREST GROUPS

It is difficult indeed to know which pressures for changes in the public schools stem from the insidious influence of selfish interests, and which stem from the justified demands of a minority group fighting for its right to be heard in the public forum. If our observations have been correct, at no time during the development of the public school system has there not been some serious debate of, and strong opposition to, the changes that were finally made.

The administrator must remember, however, that education in this country is not centrally planned and administered from a national office. Neither is it wholly controlled by state governments and the local boards of education to which they delegate certain powers. The forces affecting American education today are both complex and varied. An interesting analysis of factors influencing the changing educational scene appears in the Sixtieth Yearbook of the National Society for the Study of Education.[35] Here eight social scientists, each using his own discipline as a basis for analysis, present their views concerning these influences.

Recently, too, we have noted the activity of groups that appear to be organized specifically to question the modern development of the public schools and the motives and abilities of educators. Magazine, newspaper, radio, and television accounts of incidents occurring in some school districts where desegregation has taken place vividly describe the pressures placed upon school and government officials as they attempt to enforce the action of the courts.

In a recent publication, Campbell and others present a penetrating analysis of the role of the schools today. They also introduce the reader to groups that influence educational decision-making.[36]

It is important that the administrator gain perspective by studying those influences which have had a lasting effect on the public schools. It is easy to become harassed by local pressures and by those which for short periods of time influence public opinion, even at the state or national levels. The school administrator should be a person who can live with controversy, understand and appreciate the source of opposing positions, and have the courage to stand against opposition. He should also help the majority of the substantial citizens of the community see the educational values for

[35] *Social Forces Influencing American Education.* 60th Yearbook of the National Society For the Study of Education (Chicago: University of Chicago Press, 1961).

[36] Roald F. Campbell, Luvern L. Cunningham, and Roderick F. McPhee, *The Organization and Control of American Schools* (Columbus, Ohio: Charles E. Merrill Books, Inc., 1965).

which Americans generally have fought and the importance of continuing public interest in education.

CHARACTERISTICS OF OUR SCHOOL SYSTEM

Throughout our discussion of the development of American education we have attempted to document the fact that, although the American people have, at times, borrowed from European countries, they have built a school system that is essentially American. Certain characteristics of this system set it apart from that of any other country in the world. The administrator is introduced to them at this point so that he may reflect upon them and their implications for his behavior as he learns more about his job, himself, and the challenges of his profession.

SCHOOLS BELONG TO THE PEOPLE

Nowhere in the world do the rank and file of the citizenry have as much to say about their schools as in this country. While the state is regarded as the legally responsible agency for the development of the school system, the people, through their representatives in government or through the courts, have always limited, and continue to limit, this authority according to their will.

Furthermore, the people actively participate in school matters at the level of the school district. Any administrator who has worked on a school bond issue knows and respects the power of the citizens. Even the tenure of an educational administrator is often dependent upon the development of an educational program that is satisfactory to the people. The power of community forces is in fact so strong that there is little hope of building an adequate educational program without their support. Thus the ability to lead in community thinking about education is one of the competencies which the prospective school administrator must acquire.

OPPORTUNITY FOR ALL

Although the goal is still unachieved, America is moving toward having children of all classes attend the same schools. Rich or poor, laborer or professional, Protestant, Catholic, or Jew, white or black, the children receive essentially the same general education. In more cases than not they attend these schools together to learn, in common, the democratic values for which their country stands.

Much has already been said about the ways in which the interests of minorities have been protected by the use of such legal processes as challenging the law in the courts. But the greatest protection of all minority rights is the protection against class distinction. While it would not be argued that this country is wholly free of classes, free universal public education is one of the powerful forces that hold class distinction in check. No matter how low a child's station in life may be, his chances of rising above it are enhanced by the fact that he has an educational opportunity, at least through high school, almost equal to that of the children of families in more fortunate circumstances. This is the ideal toward which we strive. Through our schools, we attempt to diminish class distinctions, while in many parts of the world schools perpetuate them.

To realize this ideal, however, we must achieve greater equalization of educational opportunity among communities and among states. More must be done to provide opportunities for those who have ability but lack financial resources to extend their education beyond high school. Better facilities will need to be developed to accommodate children and youth whose educational needs are out of the ordinary.

PROGRAMS ARE ADJUSTED TO NEEDS

The horizontal extension of the schools—that is, widening the range of curricular offerings and the services provided by the school to minister to the needs of pupils—has been tremendous. As the school system has developed, the purposes of education have broadened, the number of pupils has greatly increased, and the range of abilities, interests, and needs of children has been extended.

Many new programs and innovations have been introduced into the schools to meet the variety of needs of our children. Among them are team-teaching programs; individualized reading programs; increased use of instructional television and other audio-visual devices; introduction of mechanical teaching aids, such as teaching machines and language laboratories; provision of guidance and counseling services in secondary schools and in some elementary schools; increased attention to vocational education and preparation; and advanced placement programs for college-bound students. Many more changes could be mentioned, all of them a part of the continuous efforts of our schools to meet the needs of all children.

Adjustment to these changes constitutes a major problem in education today. The need to expand the program is increasing so rapidly that we have neither the educational facilities nor the personnel to cope adequately with the problem. Yet here again the United States leads other countries in efforts in this direction.

PUPILS LEARN A DEMOCRATIC WAY OF LIFE

Foreign visitors to American schools express great surprise at the freedom with which school children go about their educational tasks. They show concern over the wide range in achievement that can be recognized among children in the same grade. They are amazed and bewildered on the one hand at the seeming lack of discipline and, on the other hand, at the initiative of children to see a task through to completion.

As our schools have developed, we have come to realize that responsible action, such as that required of each individual in a democracy, with a minimum of compulsion from external authority, is something to be learned. So children must learn how to be democratic, what it means to be responsible, and what the consequences of irresponsible behavior are, just as they must learn the knowledge and skills necessary for the vocation they choose to follow. The successful induction of children into a democratic society is a difficult task. No doubt the schools have made many mistakes in the attempt thus far. However, we believe the effort is characterized by the following, in varying degrees:

1. A democratic organization in which there is a recognized place for participation in planning and developing the school life by children, teachers, parents, and administrators.

2. Sufficient respect for individual differences so that administrators, boards of education, parents, laymen, and teachers are making an effort to vary the learning experiences of children to meet individual needs; and so that differences of opinion, beliefs, values, and customs, both in school and out, are given freedom of expression in making decisions.

3. Sufficient faith in the method of intelligence, so that decisions (of any consequence to those concerned) are made after appropriate processes of collecting, analyzing, and seriously reviewing and interpreting appropriate data necessary to the decision.

4. Freedom to examine the issues that are controversial in the school, community, and nation, with a view toward gaining a deeper understanding of the differences among people and of the need to perpetuate or diminish these differences.

5. The disposition to withhold judgment until it can be formulated on the basis of a reasonable amount of available data.

6. Encouragement of individual and original expression, giving proper place to initiative, but at the same time recognizing that all must play by a common set of "rules for the game."

Hence the school tends more and more to get outside the four walls, to engage in community affairs as part of the learning experiences of children and youth, and to take its place along with other agencies in assuming responsibility for the induction of students into responsible community life.

THE SCHOOL HAS A UNIQUE ROLE

As the purposes of the school have encompassed the total development of the child, an increasing number of duties and responsibilities have devolved upon it. Not only has the curriculum been broadened to teach children the many skills they need to take their places in society, but services too have increased both in number and kind. The major function of services to pupils has been to create those conditions under which learning takes place best.

Some people believe there is danger that the school may, in its zealousness to serve the people, actually take over functions that rightfully belong to other community agencies. The fact that the school has to bear the brunt of the criticism for the delinquency of youth indicates that people have assumed the school to be the agency of greatest influence in the child's life. In some instances this may be true. By and large, however, children and youth are educated by the experiences that are provided throughout the communities in which they grow up. The home, the church, the Y.M.C.A. and Y.W.C.A., the 4-H Clubs, the Future Farmers of America, and many other formal and informal groups, as well as the school, are educating the child.

In developing a community-wide educational program, it must be remembered that the school has a responsibility for *all* the young people of the community. No other single institution or agency has this responsibility. As a public trust, and with an equal responsibility to each of its pupils, the school is the agency upon which the American people have depended for examination, assessment, and interpretation of the many community influences on the life of its young people.

THE CHANGING CHARACTER OF EDUCATIONAL ADMINISTRATION

In the early years of our national history, schooling was a relatively simple enterprise. Children walked to school—first, to learn to read the Bible, and, later, to learn the 3 R's for broader secular purposes. The school buildings they attended were not elaborate structures. Furnishings were meager. Permissive rather than mandatory legislation was largely the governing role of the state. Local autonomy permitted people to have good schools or poor ones.

Probably the little red schoolhouse, which has only recently passed from the American scene, is the most characteristic symbol of the local school operation that was so jealously guarded. There was little need here for administration in the sense that we know it today. The teacher taught the children of grades one through eight, made out the attendance records, took care of his own discipline, made the fires and did other janitorial work, all as a part of the day's activities. A local board of laymen hired the teacher and made a record of the financial affairs of the district. Usually the local board "opened the school" in the fall of the year. It was the responsibility of the board to see that the school house was cleaned and painted, that the roof was repaired, that the stove was in order, that the floors were oiled, that the seats and desks were repaired and varnished, and that the coal and other supplies needed for the year were purchased. The teacher assumed the responsibility for the children while in school. The board of directors— school committee or otherwise designated local board of education—managed the business affairs. When the office of county superintendent was created in the nineteenth century, the county superintendent became the arm of the state through which local schools were regulated.

In the cities, however, the development of administration took place somewhat differently. Here, school buildings were needed to house more pupils than could be handled by a single teacher. Thus in the multiple-teacher school, someone, usually the teacher of the highest grade, became the "head teacher" or the "principal teacher." Early Latin Grammar schools of sufficient size to require more than one teacher, and later the academies, often referred to the head teacher as the "head master," a name still used commonly in private schools. Head teachers, head masters, or principals "had charge of the building," usually kept all records, and had general responsibility for the discipline of the pupils. Before the establishment of the superintendency, these building heads were responsible to the local school committee, or some other similarly named body, which had legal responsibility for the schools and performed any necessary administrative functions.

As schools took on more complex responsibilities, and as the population of the nation congregated in the urban centers, a greater number of managerial tasks needed to be performed. The sheer weight of these responsibilities caused lay boards of education to see the wisdom of employing an administrative officer to assume such obligations. Throughout the growth of this American school system, then, there has developed an increasing awareness of the need for professional leadership and administration. This chapter has provided some of the historical setting for the educational challenges to present and future school administrators. The following chapter describes the evolution of administrative responsibility from a single managerial role to the complex administrative function required by the vast and intricate school systems of today.

SUGGESTED ACTIVITIES

1. List a few important decisions which the American people should be making about the public schools and show how these decisions would affect the schools in which you work.
2. Select one school problem about which decisions need to be made at the present time. In solving the problem, what decisions should be made at the district level? The state level? The national level? Why?
3. As an administrator, what part do you think you should play in the decision to be made in 2 above?
4. Read Chapter V, "A Country of Common People," in Counts' *Education and American Civilization*. What is the implication for the development of education in America?
5. What are the implications of the pattern of American values described by Passow (see bibliography below) for the elimination of discrimination among groups in the schools in which you work?

SELECTED READINGS

American Association of School Administrators, *Religion in the Public Schools.* Washington, D.C.: The Association, 1964.

BRICKMAN, WILLIAM W. and LEHRER, STANLEY. *Religion, Government, and Education.* New York: Society for the Advancement of Education, 1962.

CAMPBELL, ROALD F. and BUNNELL, ROBERT A. (eds.). *Nationalizing Influences on Secondary Education.* Chicago: Midwest Administration Center, The University of Chicago, 1963.

CAMPBELL, ROALD F., CUNNINGHAM, LUVERN L., and McPHEE, RODERICK F. *The Organization and Control of American Schools.* Columbus, Ohio: Charles E. Merrill Books, Inc., 1965.

COUNTS, G. S. *Education and American Civilization.* New York: Bureau of Publications, Teachers College, Columbia University, 1952.

Educational Policies Commission, *The Central Purpose of American Education.* Washington: National Education Association, 1961.

————, *The Unique Role of the Superintendent of Schools.* Washington: National Education Association, 1965.

EDWARDS, N. and RICHEY, H. G. *The School in the American Social Order.* Boston: Houghton Mifflin Co., 1963.

GOOD, HARRY. *History of American Education*. New York: Macmillan Company, 1956.

PASSOW, A. HARRY, (ed.). *Education in Depressed Areas*. New York: Teachers College, Columbia University, 1963.

SUFRIN, SIDNEY C. *Issues in Federal Aid to Education*. Syracuse, N.Y.: Syracuse University Press, 1962.

THAYER, V. T. *The Role of the School in American Society*. New York: Dodd, Mead & Company, 1960.

3

The Development and Meaning

of Administration

IN CHAPTER 1, WE WERE CONFRONTED WITH SOME BRIEF EXPOSURES to the reality of administration. In Chapter 2, we noted certain historical developments that appear to have had relevance to the evolution of schools and to the emergence of the function of administration in those schools and school systems. We shall now examine more explicitly the development and meaning of administration—first in its general sense and, second, in its application to education. We shall conclude this chapter by suggesting the place and limitations of theory in administration and by indicating specific ways in which administration will be viewed in Chapters 4 through 7.

THE DEVELOPMENT OF ADMINISTRATION

Educational administration, like many other branches of administration, has suffered from too much emphasis on the adjective and too little on the noun. To understand educational administration, one must acquire some sense of the development of administration generally. This may be found in treatises on public administration, business management, industrial psychology, military leadership, and in other writings. Analysis in all of these settings has dealt with mobilizing the efforts of a number of people toward the achievement of a common goal.

Activating members of a group toward a common objective is as old as history itself. Whether we look at the public regulation of the waterways in ancient Egypt, the duties of the magistrates in the far-flung Roman Empire, or the efficient use of resources in the German states more than 200 years ago—growing largely from the work of the Cameralists—the significance of administration becomes clear. While other sources must be consulted for a history of administration,[1] we would mention that both Alexander Hamilton and Woodrow Wilson made contributions to the understanding and practice of the field.

Some aspects of the conflict between Hamilton and Jefferson—both members of Washington's cabinet—are well known. It may not be as fully appreciated that Hamilton became the chief Federalist philosopher and perhaps its most brilliant practitioner. The Federalists must be credited with creating an administrative system from practically nothing. White explains that the system they created included an independent chief executive, a plan of effective delegation by the chief executive to the department heads, an administrative organization separate from the several states, canons of personal integrity on the part of public officers, and approval of the right of public criticism.[2]

This centralization of power and responsibility was often opposed by Jefferson, who was disposed to place confidence in legislative as opposed to executive action, and who emphasized states' rights more than federal responsibility. Hamilton, however, continued to stress the need for an energetic executive, and the customs service in his own department was perhaps the best example of his ideal of government. This page in our history serves to highlight some of the persistent issues found in administration.

In 1887 Wilson attempted to distinguish between politics and administration. He said:

. . . administration lies outside the proper sphere of politics. Administrative questions are not political questions. Although politics sets the tasks for administration, it should not be suffered to manipulate its offices.[3]

What appears to be a clear differentiation between policy and administration is probably intended for quite another purpose. The cue is in Wilson's last sentence; he was greatly concerned lest special interest groups manipu-

[1] For example, see Albert Lepawsky, *Administration* (New York: Alfred A. Knopf, 1949), Chapter 4.

[2] Leonard D. White, *The Federalists* (New York: Macmillan Co., 1948), p. 512.

[3] Woodrow Wilson, "The Study of Administration," *Political Science Quarterly*, XLI (December 1941), p. 494. Reprinted from 1887 issue.

late public officeholders and thus prevent them from serving the general welfare. Even so, the relationship between policy and administration was raised, and the question is still being vigorously debated.

RECENT HISTORICAL EMPHASES

Let us turn from this brief exploration of the emergence of the concept of administration and look more specifically at some of the recent historical emphases in administration. In each case, we shall deal with a major emphasis by citing the work of a few contributors. These contributors were in reality students of administration; they described or rationalized what was being said about administration and, at least to some extent, what was being practiced in administration. Some of them were also practicing administrators themselves, and all of them had many direct relationships with practitioners.

Job Analysis

The first approach to administration was that of job analysis. We shall note the work of two major contributors to this approach. Frederick Taylor, often called the father of the scientific management movement, was born in 1856. He studied in France, Germany, and Italy in his youth, and later earned an M.E. degree at Stevens Institute. From 1878 to 1889, he was employed by the Midvale Steel Company; first as a laborer, then as clerk, machinist, foreman, chief draftsman, and finally chief engineer. Taylor noticed that workers were in charge of both planning and performing their jobs, a situation that led, he thought, to much waste and inefficiency. His experience at all levels of industry led him to formulate his principles, which were condensed in *The Principles of Scientific Management,* published in 1911.[4]

His essential points have been summarized by Villers as follows:

1. *Time-study principle.* All productive effort should be measured by accurate time study and a standard time established for all work done in the shop.

2. *Piece-rate principle.* Wages should be proportional to output and their rates based on the standards determined by time study. As a corollary, a worker should be given the highest grade of work of which he is capable.

3. *Separation-of-planning-from-performance principle.* Management should take over from the workers the responsibility for planning the work and making the performance physically possible. Planning should be based on time studies and other data related to production, which are scientifically determined and

[4] This and other works appear in Frederick W. Taylor, *Scientific Management* (New York: Harper & Brothers, 1947).

systematically classified; it should be facilitated by standardization of tools, implements, and methods.

4. *Scientific-methods-of-work principle.* Management should take over from the workers the responsibility for their methods of work, determine scientifically the best methods, and train the workers accordingly.

5. *Managerial-control principle.* Managers should be trained and taught to apply scientific principles of management and control (such as management by exception and comparison with valid standards).

6. *Functional-management principle.* The strict application of military principles should be reconsidered and the industrial organization should be so designed that it best serves the purpose of improving the co-ordination of activities among the various specialists.[5]

Taylor and other spokesmen of the scientific management movement were influential in seeing many of their principles applied to such firms as the Midland Steel Company, Bethlehem Steel Company, Santa Fe Railway, and Acme Wire Company. Labor, on the other hand, resisted time and motion studies, and other activities which were perceived as treating men as though they were machines. The whole movement became the object of an investigation by the Social Committee of the House of Representatives in 1912. Following extended hearings, Congress attached a rider to the military appropriations bill prohibiting the use of such funds for time and motion studies.

From the perspective of our day, we find that Taylor took a narrow view of management, and that, moreover, he tended to ignore the psychological or personal aspects of mobilizing human effort. At the same time, he did demonstrate that many jobs could be done more efficiently. Even more important, his work stands as a monument to the concept that management can be studied scientifically. No aspect of administration has remained immune to this idea.

Henri Fayol was another major contributor to the job analysis approach to administration. He was born in 1841 of a family of the French *petite bourgeoisie.* At the age of nineteen, he graduated from the national School of Mines at St. Etienne. In a sense, he had four careers: twelve years as a mining engineer, sixteen years as a geologist, thirty years as the very able managing director of a large metallurgical firm, and seven years—after retirement at age seventy-seven—as a teacher of administration. In the fourth period, he undertook two main tasks: the first was the formation of a Centre of Administrative Studies; the second was an effort to persuade the French government to pay some attention to the principles of administration.

[5] Raymond Villers, *Dynamic Management in Industry* (Englewood Cliffs, N.J.: Prentice-Hall, Inc., 1960), p. 29.

Although Fayol wrote his book, *Administration Industrielle et Générale,* in 1916, it did not appear in an English translation until 1929, and it was not made generally available in the United States until 1949.[6] Containing the first two parts of the eventual treatise Fayol planned to write, it describes the necessity and the possibility of teaching the principles and elements of management. The now famous elements were planning, organizing, command, co-ordination, and control.

In the early stages of the popularization of Fayol's work, attempts were made by some to represent his approach as antithetical to that of Taylor. But at the Second International Congress held at Brussels in 1925, Fayol himself made clear that such interpretations were false. Actually, both men applied the scientific method. Taylor worked primarily at the operative level, or the bottom of the hierarchal structure, while Fayol began with the managing director at the top of the hierarchy. The work of Fayol has been reflected in the thinking and writing of Gulick, Urwick, Sears, and other students of administration. A more detailed treatment of this approach to administration will be found in Chapter 5.

Both Taylor and Fayol were concerned with industry; both believed that the processes involved in production could be analyzed and studied scientifically. While Taylor concentrated on the worker and Fayol on the manager, both had as an ultimate objective the increased efficiency of industry. To be sure, in his later years Fayol extended the application of his administrative principles to government as well as to industry. Even so, both men tended to stress organizational processes and to ignore individuals as such. The time was ripe for a new emphasis, and Mary Parker Follett helped to supply it.

Human Relations

Human relations constituted the second major approach to administration. Again the work of two major contributors will be noted. Mary Parker Follett was born in 1868. She graduated from Radcliffe College, where she followed a course devoted to economics, government, and philosophy. Throughout her life, she worked to help bring about a better-ordered society in which the individual might live a more satisfying life. This motivation was expressed when she served on the Boston Committee on the Extended Use of School Buildings from 1909 to 1911, in the help she gave to establish the Department of Vocational Guidance in Boston in 1912, in her service on the Massachusetts Minimum Wage Board for many years, and in her great interest in the League of Nations.

---

[6] Henri Fayol, *General and Industrial Management* (London: Sir Isaac Pitman & Sons, Ltd., 1949).

Her book, *Creative Experience,*[7] has been characterized by Metcalf and Urwick as follows:

. . . mainly psychological in interest and content, [it] marks a definite advance both in the crystallization of thought and in style and phraseology. Its thesis is the reciprocal character—the interpenetration—of all psychological phenomena, from the simplest to the most complex. Human relationships—the ways and work of society and of industry—are at their best when difference is solved through conference and co-operation, when the parties at interest (1) evoke each other's latent ideas based upon the facts of the situation, (2) come to see each other's viewpoints and to understand each other better, and (3) integrate those viewpoints and become united in the pursuit of their common goal.[8]

Follett contended that the fundamental problem of any enterprise, whether it be local government, national government, a business organization, or an educational system, is the building and maintenance of dynamic, yet harmonious, human relationships. She tended to reduce her principles of organization to four in number, all aspects of what she termed *co-ordination*. The principles were:

1. Co-ordination by direct contact of the responsible people concerned.

2. Co-ordination in the early stages.

3. Co-ordination as the reciprocal relating of all factors in the situation.

4. Co-ordination as a continuing process.[9]

Mary Parker Follett might be characterized as a social philosopher with deep psychological insights. She came onto the scene when the process and organizational aspects of administration had been emphasized to the exclusion, perhaps, of the values to be cherished for society and for the most adequate development of individuals in that society. As an academician Miss Follett made a contribution in both the United States and England; but she was also a woman of action. She found much stimulation in the observation of governmental and industrial organizations, and she was welcomed as a consultant by many such enterprises.

While Mary Parker Follett became the first great exponent of the aspect of human relations in administration, it remained for Elton Mayo and his colleagues to supply empirical data in support of such a view. Mayo was born in Adelaide, Australia, in 1880, and received A.B. and M.A. degrees from the University of Adelaide. For twenty years, he served as the senior

[7] Mary Parker Follett, *Creative Experience* (New York: Longmans, Green, 1924).

[8] Henry C. Metcalf and L. Urwick (eds.), *Dynamic Administration* (New York: Harper & Brothers, 1942), p. 14. The collected papers of Mary Parker Follett with an introduction by the editors.

[9] *Ibid.,* p. 297.

professor in the Department of Industrial Research of the Harvard Business School. From 1923 to 1932, he and his associates were connected with the now famous experiments done at the Hawthorne plant of the Western Electric Company, near Chicago.

Industry had long assumed that wages and physical working conditions were the chief factors in employee motivation. The first experiment at Hawthorne, 1923–26, was quite simply designed to test the effect of one of these physical conditions—illumination—on worker production. It was found that illumination was not significantly related to production. In the true scientific spirit, the results of the experiment were accepted as proof that the basic assumption needed reconsideration.

A second inquiry was conducted to explore the problem more fully. A group of six girl operatives was selected for study to determine what factors might be related to their job productivity. It was found that whatever factors were changed—whether rest periods, length of day, or methods of pay-ment—and whatever way they were changed, even if the change meant returning to the original conditions, production continued to increase. Moreover, the girls were more and more satisfied with their jobs, and their attendance continued to show greater regularity. Findings of this nature were secured almost without exception over a five-year period of meticulous experimentation between 1927 and 1932.

Mayo has explained the findings as follows:

. . . What the Company actually did for the group was to reconstruct entirely its whole industrial situation.

. . . the consequence was that there was a period during which the individual workers and the group had to re-adapt themselves to a new industrial milieu, a milieu in which their own self-determination and their social well-being ranked first, and the work was incidental.

. . . The Western Electric experiment was primarily directed not to the external condition but to the inner organization. By strengthening the "temperamental" inner equilibrium of the workers, the Company enabled them to achieve a mental "steady state" which offered a high resistance to a variety of external conditions.[10]

Clearly, this and similar experiments demonstrated that economic and mechanistic approaches to human relations in industry were inadequate. While wages and working conditions are important to the worker, they rank second to what Mayo called "a method of living in a social relationship." Apparently, the girls in the Hawthorne experiment had gained a sense of playing an important part in a project instead of being mere cogs in a large productive enterprise.

[10] Elton Mayo, *The Human Problems of an Industrial Civilization* (Boston: Gradu-ate School of Business Administration, Harvard University, 1946), pp. 73, 75.

Mayo's work has been subjected to much examination, and some students find two major biases in his experiments.[11] He may have had a management bias, since he was employed by business to help business solve its problems. He may also have had a clinical bias, in that he began with observation and not with theory. Apparently, Mayo did have some disdain for theory and had more faith in empiricism. Regardless of these criticisms, however, one must recognize that through long and meticulous experimentation Mayo and his associates collected a large body of data that make it clear that what goes on inside the worker is even more significant for production than what goes on outside.

Were one to accept the work of Follett and Mayo uncritically, one might assume that adequate human relations is the sum total of administration. Indeed, the so-called "democratic" emphasis in administration of the 1940's and 50's may have sprung from the work of these contributors or, more likely, the inadequate interpretations of some of their disciples. Fortunately, Chester Barnard had turned his great talent to the examination of administration.

Behavioral Science and Administration

Chester Barnard appears to have been the first to relate administration to the behavioral sciences. Born in 1886, Barnard attended Harvard College from 1906 to 1909. He served for many years as the president of the New Jersey Bell Telephone Company and for four years as president of the Rockefeller Foundation. During this time he demonstrated an unusual capacity to deal with theoretical abstractions and with practical problems of management. He found himself consulting with clergymen, military men, government officials, university officials, and leaders of widely diversified businesses on problems of organization.

In 1937, he prepared eight lectures for the Lowell Institute in Boston. These lectures, revised and expanded, became his very important book, *The Functions of the Executive*.[12] Barnard himself suggests that the book has two parts: ". . . an exposition of a theory of co-operation and organization" and "a study of the functions . . . of executives in formal organizations." The book emphasizes the universal character of formal organizations and stresses the need for a theory to explain their behavior.

The development of an appropriate theory, Barnard suggested, has been retarded because of a misconception about the nature of authority, a misconception growing out of interpretations of the church; and because of

[11] See Delbert C. Miller and William H. Form, *Industrial Sociology*, 2nd ed., (New York: Harper & Brothers, 1964), pp. 78–83.

[12] Chester I. Barnard, *The Functions of the Executive* (Cambridge: Harvard University Press, 1938).

the unwarranted emphasis given to the economic motivation of man. He saw an organization as a complex social organism—an organism whose peripheral aspects had been dealt with by the various social sciences, but whose core had never been analyzed. His own work did much to promote analyses of organizations as such.

A formal organization, Barnard maintained, is

. . . an impersonal system of co-ordinated human efforts; always there is purpose as the co-ordinating and unifying principle; always there is the indispensable ability to communicate, always the necessity of personal willingness, and for effectiveness and efficiency in maintaining the integrity of purpose and the continuity of contributions.[13]

While Barnard dealt mainly with formal organizations, he also pointed out that in each formal organization there are informal organizations. He characterized informal organization as the contacts or interactions of people without a specific conscious joint purpose. While these organizations may not be governed by joint purposes, such informal interactions do change the experience, knowledge, attitudes, and emotions of the people affected. Since informal organization may perform important roles in a formal organization by way of communication and even in terms of helping build self-respect in organization members, Barnard thought that informal organization could not be ignored.

One of Barnard's major contributions was the concept of effectiveness and efficiency. Effectiveness is system-oriented and has to do with the achievement of the organization goals. Efficiency, on the other hand, is person-oriented and has to do with the feelings of satisfaction a worker derives from membership in an organization. For the first time, the interrelationship of organization achievement and individual satisfaction was noted. This conception did much to put the work of Taylor and Fayol, who had concentrated on organization achievement, and Follett and Mayo, who had tended to emphasize individual satisfaction, in appropriate perspective.

A second contributor to the science of administration was Herbert A. Simon. Simon was born in 1916 and received A.B. and Ph.D. degrees from the University of Chicago. His graduate work was in political science and he became particularly interested in public administration. His Ph.D. dissertation became the basis for *Administrative Behavior*,[14] the book that established him as a scholar in the field. Simon has spent much of his professional career at Carnegie Institute of Technology as a professor of administration.

[13] *Ibid.,* pp. 94–95.

[14] Herbert A. Simon, *Administrative Behavior* (New York: Macmillan Co., 1945).

Simon contended that he wrote *Administrative Behavior* in an attempt to develop a set of tools—a set of concepts and a vocabulary—suitable for describing an organization. He did give meaning to such terms as administrative behavior, decision-making, organization, rational behavior, and many others. He relied not only on political science to develop his concepts, but on economics, psychology, and sociology as well. In a very real sense he used the behavioral sciences to explain organizations and the behavior of people in them. In a number of books and journal articles, Simon has continued to provide additional insight into the field of administration.

Following Barnard and Simon, a great many behavioral scientists have turned their attention to the study of organizations and the administration of organizations. Moreover, some practicing administrators recently turned professors have discovered that some of the concepts of the behavioral sciences are very useful in describing organizational and administrative phenomena. This joining of behavioral science and educational administration is caught up in the title of a recent yearbook of the National Society for the Study of Education.[15] In that document the contributions of many other behavioral scientists are noted.

Roughly speaking, the three periods in the development of administration might be established as follows: job analysis, 1910–1930; human relations, 1930–1950; and behavioral science, 1950 to the present. But the transition from one period to the next has been neither complete nor uniform. Moreover, there is something to be said for job analysis and for human relations. Hopefully, the scientific study of administration will provide a way by which these and other approaches can be more adequately examined.

THE DEVELOPMENT OF EDUCATIONAL ADMINISTRATION

We have examined some of the major developments in the general field of administration. We shall turn now to developments in educational administration.

EARLY SCHOOL ADMINISTRATION

It seems appropriate to recall that for most of our history the organization and management of schools has been a function of laymen and not of

---

[15] National Society for the Study of Education, *Behavioral Science and Educational Administration,* Sixty-third Yearbook, Part II (Chicago: University of Chicago Press, 1964).

professional administrators. Suzzalo has traced, with considerable care, the supervision of the schools in Massachusetts.[16] For almost two hundred years, the school committee was, in one way or another, made up of the town selectmen. It was 1827 before school government was differentiated from general government, and it was some years later before the lay school committee or board of education was ready to employ a school administrator. Thus school administration did not evolve as a field of practice until the latter part of the nineteenth century, nor become a field of study until the twentieth century.

While much of our discussion above has dealt with major concepts and ideas about administration, any consideration of the development of educational administration must deal chiefly with its practice. The development of concepts about educational administration and the testing of those concepts empirically is at best a relatively new and unexplored field.

State and county school administration have both played important parts in the development of educational administration in America, but the major surge has been at the local level, chiefly in the growth of the school superintendency and of the school principalship. This phenomenon is largely a result of the decentralization of education in this country. The usual connotation of school administration to this day is local school administration. Any other meaning requires an adjective such as state school administration or county school administration.

Leadership in local school administration came first in our cities. Gradually, as multiple school districts within a single city were merged, the board of education found itself in need of a full-time executive. The first cities to establish the office of the superintendent of schools were Buffalo and Louisville in 1837, and St. Louis and Providence in 1839.[17] The practice soon spread throughout the country. Although a number of cities were unsuccessful in their experimentation with the office and abolished it for a while, they eventually returned to it as the best solution to meet the need for district-wide administration. Duties varied from city to city, with some stressing the examining and visiting function while others placed emphasis on business and clerical functions.

In the beginning, the variations in the duties to be performed, the uncertainty regarding the competence needed for the position, and the lack of any specific preparation for it made it difficult to secure people who could serve satisfactorily. Adams spoke disparagingly of the early superintendent, saying that "the ordinary superintendent is apt to be a grammar school

[16] Henry Suzzalo, *The Rise of Local School Supervision in Massachusetts*. Teachers College Contribution No. 1 (New York: Teachers College, Columbia University, 1906).

[17] Theodore Lee Reller, *The Development of the City Superintendency of Schools in the United States* (Philadelphia: published by the author, 1935), p. 7.

teacher run to seed, or some retired clergyman or local politician out of a job." [18] Northend, writing of the situation in Connecticut, described the candidates for the position as follows:

Lawyers, whose business could not "wane" because it never "waxed"; doctors, whose patients were not troublesomely numerous; clergymen, afflicted with bronchitis or some other malady, or not overburdened with hearers; office seekers of various kinds and all sorts of "do nothings" all become suddenly and wonderfully impressed with the importance of common schools, accompanied by a sort of feeling that in themselves was the only power for truly elevating those schools. [19]

But this was not the general evaluation of the superintendency, or the position would not have survived. The outstanding contributions of some of the early superintendents —such as Gove of Denver, Jones of Cleveland, Philbrick of Boston, and Harris of St. Louis—are recorded as examples of the sort of leadership that was being sought for the schools. However, the controversy over the need for the position and the brilliance of a few people holding the office had caused a thorough examination and study of the superintendency.

The growth of cities not only created populous school districts, but also populous attendance areas for single schools. The increased size of schools, in conjunction with the new practice of classifying pupils by grades, led to the need for an executive or principal for each school building. This official was first called a principal teacher, and we learn that Cincinnati had designated principal teachers for each school within that city as early as 1838. Quincy School in Boston in 1847, however, was probably the first school to have a full-time executive or supervising principal. [20] St. Louis reported in 1859 that all schools of that city had been placed in charge of full-time administrators. This practice is now common in city schools over the country.

To begin with, the work of the principal—particularly while he was still the principal teacher—was largely clerical in nature. Reports on enrollment and attendance, and other matters, were needed in the central office. With the increase in enrollments, pupils had to be classified—by grade and otherwise—and assigned to teachers and rooms. As time went on, instruction, particularly in the upper grades, was departmentalized. These and other developments tended to highlight the organization and management

[18] Charles Francis Adams, quoted in J. D. Philbrick, "Which Is the True Ideal?" *Education* I (January 1881), 300–302.

[19] *Connecticut Common School Journal and Annals of Education,* VIII (August 1960).

[20] Paul R. Pierce, *The Origin and Development of the School Principalship* (Chicago: University of Chicago Press, 1934).

functions of the principal. In recent decades, these clerical and management functions of the principal have received less stress, and his instructional leadership role more.

While educational administration has tended to focus on the superintendent of schools as the chief executive officer of the sehool system and on the principal as the executive officer of a single school within a school system, it should be clear, as will be made explicit in Chapter 14, that there are many other administrative positions in education. All of these administrative personnel have unique and complementary roles to perform, as we shall see in Chapter 8.

FEW SCHOLARS

We can find in the history of American education a number of notable administrators. On the other hand, there are relatively few notable scholars of administration. Yet the contributions of such men as Cubberley of Stanford, Strayer of Columbia, Judd of Chicago, Hart of California, and Reeder of Ohio State should not be overlooked. These and a number of other men had a hand in shaping the organization and management of public education in this country. Each of these men, moreover, had hundreds of students who became school administrators and occupied major administrative posts at all levels of education.

Many of these early professors of educational administration approached school administration through the school survey. The surveys of Boise, Idaho, in 1910, and of Montclair, New Jersey, and Baltimore, Maryland, in 1911 appear to be the first.[21] Such surveys provided some of the first literature in educational administration; and indeed, some of the early ones are still very useful reading.

Since the chief purpose of the survey, however, was to improve practice, the approach often dealt with what *ought* to be, in place of determining basic relationships. The surveys tended to reflect the value judgments of the surveyors and, as such, often proved most useful in pointing the way to improved practice. At the same time, such surveys were not designed to deal with basic concepts or to test such concepts in an empirical setting.

More than anything else, these early students of educational administration approached the field from the standpoint of job analysis. They observed administrators at work, noted the tasks they were required to perform, and then suggested how these tasks might be performed more effectively. Consciously or unconsciously, perhaps both, this attitude was a reflection of

[21] Dan H. Cooper, "School Surveys," *Encyclopedia of Educational Research* (New York: Macmillan Co., 1960), pp. 1211–16.

the work Taylor was doing in scientific management. In 1913, Bobbitt devoted a long article to principles of management and their applications, as he saw them, in school systems.[22]

The faithful application of Taylor's principles to school operation is illustrated in the following statement from Bobbitt:

> The primary functions of educational directors and supervisors, as relating to methods, are therefore: first, the discovery of the best methods of procedure in the performance of any particular educational task; and second, the giving of these discovered best methods over to the teachers for their guidance in securing a maximum product. Since so few methods, demonstrably the best, have yet been discovered with entire certainty, it is impossible yet to devote any very large amount of time to the function of distribution of this information to the teachers. This leaves the major work at the present moment in the realm of discovery of best methods, it would appear.[23]

The early textbooks in educational administration written by Cubberley, Strayer, Reeder, and others may not have followed Taylor as faithfully as did Bobbitt, but their approach was essentially that of job analysis. Callahan[24] has made a penetrating analysis of how the schools, particularly during the period from 1910 to 1930, responded to the cult of efficiency that appeared to characterize the business ideology, and perhaps the entire American culture, of that time.

A somewhat similar approach or theory of educational administration is found in the work of Sears—for many years a professor at Stanford University. He was familiar with the work of Fayol, Gulick, Urwick, and other students of public administration. In a notable book, he attempted to adapt the administrative process—first suggested by Fayol—to the administration of the public schools.[25] Sears saw the process as including the following activities: planning, organization, direction, co-ordination, and control. After developing each aspect of the process, he related the whole to such concepts as authority, delegation, and policy-making. Further treatment of the process will be given in Chapter 5.

---

[22] Franklin Bobbitt, "Some General Principles of Management Applied to the Problems of City School Systems," *The Supervision of City Schools,* Twelfth Yearbook of the National Society for the Study of Education, Part I (Chicago: University of Chicago Press, 1913), pp. 7–96.

[23] *Ibid.,* p. 53.

[24] Raymond E. Callahan, *Education and the Cult of Efficiency* (Chicago: University of Chicago Press, 1962).

[25] Jesse B. Sears, *The Nature of the Administrative Process* (New York: McGraw-Hill Book Co., 1950).

While Sears appears to have been one of the few scholars of educational administration, his contribution has created no great stir—a lack of general recognition that may be due to a number of circumstances. First, since Sears' major treatment of the administrative process appeared after his retirement, he had little opportunity to work directly with other students of administration. Second, and perhaps more significant, only in recent years have professors and some practitioners of educational administration become interested in theoretical approaches to the field. Third, the process is a useful concept in administration, but it has not stimulated the formulation of many hypotheses to be tested.

Taylor's concept of scientific management in industry, we have seen, had a counterpart in education given its clearest expression by Bobbitt; likewise the formulation of Fayol became a major inspiration to Sears, who adapted it to educational administration. In both cases there was an attempt at job analysis—Bobbitt concentrating on the work of the teacher and supervisor, Sears concentrating on the work of the administrator. The emphasis on human relations supplied by Follett and Mayo has also influenced educational administration. This emphasis was reflected in the "democratic administration" movement. Democratic administration had many exponents,[26] but for the most part they dealt in hortatory expositions and did little to give greater insight into the realities of school organizations and their operation.

SOME RECENT DEVELOPMENTS

Scholarship in educational administration, generally meager during the first part of the present century, seems to be getting some genuine bolstering in the last decade or two. Four major events, each of which will be dealt with briefly, have been part of this dramatic development.

In 1947, the first meeting of a group later to be known as the National Conference of Professors of Educational Administrators was held at Endicott, New York. This meeting was largely the idea of, and was made possible through the influence of, Walter D. Cocking. The succeeding annual meetings of NCPEA have permitted those who teach educational administration to become acquainted with each other, have encouraged an examination of what is known and what is not known in the field, and have helped shape the other events noted here.

A second event of great importance to educational administration was the Cooperative Program in Educational Administration underwritten, to a large extent, by the W. K. Kellogg Foundation. From its beginning in 1950

---

[26] For instance, see G. Robert Koopman, *et al., Democracy in School Administration* (New York: Appleton-Century-Crofts, Inc., 1943).

until most projects were closed out about a decade later, Kellogg spent about $7 million on the program. This money was supplemented by the funds of many universities, state departments of education, and local school districts. Eight Kellogg centers were established in the United States and one in Canada; each of them was encouraged to develop a regional program devoted to the improvement of educational administration.

Initially, CPEA placed more emphasis on the improved practice of administration than on its study. It soon became apparent, however, that improved practice was dependent, in part, upon more knowledge about administration. Some participants in the CPEA program found substantial stimulation in studies done in public and business administration, and in the concepts and research findings of the social sciences. Thus, in the closing period of CPEA, theory and research in educational administration emerged as the most important concern of several of the centers.[27]

One of the CPEA centers, Teachers College at Columbia University, proposed that the major universities with programs in educational administration form an organization for the purpose of continuing the work thus started. Hence, in 1956, representatives from thirty-three universities organized the University Council for Educational Administration. At first the Council was located at Columbia University; in 1959, UCEA was incorporated under the laws of Ohio and moved to the campus of The Ohio State University. The W. K. Kellogg Foundation made substantial initial and subsequent grants to UCEA to help the new organization get established.

UCEA has three major purposes:

1. To improve the pre-service and in-service training of school administrators.

2. To stimulate and produce research in educational administration.

3. To disseminate materials growing out of research and training practices.

Among its activities, UCEA has organized career seminars for professors of educational administration, participated in large-scale research projects, set up a number of task forces on particular problems in administration, sought foundation and government assistance for fellowships and other aspects of training programs, alerted member institutions to possible sources of support for research and training projects in administration, and pub-

[27] More information about the influence of CPEA may be found in Hollis A. Moore, Jr., *Studies in School Administration* (Washington, D.C.: American Association of School Administrators, 1957); and, Roald F. Campbell and Russell T. Gregg (eds.), *Administrative Behavior in Education* (New York: Harper & Brothers, 1957).

lished a number of books and monographs growing out of its many activities.

From the beginning, UCEA has maintained a small but competent central office staff. Staff members have visited member institutions, have ascertained much about the interests and strengths of those institutions, have helped bring professors of similar interests in different institutions into touch with each other, and have, in general, served as an important communication link among about fifty universities now belonging to the organization. UCEA, like CPEA and NCPEA, continues to be useful in helping students of administration define the field and learn more about it.

In reviewing recent developments in educational administration, a fourth event also seems important. The American Association of School Administrators had taken a part in urging the Kellogg Foundation to support CPEA and had maintained a relationship with that program from the beginning. In 1955, AASA created the Committee for the Advancement of School Administration and received a grant from Kellogg to help it become operative. The purpose of that Committee was to assist in getting action designed to improve the pre-service and in-service programs of preparation for school administrators.

The Committee for the Advancement of School Administration has done much to communicate research findings in administration to school administrators; to encourage national, regional, and local groups to work for improved school administration; to help develop plans for the accreditation of training programs for administrators; to urge more adequate regulations for certification in all the states; to influence boards of education regarding procedures to be used in selecting administrators; and to make its concerns about improved training clear to universities with programs in administration. Another noteworthy step taken by AASA at the behest of the Committee was approval, by vote of its members in 1959, of the completion of a two-year accredited graduate program as a requirement for membership, which became effective in 1964.

Recent developments in educational administration have affected both students and practitioners. Those who would teach administration are becoming more conscious of the place of theory and careful research in the field. Selection and training, moreover, are also receiving additional attention. Criteria for selection are being established, and selection procedures developed and evaluated. New approaches in instruction, such as the case method and the use of simulated material, are being used and appraised. A recognition that good training and research programs are expensive is also dawning. In this whole effort those who practice administration are, for the most part, supportive, as these efforts to raise standards for organization membership and certification suggest. Indeed, the whole field is characterized by challenge and excitement.

An Overview of Educational Administration

PURPOSE AND ACTIVITIES OF ADMINISTRATION

As we see it, the central purpose of administration in any organization is that of co-ordinating the efforts of people toward the achievement of its goals. In education these goals have to do with teaching and learning. Thus, administration in an educational organization has as its central purpose the enhancement of teaching and learning. All activities of the administrator—whether working with the public, the board of education, or the professional staff—should ultimately contribute to this end.

To enhance teaching and learning, administrators are required to perform three major functions: (1) to discern and influence the development of goals and policies; (2) to establish and coordinate an organization concerned with planning and implementing appropriate programs; and (3) to procure and manage resources, money, and material necessary to support the organization and its program.

While all three of these administrative functions have the improvement of teaching and learning as their end purpose, more than the classroom is, clearly, involved. In order to influence goals and policies, the administrator must work with the board of education and the lay community, as well as with the school organization itself. To establish the organization, the administrator must see that the proper personnel are selected for it; then he must see that the efforts of these personnel are co-ordinated. To secure resources, the administrator must secure approval from three sources—the board of education, the voters of the school district, and the appropriate state and national agencies.

Clearly, the managerial decisions of administrators may be pointless unless they are geared to the implementation of programs that have, in turn, grown out of the goals. Or, to put it differently, administrators who raise money, build buildings, institute accounting procedures, set up computer programs, organize transportation systems, and do many other things without visualizing a clear relationship between these activities and the teaching and learning programs they are to enhance, may forget that administration is always instrumental, not primary. For administrators to relate managerial acts to program decisions requires some knowledge of education—its purposes and procedures. It is at this point that the school administrator transposed from business or the military may encounter some difficulty.

In suggesting that the administrator not only discern but influence goals and policies, we recognize that we have departed from the formulations of some students of administration.[28] But this is more than a mere difference of opinion. In a study of 272 school districts in Illinois, Allison[29] found that boards of education rely heavily on the recommendations of their superintendents on both policy and implementation matters. In effect, we are suggesting that the division between policy-making and administration is not a clear one, and that inevitably the administrator influences policy even as he attempts to discern and clarify policy. This influence is a function of both the knowledge and the values of administration. To the extent that the administrator knows something about education, he can supply information, note alternatives, and suggest probable outcomes. His professional orientation or values permit him to prefer one alternative above another and to explain the reasons for his choice. At this point he is speaking as a professional and giving professional information, which any lay group needs if policy is to be well conceived.

To be sure, the administrator may find it desirable to use other professionals more expert than he in many aspects of education. Thus the contributions of the philosopher, the sociologist, the psychologist, the curriculum theorist, and the able teacher may all be used. Even so, someone must serve as the generalist to suggest how these various specialties are to be related to the problem at hand. While this function may be shared with able laymen, it is also a role that administrators can not escape.

Obviously, it is at the level of policy-making that professional knowledge and values must make sense to laymen. With knowledge exploding in every field of study, this juncture of special and general understanding is becoming fraught with more and more difficulty. In every public endeavor, however—whether foreign affairs, public health, or public education— there seems to be no alternative to the forging of policy decisions by laymen who have been enlightened by the experts. We are suggesting that foreign affairs are too important to be left to the army, public health too important to be left to the medical profession, and public education too important to be left to the educators. However, we are also insisting that laymen would make even more blunders in these areas if they refused to use the specialized knowledge available to them.

ADMINISTRATION IN A COMPLEX WORLD

To this point we have dealt with the major purposes and activities of administration quite in isolation. Actually, these activities go on in a most

[28] John Walton, *Administration and Policy-making in Education* (Baltimore: Johns Hopkins Press, 1959).

[29] Howard C. Allison, "Professional and Lay Influences on School Board Decision-Making." Unpublished Ph.D. dissertation, Department of Education, University of Chicago, 1965.

complex world—a fact we shall now note. In the first place, the world is an ever-expanding one geographically. Although we may begin with an attendance area in which we have a single school, we soon discover that this attendance area is part of a school district, that the district is part of a state, that the state is part of the nation, and that the nation is part of the world; and we are now in a period in which we are constantly reminded that this world is part of a mammoth universe.

The administrator of the attendance area, the principal, can not perform his major administrative functions without reference to the larger world. Policy decisions are not a product of the people of the local school community alone, but often reflect the desires of the people of the school district, the state, and in some sense the world beyond. In like manner program decisions are not made by the professionals of a single school in isolation. The professionals at the district, state, and national levels have an influence on these decisions.

Second, the administrator's world is most complex sociologically. Many people and groups of people performing different roles are involved. In a school district, for instance, there are lay citizens who hold expectations for schools and school administrators, who determine the membership of the board of education, and to some extent the expenditure level of the district. The board of education becomes a major interstitial body between school and community and also determines, within limits, the policies of the school district. The superintendent of schools finds that he must deal with the aspirations and expectations of the people and serve as executive officer and professional adviser to the board of education. But the superintendent also has a professional staff composed of supervisors, principals, and teachers. These people perform different roles in the school system, and somehow their activities must be co-ordinated toward common objectives.

Third, the administrator's world is complex in terms of the many public services to be provided by government. In addition to public education, there are health and welfare, fire and police protection, public roads, and other public services. This means, particularly at district and state levels, that support for public education is always in competition with support for other public services. Inevitably, such a condition places the school administrator within all the complexities of the political world.

Not only must schools compete with highways and welfare; all public services must compete with private services. In government there is the perennial question: Shall we leave matters to individual initiative, or shall we use tax resources to provide the service for all? Clearly there is need to do some of both, a concept Galbraith has called social balance.[30] With

---

[30] John K. Galbraith, *The Affluent Society* (Boston: Houghton Mifflin Co., 1958).

growth in any private realm (let us say the manufacture of more automobiles) there is also need for growth in the public realm—in this case the building of more highways.

We have shown that the world of the administrator is a complex one geographically, socially, and politically. Let us now examine a little more carefully the legal relationships between state and school district. The legal responsibility for education rests with the state. The state through the legislature has established school districts to help the state perform its educational function. The legislature has also created boards of education to preside over these districts, and the boards have the powers delegated to them by the legislature. In legal theory the districts are the creatures of the state, not the product of local autonomy. When there is need to alter districts or school boards, the state can take such action.

It is within this legal framework that the school district and legislature interact, that the superintendent of schools and the state superintendent interact, that the professional staff of a school district and the professional staff of the state department interact. But these legal relationships can not ignore the geographical, sociological, and political relationships we have already noted. We must recognize, too, even though space does not permit discussion here, that the psychological needs and dispositions of people provide still another dimension in the complex world of the administrator.

The major functions of administration must go forward within this complex geographical, social, political, legal, and psychological world. Not all administrators perform all of these activities. We suspect that an able superintendent of schools actually performs at all three levels—he discerns and influences goals and policies, establishes and co-ordinates an organization, and procures and manages resources. Most school principals, on the other hand, probably concentrate more on co-ordinating the efforts of staff members in building a total program and somewhat less on seeking resources to support the program. Supervisors of instruction, even more than principals, probably devote most of their efforts to co-ordinating staff activities as they relate to instructional programs.

But whether differentiated by position or by level of operation, administration operates in a complex and interdependent world. To approach administration in terms of one set of dimensions yields only a partial view of the phenomenon. He who concentrates, for instance, on intra-organizational behavior will soon run aground, for extra-organizational influences are also inevitable.[31]

---

[31] This point is elaborated in Roald F. Campbell, Luvern L. Cunningham, and Roderick F. McPhee, *The Organization and Control of American Schools* (Columbus: Charles E. Merrill Books, Inc., 1965).

Unique Aspects of Educational Administration

As noted earlier, educational administration has much in common with public administration, hospital administration, business administration, and administration in other organizational settings. This recognition represents a gain, for the insights and research findings thus available to educational administration have been multiplied many times.

Still, this new-found knowledge has caused some uneasiness. Perhaps dwelling on common elements in administration, useful as such an approach is, oversimplifies the picture. Instead of trying to define either common or unique elements, it might be useful to develop some continua on which administration in a variety of organizational settings might be placed.

Parsons has suggested three levels of systems within organizations—the technical, managerial, and institutional levels.[32] In schools, for example, teaching is at the technical level of operation, action to direct the efforts of groups of teachers toward a common goal or program is at the managerial level, and moves to seek financial support for the school from the larger society are at the institutional level. In the study of administration, according to Parsons, we have dealt mainly with the managerial level and have neglected the technical and institutional levels somewhat.

As we think of various kinds of organizations in our society and realize that all organizations, whether public or private, must be legitimized by that society, we find questions that might be asked regarding any organization:

1. What is the service that the organization is designed to provide?

2. What is the nature of the activity in which the organization will engage to perform this service?

3. What are the characteristics of the people who work in the organization?

4. How may the activities of the organization be appraised?

These considerations led us to develop six continua. Two of these, cruciality and visibility, were in response to our first question on the service to be rendered. Two others, complexity and intimacy, were in response to the second question on the nature of the activity. Staff professionalization grew out of question three on characteristics of the people. Difficulty of appraisal seemed to be a part of the general appraisal problem

---

[32] Talcott Parsons, "Some Ingredients of a General Theory of Formal Organizations," in Andrew W. Halpin (ed.), *Administrative Theory in Education* (Chicago: Midwest Administration Center, University of Chicago, 1958), pp. 166–85.

found in question four. While other continua may have been developed, these six will be discussed as one way of suggesting what may be unique about educational organizations and their administration. The organizations cited are for illustrative purposes only and organizational activities have been oversimplified to make the major point.

CRUCIALITY TO SOCIETY

Cruciality to society, as a continuum, obviously rests at the institutional level. We are suggesting that important as the making of ping-pong balls is to some people, this activity is not as crucial to society as fire protection. Likewise, important as fire protection is, we suspect that if a choice had to be made between schools and fire departments, society, particularly our kind of society, would choose schools. Or, to put it differently, we suspect that our society would settle for minimum fire protection before it would settle for minimum school programs.

LEAST CRUCIAL ——————————→ ——————→ ——————→MOST CRUCIAL

FACTORY:	FIRE DEPARTMENT:	SCHOOL:
PING-PONG	FIRE	TEACHING
BALLS	PROTECTION	AND LEARNING

The crucial place of the school in our society has been suggested by Thelen and Getzels:

But education as a system is also unique in certain respects. It is a system whose major functions seem to be delegated to it by the other systems, and, to a degree, the effective functioning of the other systems depends directly on the effective functioning of the educational system. Our geographer, for example, wants education to prepare us for the wise utilization of natural resources; in this sense the school is very much part of the geographer's domain. Our political scientist wants education to prepare us for the wise exercise of political power; in this sense the school is part of *his* domain. Our economist wants education to prepare us for the wise selection of economic alternatives; in this sense the school is also part of *his* domain. In short, the educational system seems unique in the range of its functions and the centrality of its relationship, at least theoretically, to the other social institutions. It is the institution that is charged with responsibility for the "socialization," "politicalization," "acculturation," and so on of the child (and other newcomers) in our society.[33]

The cruciality continuum has interesting implications for the fiscal dependent-independent argument in education. To place all public services

[33] Herbert A. Thelen and Jacob W. Getzels, "The Social Sciences: Conceptual Framework for Education," *School Review,* LXV (Autumn, 1957), p. 346.

at the same point of cruciality to society seems unrealistic. Thus, those who would have all-purpose government, or fiscal dependence for education, whether at local, state, or national levels, should also devise ways by which services thought by citizens to be most crucial to society can be given priority. Similarly, those who would have special-purpose government, or fiscal independence for education, should recognize that some mechanism for weighing the need of various public services is necessary. Under either system, cruciality to society ought to determine the allocation of public financial resources.

PUBLIC VISIBILITY AND SENSITIVITY

The continuum of public visibility and sensitivity seems to reside at the institutional level. Here the factory as an organization, particularly in its internal operations, is far less visible than the college and the school. Furthermore, the management of the factory need not be particularly sensitive to public opinion except as that opinion is connected with the product of the factory. To be sure, in times of labor crises, management must tell its story to the public; but such circumstances are the exception, not the rule.

LEAST VISIBILITY AND SENSITIVITY⟶MOST VISIBILITY AND SENSITIVITY

| FACTORY | COLLEGE | SCHOOL |

In contrast, the school, particularly the public school, highly visible at all times, must be sensitive to its many publics. The high visibility is connected in part with the intimacy of relationships discussed below. Even more important is the fact that most schools are a public, not a private, enterprise. But, as school administrators soon discover, there is not one but many publics, which often hold sharply different views about the task of the school. In spite of the high visibility of the school, it is only in recent years that school administration has begun a serious examination of the relationship of the school to the broader society and the implications of that relationship to administrative behavior.

COMPLEXITY OF FUNCTION

The continuum of complexity of function applies to the technical level of the organization. Some organizations perform more complex technical functions than others. The exact placement of the four organizations on the continuum might be argued, but the process of teaching and learning, at least to one who knows little about making bolts, seems to be complex.

In teaching and learning, for instance, the teachers who are charged with the responsibility of guiding the process are not in complete control of it. The learners may or may not respond to the stimulation provided. In contrast, workers who guide the process of bolt-making seem to be more nearly in control of their materials.

LEAST COMPLEX ———————⟶   ——————⟶   ——————⟶ MOST COMPLEX

FACTORY:	GOVERNMENT:	SCHOOL:	PSYCHIATRIC STAFF:
MAKING	COLLECTING	TEACHING AND	CHANGING
BOLTS	TAXES	LEARNING	PERSONALITY

Still, the task of teaching and learning is probably not so complex as the task that confronts a psychiatric staff. Perhaps a more explicit way of making the point would be to say that in terms of results acceptable to the organization, the teaching-learning task is less complex than personality change as attempted in the psychiatrist-patient relationship. Learning and bolt-making, for that matter, may both be highly complex processes, but we are concerned here with results acceptable to the respective organizations.

The main point seems to be that in each organization the administrator must have some knowledge of the complexity of the task acceptable to his organization if he is to function as co-ordinator of the organization.

INTIMACY OF NECESSARY RELATIONSHIPS

The continuum of intimacy, too, may be applied to the technical level of the organization. Exact placement of various organizations on the continuum is unnecessary to illustrate the point that relationships necessary to achieve organizational goals vary in intimacy from organization to organization. They are least intimate in a bolt factory, somewhat more intimate in tax-collecting by a government agency, appreciably more intimate in a school, and perhaps even more intimate in a hospital.

LEAST INTIMATE ———————⟶   ——————⟶   ——————⟶ MOST INTIMATE

FACTORY:	GOVERNMENT:	SCHOOL:	HOSPITAL:
MAKING	COLLECTING	TEACHING CHIL-	TREATING
BOLTS	TAXES	DREN AND YOUTH	THE ILL

It should be noted that school organizations involve the relationship of teacher to pupil, pupil to pupil, teacher to teacher, teacher to parent, and pupil to parent. Nor are school relationships confined to the formal learning of skills or knowledge. Because all human behavior is interrelated and much learning is concomitant in nature, these relationships often spill over into problems of person adjustment, family membership, and social acceptance. Only in medical practice, in hospital care, and perhaps in the church, are personal relationships more intimate.

STAFF PROFESSIONALIZATION

Staff professionalization seems to be part of a managerial continuum. We are using the term professionalization to represent competence that requires specialized preparation through which the individual acquires in marked degree the knowledge and values of his colleagues. Factories have relatively fewer professionals than skilled and unskilled workers. In a hospital, doctors and nurses are professionals, but practical nurses, nurses aides, and attendants of various kinds are not.

LEAST PROFESSIONALIZATION ⎯⎯⎯⎯⎯⟶ MOST PROFESSIONALIZATION

FACTORY   HOSPITAL   SCHOOL   COLLEGE

In a school, however, teachers and administrative personnel make up two-thirds to three-fourths of all employees. They at least tend to be, and many are, professional in education and outlook. On this continuum, the college ranks higher than the school only because, on the average, college teachers possess more specialized knowledge than school teachers.

To the extent that personal dispositions of the staff are affected by professional values, superior intelligence, and articulate communication, it seems clear that administrators in schools must pay greater attention to personal dispositions than administrators in factories. Conversely, school administrators can rely less on standard operating procedures than can administrators in industrial plants.

DIFFICULTY OF APPRAISAL

The appraisal continuum also seems to reside at the technical level of the organization. While we do not wish to underestimate the difficulty of the process of appraisal in sales organizations and manufacturing concerns, it does seem that sales and production are fairly simple indexes of performance.

LEAST DIFFICULT ⎯⎯⎯⟶⎯⎯⎯⟶⎯⎯⎯⟶ MOST DIFFICULT

SALES	MANUFACTURING	SCHOOL:	CHURCH:
ORGANIZATION:	ORGANIZATION:	CHANGE IN	INNER AND
SALES	PRODUCTS	BEHAVIOR	OUTER CHANGE

The school, in contrast, must be concerned with change in behavior, to use behavior in a broad sense. The change may involve knowledge, skills, or attitudes—all of which, presumably, influence behavior itself. But these changes are not immediately or easily perceptible. Often procedures or instruments have to be devised to measure change. But even when special instruments or procedures are used, students may, particularly in short-run evaluation, give what they believe to be appropriate responses. Sustained changes in behavior can be determined only over a period of years and by the accumulation of evidence from many sources. Obviously, the delay and the complexity of the evidence make useful feedback to the school for the purpose of revising practices most difficult.

Evaluation of a church program may be even more difficult than evaluation of a school program, for faith adds a transcendental dimension. The appraisal of school and college programs seems to be fraught with problems. Perhaps only the problems of appraising church programs are more difficult.

The six continua shown here offer a way of analyzing the common and the unique features of administration in various institutional settings. It is significant that three of the dimensions reside at the technical level, two at the institutional, and only one at the managerial level of organizations. This analysis suggests that the common elements in administration tend to be found at the managerial level, and the differentiations at the technical and institutional levels.

THEORY IN ADMINISTRATION

Some of the concepts dealt with above illustrate the quest for administrative theory characteristic of the last decade or two. In attempting to answer the question, "What is theory?" we have two alternatives. We can go full distance and side with Halpin[34] and Griffiths,[35] who both rely on Feigl[36] for a hypothetico-deductive definition. Or we can follow Walton, who suggests that we approach theory through such steps as observation, identification, definition, systematic classification, analysis, and finally, a hypothetico-deductive system.[37]

[34] Andrew W. Halpin (ed.), *Administrative Theory in Education* (Chicago: Midwest Administration Center, University of Chicago, 1958), Chapter I.

[35] Daniel E. Griffiths, *Administrative Theory* (New York: Appleton-Century-Crofts, 1959).

[36] Herbert Feigl, "Principles and Problems of Theory Construction in Psychology," in *Current Trends in Psychological Theory* (Pittsburgh: University of Pittsburgh Press, 1951), p. 182.

[37] John Walton, *op. cit.*

Our favorite definition of theory comes from Einstein:

In our endeavor to understand reality we are somewhat like a man trying to understand the mechanism of a closed watch. He sees the face and the moving hands, even hears it ticking, but he has no way of opening the case. If he is ingenious he may form some picture of a mechanism which could be responsible for all the things he observes, but he may never be quite sure his picture is the only one which could explain his observations. He will never be able to compare his picture with the real mechanism and he cannot even imagine the possibility or the meaning of such a comparison. But he certainly believes that, as his knowledge increases, his picture of reality will become simpler and simpler and will explain a wider and wider range of his sensuous impressions.[38]

Perhaps Einstein provides the most significant cue in what has been said up to now—"our endeavor to understand reality." In this context, the development of theory is the process whereby we describe reality more and more accurately.

Since the social sciences are newcomers to the scientific field, administration deals with most complex problems, and any theory seems to deal with but a few of the variables found in these phenomena, we are willing to keep the definition broad at this time. In the development of theory careful observation is a step above careless observation. Systematic classification is superior to no classification. To be sure, a series of related concepts from which we may derive testable hypotheses is theory of a higher order.

In any case, let us note some of the characteristics of theory. Theory is conceptual; it exists only in one's mind. Theory is not right or wrong; it is useful or not useful. At best, theory explains what is—never what ought to be. Theory, if it be useful, has within it the seeds of its own destruction and reconstitution. In other words, theory suggests a process of thinking, not a recipe for action.

Recent interest in theory has led both students and practitioners of administration to expect a full-blown, grand theory of educational administration. Certainly no such manifestation is currently available, and we suspect that its formulation is a long way off. On the other hand, a number of stimulating and useful theories are available. March and Simon have assessed the literature on organizational theory. They suggest that back of every proposition about organizations is a set of assumptions regarding the behavior of people. They grouped these propositions as follows:

1. Propositions assuming that organization members, and particularly employees, are primarily *passive instruments*, capable of performing work and accepting directions, but not initiating action or exerting influence in any significant way.

[38] Albert Einstein and Leopold Infeld, *The Evolution of Physics* (New York: Simon and Schuster, Inc., 1938), p. 33.

2. Propositions assuming that members bring to their organizations *attitudes, values*, and *goals*; that they have to be motivated or induced to participate in the system of organization behavior; that there is incomplete parallelism between their personal goals and organization goals; and that actual or potential goal conflicts make power phenomena, attitudes, and morale centrally important in the explanation of organizational behavior.

3. Propositions assuming that organization members are *decision-makers and problem-solvers*, and that perception and thought processes are central to the explanation of behavior in organizations.[39]

The view of Taylor, described briefly earlier in this chapter, appears to be based on the proposition that people are rather passive instruments. Barnard, as noted earlier, tended to accept the proposition that members bring to an organization their attitudes, values, and goals. Simon, as noted above, appears to have been the first person to suggest decision-making as a central proposition.

For the practitioner, theory is perhaps most useful in furnishing a number of concepts, or sets of spectacles, with which to view his situation. Such concepts were noted in the work of Taylor, Fayol, Follett, Mayo, Barnard, and Simon. In this chapter we have presented an overview and have suggested the meaning of administration. In Chapters 4 through 7 we shall describe four different ways of viewing administration. Perhaps only Chapter 7 can be seen, in any sophisticated sense, as a theory of administration, but each of the other approaches is a useful way of viewing the field. Taken together, these chapters illustrate the difficulty of subjecting a most complex phenomenon to a single theoretical formulation.

SUGGESTED ACTIVITIES

1. For one school district, suggest practices that seem to be related to (a) the scientific management or job analysis movement and (b) to the human relations emphasis in administration.
2. Note the duties suggested for the superintendent, principals, supervisors, and teachers in the rules and regulations of a city school district. How would you improve the statement? What assumptions are back of your recommendations?
3. Interview a superintendent of schools concerning his major activities.
4. Interview five teachers concerning their view of the major activities of the superintendent. Analyze similarities and differences in perceptions.

[39] James G. March and Herbert A. Simon, *Organizations* (New York: John Wiley & Sons, Inc., 1958), p. 6.

SELECTED READINGS

BARNARD, CHESTER I. *The Functions of the Executive.* Cambridge: Harvard University Press, 1938.

CALLAHAN, RAYMOND E. *Education and the Cult of Efficiency.* Chicago: University of Chicago Press, 1962.

FAYOL, HENRI. *General and Industrial Management.* London: Sir Isaac Pitman & Sons, Ltd., 1949.

HALPIN, ANDREW W. (ed.). *Administrative Theory in Education.* Chicago: Midwest Administration Center, University of Chicago, 1958.

MARCH, JAMES G., and SIMON, HERBERT A. *Organizations.* New York: John Wiley & Sons, Inc., 1958.

MAYO, ELTON. *The Human Problems of an Industrial Civilization.* Boston: Graduate School of Business Administration, Harvard University, 1946.

METCALF, HENRY C., and URWICK, L. (eds.). *Dynamic Administration.* New York: Harper & Brothers, 1942. The collected papers of Mary Parker Follett with an introduction by the editors.

National Society for the Study of Education, *Behavioral Science and Educational Administration,* Sixty-third Yearbook, Part II. Chicago: University of Chicago Press, 1964.

SIMON, HERBERT A. *Administrative Behavior* (2nd ed.). New York: The Macmillan Company, 1957.

TAYLOR, FREDERICK W. *Scientific Management.* New York: Harper & Brothers, 1947.

4

The Administrative

Tasks

IF ADMINISTRATION IS TO FACILITATE TEACHING AND LEARNING, as we maintained in the preceding chapter, it becomes necessary to examine the major tasks necessary for the achievement of such a purpose. In this chapter we shall suggest the nature and scope of these tasks. We shall show something of the interrelationships among these tasks, though we cannot treat the detailed techniques to be employed in the achievement of them. Such a treatment requires books, not a single chapter!

The task approach to administration is not characterized by any highly developed theory. At best, the organization of the tasks into operational areas is a taxonomy. This classification, however, brings a certain order to the field which will prove useful to both student and practitioner of administration.

The administrative tasks or operational areas of administration may be grouped into categories. We think the six categories shown below represent a convenient grouping:

1. School-community relationships.

2. Curriculum and instruction.

3. Pupil personnel.

4. Staff personnel.
5. Physical facilities.
6. Finance and business management.

The principal of a school and the superintendent of a school system ordinarily have many tasks to perform in each of these operational areas. In large schools or school systems, assistants to principals and superintendents may be given limited responsibilities in one or two of the operational areas. For example, a high school principal may have a vice-principal in charge of pupil activities, discipline, and attendance, to assist him. Or a superintendent of schools may have a director of curriculum and a business manager to assist him. Or a county superintendent may have an elementary supervisor as a major staff member. In these cases a team of administrators has been formed to work at the administrative tasks.

The organization and treatment of administrative tasks in this chapter should in no sense imply that one administrator or even a team of administrators can or should do these things alone. Other people are nearly always involved. These people may be citizens, school board members, or members of the teaching or non-teaching staffs of the school. In some cases the tasks are achieved with the assistance of these people, in other cases entirely by them, and in still other cases these people advise the administrator regarding the tasks. It should be clear, however, that the responsibility for seeing that these jobs are done rests with the administrator. The nature of each of the major operational areas will now be suggested.

SCHOOL-COMMUNITY RELATIONSHIPS

Because education in our country is largely a public venture, and because in the final analysis it can be no better than the citizens of a community will have it, school-community relationships represent both a point of beginning and a continuing concern for any school administrator. As suggested in Chapter 3, we are defining community in operational terms only as the attendance area for a single school or the school district for a school system. While the tasks incident to school-community relationships are numerous, we shall limit our discussion to what seem to be certain focal points.

CHARACTER OF THE COMMUNITY

School communities may be characterized as urban or rural, as farm or non-farm, as industrial or residential, as middle-class or lower-class. Such common designations may provide the school administrator with some clues as to how he is to work with his community. In actual practice, however, school communities may not lend themselves to such easy categorizing, and such rubrics may not constitute useful approaches to relating school and community.

Bullock was concerned with the community characteristics that the school administrator needed to understand.[1] After preliminary testing he determined that the following questions were important:

1. What is the general community level of approval or disapproval of the school program?

2. What kind of educational philosophy does the community hold?

3. What degree of prestige do teachers as an occupational class hold in the community?

4. What kind of community is this with regard to such characteristics as cohesiveness and unity of action?

5. How does this community define the role of the school administrator?

6. How receptive is this community to change and innovation?

Bullock then proceeded to develop some scales which an administrator might use in a school community in an attempt to answer the questions enumerated above. In one city school district, for example, he found that the level of school approval varied significantly in terms of the geographical location, occupational category, organizational membership of residents, and the amount of formal education completed by residents.

The pertinence of school-community relationships to the other tasks of administration may be seen in the further examination of some of Bullock's questions. According to him, the level of community approval is related to the level of the program for which a community would be willing to spend money. The educational philosophy of a community has a bearing upon the curriculum of the school. The willingness of a community to accept the leadership of teachers in instructional matters is, in part, a function of the prestige in which teachers are held. Community cohesiveness is pertinent to community decisions regarding school building expansion, as it is to other community decisions. Perhaps enough has been said to illustrate how necessary it is that a school administrator understand the composition and character of his school community.

[1] Robert P. Bullock, *School-Community Attitude Analysis for Educational Administrators* (SCDS Monograph #7, Columbus, Ohio: The Ohio State University, 1959), 112 pp.

DESIRES AND ASPIRATIONS OF CITIZENS

Some of what was said above has implications for the assessment of the desires and aspirations that citizens have for their schools. We need to note specifically, however, that this is another impqrtant aspect of school-community relationships. There are many ways by which assessment might be made, such as through informal conversations with citizens and through the use of rating scales like those developed by Bullock and referred to above.

A number of studies done at the University of Chicago have dealt with the task of the public school as perceived by various sub-publics.[2] Occupation and amount of schooling were found to be the best predictors of educational belief. Fair predictors were also geographic region in which one lives, age, race, and religion. Interestingly enough, the type of community in which a person lives, income, sex, and participation in school programs did not prove to be closely associated with educational viewpoint. Some useful instruments for the assessment of public perceptions were also developed as part of these studies.

The building of a realistic expectation of what the public schools can and should do in a community represents one of the major tasks of any school administrator. Only with such understanding can school procedures make sense to citizens and lead to significant advances in school programs.

INFORMATION ABOUT THE SCHOOL

We do not subscribe to the public relations concept of "selling" the public schools to the people. Actually, the people already hold title to the public schools. We do believe, however, that after school and community representatives reach agreement on programs and those programs are put into operation, there must be full and frequent reporting to the community on their progress. Thus, dissemination of information about the school to the community is an important obligation of any administrator.

Indeed, information needs to be disseminated on many subjects. It might pertain to a new emphasis in mathematics, a new method of reporting pupil progress, a program for the in-service education of teachers, the extension of the school plant, changes in the tax resources of the school district, the development of school board policies, or any number of other items. Unfortunately, school reporting in some districts still deals more extensively with athletics and the marching band than with any other aspects of the instructional program. Perhaps administrators who report

[2] Lawrence W. Downey, *The Task of Public Education* (Chicago: Midwest Administration Center, University of Chicago, 1960), 88 pp.

to the public would do well to remember to report progress toward the major purposes of education.

Just as there are many things to report, there are many ways of reporting. Inevitably school pupils become conveyors of school news. Teachers, too, have many community contacts and are often sources of information about schools. Many schools have found letters to parents, room meetings for parents, and regular P.T.A. sessions useful aids in reporting. Some central offices print short brochures about school matters to be included with the report cards of pupils. Other school districts issue annual reports either as booklets or as special editions of the local newspaper. Coverage of school news by newspaper, radio, and television is, of course, a common and important means of disseminating information about the school.

A three-year study on the "understanding" existing between communities and their schools, undertaken at Stanford University, has yielded a number of useful insights.[3] For instance, evidence was found that people generally value education enough to try to understand its problems, that an understanding is essential to any stable support of public education, and that understanding is the result of effective communication. In larger districts, more importance was attached to the role of mediating agencies such as mass media, the Parent-Teachers' Association, and the board of education as vehicles of communication. In smaller districts, more face-to-face communication was seen as a significant factor in successful school-community relations.

ROLE OF THE SCHOOL

Another aspect of school-community relations is the development of a consensus on the role of the school in the community. That the establishment of such a consensus is not so simple as it once was is attested by a statement from the White House Conference on Education:

The basic responsibility of the schools is the development of the skills of the mind, but the over-all mission has been enlarged. Schools are now asked to help each child to become as good and as capable in every way as native endowment permits. The schools are asked to help children to acquire any skill or characteristic which a majority of the community deems worthwhile. The order given by the American people to the schools is grand in its simplicity; in addition to intellectual achievement, foster morality, happiness, and any useful ability. The talent of each child is to be sought out and developed to the fullest. Each weakness is to be studied and, so far as possible, corrected. This is truly a majestic ideal, and an astonishingly new one. Schools of that kind have never been provided for more than a small fraction of mankind.

[3] Richard F. Carter, *et al.*, "Communities and Their Schools," Co-operative Research Project #308 (School of Education, Stanford University, 1960), 228 pp.

Although it is new, this ideal of schools which do everything possible for all children is a natural development in the United States. The moving spirit of this Nation has been from the beginning a sense of fairness. Nowadays equality of educational opportunity for adults means little without equality of educational opportunity for children. Ignorance is a greater obstacle than ever to success of most kinds. The schools have become a major tool for creating a Nation without rigid class barriers. *It is primarily the schools which allow no man's failure to prevent the success of his son.*[4]

The social, as well as the educational, purpose of the school is also emphasized in a recent study of the Chicago schools:

The future of the city is bound up with the program of the public schools in two basic ways.

First, the schools help to give the next generation and the present generation of citizens and workers the knowledge and the understanding and the attitudes that make them good, bad, or indifferent citizens, workers, and parents.

Second, the program of the schools is the greatest single factor in the decision of middle-income people to live in the central city or to live in the suburbs, and to live in one section of the city or another.[5]

The administrative task suggested here is two-fold. There is first of all the stimulation of school workers and lay citizens in thinking about the role of the school in a particular attendance area or school district, with, of course, the clear recognition that state, regional, national, and world forces also impinge upon every locality. Second, this consideration must be continued until agreements can be reached which will serve as operating bases for the schools.

ROLE OF OTHER COMMUNITY AGENCIES

As lay citizens and school people work together to determine for a particular school community the role of its school or school system, they will inevitably have to give attention to the roles to be played by other community agencies and organizations. These organizations and agencies include the home; the churches; the city or county government; farm, labor, or business associations; public libraries; newspapers, radio, and television stations; and many others. In the total development of a community each of these agencies has a part to play.

[4] The Committee for the White House Conference on Education, *A Report to the President* (Washington: U.S. Government Printing Office, 1956), p. 9. (Italics in original.)

[5] Robert J. Havighurst, *The Public Schools of Chicago* (Chicago: Board of Education, 1964), p. 28.

Goldman examined the perceptions held by educators, non-educators, and high school students regarding the roles of the high school, the family, and the church in the development of a number of qualities in the high school graduate.[6] Educators and non-educators agreed that the family should hold primary responsibility for developing most of the qualities of the ideal graduate. To the high school was assigned the responsibility for developing the theoretic and political qualities, while the family was seen as having primary responsibility for developing the religious, economic, altruistic, hedonistic, social, æsthetic, and ethical qualities. While the students themselves saw the church as having primary responsibility for the religious quality, neither educators nor non-educators were of that opinion.

These findings suggest that more work needs to be done in assessing the perceptions people hold regarding the role of the school and the roles of other community agencies in the total program of education. Moreover, current perceptions in any particular community, we suspect, need not be ultimate perceptions. Again, the need to work out community understandings and programs becomes apparent.

In the operational area of school-community relations, we have suggested that the administrative tasks include those of ascertaining the composition and character of the community, and of determining the desires and aspirations the people have for the public school. We have also indicated that with such data at hand administrators must stimulate the development of some agreements in a community regarding the roles of the public school and of other community agencies.

CURRICULUM AND INSTRUCTION

A second, and in a sense the basic, operating area for the school administrator is that of curriculum and instruction. By curriculum and instruction we mean those activities in which school workers, sometimes assisted by lay citizens, engage to plan, implement, and evaluate an instructional program.

We recognize, too, that in the final analysis change in instructional content or method does not come through mere talking about it. Actually, changes occur when the understanding and skills of teachers and other workers change. To be effective, therefore, curriculum development activities should provide ways by which school workers may acquire new insights or develop new skills. Such insights and skills are related to the following

---

[6] Samuel Goldman, "Sub-Public Perceptions of the High School Graduate and the Roles of Institutions in His Development." Unpublished Ph.D. dissertation, Department of Education, University of Chicago, 1961.

curriculum categories: determination of objectives, the development of a program of instruction, the use of instructional procedures, and the appraising of instruction. Each of these will be treated briefly here.

DETERMINING OBJECTIVES

Each school staff needs to develop, in the light of all the evidence available, a concept of the specific objectives of the school or school system in a particular community. Setting the conditions so that this procedure can be carried out effectively is another important administrative task.

General statements of policy, like those found in *Goals for Americans,* are provocative.[7] Gardner suggested, it will be recalled, that "our schools must prepare all young people, whatever their talents, for the serious business of being free men and women."[8] These broad objectives seem acceptable enough until one tries to spell them out in more specific terms. For instance, in the interest of intellectual development, are youngsters going to be free to examine controversial issues such as the economics of communism? In the moral realm, to what extent can and should representatives of religious denominations be used in the school program? In what ways do we challenge the gifted and still provide for their participation in social situations with pupils of a wide range of abilities? The administrator must be concerned with these and similar questions as he tries to develop a plan whereby the professional staff can get at the objectives of the school.

What are some of the elements of such a plan? Basically, two things are necessary: to provide opportunity to learn more about the culture and its demands upon the school, and to provide opportunity to learn more about the growth and development of children and youth. These are the foundations of any kind of curriculum study.

Teachers and other school workers, to be sure, already know a great deal about the culture which determines, in part, what the school ought to be about. In a society as complex and pluralistic as ours, however, such knowledge may be fragmentary, incomplete, and even in error. A comprehension of the way federal expenditures for foreign aid may be related to our own economic well-being may illustrate the world-wide nature and complexity of our society.

Any plan for helping professional workers to make a continuous assessment of the social scene requires that they have an opportunity to examine

---

[7] John W. Gardner, "National Goals in Education," in Report of the President's Commission on National Goals, *Goals for Americans* (New York: Prentice-Hall, Inc., 1960), Chapter 3.

[8] *Ibid.,* p. 100.

the culture both first hand and vicariously. To examine first hand, people must have an opportunity to travel in their own locality, in the nation, and the world at large. Such travel can, of course, be supplemented by reading or by hearing the reports of other observers, provided such observers have the ability to see and to report.

Opportunity for extending the knowledge of teachers about human growth and learning is readily at hand. Pupils can be seen not only as people to be taught but as subjects to be studied. Actually, the challenge of teaching is probably not fully appreciated until both approaches are used. To study children and youth, however, certain conditions seem necessary. Teachers need a little time for reflection. They may also need the help of a person who is more capable in study and research approaches if their own studies are to be well conceived and executed. The administrator should try to provide these conditions.

PROGRAM OF INSTRUCTION

After the objectives of an instructional program are formulated, the job of actually determining a program to achieve these objectives still remains. Facilitating the development of such a program is also the task of the administrator. To the extent that programs are district-wide in character, the superintendent and his staff should take major responsibility to facilitate the process. To the extent that each building has autonomy in developing its own program, the building principal and his staff should take major responsibility to facilitate the process.

Many of the conditions suggested above for administrators to promote in the determination of objectives pertain also to the development of instructional programs. It seems desirable, however, to look more specifically at the behavior of administrators, particularly as such behavior may affect the work of teachers and other professional personnel as they engage in program development.

Jenkins and Blackman studied the relationship between the behavior of elementary school principals and the curriculum development activities of their staff members in a large city school district.[9] While many of the findings were suggestive only, the data do indicate rather clearly that there was no significant relationship between the verbalization of democratic attitudes by administrators and the effectiveness of those administrators in putting democracy into action. Or to put it another way, administrators may say they involve teachers in curriculum planning—they may even

---

[9] David H. Jenkins and Charles A. Blackman, *Antecedents and Effects of Administrator Behavior, SCDS Monograph* No. 3 (Columbus, Ohio: College of Education, The Ohio State University, 1956).

think that they do involve them—and at the same time this condition may not exist.

In the same study it was also found that the most effective administrators used approaches that were neither strongly "staff-centered" nor strongly "task-centered." Rather, principals who had some facility to help teachers define jobs and who at the same time were able to exhibit warmth toward teachers were the ones who, in general, had the most effective staffs in terms of developing curriculum programs.

While organizational arrangements for curriculum study were not a significant variable in the Jenkins-Blackman study, a school administrator does have certain organizational responsibilities if he is to foster program-building among his staff members. At the district level, for instance, it would seem appropriate that some kind of district-wide curriculum council be formed. This council should have on it representative teachers, principals, and staff members from the central office, so that instructional plans for the entire system might be appropriately reviewed. Existence of such a council in form only will, of course, guarantee nothing. The council must come to represent a genuine forum where ideas, not status positions, are important.

Organization of programs where instruction is scrutinized is also important at the building level. In the Denver study, for instance, a team of leaders—the principal and a curriculum co-ordinator—for each of the secondary schools was established, and their leadership activities pertaining to instructional improvement over a period of three years were examined.[10] Such a team arrangement seemed to provide a way by which the principal's office could really do something by way of working with teachers on instructional problems.

NATIONAL CURRICULUM PROGRAMS

But development and implementation of the program of instruction is no longer an activity carried on chiefly by a school district or a single school. Under the auspices of the National Science Foundation and other groups, national curriculum programs have been developed, and they have had decided impact upon the instructional practices of many schools.[11] Beginning in 1956 with the Physical Science Study Committee, with headquarters at the Massachusetts Institute of Technology, extensive programs

[10] Gordon N. Mackenzie and Stephen M. Corey, *Instructional Leadership* (New York: Bureau of Publications, Teachers College, Columbia University, 1954).

[11] Roald F. Campbell and Robert A. Bunnell (eds.), *Nationalizing Influences on Secondary Education* (Chicago: Midwest Administration Center, University of Chicago, 1963).

have also been developed in mathematics, biology, and chemistry.[12] More recently, the National Education Association has carried on an extensive project on instruction.[13] The United States Office of Education has also supported projects in English and social studies whose results may have national impact.

These national programs raise several important issues. For one, control of education in this country has, in the past, been assumed to be a state and local matter. Legally, this is still the case for the most part, but actually the influence of the national programs is widespread and pervasive. At one time, extensive teacher participation was considered essential to the development of curriculum programs. But today relatively few teachers take part in the development of most national programs; in fact, they find that they are, rather, the consumers of these programs. Although very limited resources were once available for curriculum development, the national programs have had at their disposal millions of dollars for holding conferences, developing instructional materials, hiring consultants, and organizing institutes wherein teachers might become acquainted with the programs.

In addition, these programs create new responsibilities for the administrator, who must acquire some knowledge of them in order to discuss them with his staff. He also will probably wish to encourage his teachers to attend institutes where the new programs are being presented. In any case, those involved in curriculum development at the local level can no longer ignore the ideas growing out of the national programs, nor can they ignore the instructional materials these programs make available.

INSTRUCTIONAL MATERIALS

Another closely related task for which the administrator takes responsibility is the selection and procurement of instructional materials. The teacher, to be sure, is central to adequate instruction, but even good teachers can do better when they are provided with appropriate tools.

The first task in this area is that of budget provision. Budget-building at its best assumes that program development, discussed briefly above, has gone forward, and that the materials needed to implement such a program will now become the basis for the budget request. For instance, if it has been decided that every biology student should have actual experience using laboratory equipment and supplies, the budget request will be quite

---

[12] These programs are dealt with in some detail in *The School Review*, 70 (Spring 1962) 1–147.

[13] NEA Project on Instruction, *Schools for the Sixties* (New York: McGraw-Hill Book Co., Inc., 1963).

different from one based upon a course that is to be taught with the textbook-demonstration-lecture approach.

Even assuming this kind of budget approach, however, it will usually be the administrator who must convince the superintendent's staff, the board of education, and finally the community that expenditures for instructional materials are indispensable to an adequate program of instruction. Sometimes elaborate plant and grounds—the outside façade of the school—win out over books, maps, and other instructional aids when budgets become tight. Without deprecating adequate programs of plant operation and maintenance, administrators need to be able to hold the line for budget items intimately related to the instructional program.

In the actual selection of instructional materials, teachers should play a large part. It has been found that teachers feel strongly the need to assume responsibility for those activities which have to do with instruction. It behooves administrators, therefore, to devise ways by which teacher participation in instructional matters, including the selection of instructional materials, can be encouraged. It should be recognized, however, that since such participation does take time, it must be regarded as a part of the total load of the teacher.

When budget provision for instructional materials has been made and when teachers have assisted in the actual selection of materials, there still remain the problems of procurement and delivery. These are tasks which the administration of a school district should perform with the greatest possible dispatch. Nothing is as exasperating to a teacher as to participate in a budget-building or a materials-selection program and then have purchase or delivery of materials delayed indefinitely by administrative red tape. The principal and the superintendent must cut through any such maze or avoid creating it.

APPRAISING INSTRUCTION

Another major responsibility confronting any administrator in the area of curriculum development is that of appraising instruction. Some industries allocate as much as one-sixth of their manpower to quality control. In education, unfortunately, evaluation has tended to be done with the left hand, if at all.

Space here will not permit a full treatment of evaluation. It does seem appropriate to suggest, however, that evaluation as a process has the following steps:

1. The formulation of objectives.
2. The definition of these objectives in behavioral terms.

3. Determination of places where these behaviors may be observed.

4. Selection or development of instruments upon which to record these behaviors when observed.

5. Appraisal and interpretation of the evidence thus collected.

If done carefully this process is, of course, a rather laborious one. All aspects of an instructional program probably can not be submitted continuously to such a careful procedure. On the other hand, the spirit of the evaluative approach can be applied much more generally than is now the case. Essentially, such an approach stresses careful formulation of purposes and collection of evidence in terms of those purposes.

Administrators need to help school workers and lay citizens alike to see that evaluation is a necessary complement to planning and doing. If we devise a new program for the teaching of reading, we must, of course, try it out, and we must evaluate, as best we can, how effective the program has been. Planning, doing, and evaluating are, in a real sense, just parts of a whole.

If this view is taken, it becomes clear that teachers must have time to participate in planning and evaluating as much as in doing. Such a statement has implications for teacher selection, job expectation, and teacher load. Moreover, the assistance of specialists in evaluation should probably be made available to teachers and others in the school system if the process is to be done well. It seems clear that only with regular and adequate evaluation can the administrator fulfill his responsibilities to his staff, his board of education, and his community. People have a right to know "how we are doing."

We have suggested that, in the operational area of curriculum and instruction, administrators have the responsibility for setting conditions that will promote the determination of objectives, the development of instructional programs, and the procurement of instructional materials. We have also indicated that, as programs are planned, plans for their evaluation should be formulated.

PUPIL PERSONNEL

Curriculum and instruction as discussed above had to do essentially with that part of the school program which is concerned with regular classroom instruction. Activities included within the operational area of pupil personnel embrace those services to pupils that supplement regular classroom instruction. Except in schools with very small enrollments, the chief role of the administrator in the pupil personnel area is one of integrating the personnel functions with instruction and of co-ordinating the various kinds of personnel services. Recent developments, such as special programs for the talented and the growth of external testing, have placed even more emphasis on pupil personnel services. A discussion of a few of the major tasks in pupil personnel follows.

PUPIL INVENTORY AND ORGANIZATION

Some staff member in a school or school district must first of all determine how many youngsters there are of school age in the attendance area or district. He does so by means of a school census, by the keeping of enrollment and attendance data, and by other means that will be discussed later. It is usually necessary that the number of pupils be determined by grade level and by school or attendance area.

With this information in hand, the administrator is in a position to determine to what extent school rooms in the existing buildings will house the pupils of the district. If certain buildings appear to be overcrowded and others have capacity to spare, the administrator may find that attendance boundaries need to be altered. In recent years, with charges of de facto segregation in many cities, the establishment of attendance areas has taken on new significance. The social and racial composition of the attendance area is fully as important as the consideration of number of pupils to be enrolled in the school.

The continual or yearly enumeration of pupils also furnishes one of the bases for determining new building needs. Often this enumeration furnishes data having to do with the direction of growth in a school district. In city school districts, particularly, population growth is usually toward the outskirts or even beyond the boundaries of the district to the suburbs. At the same time, enrollments in schools near the center of the city may actually be decreasing.

Enrollment data also furnish the administrator with the best single index of teaching personnel needed by grades, by subject area, and by school or attendance area. For example, if the projected enrollment data for a new elementary school indicated that 456 pupils would attend, and if the district had a policy of providing a teacher for each 28 elementary pupils, it is clear that the new school would require no fewer than 16 teachers.

Up to this point we have spoken of gross enumeration of pupils. It is also necessary that much be known about the characteristics of the pupils found within a school district. How many are gifted, how many are slow learners, how many are hard of hearing, how many are orthopedic cases? Ordinary census or enrollment data will not, of course, provide the kind of information suggested here. The identification of pupils with special problems will require the co-operation of teachers, parents, and specially trained personnel. Again, however, such information is necessary in order that a school or school system can plan a program of services for all, including its deviate pupils.

PUPIL ACCOUNTING

We have already alluded to the first task of pupil accounting, the enumeration of pupils. Ordinarily a school census system is established to help with this task. There is a compulsory education law in every state, and a school census is a necessary step in the enforcement of such laws. While census-taking was once seen as a yearly task, many school systems now use the continuing census approach. Specific procedures to be followed have been described in detail elsewhere.[14]

Another task facing every school system is the development and the operation of a pupil-accounting system. A plan for dealing with pupil absence and tardiness must be developed. If such a plan is to be followed by teachers and principals as part of their regular duties, it needs to be relatively simple. If specialized attendance personnel are to be employed, the plan may be somewhat more ambitious. In any case, teachers should have some voice in deciding upon the plan, and their own part in its operation will need to be clearly understood.

It seems appropriate to say at this point that the "hooky cop" approach to attendance leaves much to be desired. There is usually substantial cause back of non-attendance of school pupils. The school needs personnel who can both determine these basic causes and work toward their alleviation. Such causes often reside in the family, or the culture of which the family is a part, and thus non-attendance may actually be a social symptom toward which school workers, social agencies, and society itself ought to be directing their efforts.

Another duty common in pupil accounting is the issuance of work permits. In most states pupils may be excused at age fourteen or sixteen if they are needed to help support a family or if they can benefit no further from school attendance. These are important decisions in the life of a child and should be made only after facts are ascertained and appropriate counseling has been given the pupil and the family. In small school districts, principals and superintendents ordinarily perform these functions. In larger districts, specialized personnel are usually employed.

[14] Wm. A. Yeager, *Administration and the Pupil* (New York: Harper & Brothers, 1949), Chapter 5.

PUPIL PERSONNEL SERVICES

A very important aspect of the pupil personnel area is the provision of appropriate pupil personnel services. Large school districts may have services such as the following:

1. Child study.
2. Guidance and counseling advisement.
3. Testing.
4. Visiting teacher and social worker.
5. Speech and hearing therapy.
6. Medical and nursing.
7. Special education
   a. Physically handicapped
   b. Emotionally disturbed
   c. Mental deviates
   d. Gifted.

To some of these services we have already alluded. For instance, tests and measurements would be helpful in any program of evaluation; the school social worker might be skilled in getting at causes behind non-attendance of pupils. Some school systems see special education as a part of the curriculum program, but even so the workers in special education need to have close affiliation with the workers in the pupil personnel area.

If pupil personnel services are really going to supplement regular classroom instruction, it seems quite clear that some specialized personnel will be necessary. The welfare federation of a large city has suggested that a minimum staff for pupil personnel services should be composed of specialized people for each of the following:

1. Director (or co-ordinator) of pupil personnel services.
2. Health service.
3. Secondary school counseling service.
4. Speech and hearing therapy.
5. Child study service (psychological service and psychiatric consultation).
6. School social work service.

To be sure, small school districts cannot ordinarily employ all of the specialists suggested above. Such districts might start by getting one guidance counselor and by determining where the other services could be obtained on a part-time basis. For instance, in many states the county or intermediate school district is becoming a service unit to smaller school districts. In such cases most of the services noted above can be provided on a co-operative basis. Again, the job of the administrator is that of seeing that these services are made available and co-ordinated.

CONTROL OF PUPIL BEHAVIOR

While schools should attempt to determine the cause of misbehavior in pupils, and to treat the cause and not the symptom of such actions, there are times when pupils must be corrected or disciplined. Policies governing these matters should be clear, and the responsibilities of teachers and other staff members in this area should be understood. Competent teachers can and should exercise appropriate controls over their pupils. Actually, and contrary to the views of some beginning teachers, pupils prefer those teachers who are seen as fair, helpful, setting high standards, and allowing no "monkey business."

Even with the best of teachers, however, there are times when the principal, guidance counselor, or some other non-teaching staff member is placed in the role of disciplinarian. Many contend that guidance counselors and other pupil personnel workers should have no disciplinary function; that function, they insist, should be carried by the principal or some other administrative officer. The logic behind such an argument is that the guidance counselor should be individual- and not group-oriented—or, perhaps better stated, pupil-centered in place of school-centered.

In general, we accept this position; but carried to its extreme it would mean that both guidance counselors and principals would become less effective than they should be. When it is necessary for a principal to take part in a discipline problem, he should get the best picture possible of the circumstances surrounding the misbehavior prior to arriving at a plan of action. Some of this information he may get from the pupil, some he should get from those workers who have specialized knowledge and the competence to place such knowledge in its appropriate context. The best diagnosis possible is needed if the principal is to be effective in helping youngsters toward the ultimate goal of self-discipline.

We have suggested that in the area of pupil personnel the major administrative tasks have to do with pupil inventory and organization, pupil accounting, provisions for pupil services, and control of pupil behavior. These services should complement the program provided all pupils through regular classroom instruction.

STAFF PERSONNEL

To implement any of the programs suggested above under curriculum development or pupil personnel, appropriate staff must be provided. Here, therefore, we should like to examine staff personnel as one of the major operational areas in administration. Our discussion will be focused on certificated personnel such as teachers, guidance workers, and administrators. Many of the approaches suggested also have application to non-certificated personnel (custodians, lunchroom workers, and bus drivers). Some additional comments regarding non-certificated personnel will be made when business management is discussed.

PERSONNEL POLICIES

In personnel administration, as with all other aspects of administration, one of the first tasks is the development of appropriate personnel policies. Often school districts recognize the necessity for personnel policies even before they see the need for more general policy statements. Perhaps a word should be said here about the meaning of policy. As we use the term here, and as it might be applied more broadly to school administration, policies refer to a set of guiding principles that establish a framework to give consistency to a school board's actions. In a sense, then, a policy statement represents the framework, in terms of law and of the philosophy of the board, upon which action is to be based.

To be sure, many boards of education will need help in thinking through possible alternatives if they are to express what we would deem sound personnel policies. This means that the administrator will think with both staff members and lay citizens concerning policy matters, and from such deliberation will gain assistance in arriving at policy statements to be recommended to his board of education. These policies will probably most often pertain to working conditions and to the salary program.

Personnel policies pertaining to working conditions, we believe, should meet the following criteria:

1. Appear reasonable and not capricious.

2. Have a positive and not a punitive flavor.

3. Be suggestive and not merely prescriptive.

4. Establish the fact that full information on school operation is available to teachers.

5. Provide clear channels of communication.

6. Make plain the bases for promotion.

7. Provide for staff participation in the formulation and operation of policies.

One illustration of policy statement, having to do with the participation of staff personnel in policy formation, has been taken from the handbook of a city school district. The statement follows:

Personnel policies for the Union District shall be co-operatively formulated and written in concise form. In the development of the same the Superintendent is directed to create and maintain a committee system in which the teaching personnel and all others affected by the policies under consideration may participate in their formulation.

The Committee (a) may direct their recommendations directly to the Board through the Superintendent and he is directed not to interrupt, obstruct, or delay transmittal of said recommendations. The Superintendent will provide every means whereby the certificated personnel receive full information and explanation of all personnel policies, rules and regulations that may affect them directly or indirectly. Copies of such policies shall be distributed at least once each year to all employees not having the same. Professional Standards and Staff Relationships will also be discussed in at least one meeting per year.

Personnel policies shall be reviewed at least once per year by a joint committee of teachers, administrators, and board members.[15]

It will be noted that the place of the committee system has been made clear. Participation of staff members in discussing major school problems is given official endorsement, and the need for face-to-face communication among the superintendent, professional staff members, and board of trustees is recognized.

The increasing militancy of teachers and teachers' organizations has added a new dimension to the problem of formulating personnel policies. The day when school boards and administrators could take a rather paternalistic attitude toward teachers seems to be drawing to a close. Teachers' associations and unions are ever more frequently demanding some type of collective relationship with the board of education. While AFT locals strive for formal contractual arrangements, NEA affiliates seek co-operative relationships, such as a joint committee of teachers, administrators, and board members. But this is not to say that NEA affiliates do not bargain as strongly as AFT locals; on the contrary, many of them have and do.

In a study of bargaining in a number of districts, Stephens was able to develop the following typology:

1. Formal collective bargaining or negotiation.
   a. Recognition contract.
   b. Policy contract.
2. Active bargaining or negotiation.

---

[15] Union School District, San Jose, California, "Policies, Rules and Regulations, and Administrative Code." Not dated, p. 31.

3. Intermediary committee.

4. Informal or nominal contacts.

5. Essentially unilateral action by the board of education.

6. Complete absence of any organized teacher influence.[16]

Stephens concluded that collective relationships in public education require organized teachers' groups. These groups maintain their identity over a period of time and seek the loyalty of the largest possible number of teachers in the district; they seek the standardization of personnel policy and the application of such policy to all members of the group, if not to all teachers in the district. Methods of persuasion are used which reveal the base of power inherent in the membership of large numbers of teachers. Such a position of strength is gained only by substantial membership in proportion to total potential membership. Power is also enhanced by the maintenance of the relationship over a period of time, by the establishment and extension of opportunities to bargain with the board, and by affiliation with mass state and national teachers' organizations.

It seems quite clear that the job of developing personnel policies pertaining to salary programs and working conditions is a task confronting the administrator. This task will require the co-operation of many people, including representatives of teachers' organizations, but the coordination of this effort is the proper function of administration.

SECURING PERSONNEL

The administrator must also determine the kinds and numbers of people needed to man the various programs of the school and must then proceed to secure the people. This task, always a critical one, has become in recent years, with the general manpower shortage, a most difficult one. Since teachers and other professional workers will probably be in short supply for years to come,[17] a brief analysis of reasons back of this shortage may be in order. The lack of teachers is due to a number of factors including the following:

1. Expanded school services.

2. Great increase in school enrollments.

[16] Kenton E. Stephens, "Collective Relationships Between Teachers' Organizations and Boards of Education." Unpublished Ph.D. dissertation, Department of Education, University of Chicago, 1964.

[17] See annual studies of teacher supply and demand made by the Research Division of the National Education Association.

3. Low birth rates of 1930's, providing fewer college students in the 1950's.

4. Continued competition in labor market for highly trained people.

5. Expanded occupational opportunities for women.

With respect to some of these factors the tide has turned: college enrollments are on the increase, a greater percentage of women are attending college, and a high proportion of college graduates are expressing an interest in teaching. Even so, manpower for any occupation requiring extensive training will remain in short supply, particularly if the economy remains at a high level.

These circumstances suggest at least two courses of action for the administrator. He must find ways of helping lay citizens understand the facts pertaining to the manpower shortage, and he must help them see its implications, particularly from the standpoint of the teacher shortage. Only as citizens become thoroughly aroused about the matter will higher levels of compensation and more desirable working conditions for teachers—such as reasonable size of classes—be fully supported by the public.

A second task for the administrator, in view of the manpower situation, is the establishment of employment, assignment, induction, and supervision procedures which will attract and hold capable people. Teachers prefer to work in schools and school systems where they feel wanted, where they feel that the program is on the move, where they feel that their contribution is important, and where they feel that the "boss" is understanding and fair. Important as adequate pay is, a number of studies have shown that work conditions are even more significant.[18]

In essence the personnel policies of boards of education and the personnel practices of administrators can do much to relieve the teacher shortage. This is particularly true at the point of encouraging teachers not to drop out of the profession after they have entered it. Moreover the personnel policies and practices that tend to keep teachers in the profession are the same factors that help teachers perform at their highest levels. In short, the relationships an administrator establishes with his staff to achieve the purpose of the school may well be the essence of administration.

Perhaps brief mention should be made of the procedures to be followed in the selection and assignment of personnel.[19] The first task confronting the administrator is the preparation of a job description. Ordinarily, responsibility for the preparation of this statement will be given to the building principal. He may, of course, consult his staff in the process of deciding

[18] For instance, see Francis S. Chase, "Professional Leadership and Teacher Morale," *Administrator's Notebook.* 1 (March 1953), No. 8.

[19] For more detail see Wm. B. Castetter, *Administering the School Personnel Program* (New York: Macmillan Co., 1962).

just what is needed for a particular job. Moreover, it must be assumed that job openings are determined within the framework of personnel policies that have been previously formulated.

With job descriptions in hand the superintendent is in a position to seek candidates from a file of applicants, from college placement bureaus, and from other sources of supply. The objective will be to find the best possible people for each of the openings. Often good people must be approached in terms of professional opportunities present in the school system and not merely in terms of an available vacancy and salary to be paid. In other words, selection of personnel is a two-way process: the prospective teacher is appraised by the school system, and the school system is appraised by the teacher. In this kind of approach the superintendent will often find that principals and teachers in the school where the teacher may be placed are key people in the exploration.

When the candidate and the school system have reached agreement, the superintendent is in a position to recommend the prospective teacher to the board of education for employment. It should be quite clear that seeking out and selecting candidates is a professional task. Actual employment of the teacher is, of course, the prerogative of the board of education.

SUPERVISING PERSONNEL

After personnel have been employed and assigned to various positions of responsibility within a school system, there is still the need for the administrative leader—be he called superintendent, principal, or supervisor—to supervise the work. Three terms—supervision, curriculum development, and in-service education—are closely related. Each suggests that teachers and administrators need to work together to decide what the program ought to be, how it should be implemented, and how it is to be evaluated. For detailed treatment of these tasks other sources should be consulted.[20]

One of the first tasks in supervision is that of teacher orientation. Whether teachers are beginning their first year of teaching or joining a new school system, certain induction procedures are in order. Often these involve helping new people understand the terms and conditions of employment, become acquainted with the community, develop an understanding of the school system and the people in it, and adjust to the job. The process, which may begin even before employment, probably will not be completed until the end of the first year of service.

It should be quite clear that the working relationships existing between the administrator and his staff and among the members of the staff, dis-

[20] For example, see Wm. H. Burton and Leo J. Brueckner, *Supervision—A Social Process* (New York: Appleton-Century-Crofts, Inc., 1955).

cussed earlier in this chapter, have much to do with staff productivity. Stated otherwise, the development of an atmosphere of mutual respect and confidence, a commendable objective in itself, in a school situation is also a necessary condition if the purpose of the school is to be fostered. Adequate human relations are thus both ends and means.

Activities related to supervision ordinarily focus on the educational program and incidentally upon teachers and others who implement such a program. Thus supervision may include, as Burton and Brueckner suggest, such activities as the following:[21]

1. An appraisal of the educational product.

2. A study of the learner: diagnosis of learning difficulties.

3. A study of instruction.

4. A study of curriculum in operation.

5. A study of materials of instruction, including the socio-physical environment.

Each of these endeavors may suggest improvements that should be tried in practice and evaluated.

APPRAISING TEACHING EFFECTIVENESS

Administrators who have been given responsibility for the operation of a school or a school district must develop some plan of appraising the work of the certificated and non-certificated personnel who work in the school or the district. We suggest that the appraisal be based on the work or performance of the teachers or other personnel rather than on their personal characteristics. The latter involves looking at traits in isolation, an approach that has been largely discredited, as we show in Chapter 11. Moreover most of us can look more objectively at our performance than we can at our persons.

The major objective of any plan designed to appraise the work of teachers and other personnel should be that of improving performance. It seems clear that when teacher and principal, both of whom comprehend the teaching-learning process, can discuss quite frankly the performance of the teacher, some ways of improving that performance can be determined.

While the primary purpose of performance appraisal should remain that of improving such performance, certain secondary purposes may also need to be served. Decisions pertaining to the retention or dismissal of teachers must be made. Decisions to place or not to place teachers on tenure status

[21] *Ibid.*, Chapter I.

are required in many school systems. Many school districts also have a policy of promotion from within the system. Such a plan is based upon the assumption that some teachers have the competencies for such jobs as assistant principals, pupil personnel workers, and other posts, and that those competencies can be recognized. If all of these purposes are to be served well, there must also be appraisal of performance.

In recent years lay citizens and school board members in many school districts have demanded that teaching performance be evaluated in relation to salary. This issue has been debated more than it has been studied. We are convinced that if merit performance is to become a factor in salary determination, most school districts have a long process of "getting ready" for such a program. This eventuality, however, does suggest an additional reason for appraising teaching performance.

Several approaches have been made to the appraisal of teacher performance. One of these might be termed the change-in-pupil-achievement approach. Notable experimentation along this line has been carried out by Barr and his students.[22] It rests on the assumption that the effectiveness of teaching performance can be determined by the growth in achievement of pupils while under the direction of the teacher. While there is much to support such an assumption, influences on pupil learning other than the teacher's do not seem to be adequately recognized.

A second approach to the appraisal of teaching performance might be termed the pupil-rating method, to which Bryan has been a major contributor.[23] This plan rests on the assumption that pupils know when they are being well taught. Again, there seems to be some truth in such a contention, but it is doubtful that pupils are acquainted with all of the expectations which most school systems have for teachers. Then too, pupils in the early years of school seem less able than older pupils to make a judgment about the quality of teaching performance.

If both of the approaches noted above have limitations, what approach can an administrator use in appraising teaching performance? In our judgment the evaluation approach discussed earlier in this chapter seems to be the most fruitful one. It includes the following steps:

1. The characteristics or criteria of good teaching will be determined.
2. These characteristics will be defined in behavioral terms.
3. A method of observing and recording these behaviors will be evolved.
4. The evidence collected will be appraised.

[22] A. S. Barr, et al., "The Measurement of Teaching Ability," Journal of Experimental Education, 14 (September 1945), 1–100.

[23] R. C. Bryan, Student Reactions and Merit Salary Schedules (Kalamazoo, Michigan: School of Graduate Studies, Western Michigan University, 1958), 67 pp.

If these four steps seem formidable, the essence of this approach might be reduced to two major points: (1) there is joint decision as to what good teaching is and (2) a procedure for collecting and appraising evidence concerning good teaching is evolved.

A series of articles in a recent issue of *The National Elementary School Principal*[24] deal with the question of teacher evaluation. Conceptual approaches, actual experience with evaluation programs, and studies of evaluation procedures are reported. The problem is a complex one but apparently in some schools a cooperative definition of good teaching has been developed and acceptable procedures have been established.

In the discussion above we have suggested that the major administrative tasks in the area of staff personnel include developing personnel policies, securing personnel needed to man programs of instruction and pupil services, providing appropriate stimulation and encouragement to staff members as they work at their jobs, and appraising the performance of staff members in terms of their assigned responsibilities in the school system.

Physical Facilities

Most programs of instruction and of pupil services require some physical facilities. We include under such a term school buildings, school grounds, and equipment needed in instruction and incidental to instruction. We have also chosen to include school buses and other transportation equipment under the general term of physical facilities. The major tasks of school administration in this area are what we turn to next.

SCHOOL PLANTS FOR INSTRUCTION

We would like to emphasize the point that school plants exist to facilitate the instructional program. To be sure, these plants may be impressive or they may be beautiful, but neither monumental character nor artistic expression should be achieved at the expense of functional arrangement. Actually, we would suggest that artistry and impressiveness be achieved through assigning function its highest type of physical expression.

Perhaps we can illustrate the relationship we see between program and plant. If the program calls for self-contained classrooms, these rooms must be large enough to permit a variety of activities. If the program includes gardening or camping, clearly the plant must provide for these activities. If

[24] *The National Elementary School Principal*, 43 (November 1963), pp. 3–67.

television is to be used extensively in instruction, the plant must be designed to permit closed circuit hook-ups or other necessary arrangements. If part-time farmers are to be given help with their problems, land for agricultural demonstration should be provided. If the school is also to serve as a center for many community activities, it must be so located and so constructed as to permit such use.

Prediction of the educational program of tomorrow is hazardous, but it seems clear that education will undergo change. Hence modern designers attempt to make school plants highly flexible. The problem facing planners is well put by a recent commission report:

If the educational program never changed; if the culture were static and scientists had ceased probing into the unknown; if inventors had gone on a long holiday and discoveries and innovations were at a standstill; if popula-tion mobility had ceased and the birth rate had become a constant factor; if community life always remained the same; if towns and cities were all alike; if there were no differences in school sites; if no new jobs were being created; if no new educational needs were emerging and the specific purposes of the school were rigidly defined; if the researchers had concluded that all the answers to the problems of teaching and learning had been found; if there were no more content to be added to the curriculum; if the producers of instructional materials and equipment had ceased to experiment and had settled down to producing a standard product; if people were entirely content with present accomplishments; if the dynamic forces of society had all been securely grounded and had ceased to function, then school-building planning would be a simple matter. Stock plans and standard classrooms would be the answer to the school districts' needs for building space. But such is not the case nor is it likely to be.[25]

PLANT DEVELOPMENT PROGRAM

The many problems involved in developing a plant to house a school program are dealt with in the report mentioned above.[26] This volume details the steps to be taken in the development of a school plant program. In order to determine what school plants are needed, an administrator must have data of four kinds: a picture of the educational program to be housed, a projection of the school population to be served, a plan for usage of the existing plant, and an indication of money available for plant expansion. The character of the data needed in each of these areas will be noted briefly.

The school program is a matter of prime importance. For instance, are schools to be organized on a K6–3–3 basis or on a K8–4 basis? Are ele-mentary schools to be designed for 300 pupils or 1,000 pupils? Are rooms

[25] Report of the AASA School-Building Commission: *Planning America's School Buildings* (Washington, D.C.: The Association, 1960), p. 5.

[26] *Ibid.*, 229.

to be designed to house 25 pupils or 40 pupils? Is the seventh grade to be organized largely on a self-contained basis or on a departmental plan? Is science to be taught by the laboratory or by the demonstration method? Is team teaching, where large and small rooms are needed, to be a part of the program? Is closed-circuit TV to be provided?

These questions suggest that the plant should be built to house a program. In a recent report[27] on educational change and architectural consequences, based on a study of a number of outstanding high schools, several developments were noted. These included the following:

1. Variation in spatial arrangements, i.e., large spaces for team teaching, small rooms for seminars, and individual spaces for independent study.

2. Resource centers for books, tapes, films, records, programed learning equipment, and other materials.

3. Planning of facilities for community and recreation use, as well as for the regular instructional program.

4. Willingness to put a greater proportion of the school facility dollar into equipment and less into the outer shell of the building.

The second area of concern has to do with the pupils to be served, and in this case the administrator is dealing in futures. Such questions as the following must be answered: What changes are anticipated in the school population? How do these changes affect each grade level? How do these changes affect each part or attendance area of the district? What are the prospects of changes in district boundaries, and how are they likely to affect pupil population, including racial composition? What housing developments are in prospect, and what effect are they likely to have on pupil population?

A third body of data necessary in planning for the school plant has to do with the proposed use of the existing plant. Again, key questions must be answered. Are the present buildings safe? Are they located where they will be needed? Can they be adapted to serve the educational needs of the district? What capacities do the existing buildings have in terms of the educational program and pupil population of the future?

Results of these three types of studies begin to suggest the kind, amount, and location of school plants needed by the district. At this point the financial resources available for capital outlay must be examined. Since most districts must rely on a bond issue for capital outlay, the bonding possibilities of a district, usually limited by statute, must be noted. Moreover, practical considerations usually require that attention be given to tax levies already in effect for capital outlay and for current operation of the school. These considerations may require that the relative cost of reconditioning

[27] *High Schools 1962* (New York: Educational Facilities Laboratories, Inc., 1962).

existing buildings as opposed to costs of constructing new buildings be determined. All in all, the financial data help answer the big question of whether or not the needed plant expansion is practicable.

In a school district of any size the four kinds of data mentioned above are necessary to a program for the development of the school plant. In a small school district the superintendent will work directly with principals, teachers, and citizens on the problem. In a larger school district he may have one or more staff members who will assist with these studies. In some cases, the help of outside consultants can be secured to guide or supplement the work of local people. In any case, however, the superintendent must see that these studies are made. With such information in hand the board of education and the people of a community are in a better position to make decisions regarding the modification of the existing plant and the securing of additional plant facilities. After such decisions have been made, the superintendent will have other tasks as he works with architects and contractors, but his basic responsibility lies in the tasks enumerated above. Unless the administrator and his staff have given attention to the program to be housed, the planning aspect of the plant program will not be adequate.

In addition to a program designed to expand the physical facilities of a school district, administrators are confronted with the operation and maintenance of the existing school plant. Operation, as the word implies, has to do with the day-to-day running of the plant. The major objectives of operation are to keep the plant safe, sanitary, attractive, and in readiness for teaching and learning. All of this is to be done as efficiently as possible. Extravagance in plant operation may mean that less money is available for those aspects of the program which are more directly related to teaching and learning.

School plants, like other physical facilities, require a constant program of maintenance. Equipment wears out and must be replaced. Paint deteriorates and must be replaced. Mortar loosens and must be repaired. Roofs eventually leak and require repair. A hundred other examples could be given. Most maintenance jobs require skilled craftsmen, including plumbers, painters, electricians, masons, roofers, and many others.

A perennial issue in the plant maintenance field is how to get these skilled workmen. Should the school set up a maintenance department and employ many of these craftsmen on an annual basis so as to have them available when needed? Or should maintenance work be let out on contract at times when there is work to be done? This problem and many allied problems will require administrative attention in any school district.

As suggested above, we have made transportation a part of our discussion of physical facilities, a decision which seems to be logical for two reasons. First, the transportation service is carried on with a rather high capital investment in equipment, for which the problems of procurement and maintenance are somewhat similar to the procurement and maintenance of other equipment. Second, the transportation program is auxiliary to the instructional program in somewhat the same manner as are building facilities. Pupils are housed or transported so as to be available for instruction.

In rural areas the transportation function has become so extensive as to require in some places as much as 25 percent of the school budget. In such instances administrative responsibility for establishing the transportation program, for purchasing equipment, for securing bus drivers and mechanics, for supervising their work, and for maintaining relationships with parents of transported pupils is a major task. In all but the very small districts, supervisors of transportation are usually added to the administrative staff.

FINANCE AND BUSINESS MANAGEMENT

In a money economy such as ours, the services of personnel, the buildings, the equipment, the supplies, and the other items necessary to the operation of a school or a school system must be paid for. Thus another operational area of administration, that of finance and business management, is indicated. The administrative tasks included in this area, whether they have to do with securing revenues or making expenditures, are instrumental, not primary, in character. In other words, money is useful only as it is used to purchase a program of teaching and learning. The details of both finance and business management have been described elsewhere.[28] For our purposes, we shall deal with budget-making, securing revenue, managing expenditures, and managing non-certificated personnel.

BUDGET-MAKING

The school budget is often defined as a school program expressed in fiscal terms. Actually, a good budget will have three major aspects: the proposed program of the school district, the expenditures necessary to support such a program, and the anticipated revenues to cover such expenditures.

Again, the basic position of the instructional program is stressed. The budget should not provide simply for personnel, but rather for particular personnel to carry out particular parts of the program. The budget should not call simply for new or remodeled buildings, but rather for particular

[28] For instance, see Roe L. Johns and Edgar L. Morphet, *Financing the Public Schools* (Englewood Cliffs, N.J.: Prentice-Hall, Inc., 1960), 566 pp., and John E. Corbally, Jr., *School Finance* (Boston: Allyn and Bacon, Inc., 1962), 288 pp.

buildings with particular facilities to permit particular parts of the program to go forward. The budget should stipulate not simply money for equipment, but money for particular equipment to facilitate teaching and learning for particular parts of the program.

If the budget is to reflect the school program to the extent here indicated, it is clear that budget-building becomes a most important process within a school system. We would like to comment upon two aspects of that process.

First, it is important that the people within the school system who actually operate the program have a large part in budget-building. This means that teachers will have a real voice in suggesting what is necessary by way of working conditions, equipment, supplies, books, and other items to make instruction most effective. This means also that non-certificated employees who clean floors, repair roofs, or do other tasks will also have a voice in suggesting what is needed to do these jobs efficiently. To be sure, all of these suggestions may not be accepted, but they should be considered.

Second, it is clear that budget-making is a continuous process. It has both short-range and long-range aspects. Filling out a budget estimate for the ensuing year may be essentially a short-range task. On the other hand, teachers may work for a year or two in projecting an improved program for the teaching of the social studies. We submit that such planning is long-range budget-making as truly as it is curriculum development. In brief, we suggest that all planning for program improvement, whether it be for instruction or for services, should also be considered as budget-making.

The concept of the budget suggested here means that it is a major policy statement in any school district. Unfortunately, there are still many school districts in which the budget is seen only in its short-range aspects, where the deliberations of staff members are seldom reflected, where the program which the budget proposes to buy is meagerly portrayed, and where the format is unattractive. Such an important document deserves better treatment.

SECURING REVENUE

Another important administrative task in the area of finance and business management is the securing of revenue. The financing of schools is, of course, but one aspect of public finance. Numerous governmental services at local, state, and national levels must be financed. The securing of money for these services, chiefly through taxation, is intimately related to the general economy of the nation. These interrelationships are often not fully appreciated by citizens, or for that matter by school administrators. Benson[29] has dealt extensively with school finance as an area of public finance, and

[29] Charles S. Benson, *The Economics of Public Education* (Boston: Houghton Mifflin Co., 1961).

he has applied economic analyses to a comprehensive selection of topics in the financing of education.

School districts ordinarily receive revenues from local, state, and federal sources. Percentages of revenue received from each of these sources are shown for selected states for 1960–61 and 1964–65 in Table 4.1. It will be noted that for the United States as a whole, over the five-year period, the percentages of local, state, and federal support have remained almost identical. Indeed, for each of the states shown there has been little change over the same period. Despite this stability there is great variability among the states, from almost complete reliance upon local revenues in Nebraska to little reliance on local revenues in New Mexico. For the years shown the proportion of federal support has been a minor one, but with the enactment of recent legislation the percentage of revenues from federal sources will probably show some increase in the years ahead.

TABLE 4.1

ESTIMATED PERCENT OF REVENUE FOR PUBLIC ELEMENTARY AND SECONDARY SCHOOLS FOR SELECTED STATES BY LEVELS OF GOVERNMENT, 1960–61 AND 1964–65

	1960–61			1964–65		
	Local	State	Fed	Local	State	Fed
Alabama	22.8	69.1	8.1	29.1	63.2	7.7
California	56.3	40.4	3.3	57.1	39.5	3.3
Illinois	76.9	20.4	2.7	75.1	22.8	2.1
Nebraska	91.4	4.0	4.6	90.0	4.7	5.3
New Mexico	15.9	70.6	13.5	21.4	69.3	9.3
New York	56.4	42.4	1.2	55.1	43.0	2.0
Ohio	68.1	29.1	2.8	70.9	26.8	2.3
Texas	45.5	50.0	4.5	43.9	52.7	3.5
United States	56.3	40.1	3.6	56.2	40.0	3.8

Source: Research Division, National Education Association, *Rankings of the States,* 1961 and 1965.

At the local level, the source of school revenue is almost entirely the property tax. At the state level, legislative appropriation from the general fund is the usual practice. While revenues accruing to the states upon which legislative appropriations may draw are from several sources, the retail sales tax, the state income tax, or both, have become major sources of such revenue in most states.

In about the last quarter of a century, the federal government has become the chief tax collector. Whereas in 1929 approximately 75 percent of the taxes were collected at local and state levels, and the remaining 25 percent at the federal level, during World War II these percentages were almost reversed, thus making the federal government the chief tax collector. This shift has, of course, been accompanied by a great increase in total taxes collected and by unprecedented expenditures on the part of the federal government for services at home and abroad.

Large sums of federal money have been allocated for such services as hospital construction and road building. Because state and local sources have been shown to be inadequate for these and other public services, many doubt that public schools can be supported adequately from state and local sources alone. Certainly the flow of goods, services, and money tends to be national and international rather than local and state in character.

With the clear recognition that the various states must play a major role in financing public education, and with the likelihood that the federal government will also share more significantly in such financing, school administrators must be prepared to give leadership in public school finance at both state and federal levels. The administrator cannot see his responsibilities in the finance realm as limited to his own school district.

At the state level this means that the whole plan of state support for public education must come under the purview of the school administrator. Most states have some kind of foundation program for the financial support of schools, an arrangement which is supposed to guarantee a minimum educational program for every district of the state. School administrators must be able to help state boards of education, state legislatures, and citizens generally to understand the purposes and operations of such a foundation program. Without such study and vigilance, state aid may actually subsidize conditions that militate against good educational practice.

At the federal level, too, administrators should have insights based upon the economic realities of a highly industrialized and interdependent economy. With such insights, and with facts based upon careful research, the appropriate role of the federal government in school finance might be determined. Recent legislation enacted by the Congress suggests that the role of the federal government in financing education in the future will be an expanding one. The task ahead seems to be the evolution of an appropriate local-state-national partnership in the financing of the schools.

Though school administration should provide statesmanship in school finance at both state and federal levels, the concern with the revenues available to one's own school district must also have attention. For instance, the superintendent or members of his staff must check to see that taxes levied for the school district are properly calculated and distributed. In many states this will require close working arrangements with the county assessor and the county auditor.

In similar manner the superintendent or members of his staff must ascertain all ways by which the school district might become eligible for state funds; and when the district is eligible, he must check to see that allocations due the district are being made. Ordinarily, then, the local superintendent must have a working relationship with the state department of education.

While federal funds are a minor part of total school revenue, they are exceedingly important to many school districts. Public Laws 874 and 815, for instance, have provided federal funds for operation and capital outlay to school districts where enrollments have been increased due to population movements caused by federal installations. Recent congressional action has also authorized appreciable revenues for the improvement of vocational education and for the education of the culturally deprived. As with local and state revenues, the administrator has the obligation to determine the eligibility of the school district for federal funds and then to see that such funds are made available.

MANAGING EXPENDITURES

The management of expenditures made by a school district is another administrative responsibility. There are many tasks in this aspect of admin- istration, including purchasing, payroll operation, supply management, ac- counting and reporting, insurance management, and the keeping of a property inventory. The adequate performance of each of these tasks re- quires considerable knowledge and skill.[30] In small school districts, the superintendent will be expected to perform many of these functions. In larger school districts, specialized help may be secured, but it is still the superintendent's responsibility to see that these jobs are competently performed.

One important part of the accounting procedures of a school district is the budget-control record. As will be recalled, we advocated that the budget be formulated in considerable detail so as to depict the educational program for which the money was to be spent, and the sources from which the money was to come. With such a budget as a beginning point, a budget control system should be developed so that at least once a month the conditions of expenditures and revenues might be ascertained. Such a report can both help the superintendent and his staff in their administration of the budget, and prove an indispensable aid to a board of education in its efforts to under- stand how the school enterprise is going forward. For budget control, bookkeeping, and other aspects of business management, a machine tech- nology, including the use of computers, has been developed.

[30] John E. Corbally, Jr., *op. cit.*

MANAGING NONCERTIFICATED PERSONNEL

Ordinarily the management of noncertificated personnel is made a part of business management. In small school districts this distinction is of little consequence. In larger districts, however, the business management function, including responsibility for noncertificated personnel, is delegated by the superintendent to a business manager or assistant superintendent in charge of business. Noncertificated personnel include a wide variety of workers such as custodians, skilled craftsmen, cafeteria employees, bus drivers, and secretaries. In many school districts, these employees number approximately one-half the number of instructional or certificated workers.

For each of these categories of workers, a plan of personnel management needs to be evolved. In many respects the details of such a plan are similar to those which were developed at some length in the discussion of staff personnel above. For each group of workers, appropriate personnel policies must be developed, suitable people must be selected and employed, supervision must be provided, and appraisal of work performance made.

The components of job satisfaction for noncertificated workers are similar to those of certificated workers. People like to feel wanted, they like to feel that the institution has a desirable program, and they like to feel that their contribution is valued.

We have suggested that administrative activities in finance and business management are instrumental to the achievement of the major purpose of the school. The major tasks of this area have been presented as budget-making, securing revenues, managing expenditures, and directing noncertificated personnel.

Organizing to Achieve the Tasks

Achievement of the tasks enumerated above requires an organization or structure. The establishment of this structure represents, in a sense, an additional task area. However, we have chosen to view the development of such a structure as a way of implementing the tasks already suggested rather than as a set of additional tasks.

By structure we refer to the relationships of people as they work to achieve a common goal, and it is these relationships with which this section will deal. In this connection it is necessary to discuss briefly the meaning of formal organization, the controlling board, administrative organization, and channels for communication and participation.

MEANING OF FORMAL ORGANIZATION

Most people belong to both formal and informal organizations. A group of women may get together regularly to play bridge, a group of men may become a golf foursome, children on a particular street may become a play group, or a half-dozen members of a high school faculty may meet frequently for lunch. All of these are examples of informal organizations.

On the other hand, a business corporation, a military battalion, a church congregation, and a school district are examples of formal organizations. What are the basic differences between these two kinds of groups? There are several worthy of mention. With respect to origin, informal groups tend to be voluntary while formal groups are usually official. An informal organization may terminate when the present membership leaves, while a formal organization persists beyond its immediate membership. The task or purpose of an informal group is probably not known or, at least, not clear to outsiders, while the task of a formal group is usually adequately perceived by people out of the organization. An informal organization ordinarily has no assigned status hierarchy while a formal organization does. In an informal organization there may be little regular differentiation of assigned work (or play), while in a formal organization there is definite allocation of work responsibilities.

The people who work in a school or school district are definitely members of a formal organization. The school or school district came into being by official governmental act. The organization will go on beyond the lives of the present members. The task of the school or school district is clear to those outside the organization. In all except the smallest schools, there is a recognized hierarchy of position. The work of administrators, teachers, custodians, and other workers is clearly differentiated. This concept of the school as a formal organization is relevant to the remainder of this discussion.

We are well aware of the fact that a school or school district, in addition to being a formal organization, may have one or more informal organizations within it. A clique within a faculty, for instance, may greatly influence decisions of the faculty or of the administrator, entirely outside the formal organizational channels. It is not our purpose here to explore the ramifications of informal organizations within formal organizations. Suffice it to say that formal organization cannot replace informal organization.

CONTROLLING BOARD

As with most other formal organizations, workers of a school district are subject to the direction of a controlling board, in most states known as the board of education. In some states the terminology is board of trustees or board of directors. In all cases these boards are created by the respective state legislatures and given by them broad grants of power to organize and conduct schools within their respective school districts. In addition to the specified powers enumerated in the respective state codes, boards of education also have the powers implied as necessary to the proper exercise of the specified powers. The breadth of these responsibilities is illustrated by two sections of the laws of Wisconsin relating to the public schools:

. . . the school district board shall have the possession, care, control, and management of the property and affairs of the district. (40.29) The board may make rules for the organization, graduation, and government of the schools. . . . (40.30)

While the language shown above makes clear the fact that the board of education has complete legal control, within the limitations of state and federal law, to operate a school district, the board of education has found it necessary in actual practice to create an organization to operate the schools. In a small school district this may be a very simple organization of a few teachers and a custodian with the board itself attempting to retain the administrative function. In most school districts, however, the board of education employs a superintendent of schools as its chief administrator. In turn, the superintendent is expected to organize separate schools under the direction of building principals, and to secure instructional and non-instructional personnel, usually subject to approval of the board, to man the school enterprise.

With the employment of a superintendent of schools, the differentiation of function between the controlling board and its chief executive officer becomes a matter of importance. In general, a board of education does or should become chiefly a legislative and judicial body, while the administrative function is or should be given to the superintendent. This distinction is not as simple as it sounds and many boards and superintendents have difficulty in establishing their respective roles. Since legal control, even for administration, rests finally with the board, the superintendent cannot exercise an executive role except as his board permits.

To assist in this kind of understanding, the role of the board is often defined as part of the rules and regulations of the school district. In Cincinnati the duties of the board have been defined in the following language:

Recognizing the legal definitions of its duties, the board of education considers its major responsibilities to be:

a. To select a superintendent of schools.

b. To provide for the preparation of and to adopt the annual budget.

    c. To provide by the exercise of its taxing power the funds necessary to finance the operation of the schools.

    d. To make rules and regulations for the operation of the schools under its control.

    e. To initiate questions of policy for consideration and report by the superintendent.

    f. To consider and pass upon the recommendations of the superintendent in all matters of policy, appointment or dismissal of employees, salary schedules or other personnel regulations, courses of study, selection of textbooks or other matters pertaining to the welfare of the schools.

    g. To appraise the effectiveness with which the schools are achieving the educational purposes of the board.

    h. To inform the public concerning the progress and needs of the schools, and to solicit and weigh public opinion as it affects the schools.[31]

To perform the duties enumerated above in one or two meetings per month—all the time lay citizens can ordinarily devote to the school board—it is clear that the Cincinnati Board of Education would have to deal with questions of policy and not with the details of operation. Often the establishment of policy, upon the recommendation of the superintendent and his staff, constitutes the legislative activity of the board of education. Examination of how that policy has worked in practice, often with the help of rather complete reports supplied by the superintendent and his staff, permits the board to exercise its judicial function.

    This discussion has already implied much concerning the role of the superintendent, but let us look more specifically at that matter. Cincinnati has also defined the superintendent's job as follows:

The superintendent of schools shall be the chief executive and administrative officer of the board of education, and shall have, in addition to the powers and duties specifically imposed upon his office by statute, all executive and administrative powers and duties in connection with the conduct of the schools which are not required by statute to be exercised directly by the board or by some other officer. It shall be the duty of the superintendent to complete all executive and administrative transactions not by law or resolution required to be brought before the board of education; and to prepare all other matters of administrative procedure or policy for board approval. The enumeration in this section, or elsewhere in these rules and regulations, of specific powers and duties shall not be construed to derogate from the generality of duties hereby imposed.[32]

    In general terms the superintendent of schools should have two major functions: that of being the chief executive officer of the board of education,

[31] Cincinnati, Ohio, Board of Education, *Rules and Regulations* (1964), p. 1.

[32] *Ibid.*, p. 15.

and that of being the chief professional adviser to the board of education. These two roles must go hand in hand if a board is to have the help it needs. If the superintendent performs as executive officer only, the board will not be able to establish its policies in light of the professional knowledge with which the superintendent should be familiar. In other words, the superintendent should, with the assistance of his staff, help the board of education be its best self.

ADMINISTRATIVE ORGANIZATION

The school enterprise of many school districts is of such magnitude that a single administrator cannot give it adequate direction and supervision. In these cases an administrative organization must be established. In some districts this organization may include only the superintendent and three or four building principals; in others a much more complex structure becomes necessary.

While we maintain that no form or amount of administrative organization will, per se, guarantee an effective school system, we do believe that appropriate administrative organization can facilitate the achievement of the goals of a school system. There are some telltale signs that betray ineffective administrative organization. Some of these are: a large proportion of administrative time spent on "emergencies," unexplained delays in carrying out plans, or frequent complaints that "no one told me." These and similar breakdowns warn that the concepts and principles of administrative organization should be examined.

Let us mention some of the concepts that require attention. One of these is the question of centralization versus decentralization. In the centralized plan the superintendent's office exercises tight control over all of the schools of the district. In the decentralized arrangement building principals and their staffs are given considerable autonomy with regard to many aspects of school operation. Centralization requires a relatively large central office staff of directors and supervisors, whereas decentralization may mean that each principal will be given administrative assistance. Centralized control usually requires considerable uniformity of practice among the various schools; decentralized control ordinarily results in more diversity of practice among the schools.

Another concept in organization is that of line and staff. Line officers are usually thought of as those responsible for the operation of the major units of an organization, i.e., school district or school attendance area. Staff officers usually serve in a fact-gathering or advisory capacity or perform a specialized function for line officers, i.e., director of research or school psychologist. Since these terms have a military connotation, some educators have been prone to condemn them, a rejection which seems rather foolish, for in relatively large school organizations some line and some staff officials seem necessary. Ordinarily building principals are thought of as line people, since they are responsible for the operation of a school. On the other hand, a director of research and a director of in-service education would usually be designated as staff people. Their function is that of assisting the superintendent either by supplying him with research findings or performing some tasks in his name. While staff people do not have the responsibility for a school, they do have functional responsibility.

In any organization there is also the matter of a flat or a pyramidal arrangement. A superintendent working directly with principals represents a flat or a two-level arrangement, while a plan of organization which includes assistant superintendents and directors may mean a pyramid, or a four-level arrangement. More levels seem to increase the feeling of distance between the chief administrator and the teachers, and may easily lead to such remarks as, "Oh, I know nothing about that, for it is handled downtown."

Closely related to flat and pyramidal organization is the concept of span of control. This refers to the number of people reporting directly to a single administrator, usually the chief administrator or superintendent of schools. Often the superintendent is torn between wishing a flat organization, and having so many sub-administrators reporting directly to him that he cannot do justice to those relationships. Some students of organization think that the chief administrator should not have more than five to eight administrative assistants reporting directly to him.

Still another concept is that of horizontal and vertical organization. Assistant superintendents in charge of elementary and secondary education respectively represent a horizontal arrangement, while assistant superintendents in charge of functions or operational areas such as instruction or staff personnel represent a vertical plan.

Griffiths and others have suggested that the establishment of an administrative organization is one of the basic functions of administration. They suggest that the steps necessary in this process are as follows:

1. The purposes of the school should be stated clearly and in operational terms.

2. The conceptual framework on which the organization will be constructed must be agreed upon.

3. The functions of administration necessary to the achievement of the stated purposes must be listed.

4. The present administrative structure must be surveyed to determine which functions are being performed by whom.

5. A plan of organization must be developed consistent with the conceptual framework of organization.

6. The functions of administration must be related to specific administrative positions.

7. Job descriptions must be developed for the administrative positions to which functions are assigned.

8. The administrative positions and the job descriptions must be related to the incumbent administrators.

9. A timetable must be set up to implement the reorganization.[33]

COMMUNICATION AND PARTICIPATION

In any formal organization it becomes necessary to establish channels for communication and participation. Only through adequate communication can members of the organization remain aware of organizational goals, keep clearly in mind how their own work contributes to those goals, understand how the work of others contributes to the goals, and make suggestions for the improvement of operational procedures in the organization. The conditions suggested above make it clear that communication in an organization must flow up, down, and across.

Culbertson points out that there are many barriers to communication in an organization.[34] These barriers may include the words used in the communication, many of which carry different emotional overtones to different people; or the barrier may rest with the administrator as the communicator, particularly if he is inclined to emphasize the aspects of his office related to status; or the barrier may rest with members of the organization as communicatees, if their values and motivations are different from those of the communicator.

The role of the administrator in facilitating communication within an organization is a crucial one. For instance, Clark found in a study of the administrative behavior of high school principals that the more effective principals initiated and had more communication with staff members than did the less effective principals, and that more of it was face-to-face communication.[35]

We shall say more about what we mean by appropriate participation later, but we do emphasize that teachers should participate extensively in

[33] Daniel E. Griffiths et al., Organizing Schools for Effective Education (Danville, Illinois: Interstate Publishers, Inc., 1962), p. 309.

[34] Jack Culbertson, "Recognizing Roadblocks in Communication Channels," Administrator's Notebook, 7 (March 1959), pp. 1–4.

[35] Dean O. Clark, "Critical Areas in the Administrative Behavior of High School Principals." Unpublished doctoral dissertation, The Ohio State University, 1959.

matters that have to do with instruction. This position is supported in a study done by Sharma, who concludes:

An extensive examination of the data summarized above indicated rather clearly that the teachers participating in the study want to assume professional responsibility for all activities that concern instruction. They want more autonomy for the individual schools in which they teach. They believe that the role of citizens in the community should be limited to participation in policy making in areas other than professional matters. And finally, they report significant differences between what they desire and current practices in decision making insofar as participation by groups of teachers, the principal, the board of education, and the superintendent are concerned. In most cases, the percentages of the teachers desiring participation by groups of teachers and the principal were considerably larger than the percentages reporting such participation. On the other hand, the percentages desiring participation by the board of education and the superintendent were considerably smaller than the percentages reporting their participation.[36]

We have concluded our overview of the administrative tasks in educational administration by a consideration of organization and structure. We have suggested that organization and structure imply arrangements designed to facilitate the other administrative tasks; and all administrative tasks, it will be recalled, have their *raison d'être* in improving the programs for teaching and learning in a school or school district.

SUGGESTED ACTIVITIES

1. Compare the operational areas of this chapter with those suggested by Miller. Which categorization do you prefer? Why?
2. In the light of the criteria suggested for personnel policies in this chapter, appraise the personnel policies of your district.
3. Determine what percentage of the budget of your school district over the past ten years has been allocated for (a) instruction and (b) capital outlay and debt service.
4. Taking account of recent legislation enacted by the Congress, project the school revenues from federal sources for your state during the next three years.

[36] C. L. Sharma, "Who Should Make Decisions?" *Administrator's Notebook,* 3 (April 1955), pp. 1–4.

SELECTED READINGS

BENSON, CHARLES S. *The Economics of Public Education.* Boston: Houghton Mifflin Co., 1961.

CAMPBELL, ROALD F. and RAMSEYER, JOHN A. *The Dynamics of School-Community Relationships.* Boston: Allyn and Bacon, Inc., 1955.

CASTETTER, WM. B. *Administering the School Personnel Program.* New York: Macmillan Co., 1962.

CORBALLY, JOHN E., JR. *School Finance.* Boston: Allyn and Bacon, Inc., 1962.

MILLER, VAN. *The Public Administration of American School Systems.* New York: Macmillan Co., 1965.

Report of the AASA School-Building Commission, *Planning America's School Buildings.* Washington, D.C.: The American Association of School Administrators, 1960.

TABA, HILDA. *Curriculum Development—Theory and Practice.* New York: Harcourt, Brace and World, Inc., 1962.

YEAGER, WM. A. *Administration and the Pupil.* New York: Harper & Brothers, 1949.

5

The Administrative

Process

TO THIS POINT WE HAVE EXAMINED ADMINISTRATION from the standpoint of its development and meaning, and in terms of the major tasks confronting a school organization. We shall now look at administration as a process by which an organization makes and implements decisions. Some writers call this approach the decision-making process, but we shall call it simply the administrative process. While this view of administration has been prominent in business and public administration, it has been relatively neglected in educational administration.

THE GENERAL CONCEPT

It now seems appropriate that we examine the meaning of the term "administrative process." We shall build this definition in a historical manner by examining some of the earlier statements on the administrative process, and in a comparative way by noting discussions in educational writing and elsewhere.

EARLY STATEMENTS

As noted in Chapter 3, Fayol, as early as 1916 in his *Administration Industrielle et Générale,* dealt with what he called the "elements of management."[1] He described them as planning, organizing, commanding, co-ordinating and controlling. These components of what we would call the administrative process resulted from thoughtful observation on the part of Fayol, an engineer who had turned administrator. Urwick, a student of public administration, has this to say of Fayol:

Thus his life embraced four careers rather than one, and in each of them he was pre-eminent. As a technical man he achieved national distinction for work in mining engineering. As a geologist he propounded a completely new theory of the formation of coal-bearing strata and supported it with a detailed study of the Commentry district, almost unique as a piece of geological research. As a scientist turned industrial leader his success in both fields was phenomenal. The days of his own detailed research were over, but he applied the scientific approach to problems in every direction and encouraged those associated with him to do likewise. . . . But he always declared that that success was not due to personal qualities, but to the steady application of certain simple principles. Finally, as a philosopher of administration and as a statesman he left a mark on the thinking of his own and of many other European countries. . . .[2]

While the meaning of planning, organizing, and co-ordinating may seem clear, two of the words Fayol used above may need explanation. The word "commanding" will be better understood if one remembers that the time was 1916. Under this term, Fayol suggested that the manager should perform such activities as these: acquiring a thorough knowledge of his personnel, eliminating the incompetent, setting a good example, conducting periodic audits of the organization, bringing together his chief assistants for conference, and avoiding preoccupation with detail. Perhaps today we would use the term "directing" to include much of what Fayol meant by command.

The word "controlling" may also give some trouble. A part of Fayol's own explanation of the word follows:

In an undertaking, control consists in verifying whether everything occurs in conformity with the plan adopted, the instructions issued and principles established. It has for object to point out weaknesses and errors in order to rectify them and prevent recurrence. It operates on everything, things, people, actions. From the management standpoint it must be ensured that a plan does exist, that it is put into operation and kept up-to-date, that the human organization is complete, the summarized personnel charts in use, and that

---

[1] See translation by Constance Starrs, *General and Industrial Management* (London: Sir Isaac Pitman and Sons, Ltd., 1949).

[2] *Ibid.,* p. ix.

command is exercised in line with principles, that co-ordinating conferences are held, etc., etc.[3]

Some of our present-day writers use the term "evaluating" in much the same way that Fayol used "controlling."

Even this brief discussion may suggest that Fayol had given expression to a process that seemed to have application to the problems confronting an administrator.

Fayol's "elements" or processes of administration were derived chiefly from experience with industrial enterprises. Soon, however, students were to apply these principles to the public realm. For instance, Gulick [4] suggested how the office of the President of the United States might be organized. He asked the question, "What is the work of the chief executive?" His answer was, "POSDCoRB," which sounds a little confusing until one learns that the letters stand for activities necessary to the proper functioning of the office. Gulick himself explains these activities as follows:

Planning, that is working out in broad outline the things that need to be done and the methods for doing them to accomplish the purpose set for the enterprise;

Organizing, that is the establishment of the formal structure of authority through which work subdivisions are arranged, defined and co-ordinated for the defined objective;

Staffing, that is the whole personnel function of bringing and training the staff and maintaining favorable conditions of work;

Directing, that is the continuous task of making decisions and embodying them in specific and general orders and instructions and serving as the leader of the enterprise;

Co-ordinating, that is the all-important duty of interrelating the various parts of the work;

Reporting, that is keeping those to whom the chief executive is responsible informed as to what is going on, which thus includes keeping himself and his subordinates informed through records, research and inspection;

Budgeting, with all that goes with budgeting in the form of fiscal planning, accounting and control.[5]

Gulick acknowledged that the above formulation was an adaptation of the functional analysis previously elaborated by Fayol. Although Gulick was speaking specifically of the office of the President of the United States, he contended that this analysis would be a helpful pattern into which to place the major activities of any chief executive.

[3] *Ibid.,* p. 107.

[4] Luther Gulick and L. Urwick (eds.), *Papers on the Science of Administration* (New York: Institute of Public Administration, 1937).

[5] *Ibid.,* p. 13.

We have in the above statements the conclusions reached by two scholars, one with a background in industrial management and the other with public administration as his orientation, who tried to fathom and explain the process by which the work of an administrator, particularly a chief administrator, gets done. Soon these and other promising efforts were to be adapted to educational administration.

APPLICATION TO EDUCATIONAL ADMINISTRATION

Sears appears to have been the first writer in education to apply the administrative process to educational administration in comprehensive fashion.[6] In his book, he acknowledges indebtedness to other students of administration, including Fayol and Gulick, for their work in the field. According to him, the process includes the following activities: planning, organization, direction, co-ordination, and control. With but two minor changes, Fayol's five elements emerge in Sears' formulation. The staffing and reporting functions, as presented by Gulick, are apparently subsumed in the other activities enumerated. Moreover, Sears does not follow Gulick in including budgeting as one aspect of the administrative process. It will be noted, however, that much of what Gulick places under budgeting has to do with control, a term Sears retains as one of his major headings. Each of the five elements of the process is treated by Sears at some length.[7]

A yearbook of the American Association of School Administrators took cognizance of the administrative process.[8] After noting that administration is essentially a way of working with people to accomplish the purpose of an enterprise, it enumerates some crucial activities in this relationship. An excerpt from the section in which five crucial activities are described follows:

1. *Planning* or the attempt to control the future in the direction of the desired goals through decisions made on the basis of careful estimates of the probable consequences of possible courses of action.

2. *Allocation* or the procurement and allotment of human and material resources in accordance with the operating plan.

3. *Stimulation* or motivation of behavior in terms of the desired outcomes.

4. *Co-ordination* or the process of fitting together the various groups and operations into an integrated pattern of purpose-achieving work.

[6] Jesse B. Sears, *The Nature of the Administrative Process* (New York: McGraw-Hill, 1950).

[7] *Ibid.*

[8] American Association of School Administrators, *Staff Relations in School Administration* (Washington: AASA, 1955), Chapter 1.

5. *Evaluation* or the continuous examination of the effects produced by the ways in which the other functions listed here are performed.[9]

The above formulation of the administrative process seems to contain one new point of emphasis. For "commanding" (Fayol's term) or "directing" (the term used by Gulick and Sears), the word "stimulation" has been suggested. In view of what is known about motivating group action toward a common enterprise, this may be a significant addition.

A careful examination of the administrative process as it applies in education has been made by Gregg.[10] To him the process has seven components as follows: decision-making, planning, organizing, communicating, influencing, co-ordinating, and evaluating.

While Gregg uses many of the components with which we are now familiar, he employs certain new emphases. Decision-making, as different from and perhaps previous to planning, is introduced. Both communicating and influencing stress the necessity for mobilizing all members of the work group if the organization is to achieve its purpose. In fact, Gregg's treatment stresses time and again the necessity for involvement of staff if the administrative process is to be effective.

One of the few empirical tests of the administrative or decision-making process is found in the work of Griffiths and Hemphill.[11] In a comprehensive and careful study of the performance of 232 elementary school principals, tested in a week-long simulated situation, considerable evidence was gathered to support a formulation of the process as follows:

1. Recognizing a problem and the need to prepare to make a decision.

2. Preparing for clarification of the problem.

3. Initiating work in preparation.

4. Organizing and judging facts, opinions, and situations.

5. Selecting alternatives.

6. Deciding and acting.

A DEFINITION

Reference to additional analyses of the administrative or decision-making

[9] *Ibid.*, p. 17.

[10] Russell T. Gregg, "The Administrative Process," in Roald F. Campbell and Russell T. Gregg (eds.), *Administrative Behavior in Education* (New York: Harper & Brothers, 1957), Chapter 8.

[11] Daniel E. Griffiths, John Hemphill, *et al., Administrative Performance and Personality* (New York: Bureau of Publication, Teachers College, Columbia University, 1961).

process seems desirable before a definition is attempted. Simon has amplified the idea as follows:

It should be noted that the administrative processes are decisional processes: they consist in segregating certain elements in the decisions of members of the organization, and establishing regular organizational procedures to select and determine these elements and to communicate them to the members concerned. If the task of the group is to build a ship, a design for the ship is drawn and adopted by the organization, and this design limits and guides the activities of persons who actually construct the ship.

The organization, then, takes from the individual some of his decisional autonomy, and substitutes for it an organization decision-making process. The decisions which the organization makes for the individual ordinarily (1) specify his function, that is, the general scope and nature of his duties; (2) allocate authority, that is, determine who in the organization is to have power to make further decisions for the individual; and (3) set such other limits to his choice as are needed to co-ordinate the activities of several individuals in the organization.[12]

In the above, Simon helps us see that the decision-making with which we are concerned is not *individual* but rather *organizational* decision-making. The administrator occupies a key spot in the process, but even so he is not permitted to make arbitrary decisions or give arbitrary directions.

In a statement on administrative theory, Litchfield sets forth major and minor propositions having to do with the administrative process.[13] Excerpts from his statement follow:

First major proposition: The administrative process is a cycle of action which includes the following specific activities:

A. Decision making
B. Programing
C. Communicating
D. Controlling
E. Reappraising

Minor proposition: Decision making may be rational, deliberative, discretionary, purposive, or it may be irrational, habitual, obligatory, random, or any combination thereof. In its rational, deliberative, discretionary, and purposive form, it is performed by means of the following subactivities:

a. Definition of the issue
b. Analysis of the existing situation
c. Calculation and delineation of alternatives.
d. Deliberation
e. Choice

[12] Herbert A. Simon, *Administrative Behavior,* second edition (New York: Macmillan Co., 1957), pp. 8–9.

[13] Edward H. Litchfield, "Notes on a General Theory of Administration," *Administrative Science Quarterly* (June 1956), pp. 3–29.

Minor proposition: Decisions become guides to action after they have been interpreted in the form of specific programs.

Minor proposition: The effectiveness of a programmed decision will vary with the extent to which it is communicated to those of whom action is required.

Minor proposition: Action required by a programmed and communicated decision is more nearly assured if standards of performance are established and enforced.

Minor proposition: Decisions are based on facts, assumptions, and values which are subject to change. To retain their validity, decisions must therefore be reviewed and revised as rapidly as change occurs.

While Litchfield's propositions are submitted as hypotheses to be tested, they appear to us, even in their present form, to represent a most understandable description of what is involved in the administrative process. There is clearly a flow from decision-making, to program formulation, to communication and motivation about program, to checking and controlling standards of performance, and to continual reappraisal.

Dill [14] prefers to characterize the entire process as decision-making. He suggests that the process includes an agenda-building phase or intellectual activity; a commitment phase or "choice" activity; an implementation phase; and an evaluation phase. Dill also points out that to understand how decisions are actually made, we need to know about the environments in which decision-makers work and about the complexities of interpersonal and intergroup relations in decision-making. We are also indebted to Dill for noting ways by which decision-making has been improved. These improvements include rapid advances in the capacity to define and collect data, and progress in the development of models that assist in predicting the consequences of decisions.

Clearly, the decision-making or administrative process, while variously defined and still subject to further refinement, represents a useful concept. For our purpose here, we shall define the administrative process as *the way by which an organization makes decisions and takes action to achieve its goals.*

STEPS IN THE PROCESS

For our purpose, we propose that the process is cyclical and contains the following components:

[14] Wm. R., Dill, "Decision-Making," in National Society for the Study of Education, *Behavioral Science and Educational Administration,* Sixty-third Yearbook, Part II (Chicago: University of Chicago Press, 1964), Chapter 9.

Decision-making
Programing
Stimulating
Co-ordinating
Appraising

It is obvious that our selection of terms is eclectic. For this we make no apology. Much as we tended to agree with the Litchfield formulation, we have made certain modifications which we think describe somewhat more accurately what goes on in educational administration.

Lest this formulation seem too pat and its application too obvious, we refer to a warning given by Halpin:

Unless one is extremely careful he can easily be tempted into talking about "process" as if it were a free-floating affair, detached from the behavior of individuals. . . . An outside observer can never observe "process" *qua* "process"; he can observe only a sequence of behavior or behavior-products from which he may infer "process." [15]

These words bring us to emphasize the point that the administrative process is a conceptualization—not an observed phenomenon. It appears, however, that such a conceptualization can be a useful guide to the practicing administrator, and that it can suggest ways by which researchers may submit the idea to further testing. Each of the five components of the administrative process suggested above will now be discussed.

DECISION-MAKING

Decision-making, at least to the observer, can be rational or irrational. Obviously, we are concerned with decision-making as a rational matter. Whatever the decision is, the issues and problems involved must first be clarified. In other words, the problem must be defined. Secondly, the existing situation must be analyzed, often requiring the gathering and interpretation of data. At this point, consideration must be given to the possible alternatives, and the consequences of each alternative course of action weighed. Finally, a choice must be made; a course of action must be determined.

Let us illustrate this step in the administrative process. Suppose there is public demand to teach reading more effectively. The school as an organization needs to ask such questions as, Who is making the demand? What are they seeking? What seems to be the motivation behind the demand? These questions will help in getting at the issues and defining the problem.

---

[15] Andrew W. Halpin, "A Paradigm for Research on Administrative Behavior," in Roald F. Campbell and Russell T. Gregg (eds.), *op. cit.*, p. 195.

The next step is that of determining the existing situation. What is the character of the pupil population to whom reading instruction is given? How do these pupils achieve on various kinds of reading tests? From data gathered to answer these two questions, the school may be in a position to determine to what extent and in what ways the demand for more effective reading instruction is justified.

Suppose the reading tests reveal that the youngsters are not quite up to national norms, particularly for above-average pupils, as we shall say the youngsters in our example are. Suppose further that the achievement of pupils in some buildings does seem to meet expectations, while achievement in other buildings falls appreciably below expectations. With such information collected and interpreted, what are the alternative courses of action? What are the consequences of each possible action? For instance, the school can do nothing, or it can pursue any one of several courses of action. The test results could be circulated to each of the principals, or to the teachers. An in-service program on reading instruction for all teachers in the system might be organized, or such a program might be organized in just certain buildings or for certain teachers. Additional materials for reading instruction might be purchased. From among these and other alternatives, one or more choices must be made. Even the choice to do nothing is a choice.

This choice may finally be made by the superintendent of schools, but note what has prefaced such a choice. In all probability, other administrative staff members, and possibly teachers and citizens, were involved in answering the questions concerning the sources of the demand for improved reading instruction, and the motivations behind such demands. A whole research department may have been involved in determining what the youngsters are like and how they read. An assessment of teacher opinion concerning many aspects of the problem may have been taken. A review of the alternative courses of action may have been deliberated at length in a meeting of the school principals and the central office staff. Only after analyzing all of the cues supplied by the involvement of these various people in the organization does the superintendent make the decision. In a real sense, the decision is an organization decision.

PROGRAMING

Once a major decision is made, there are a number of implementing decisions to be made. This aspect of the administrative process is often called organizing, but the word "programing" seems to describe it somewhat more accurately. In programing, arrangements for the selection and organization of staff for housing, equipment, and budget must be made. The nature of these tasks has been described in some detail in Chapter 4.

At this point, it is necessary to point out that the material treated in Chapter 4 is but a part of the larger framework of the administrative process.

Let us refer once again to our example of unsatisfactory reading achievement. Suppose one decision made in that situation included establishing an in-service education program for teachers on reading instruction. Such a decision requires considerable programing. For instance, which teachers are to be involved? Who will serve as instructors or resource persons to these teachers? Who will actually organize and conduct the program for the school district? What kinds of meetings will be arranged and what kinds of meeting facilities are needed? What equipment and materials are needed for such a program? What will the program cost and how is it to be budgeted? Finally, how is this new expectation of teachers related to their other work responsibilities? Only after such questions as the above are considered, answered, and acted upon can the decision to offer an in-service program to teachers be said to be programed.

Again, this tends to be organization action rather than a one-man performance. Teachers and principals may help the superintendent decide which teachers are to be included. A planning committee composed of teachers, principals, and supervisors may be organized to help in picking the reading consultants and in making other plans. A particular supervisor may be asked to take over the detailed organization and direction of the program. Meetings may be scheduled in buildings that are central to the group participating and room arrangements made with the principals of those buildings. The supervisor in charge and the consultants engaged for the program would probably determine equipment and materials needed. For all of these activities, the superintendent would need to allocate money from the school budget. If the current budget did not permit such allocation, the program might have to be delayed until budget provision could be made. Such provision might require action by the board of education in adopting the budget. In all of these activities, an organization has programed its decision.

STIMULATING

The third step in the administrative process, it will be recalled, has at times been called command, and at other times, direction. While any administrator may on occasion need to command and on other occasions to direct, we feel the better term for what is involved here is "stimulating."

To be sure there are several kinds of stimulation. At one level, the organization or the administrator acting for the organization can exercise considerable pressure upon an individual in that organization. Seldom, if ever, can a status leader in an organization free himself completely from exercising some such influence. At another level, however, stimulation can be much more rational. In other words, members of the organization also examine the evidence and come to recognize that certain courses of action are desirable. It is our belief that effective administrators act nearer to the rational level of stimulation than to the pressure level.

We do not wish to oversimplify this problem. Stimulating members of an organization to action is as complex as human personality itself. What seems to be effective in an administrator's relationship with one person may not be effective with a second. There is no cook-book procedure or "never-fail recipe" for stimulation, although certain kinds of activities seem useful in many situations. One of these is involvement. Teachers wish to have a part in deciding school policies, particularly those having a direct relationship to the instructional program. Such involvement gives many teachers a sense of identification with the organization and greater readiness to do what is needed to help the organization achieve its goals.

Communication has also been found to be of great importance to the stimulation of organization members. Communication needs to be of three kinds: down, up, and across. The Hawthorne studies[16] and other research have demonstrated that when members of an organization are "in on the know," when they understand clearly what is being attempted by the organization, they tend to be more productive. Face-to-face communication appears to be very important if organization members are to be motivated to do their best.

Let us use our reading example above to illustrate stimulating as a part of the administrative process. Even after the decision to provide an in-service education program for teachers on reading instruction has been programed, there is still the question of stimulating the teachers who need help to become interested in getting it. Of course, they might be required to take the program; but if so, the question remains as to how they can be stimulated to do something about improving their teaching techniques. This is clearly the problem of building attitudes, again not a simple matter.

However, if teachers have been involved in the decision to initiate the program, and if some of their own wishes as to time and place of meetings have been taken into consideration, their attitudes toward the program are probably different from what they might have been if the decision had been merely thrust upon them. Moreover, if test results on the reading program and interpretations of those results have been shared with the teachers, the need for improved reading instruction will probably be as apparent to teachers as to administrators. In the case of a teacher who particularly needed to get into the program, the principal might find no substitute for a frank face-to-face conference in which, among other things, a review of the test results of the pupils of that teacher would be made.

[16] See F. J. Roethlisberger and W. J. Dickson, *Management and the Worker* (Cambridge: Harvard University Press, 1939).

As with the other aspects of the administrative process, stimulating is not merely personal behavior on the part of the administrator. Ideally, stimulation should be directed toward the achievement of the purposes of the organization, not merely toward the personal satisfaction of a status leader. Moreover, the work group itself may often provide or contribute to the stimulation needed to get individual members of an organization to increase their contributions to the organization.

CO-ORDINATING

A further aspect of the administrative process is that of co-ordinating. This activity involves bringing into appropriate relationship the people and things necessary for the organization to achieve its purposes. Often, in co-ordinating, the goals of the organization must be reviewed and made explicit. At times, standards of performance necessary to the achievement of such goals need to be noted. Members of the organization may need to be held to meeting such standards.

The place of co-ordination may also be illustrated in our reading example. The in-service program was set for a particular time. Equipment and materials had to be made available at that time, not at some other time. Perhaps an important purpose of the school, the teaching of literacy, had to be reiterated and re-emphasized. The organization had to become involved in the business of setting standards for the in-service program to be made available to teachers. Not just any resource people would do. Consultants who could serve at a suitable level or standard were sought. Presumably, those teachers who took the in-service program were not permitted merely to "sit in." Work expectations were established, and all participants required to meet them.

Some of this may make it appear that the administrator manipulates the members of the organization. In a sense this may be true; however, the control implied is for the purpose of organization achievement, not individual aggrandizement. Ordinarily, no member of an organization has the vantage point occupied by the administrator of that organization. Hence no one, as a rule, can see as clearly as he the relationships among people, the allocation of tasks, and the division of labor necessary to organizational achievement. Two extensions of this argument seem to be necessary. In the first place, in order for the administrator to see the relationships of people and things necessary for the achievement of the organization's purposes, one assumes administrative competence. Moreover, co-ordination will not proceed at a high level unless the members of an organization recognize both the administrator's role and their own roles in co-ordinating activities.

The administrator is the key person in helping all members of an organization understand the need for co-ordination and the role each person is to play. When he becomes lax in his co-ordinating role, confusion, in-effectiveness, and job dissatisfaction nearly always follow.

APPRAISING

The last step in the administrative process, as we see it, is that of ap-praising. Some writers in the field use the term evaluation; and, to be sure, the two terms have many of the same connotations. Because we have used evaluation in a somewhat broader sense in Chapter 4, we have chosen the word "appraising" as more suitable to describe one aspect of the adminis-trative process.

It seems clear that administrative decisions and subsequent actions, if they are rational, are based upon certain facts, values, and assumptions. In time, any or all of these bases may change, and such change may make both the decision and the implementing action obsolete. The need for con-tinuous appraisal, or reappraisal as Litchfield calls it,[17] is apparent.

There would appear to be two purposes or concerns in appraisal. They might be stated as follows: (1) To what extent and how well have the organizational objectives been met? (2) To what extent and how well has the organization been maintained? A variation of the latter question might be: To what extent and how well have the members of the organization grown in competence? These points emphasize the fact that organizations do not exist just for fun but rather to achieve some specific purpose. In the case of the public school, the purpose includes the teaching and learning of literacy and critical thinking. In appraisal, then, key questions would have to do with how well literacy and critical thinking are being taught and being learned.

But an organization must also take the long view. In addition to looking at the degree to which its objectives are being met at the moment, it must also be aware of how well the organization is being maintained so that it may continue to achieve its ends. Excessive teacher turnover, for instance, implies that the organization is not being maintained. Moreover, unless the members of an organization continue to grow in competence, the organiza-tion cannot be well maintained. It follows that, in public education, teachers and administrators are continually confronted with new challenges and op-portunities to meet those challenges.

Let us see if appraising can also be applied to our reading example. The in-service program on reading instruction for teachers has gone for-ward. The results of such a program now need to be assessed. Such ques-tions as the following should be asked: Did the people who needed help in the teaching of reading enroll in the program? Was the program of such a nature that actual assistance was given? In what ways have the practices

---

[17] Litchfield, *op. cit.*

of teachers changed as a result of the program? Have these changes in practices produced more effective reading on the part of pupils?

The last two questions are key ones. If teaching practices have been shifted toward established criteria of good teaching, one kind of evidence concerning the effectiveness of the in-service program has been obtained. At best, however, this is a kind of intermediate or inferred evidence. The real test comes in determining whether or not the youngsters, on the basis of the established criteria, are actually reading more effectively. This last tends to be a kind of ultimate evidence as opposed to intermediate evidence. We suspect that many workers in education have been too willing to settle for intermediate in place of ultimate evidence.

Perhaps we need to say a word about criteria. The establishment of criteria, the bases used in so much appraising, particularly in education, is a value process. In other words, what we consider to be effective reading is a result of the values that professionally sophisticated or informed people hold for effective reading. Comprehension as opposed to mere word-calling is an example. In appraising, then, the organization applies values as well as facts to determine how well it is doing.

An appraisal of the reading ability of youngsters before and after the in-service program may suggest to what extent the organization is achieving its purpose so far as reading instruction is concerned. But what about the maintenance of the organization? Now another set of questions, such as the following, must be asked: Have the teachers who participated in the in-service program identified more fully with the organization? In case the school needs to tackle another problem, are they disposed to help with it? Did the in-service experience result in increased professional competence and a feeling of increased professional status? If these questions can be answered in the affirmative, there has been organizational maintenance as well as organizational achievement.

A CASE REPORT

To illustrate further the administrative process we shall next present an actual case report. Subsequent to the presentation of the case, we shall point out certain applications of the administrative process which were followed in the case.[18]

CENTRAL CITY, U.S.A.

During the past decade a number of new industries had settled in Central City, and its population had grown to about 40,000. The leaders of these industries found that as they recruited technical and professional

[18] The initial report on this case was written by Thomas B. Southard.

personnel for their plants, the adequacy of the local public schools became a question of considerable importance. The schools may have been appropriate for a conservative city of yesterday, but they did not appear to be good enough for the emerging leaders of the community.

This feeling led to the nomination of a slate of three candidates for the board of education who were pledged to improve the schools. These men were elected to the board, and they then began "to cut their eye teeth." Within a few months the board secured state university personnel to help them make a study of their school plant needs. About the time the study findings were reported, the board also employed Mr. Smith, a promising young administrator, as its new superintendent of schools. As this point, many of the problems with which the board had been struggling, including the passage of a large bond issue, were placed in Mr. Smith's lap.

Mr. Smith recognized that it would be no easy task in Central City to pass a bond issue of the size that would be required to meet the needs that were so apparent. The area of Central City had doubled in the last five years, and the survey currently completed by the state university indicated that the enrollment in the schools had increased 40 percent in the last ten years. The survey recommended a new senior high school to accommodate ultimately 2400 students and three additional elementary schools with a total of forty-two elementary classrooms. Central City had not made any sizable capital outlay for school construction for over twenty years, except for additions to elementary schools provided by a $2.5 million bond issue about five years earlier. The issue had failed to receive the simple majority required for passage in the regular election and had scarcely met the 60 percent favorable vote required at a special election. It was apparent to Mr. Smith that if an issue were to be passed this time, the community must see the need for it and feel involved.

The first step was to translate the needs indicated by the survey into dollar amounts. Mr. Smith contacted an architectural firm and, with board approval, retained them on a per diem basis to secure these estimates. The estimate totaled approximately $10 million. To acquire such a sum would require Central City to vote bonds up to the statutory limit of 10 percent of its total assessed valuation.

The problem was now clear. Central City had not kept up with school needs over a long period. Buildings were old and run down. Taxes over the years had been among the lowest in the state, and a certain pride in the low tax rate seemed to be held by at least the older people in the community. There seemed to be also a general dissatisfaction with present school administration, especially among the industrial leaders and the younger people in the community. The problem facing Mr. Smith was, how could such a large issue be passed? What group or groups should spearhead the campaign? How could this modern Rip Van Winkle be awakened to the needs of its schools?

One of the first steps that Mr. Smith took was to meet in his home with the members of the board of education, perhaps ten or twelve times, to "talk shop." Technically speaking, his purpose was to strive for some common perceptions of the campaign on the part of the board of education and himself, with emphasis on the objectives of the campaign and the respective roles of the board and the superintendent in their achievement. During the meetings, the state university survey was inspected and its recommendations discussed. The place of the school in the community was discussed. Mr. Smith familiarized himself with board policies, although the board had no written statement of policy. These informal get-togethers also enabled new and old board members to get acquainted.

Soon Mr. Smith developed a tentative plan for the campaign and prepared a brochure entitled *The Fact of the Matter Is.* The plan had emerged in concert with the board during the informal meetings. The board agreed that the supporting data were appropriate for use in the campaign.

In addition to meeting with the board of education, Mr. Smith made a conscientious effort to become acquainted in the community. By invitation, he joined the local Rotary Club and became well acquainted with a number of leading citizens in the city. He also became a member of the Chamber of Commerce. More by chance than design, one of the most influential leaders of Central City took Mr. Smith under his wing and agreed to help in any way he could for the betterment of the schools and the passage of the bond issue.

The next decision that faced Mr. Smith was who should spearhead the campaign. This was not a simple matter. By this time, Mr. Smith had become acquainted with people representing all service clubs of the community and had acquaintances in each who were sympathetic to the school problem. At the November election, however, a city manager plan backed by the Chamber of Commerce had been defeated; and the expressway issue backed by the Kiwanis Club and independent groups had barely passed. A two-mill school-operating levy supported by the P.T.A., on the other hand, had passed rather easily. It seemed, therefore, that a school bond issue in Central City might be initiated by the local P.T.A. Council.

Mr. Smith was aware, nevertheless, that a two-mill operating levy and a $10 million bond issue were indeed two different things. Historically, Central City had never turned down an operating levy, but bond issues had been defeated. The P.T.A. of course cut across many lines and represented some 6,000 votes. It also had among its members people from all the service clubs in the community.

The greatest single item that concerned Mr. Smith was whether or not the P.T.A. Council had the proper type of leadership to conduct a suitable campaign. After meeting with the P.T.A. leaders, Mr. Smith concluded that it would be best for the P.T.A. Council to spearhead the campaign but that it also seemed wise to organize an advisory committee on the ways and means, or professional know-how, of campaigning. The latter group was to remain in the background to help in any way possible.

The advisory committee was formed by invitation. Its members numbered twenty-three and represented all facets of community organization: radio stations, newspapers, ministers, social groups, labor organizations, financial groups, parochial school leaders, and the federated women's clubs. To co-ordinate this group and to work out relations with the P.T.A. Council, the president of a local bank donated the full-time services of his public relations director. This man, Mr. Fair, worked closely with Mr. Smith in all phases of the actual campaign.

The leaders of the P.T.A. Council and the advisory committee met frequently with Mr. Smith to work out the details of the campaign, after the P.T.A. Council had officially endorsed the bond issue. The first phases of discussion centered around a calendar of activities leading up to election day, May 7. It was decided that a short, all-out effort would be more effective than a campaign over a long period of time. The group first met in December. The all-out effort was to be confined to three weeks before election; dissemination of factual information was to start immediately, but was to be built up slowly.

The committee thought that as a new superintendent Mr. Smith should avail himself of every opportunity to speak publicly, as it seemed important for the residents of Central City to become acquainted with him. Mr. Smith complied by making sixty-nine public addresses between August 1 and May 7.

The campaign actually got under way about mid-December. Before it began, however, the board of education reviewed and approved the whole operation, including committee appointments. Mr. Fair, the co-ordinator, worked with both the P.T.A. Council and the advisory committee to establish a budget after the campaign had been outlined. The budget, which amounted to $3,000, was raised through contributions from local P.T.A. units and local industry. Close records of expenditures were kept and filed with the board of elections within ten days after May 7.

The overall campaign included the following activities:

1. Public addresses to civic groups were given by Mr. Smith from December to the following May.

2. Beginning in late March, school pupils participated in a poster contest on paper furnished by the P.T.A. The poster paper was bordered like a school slate. This same slate theme was carried through on all signs and billboards.

3. A speakers' bureau of teachers, students, and board members was organized and speakers were made available.

4. Daily newspaper releases were made from April 1 to May 7.

5. Students, citizens, and lay leaders were interviewed by the local radio beginning April 1.

6. Daily advertisements were carried in local newspapers from April 29 to May 7.

7. Advertisements at station breaks on the local radio were broadcast during the last week of the campaign.

8. A weekly fifteen-minute discussion, "Inside Central City Schools," was broadcast by the local radio for a month prior to May 7.

9. Twenty thousand handbills were devised by local Chamber of Commerce officials and Mr. Smith and were handed out by P.T.A. mothers on a house-to-house canvass starting two weeks before election.

10. Fourteen billboards covering all routes into and out of the city were rented for five weeks prior to election.

11. Seven thousand copies of *The Fact of the Matter Is* were distributed through the student body.

12. One thousand professional posters were placed in stores and offices.

13. A thirty-two-page tabloid was organized by the high school journalism group and placed as an insert in the daily newspaper on the Saturday before election. This tabloid included pictures, articles by citizens and teaching staff members, a historical account of the schools in Central City, endorsements by local leaders of business and labor, and accounts of interviews with community leaders.

14. Forty of the forty-five churches in Central City, including church denominations with parochial schools in Central City, devoted their sermons to the bond issue on Sunday, May 5.

15. Twenty-one sign boards (4' x 8') were constructed by the high school industrial arts department with material furnished by the P.T.A. and placed in front of each school at least one month before the election.

16. The campaign was climaxed by a torchlight parade the night before election involving approximately 4,000 students, 500 parents, a float representing each local P.T.A. unit, the labor union band, three high school bands, the board of education, and the superintendent of schools. The high school band director assumed the responsibility of organizing and co-ordinating this huge parade.

17. At noon on the day of election, a small printed reminder to vote was sent home with each student.

Two weeks before the election, when no organized opposition had appeared and many of the people normally against changes had rallied behind the proposal, Mr. Smith sensed that the issue would pass. The parade was indeed the climax of the entire campaign. Mr. Smith could feel the community spirit and enthusiasm at its peak with approximately five thousand people parading and twenty thousand onlookers. After the election, the official count revealed that 68.14 percent of the voters had voted in favor of the bond issue. The building program could now proceed.

In retrospect, Mr. Smith saw many additional values in the campaign other than the successful passage of the bond issue. First, his appearance before many community groups afforded opportunity for him to become acquainted, and the successful passage of the issue could be interpreted as community confidence in the change of administration. Further, new channels of communication were established, which Mr. Smith felt must remain open. With such broad involvement of lay people in the campaign, Mr. Smith noticed that the passage of the bond issue had resulted in a feeling of community pride and accomplishment. Mr. Smith looked forward to continued community participation in solving the school problems in Central City, U.S.A.

SOME INTERPRETATIONS

The following is our interpretation of the application of the administrative process in the case reported above. For the purposes of this chapter, we have reviewed this case to discover examples that will illustrate each of the five steps in the administrative process.

Decision-making

The decision that new buildings were needed in Central City and that a large bond issue should be submitted to the electors of the school district was a long time in the making. Actually, the process began with community dissatisfaction with the school program, particularly as expressed by certain industrial leaders, and the election of a slate of three new members to the board of education. These new members were committed to do something about existing educational conditions, including possible provision for a larger educational plant. This is an interesting example of a decision initiated by citizens and board members despite the relative inactivity of the retiring superintendent of schools. It illustrates again that decision-making is an organizational process and not the whim of a single person, even though he is the chief administrator.

The reconstituted board of education and, presumably, the retiring superintendent were not content to accept dissatisfaction on the part of certain citizens as sufficient evidence that additional facilities should be provided. Such feelings were probably part of the motivation that caused the board to employ consultants from the state university to determine the facts in the case. In the study that followed, population growth was ascertained, the condition of the existing plant was appraised, and the extent of need for additional facilities determined. These data were probably more objective and more complete than they would have been had they been gathered without outside assistance. With such data in hand, the board of education had taken an important step in its decision-making activity.

The new superintendent of schools, who took over at this time, helped the board interpret the survey. He also helped clarify the probable cost of the projected building program, ascertained the bonding capacity of the district, and made some assessment of the probable reception the bond issue would get with the people of the community.

The new superintendent also developed a tentative plan for the bond campaign. In this process, various alternatives were undoubtedly considered. Note the ten or twelve meetings that were held in the new superintendent's home. Only with the acceptance of the tentative plan of the superintendent could it be said that the school district had made a choice: to try for $10 million with which to construct a high school and three elementary schools.

Programing

Like decision-making, programing is well illustrated in the case. There was first the question of who would give leadership to the bond issue campaign. This case illustrates one kind of staffing for school purposes, in which many of the leaders were lay people, rather than professional educators, who contributed their services rather than serving as paid employees of the school system. As it turned out, there were several community leaders who assisted the superintendent and the board of education, including P.T.A. leaders, members of an advisory committee of influential citizens, and Mr. Fair, whose services were loaned by one of the bankers.

A related question was how these leaders should be organized. In a sense, the new superintendent at this point created for himself an *ad hoc* advisory council composed of P.T.A. leaders, advisory council members, and Mr. Fair. This council was to deal with the decisions necessary to implement the basic decision made by the board of education, as already discussed. It should also be noted that many aspects of implementation or programing were also reported back to the board of education in order to keep them fully informed.

The programing actually covered the development of seventeen activities to publicize the bond campaign. These activities included speeches by the superintendent, publicity by radio and newspaper, house-to-house canvas by P.T.A. workers, preparation of a special edition of the newspaper by pupils, expressed support by ministers, and a torchlight parade.

As in most programing, there was also the question of budget allocation. In this case $3,000 was required. Since state law prohibited the use of school funds for such purposes, other sources of revenue had to be found. Again, the implementing character of the programing step in the administrative process can be noted.

Stimulating

It was previously suggested that in stimulating people to action the administrator often uses the processes of involvement and communication. These devices were used extensively in Central City. To begin with, the plan of the campaign was developed by the superintendent in a series of informal conferences with the board of education. Board members could undoubtedly say with considerable justification, "This is our campaign." Significantly, it did not become Mr. Smith's campaign.

Involvement and communication were again in evidence in the many contacts Mr. Smith established with community leaders, with the P.T.A. Council, and with the appointed advisory committee. A part of Mr. Smith's own enthusiasm for the project rubbed off on a great many other people in Central City. But there was more than enthusiasm. The new board of education was made up of people in whom many community leaders had confidence. The board had studied the problem, had secured outside consultation to examine the building needs, had employed a competent young superintendent to assist them, and had approved a tentative proposal. There was now the question of getting this proposal accepted as a community-wide goal and not as just a goal of the board or of the superintendent. It was with this objective in mind that the superintendent built the factual analysis of the extent of the need.

Another example of communication is found in the sixty-nine speeches made by the superintendent. Had he not been a new superintendent, we think that this would have been too many speeches for any one leader. Under the circumstances, many community groups needed a face-to-face relationship with their new school administrator. His speeches may have seemed like too much one-way communication. We understand, however, that after the presentation, in most cases, the audience was given an opportunity for questions. We suspect that many of these speeches provided the basis for discussions among members of various groups. A good part of that talk probably got back to the superintendent and the board of education. If this was the case, two-way and not merely one-way communication was in operation.

Co-ordinating

In this case there is also evidence of considerable co-ordinating. First of all, the new superintendent, Mr. Smith, had to work out an understanding of his own role and the roles of the board of education, of the *ad hoc* advisory council, and of Mr. Fair in the bond campaign. This he did not do simply by assigning the various roles. While Mr. Smith probably had some idea as to the appropriate role each group or person should play, he discussed these ideas in numerous conferences, and in that process he probably arrived at many modifications of his original ideas. It is significant to note the crucial place that role definition, as a part of co-ordination, has in the administrative process. Unless it is well managed, misunderstanding, confusion, and conflict are likely to follow.

In this case the question of time was also important. The plan involved the release of information on the building problem from December to the following May, a gradual build-up in campaign activity, and an intensive campaign during the final three weeks. This plan was probably based on knowledge of advertising principles, assessment of resources available for campaign activities, and judgment as to how the budget could be most effectively allocated.

In the time span noted above, there was the question of when each of the seventeen activities should take place. Moreover, there was the problem of which people could do these activities most appropriately. It would seem to require some co-ordinating genius to fit together the efforts of preachers, industrial arts pupils, radio announcers, newspaper editors, P.T.A. workers, and the organizer of a torchlight parade. This "fitting together" is a most important aspect of the co-ordinating part of the administrative process.

Since most of the workers in this case were volunteers, high commercial standards could not be set and maintained. Nevertheless, the setting of standards, as an aspect of the co-ordinating process, was not entirely lacking. Mention was made of the fact that the posters in the stores and business offices were "commercial" posters. Presumably, the rented billboards were also of commercial quality. One suspects too that the signs made by the industrial arts pupils to be placed in front of the school buildings were signs of good quality, or they would probably not have been displayed.

Appraising

In appraising, it will be recalled, we were concerned with both organization achievement and organization maintenance, including the growth of the people within an organization. Does our case also illustrate this aspect of the administrative process? Perhaps so, to some extent. The bond issue was approved by 68 percent of those voting, which is a rather objective measurement of one kind of achievement. But it is not an achievement about which a school administrator can become too sanguine. Three of every ten voters were still not convinced that the projected building program was a desirable thing for Central City. This sort of opposition serves to chasten an administrator and to prevent him from becoming overconfident.

Even before the election Mr. Smith did some appraising. He noted that no organized opposition to the bond issue had developed. He felt the community enthusiasm on the night of the parade. This last observation was perhaps more precarious than the first. Even so, these events illustrate that appraising as a part of the administrative process is not something that is done after all action has been taken. Actually, each step may be appraised as it is taken, even though quite informally.

Mr. Smith also saw some additional values in the campaign. He thought new channels of communication between school and community had been established. The involvement of lay people in the school program also seemed to Mr. Smith to be a real gain. These observations deserve comment. First of all, appraisal is usually made in terms of certain criteria or value judgments. Mr. Smith used the word "value" to refer both to communication channels and to lay-citizen involvement. In other words, these things are important only to the extent that one's value framework includes them.

It may be premature to speak of "new channels of communication" or "extended lay involvement." The real appraisal on these items comes after some years of school-community interaction, for these phenomena are usually not built into habitual community behavior through one experience. This circumstance illustrates the point that appraisal is a long-term, as well as a short-term process.

OTHER OBSERVATIONS

The analysis of the Central City case from the standpoint of the administrative process brings out certain other aspects of the process. First, it should be quite clear that decision-making, programing, stimulating, co-ordinating, and appraising are simply ways of conceptualizing the administrative process. There is considerable unity among these components. They do not necessarily represent a sequence of acts in administration. In fact, the same act on the part of the administrator may both stimulate and co-ordinate. Involvement of a person in the basic decision may do much for him by way of stimulation and co-ordination later. And the programing of pupils, editors, P.T.A. workers, radio men, and ministers into the bond campaign in Central City was at the same time stimulation and co-ordination.

We would also suggest that the administrative process is, in a sense, a cyclic process. Each time the process is applied to an administrative problem and that problem is solved or appropriate action is taken, other or subsequent problems, which also require application of the administrative process, result. With the passage of the bond issue in Central City, for instance, many other problems emerge. One of these has to do with the facilities that are to be provided in the new high school building. The answer to that question, and many others, will again require decision-making, programing, stimulating, co-ordinating, and appraising.

This brings us to our last point. The administrative process is an economical method of approaching administrative problems. To be sure, the substantive content of problems and the situational factors surrounding them will differ. A bond campaign is not identical to building the educational specifications for a new high school plant. Both are different from the establishment of an in-service education program for teachers. Each of these problems must be approached in terms of the conditions found to pertain in a particular school community at a particular time. But all three problems can be approached intelligently by application of the administrative process. Thus, knowledge about the administrative process and the ability to apply it do much to make one an effective administrator.

SUGGESTED ACTIVITIES

1. How do the views of Barnard, Griffiths, Simon, or Dill with respect to the administrative process compare with those presented in this chapter?
2. Read the case, "Since September," presented in Chapter I of Campbell and Gregg, *Administrative Behavior in Education,* and indicate to what extent the administrative process, as described in this chapter, was followed by Mr. Miner.
3. Using the elements of the administrative process as described in this chapter as criteria, appraise the steps taken to solve an administrative problem in your school.
4. Interview a superintendent or principal concerning steps taken in the solution of one of his administrative problems. Write up the case and analyze the extent to which the administrative process as described in this chapter was followed.
5. Develop a research proposal to test any one of the hypotheses listed in or suggested by the Litchfield article.

SELECTED READINGS

BARNARD, CHESTER I. *The Functions of the Executive.* Cambridge: Harvard University Press, 1938.

DILL, WM. R. "Decision-Making," in National Society for the Study of Education, *Behavioral Science and Educational Administration,* Sixty-third Yearbook, Part II. Chicago: University of Chicago Press, 1964, Chapter 9.

GREGG, RUSSELL T. "The Administrative Process," in Campbell, Roald F. and Gregg, Russell T., eds. *Administrative Behavior in Education.* New York: Harper & Brothers, 1957. Chapter 8.

GRIFFITHS, DANIEL E. *Administrative Theory.* New York: Appleton-Century-Crofts, Inc., 1959. Chapters 4 and 5.

GULICK, LUTHER and URWICK, L., *Papers on the Science of Administration.* New York: Institute of Public Administration, 1937. Chapter I.

LITCHFIELD, EDWARD H. "Notes on a General Theory of Administration," *Administrative Science Quarterly,* 1 (June 1956), pp. 3–29.

SEARS, JESSE B. *The Nature of the Administrative Process.* New York: McGraw-Hill, 1950.

SIMON, HERBERT A. *Administrative Behavior* (2nd ed.). New York: Macmillan Company, 1957. Chapter I.

6

Leadership Behavior

and Educational Administration

HAVING VIEWED EDUCATIONAL ADMINISTRATION in terms of its meaning and purpose, its tasks, and its process, we shall now look at the administration of the school from the standpoint of the leadership behavior expected of those who occupy status positions. This chapter has two major emphases: (1) a development of the meaning of leadership and (2) the implications of knowledge about leadership for administrative personnel in the school.

Both leadership and administration have been defined in a number of ways; however, the concepts involved in most of these definitions have a tendency to overlap. Thus, in order to reach a better understanding of the meaning and implications of both leadership behavior and administrative behavior, we must try to determine if there is any real distinction between them.

The fact that our time is characterized by the most rapid and diverse changes in the history of mankind leads us to believe that any adequate definition of leadership must include heavy emphasis upon change and its effects. We may define leadership as "the initiation of a new structure or procedure for accomplishing an organization's goals and objectives or for changing an organization's goals and objectives." [1] Note that the emphasis of this definition is clearly focused upon the initiation of change. As one writer has stated: ". . . the leader is concerned with initiating changes in established structures, procedures, or goals; he is disruptive of the existing state of affairs." [2]

Leaders then, according to the above definition, are seen as powerful agents for change. But at least one writer sees *administrators* in a much different light. According to Lipham:

> The administrator . . . may be identified as the individual who utilizes existing structures or procedures to achieve an organizational goal or objective.
>
> . . . .
>
> . . . the administrator is concerned primarily with maintaining, rather than changing, established structures, procedures, or goals. Thus, the administrator may be seen as a stabilizing force.[3]

Although these definitions distinguish between the act of leadership and the act of administration, they do not imply that one act is, in and of itself, more important than the other. Clearly, the administration of any organization in modern society requires both change and maintenance properties. Both are important. To survive, an organization must not only change itself to adapt to and influence environmental changes, it must also maintain some degree of stability. The condition of the organization and of its environment will determine which act is most important at any given point in time.

If we recognize the need for adaptive change in modern society, and if we equate one phase of administration with implementation and encouragement of organizational change, then we must understand some of the aspects of the nature of leadership. Some of the findings of social scientists about leadership in general provide an appropriate setting for this discussion.

SOME PRELIMINARY CONSIDERATIONS

Various approaches to the study of leadership have been made. In general, they may be characterized by the attempts that investigators have

[1] John K. Hemphill, "Administration as Problem Solving," in Andrew W. Halpin, *Administrative Theory in Education* (Chicago: Midwest Administration Center, University of Chicago, 1958), p. 98.

[2] James M. Lipham, "Leadership and Administration," in *Behavioral Science and Educational Administration* (Chicago: 63rd Yearbook of the NSSE, Part II, the University of Chicago Press, 1964), p. 122.

[3] *Ibid.*

made to identify leaders, to determine what leaders are like, and to determine what leaders do. We shall review briefly the major generalizations resulting from these approaches.

WHO ARE THE LEADERS?

An assumption underlying the work of some students of leadership has been that there is a group of people, called leaders, who are distinguishable from others, called followers. Thus, various attempts have been made to identify the leaders. In a recent publication, Bell, Hill, and Wright have summarized many of the efforts to identify leaders in public life.[4] Interestingly enough, they conclude that leaders are found among holders of status positions; power people in the community who are not necessarily office holders but who, for some reason, wield power; active volunteers in the community; opinion-influence people from many walks of life whose judgment in limited areas of decision-making is respected; and events-oriented people who seem to rise to the challenge of a given occasion or circumstance.[5]

Authorities differ in their conclusions about the number of people who actually lead. Hunter, for example, suggests that between 100 and 300 people constitute the nucleus leadership group in our national government.[6] McCamy and Corradini, on the other hand, identify as many as 7300 government leaders.[7] Other estimates range from 700 to 5000 such leaders. Obviously the difference in the number of persons identified depends upon the limits that the investigator sets on the extent and kind of influence a person must exert to be classified as a leader.

Like differences exist in the number of people classified as leaders in any of the categories mentioned above. Who the leaders are seems to depend upon a number of factors, among which are (1) who the investigator is, (2) the method employed in identification, (3) the definition of "leader," and (4) the people to whom the investigator goes to get opinions about leaders.

While investigators disagree about numbers and the identification of specific individuals, they are practically unanimous in agreeing that while

[4] Wendell Bell, Richard J. Hill, and Charles R. Wright, *Public Leadership* (San Francisco: Chandler Publishing Company, 1961).

[5] *Ibid.*, Chapter II.

[6] Floyd Hunter, *Top Leadership, U.S.A.* (Chapel Hill: University of North Carolina Press, 1959).

[7] James L. McCamy and Alexandro Corradini, "The People of the State Department and Foreign Service." *American Political Science Review*, 48 (December 1954), pp. 1067–82.

leaders are found *among* those who hold "top" positions or "headships," not all who hold such positions, by any stretch of the imagination, can be called leaders. Social scientists seem to agree that leaders may be found among all strata of society. There is some, but by no means common, agreement that all normal people have some capacity for leadership and, possibly, at given times, under certain circumstances, do lead. There is considerable agreement that leaders differ in their range of influence and that for all leaders the range is limited in some respects. Finally, people may be leaders in some situations but not in others. For example, Dahl,[8] in his study of New Haven, found that "the small group that runs urban redevelopment is not the same as the small group that runs public education, and neither is quite the same as the two small groups that run the two [political] parties." [9]

WHAT ARE LEADERS LIKE?

Are leaders and followers different kinds of people? Is there an identifiable personality type that can be counted upon to become a leader? Jennings, after an analysis of the behavior of prominent leaders, identifies three personality types: the princes, power seekers; the heroes, those dedicated to noble causes; and the supermen, the inner-directed value creators.[10] While he argues that in modern society we have discouraged personal leadership, he is hopeful that the person whom he identifies as the superior man can again emerge as the respected leader.

Lasswell theorizes that there is a political personality type and that this type of person values obtaining and using power.[11] He advances the proposition that, for such people:

. . . the accent on power rather than on some other value in the social process has come because limitations upon access to other values have been overcome by the use of power. In the broadest sense, therefore power is a defense.[12]

---

[8] Robert A. Dahl, "A Critique of the Ruling Elite Model," *American Political Science Review,* LII (June 1958), pp. 463–469.

[9] *Ibid.,* p. 466.

[10] Eugene E. Jennings, *An Anatomy of Leadership* (New York: Harper & Brothers, 1960).

[11] Harold D. Lasswell, *The Political Writings of Harold D. Lasswell* (Glencoe, Illinois: The Free Press, 1951).

[12] Lasswell, "The Selective Effect of Personality on Political Participation," in Richard Christie and Marie Jahoda (eds.), *Studies in the Scope and Method of "The Authoritarian Personality"* (Glencoe, Illinois: The Free Press, 1954), p. 206.

However, Lasswell also argues that "intensely power-centered persons tend to be relegated to comparatively minor roles." [13] Finally, he goes on to say that "all top leaders in democratic and totalitarian regimes . . . tend to be recruited from personality patterns that are not primarily oriented toward power." [14] If this is true, he has not produced sufficient evidence to verify the existence of a political personality type or to describe the motivations that lead people to pursue political careers.

Much of the early research on leadership was characterized by efforts to identify *personality traits* by which leaders could be distinguished from other people. These efforts have been only partially successful. Gibb summarizes the search for the traits of leaders as follows:

In the study of the relation between personality traits and leadership, two things seem to be well established at this time. In the first place, . . . numerous studies of the personalities of leaders have failed to find any consistent pattern of traits which characterize leaders. The traits of leadership are any and all of those personality traits which, in any particular situation, enable an individual to (i) contribute significantly to group locomotion in the direction of a recognized goal, and (ii) be perceived as doing so by fellow members of the group.[15]

Gibb goes on to explain that there is evidence that certain personalities do affect group behavior and that it is altogether possible that failure to identify leadership traits positively may be due not to their absence, but to inadequate measurement, the lack of comparability of data from different kinds of research, and the inability to describe exactly what leadership is and how it works.

One of the most comprehensive summaries of research on leaders in many fields of endeavor was made by Stogdill.[16] He examined 124 studies on personality traits as they relate to leadership and concluded that:

A person does not become a leader by virtue of some combination of traits, but the pattern of personal characteristics of the leader must bear some relationship to the characteristics, activities, and goals of the followers. Thus, leadership must be conceived in terms of interactions of variables which are in constant flux and change.[17]

[13] *Ibid.*, p. 222.

[14] *Ibid.*, p. 224.

[15] Cecil A. Gibb, "Leadership," in Gardner Lindzey (ed.), *Handbook of Social Psychology*, Vol. II (Cambridge, Mass.: Addison-Wesley Publishing Company, 1954), p. 889.

[16] Ralph M. Stogdill, "Personal Factors Associated with Leadership, A Survey of the Literature," *Journal of Psychology*, XXV (1948), 35–71.

[17] *Ibid.*, p. 64.

Further analysis of Stogdill's work indicates that there is some evidence to support the fact that leaders excel in intelligence, scholarship, dependability, activity and social participation, and socio-economic status. The qualities, characteristics, and skills required in a leader are determined, however, in large measure by the demands of the situation in which he functions.

Myers, in an attempt to find factors helpful in the preparation of school administrators, made a similar analysis of approximately 200 studies of leadership.[18] He could find no physical characteristics that are significantly related to leadership. He found that leaders were slightly higher in intelligence than other members of their group, that knowledge, insight, initiative, co-operation, originality, ambition, persistence, emotional stability, judgment, popularity, and good communication skills seemed to be significant. His conclusions are similar to those of Stogdill, namely that "these characteristics denote qualities of an interactional nature" and that "no single characteristic is a possession of all leaders." [19]

Researchers find also that the characteristics of leaders differ according to the situation. What confuses the picture even more is the fact that the characteristics of leaders may be found also among people who do not lead. It seems that in one respect, however, leaders tend to be different from other people. This difference is in their disposition to use their innate abilities to work with other human beings in ways that influence the decisions people make.

WHAT LEADERS DO

We have been saying that leaders are persons who affect the behavior of others. This is true whether or not they occupy positions of status, belong to the power elite, make outstanding contributions in their fields of endeavor, or emerge within their groups as individuals whose insight and judgment command the respect of their peers. Most people are not identified as leaders because of their influence on one other individual. People who become identified as leaders affect the behavior of a group of people.

Affect Group Behavior

As a result of his study Stogdill concludes that:

It is primarily by virtue of participating in group activities and demonstrating his capacity for expediting the work of a group that a person becomes endowed with leadership status.[20]

[18] Robert E. Myers, "The Development and Implications of A Conception of Leadership Education" (Doctoral Dissertation, University of Florida, 1954), pp. 105–6.

[19] *Ibid.*, p. 107.

[20] Stogdill, *op. cit.*, p. 64.

According to this view, then, it is what a person does, rather than who he is or what position he holds, that makes him a leader. Any or all members of a group may at some time or another perform a leadership act by helping to clarify a goal, encouraging individuals to speak, bringing a discussion to the point of action, or otherwise affecting *functionally* the behavior of the group. Here the leadership act is primarily that of helping the group get on with the task at hand.

Knickerbocker, another student of group behavior, proposes that:

> . . . leadership exists when a leader is perceived by the group as controlling means for satisfaction of their needs. Following him may be seen either as a means to increase need satisfaction or as a means to prevent decreased need satisfaction.[21]

Notice here that the emphasis is upon group satisfaction. In our earlier reference to the work of Gibb these same two dimensions were alluded to: helping get the task done and keeping the group in good working order.

The weight of evidence from research leads to the conclusion that more can be learned about leadership by centering attention upon *leadership acts* than upon leaders. The *essential element in leadership is that acts take place which affect behavior,* not that a particular person be present when these acts are performed or that a particular person supply these acts.

What specifically can a person do to affect group behavior? There are many who have suggested answers to this question. Ross and Hendry summarize these answers by suggesting that a leader affects the viscidity of a group, i.e., the way in which the members pull together; its hedonic tone, or geniality of member relationships; its syntality or "group personality"; and its goal analysis and achievement. The leader affects the group in these ways by initiating action, facilitating communication, establishing structure, and implementing his own philosophy in the manner in which he leads.[22] Perhaps the most extensive list of dimensions by which one could measure his influence upon a group is that set forth by Hemphill. His fifteen group dimensions are size, viscidity, homogeneity, flexibility, permeability, polarization, stability, intimacy, autonomy, control, position, potency, hedonic tone, participation, and dependence.[23] He found two dimensions—*viscidity,* the feeling of cohesion in the group, and *hedonic tone,* the degree of satisfaction of group members—to correlate more highly with leader behavior than did

[21] I. Knickerbocker, "Leadership: A Conception and Some Implications." *Journal of Social Issues,* 4, 3:23–40, 1948, p. 33.

[22] Murray G. Ross and Charles E. Hendry, *New Understandings of Leadership* (New York: Association Press, 1957), Chapter III.

[23] John K. Hemphill, *Situational Factors in Leadership* (Columbus, Ohio: The Ohio State University, 1949), pp. 31–33.

the other dimensions.[24] His work emphasizes the fact that working with people in groups is a very complicated enterprise and that there are many characteristics of the group itself that may affect group achievement.

One could ask, as Jennings does, whether such lists do not merely show the scientists' bias. For instance, with their interest in group solidarity, are not scientists, in reality, seeking ways to promote it? Thus, although each of the acts mentioned above is supported by the work of a number of sociologists, can it be defended by scientific investigation? Are there not times when group solidarity may need to be shattered in order to get the members of a group to permit anything other than the status quo? Is it not true that some organizations and institutions outlive their usefulness? And, if so, is it not true that some leader must perform the unpopular act of arranging for their demise?

A good example of this is the action that many school administrators take to eliminate certain inefficient school districts, often against the will of their patrons. Other examples could be cited. Suffice it to say here that leadership probably involves some risk. In a sense, the course that a leader proposes is a hypothesis that must be tested in social action. Fortunately, it is often tested not only in the small group which it affects most intimately and immediately, but also in a larger social setting. Thus the leadership act which appears unsuccessful in its immediate setting may succeed in meeting the goals of a larger group.

Range in Leadership Styles

What the leader chooses to do, when he does it, and the manner in which he acts constitute his leadership style. It is obvious that leaders have different styles; hence there is a tendency among the writers in this field to set up various leader stereotypes. One of these is the "autocratic" leader who makes decisions for the group, talks more than he listens, and even ignores or frustrates the personal needs of his group members. People follow such leaders for many reasons, one of them being that "it is easier that way." People are relieved when someone in the group "takes over," makes the decisions, and relieves them of the responsibility for doing so. Sometimes, too, the autocratic leader is followed because people fear his power; not to follow him would result in consequences they would not like to face. Perhaps there are occasions, too, when people have experienced so much inertia in the group that they are relieved to have action— almost any action.

One way of thinking about styles of leadership is to relate them to the partial theories that have been used to explain leadership. One's style may

[24] *Ibid.*, pp. 51–57.

reflect, to some degree, one's acceptance of a given theory. We submit that the person who holds strongly to a "personal leadership theory" may sense that much responsibility rests on his shoulders, that he was chosen because of his superior competence, or that he must use the power of his position. Indeed, beliefs leaders hold for themselves are very compelling ones. They are sufficient to cause the leader to think of his group as followers who need him. He could be dictatorial, paternalistic, or benevolent. However, he remains aloof from the group and leads from a safe distance in front of them.

A different style of behavior may result when the leader perceives all leadership acts as a "function of group interaction." Then he must somehow become a part of the group. He works behind the scenes. His action is catalytic. What the group does is more important than his own action. He facilitates the emergence of leadership on the part of others. He structures relationships in such a way that the group works more efficiently and harmoniously. He is an organizer and a co-ordinator.

Still a different style may be noted in the proponent of the "situational approach" to leadership. To him the events make the man. He tends to move as he finds events and circumstances compatible with his personal liking or competence. He may be opportunistic. He may be accused of doing the expedient thing but, for the time, his action is appropriate. He times his actions well. He is a student of the situation and what it seems to require. He can meet this demand.

Other leadership styles may come to the mind of the reader as he examines the behavior of groups he is privileged to observe. The student is warned, however, against the common fault of creating an administrative stereotype and behaving as though it actually existed. While there is a tremendous range in leadership styles, it is most probable that administrators use some portions of several styles as times and circumstances differ.

Leadership Behavior

Shartle and the members of his staff who conducted the Ohio Leadership Studies point to two criteria of leadership behavior sometimes called the "human relations" and the "get out the work" dimensions.[25] Halpin[26] and

[25] Carroll L. Shartle, *Executive Performance and Leadership* (Englewood Cliffs, N.J.: Prentice-Hall, Inc., 1956), p. 120.

[26] Andrew W. Halpin, "The Leader Behavior and Leadership Ideology of Educational Administrators and Aircraft Commanders," *Harvard Educational Review,* 1955, 25, pp. 18–32.

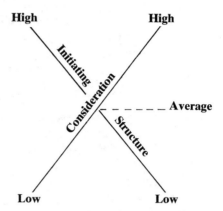

Figure 6.1   Dimensions of Leadership Behavior

Hemphill [27] refer to them as "consideration" and "initiating structure." Figure 6.1 shows these two dimensions graphically.

Leaders whose leadership acts were measured on the Leader Behavior Description Questionnaire showed high *consideration* for others when they exhibited a real interest in the personal needs of the members of the group even while they were taking initiative in getting the work done. High loadings on the *initiating structure* dimension resulted from behavior that tended to clarify goals, organize for the completion of tasks, and emphasize standards of production.

Authorities agree that at least these two criteria—*getting the job done* and *maintaining the solidarity of the group*—are appropriate measures to use to appraise the effectiveness of leadership behavior. Miles would add the criterion of *learning*.[28] He maintains that unless the members of the group have gained something either in knowledge about the task at hand, skill in working together, or improved organization in getting the work done, the quality of the leadership leaves something to be desired. Stogdill also names three criteria for evaluating the effectiveness of group behavior. They are *production, morale, and integration*.[29]

[27] John K. Hemphill, "Leadership Behavior Associated with the Administrative Reputation of College Departments," *Journal of Educational Psychology*, Vol. 46, No. 7, November 1955.

[28] Matthew B. Miles, *Learning To Work in Groups* (New York: Teachers College, Columbia University, 1959), p. 19.

[29] Ralph M. Stogdill, *Individual Behavior and Group Achievement* (New York: Oxford University Press, 1959), Chapter VI.

Halpin, Miles, Shartle, and Stogdill all maintain that none of the dimensions used as a single criterion is an effective measure for leadership in the society of which we are a part. These dimensions are not mutually exclusive. Growth along one dimension affects growth in the others. Thus morale is not merely a sentimental liking among members of the group arrived at by the "kaffee-klatsch." Morale is achieved in part from the satisfaction of a job well done, or from the feeling that progress has been made in the co-ordination of individual efforts to achieve the organizational task. It is attained through co-operative and satisfying work as well as through pleasant work conditions and camaraderie.

From this discussion and reference to the research, one can generalize that leadership behavior is not necessarily associated with position or status. It is an act which affects others. Leadership behavior gets into the mixture of behaviors already present in the group. This interaction results in new activity—activity that would not have been possible without an act of leadership.

THE SETTING FOR LEADERSHIP BEHAVIOR

Obviously, for the purposes here, the statement that leadership takes place in groups is too simple an answer. School administrators, like status leaders in many institutions, find that the organizational behavior with which they are working is a complex network of the behaviors of many groups. The setting, then, for their leadership behavior is a formal organization that has both internal and external group relationships.

While the task of leadership within a group itself is that of getting individuals to work together harmoniously to achieve group ends, the task of leadership in formal and complicated organizations extends the responsibility to one of obtaining co-operative and harmonious working relationships among groups. For the school administrator this is not a simple task, because his leadership must affect a number of reference groups.

Staff employees, both professional and nonprofessional, are grouped formally around the activity of the school system as a whole and in each of the attendance units of the district. Within these groups, organized to accomplish the school's purpose, there are informal associations and groupings. The board of education, the parent-teacher organizations, community groups representing, either formally or informally, the wider community interest, or specialized interests—all have concerns for the schools and represent groups with which school leaders in any community must work.

Working unilaterally with any one of these groups may not bring about the harmony desired. It may be that a change which is functional in its effect, or has no effect, upon one group or system may act quite differently upon other groups or systems. Therefore, building a larger organizational framework in which both internal and external groups play appropriate roles is a goal toward which school administrators strive. Such an achievement is not a mere accident, nor does it come easily even when leaders have given it long and careful thought.

A THEORY OF ORGANIZATIONAL ACHIEVEMENT

Fortunately, complex formal organizations have become the subject of study by a number of social scientists. In the early 1900's, Tarde attempted to describe societal behavior as the sum total of individual behaviors.[30] The transmission or initiation of behaviors among individuals seemed to be the basis for his explanation of social behavior. Durkheim, however, held that individual and social behavior, while mutually interdependent, must be explained in terms of different sets of principles.[31] Among the contemporary sociologists, Parsons has done much to stimulate research and experimentation in large, complex organizations through his own study of the consequences of certain input variables on the achievement of groups.[32]

The work of these men and others has had a profound effect upon Stogdill, whose theoretical formulation presented here has definite implications for those who attempt to influence groups. In explaining how his theory works Stogdill reminds us that "an organized group may be regarded as an input-output system in unstable balance." [33] That is, the group takes on something from outside itself which influences it—makes it different from what it would be if the group existed alone. In turn, as this difference in behavior takes place, the group "puts out" (contributes) differently from the way it would were the influence not felt. The structure of his theory is presented in Figure 6.2[34]

Despite the risk of paraphrasing Stogdill too briefly, we shall state an application of his theory to leadership behavior. Stogdill reminds us that one model we can use to understand the achievement of an organization is to think of what goes into the organization through its members (inputs), how the inputs are modified by the formal structure developed to get the work done, and the roles that members play in the organization. As Stog-

---

[30] G. Tarde, *The Laws of Initiation* (translated by E. C. Parsons) (New York: Holt, Rinehart and Winston, Inc., 1903).

[31] E. Durkheim, *The Division of Labor in Society* (translated by G. Simpson) (Glencoe: Free Press, 1947).

[32] Talcot Parsons, *The Social System* (Glencoe: Free Press, 1951).

[33] Stogdill, *op. cit.,* p. 13.

[34] *Ibid.,* p. 13.

Member Inputs	Mediating Variables		Group Outputs
Behaviors	*Formal Structure*	*Role Structure*	*Achievement*
Performances	Function	Responsibility	Productivity
Interactions	Status	Authority	Morale
Expectations	(Purpose, Norms)	(Operations)	Integration

Group Structure and Operations   Effects

Figure 6.2   Structure of a Theory of Organization Achievement

dill puts it, "The end effects of these personal and interpersonal behaviors, mediated through group structure and operations, are exhibited in the form of group achievement.[35]

Thus we see that in the operation of the model, movement is predominantly from left to right, although any of the mediating variables may affect any or all of the input variables. Each of the four sets of variables may be considered singly or in combinations of two or three. No implication is to be drawn that *productivity* is affected by a simple interplay of *function* and *responsibility* upon *performance*. Actually there is a vertical movement here, also. That is, the performance of members of a group is affected both by interaction among themselves and the expectations they hold for each other, as well as by the expectations that they perceive others (even those outside of the organization) hold for them.

Whether one is working within a single group where the members are individuals, or with a complex organization where the members are groups, one might hypothesize the manner in which these variables play upon each other and in combination to obtain certain effects. Affecting group behavior or the behavior of individuals (leadership, as thus far defined), according to this model, may be closely akin to the arrangements and conditions that are made to facilitate the input of members as they move toward organizational achievement.

The school administrator using this model would surely assess the kinds of "input" that can be expected of the groups and individuals with whom he works. Group members who have been active participants in decision-making could be expected to perform with greater competence in this respect than would those who have had little or no such experience. Many studies have suggested that the expectations of members of a group are varied and

[35] *Ibid.,* p. 14.

often conflicting. The administrator needs to know what these expectations are. One way to operate in terms of them would be to postulate how these expectations might affect behaviors under certain kinds of structuring that he might arrange. Checking his proposition in terms of group output would provide him valuable information for making arrangements in the future.

Note that the model suggests a number of mediating variables. The administrator may attack the problem of organizing, facilitating, and structuring individual and group behavior at a number of places. In some instances his most important job may be to get group agreement on the formal structure of the school and the roles that individuals play in it. In other situations it may be a problem of the clarification of purposes, of the status of individuals in the hierarchical structure, or of whether authority is commensurate with responsibility. The imaginative and creative administrator will think of many combinations or arrangements of these variables that might be used to improve the total organizational output of the school. The model suggests that his work is not done, however, until he has measured the effectiveness of his arrangements. The effects of his acts are measured by the output variables: achievement, productivity, morale, and integration. Gains might be made, Stogdill suggests, if but one of these effects results. The real intent of the model, however, is to suggest that if leadership behavior is effective, it should be possible to measure gains in what the school actually achieves in terms of its purposes, improvement in the productive means employed and in staff morale, and in terms of the integration or meshing of individual efforts into a co-operative institutional effort.

THE MEANING OF LEADERSHIP

We have already alluded to a number of definitions of leadership. A dictionary states that leadership is *action or behavior among individuals and groups which assists them in moving toward goals that are increasingly mutually acceptable.* For those who are viewing administration from the standpoint of leadership, such a definition is helpful, but to have operational meaning it needs amplification. One's concept of leadership grows in meaning as one studies the experiences of others and tests the hypotheses that emanate from theoretical formulation. Research in the fields of psychology, sociology, anthropology, business administration, public administration, and education support the following propositions:

1. Leadership is directed toward changing the behavior of people. Changes in people's behavior are manifestations of changes in their goals, perceptions, understandings, insights, values, beliefs, motivations, interrelationships, habits and/or skills. To bring about changed behavior in people, leadership behavior alters one or more of these factors.

2. Leaders serve as catalysts to help stimulate the activities of all those who contribute to an organization. Therefore, leadership is a function of the interaction and change that takes place among individuals and groups.

3. The quality of the interaction of persons in a group may be recognized by the initiative, originality, communicativeness, empathy, understanding, morale, and performance which they exhibit.

4. Leadership is not necessarily related to status or position. In fact, status assignments may either enhance or reduce one's effectiveness as a leader. Such assignments place individuals in group situations where their behavior is more readily perceived by others. This makes leadership easier for some, more difficult for others.

5. Normal people at all levels of the hierarchical structure of an organization, institution, or society have some capacity for leadership, and possibly do exhibit such behavior at some time and under certain circumstances.

6. Leadership behavior is not necessarily associated with the degree of observable overt action of people. The quality of the leader's ideas is often a more potent force than the loudness of his voice.

7. The demands upon people vary with the situation. Therefore, people who perform as leaders in one group or situation may not so perform in others.

8. People who exhibit leadership behavior in several kinds of situations, and are so perceived by others, generally become known as leaders. Others, while equally effective in a limited number of situations, often fail to acquire the label.

9. Institutional changes are dependent upon the amalgamation of changes in individuals. Leadership behavior in formal organizations must employ such processes as grouping, organizing, programing, and rearranging relationships. (See Chapter 5.)

10. Leadership results in an ordering of events according to importance. Selznick refers to this effect as placing a higher priority on the critical rather than the routine decisions which an organization makes.[36]

11. Appointment of a person to a status position with a responsibility for leadership implies that authority is attributed to him by the persons making this appointment.

12. Leadership behavior disrupts the balance of forces in a group, and this imbalance causes group action to move in some directions. In exercising this behavior, leaders may be aggressive and exert pressure upon the group, or they may work as a leavening influence or catalyst within a group, but they are never neutral.

13. The leader does not determine the norms for the group; groups generally accept leaders who best exemplify their norms. Every group has certain critical norms which the leader cannot ignore.

[36] Philip Selznick, *Leadership in Administration* (White Plains, New York: Row, Peterson & Company, 1957), pp. 56–61.

14. The effectiveness of leadership behavior is measured in terms of productivity (achievement of accepted goals), maintenance of group solidarity, and a manifestation of the fact that group members are growing more proficient both individually and collectively.

IMPLICATIONS FOR EDUCATIONAL ADMINISTRATORS

Social change is exerting a tremendous influence on the goals, organization, nature, and direction of American education. In discussing the need for more and better educational leadership, Hencley[37] lists six dimensions of change which impinge upon education today:

1. Satellite competition, cold wars, and world-wide ideological conflicts are continuing to reaffirm the important role of education in the affairs of men.

2. The current population explosion, the increased mobility of the American population, and the phenomenal growth of metropolitanism are generating unusual educational problems.

3. The growth of automation and technology raise basic questions about the adequacy of current educational goals.

4. Dramatic increments of new knowledge and the impact of science are radically affecting established patterns of living.

5. Rapid shifts are occurring in world conceptions of morals, power, economics, and freedom.

6. The forces surrounding the schools are powerful and pervasive; they are creating strong societal demands that quantity in education be matched with quality and that universality be paralleled by excellence.[38]

These factors highlight the critical need for sound appraisal and analysis of the appropriate professional and social roles of educators in general and of educational leaders in particular.

The critical role of administrators as introducers of change has been documented by Brickell[39] in his 1961 report to the Commissioner of Education of the State of New York. In summarizing his findings regarding the process of change within local school districts in New York, Brickell reported that:

---

[37] Stephen P. Hencley, "Forces Shaping the New Perspectives," in Jack Culbertson and S. P. Hencley (eds.), *Preparing Administrators: New Perspectives* (Columbus, Ohio: The University Council for Educational Administration, 1962), pp. 1–8.

[38] *Ibid.,* pp. 1–5.

[39] Henry M. Brickell, *Organizing New York State for Educational Change* (Albany, New York: State Department of Education, 1961).

New types of instructional materials are introduced by administrators. Re-arrangements of the structural elements of the institution depend *almost exclusively* upon administrative initiative. Teachers are not change-agents for innovations of major scope. Even when free to guide their own activities, teachers seldom suggest distinctly new types of working patterns for themselves.

The administrator may promote—or prevent—innovation. He cannot stand aside, or be ignored. He is powerful not because he has a monopoly on imagination, creativity, or interest in change—the opposite is common—but simply because he has the authority to precipitate a decision.[40]

Brickell's findings are supported by several contributors to the 1964 compilation of reports on innovation and change edited by Matthew Miles.[41]

We, of course, concur with Brickell when he writes that "administrators do not have a monopoly on imagination, creativity, or interest in change." [42] But we must recognize the fact that administrators who lack these characteristics will find it extremely difficult to become leaders in any real sense. However, there is one more characteristic that is probably even more indicative of leadership ability, and that is an administrator's gift for developing leaders from within the school environment and organization. This ability, in fact, may well be the ultimate test of any true leader.

In a democratic society where the schools are expected to contribute to the democratic way of life, citizens do not elect or appoint their school heads out of honor or reward for past achievements. Rather, people are appointed to such positions because it is believed that they can assume the responsibilities of leadership. Thus, while certain privileges accompany such appointments, it is the responsibility incumbent upon school officials that is pertinent here.

LEADERSHIP RESPONSIBILITIES OF SCHOOL OFFICIALS

In Chapter 4 the administrative tasks were discussed. It is obvious from the present chapter that there was no intention to label every act that an administrator performs as one of leadership. Part of his responsibility is one of maintenance. Nevertheless, there are many points at which decisions must be made co-operatively. Individuals and groups must be challenged to view education in a new light and to behave in a manner different from that to which they are accustomed. This is true in each of the areas of administrative responsibility described here.

[40] *Ibid.*

[41] Matthew Miles, (ed.), *Innovation in Education* (New York: Bureau of Publications, Columbia University, 1964).

[42] Brickell, *op. cit.*

Define Goals and Objectives

Certainly, the definition and determination of goals is one area in which real leadership is needed. The public generally is confused about the desired outcomes of education. Every national emergency seems to cause us to press a new panic button. Such anxiety is manifested in the many and diverse pressures that are put upon the schools to do something different from whatever they are now doing.

We recall clearly that during World War I it was unpatriotic to teach foreign languages in the school; in some states this practice was even made illegal. Now, however, as the international crises become more severe, the urgency to teach foreign languages is increased. In some circles it would almost appear that knowledge of foreign language is considered a panacea for the achievement of better international understanding. In making these and other educational decisions people have difficulty in deciding whether Rickover or Conant is the educational "Messiah." In other instances they seem to prefer to rely on decisions by the legislature rather than trust the guidance of professional educators or of other spokesmen.

The problem of bringing the professional staff of the school, the vocal members of the community, and the members of the board of education to a common agreement on goals is, indeed, a formidable one. Perhaps this is the most difficult of all tasks which a superintendent of schools faces today. He cannot be neutral here. He must stand up to the challenge. Failure to do so is an abdication of leadership responsibility and usually ends in professional suicide.

This task is no longer a limited one. The importance of education is being determined and judged on a much larger stage than ever before:

No longer are contributions of educational leaders judged to be of importance only within the contexts of local school districts; education has attained national and international significance. Today, the educational administrator is the key leader of a significant social institution. Effectiveness in his position requires breadth and vision in comprehending the meaning of widespread change, and wisdom in assessing the implications of change for the educational enterprise. Equally important, the educational leader requires the stature and competence necessary for formulating and promoting educational policy in a highly complex matrix of social and ideological conflict.[43]

The administrator today, and most assuredly tomorrow's administrator, will be called upon to assume a leadership role in promoting constructive solutions to major social problems through *education*.

The superintendent's only recourse is to arm himself with professional knowledge, knowledge of his community, his people, his staff, and his pupils,

[43] Hencley, *op. cit.*, p. 6.

so that as a leader he is in a position to bring to decision-making groups propositions that have been well considered. This means that the school superintendent and his staff must be students of the many factors and forces to be resolved in such decision-making. As a result of this study he should seek a clarification of the values that people hold for education as the basis for arriving at a rational and operational definition of goals and objectives.

Facilitate Effectiveness in Instruction

The major factor in effective instruction is the effective teacher. We have read and heard many arguments for and against merit-rating of teachers and compensation in terms of competence. Any large or complex organization will probably have certain areas of ineffectiveness in its operation. There can be little doubt that some of the ineffectiveness in schools results from poor teaching. There is a great range in the effectiveness of teachers, not only among schools in general, but within each school. Can the range in teaching effectiveness be decreased by reducing the proportion of poor teachers or by the encouragement of excellence through higher compensation of the good ones?

Whatever answer one chooses to give to this question, the problem is complicated by the ever-increasing number of pupils entering our schools and the consequent increase in the number of teachers needed. Money differentials may help solve our problem, but so far they have not provided a completely satisfactory solution. The leadership approach is characterized by the assumption that the quality of instruction can be improved by centering attention on the problem within the school itself. The evidence that leadership is being exercised to improve instruction would certainly be manifested in (1) the provisions made for evaluating the effectiveness of instruction; (2) the nature of the hypotheses established for improving practices; (3) the amount and kind of experimentation, exploration, and creativity shown by the group; (4) the provisions made for the acquisition of new skills and the utilization of a variety of resources for teaching; and (5) the opportunities provided teachers to grow in understanding of how children learn and what pressures and demands are being made on them as they advance through school.

Build a Productive Unit.

The many individual contributing parts of the school must be synchronized into one complete productive unit. The parts must not be working against each other or out of relationship to each other. The child has enough problems to solve in integrating his learning without the added burden of rationalizing the disjointed efforts of the several parts of the school.

The problem is so to structure and organize the school that the many teachers and other school employees carry out their tasks in a manner that achieves the school's purposes, not only with optimum effectiveness, but also with a high level of morale. It might appear to some people that such an organization is built in the central office. It is more correct to say that central office personnel, under the guidance of the chief administrator, are the designers of organization. By applying the theories of small and large group organization to the situation, we conclude that leadership behavior prompts organizational changes which stimulate a higher level of co-operation and expertness in the achievement of goals.

Organizational change, then, permeates the entire system. Although it could be imposed upon the working members, unless it is accepted by them ineffectiveness is bound to result. When members of the school staff can perceive organizational changes as improving their effectiveness, they become co-operative partners in effecting such changes. In terms of our criteria for the effectiveness of leadership, an ideal in organizational change is achieved when the following conditions exist: goals and objectives are clarified and accepted mutually; the functional roles and assignments of individuals and sub-groups are defined co-operatively; relationships among individuals and group responsibilities are understood and accepted; a functional hierarchical arrangement is sanctioned; communication flows easily and amiably among the various sectors of the school and from one echelon of authority to the other; and finally, as a consequence of this behavior, a high degree of satisfaction is reached concerning the productivity of the school.

Provide a Climate for Professional Service

Little would be gained here by debating the issue of whether or not teaching is or will become a profession. Suffice it to say that teachers and other school workers grow in effectiveness under appropriate conditions. The provisions mentioned above contribute to such growth. However, unlike organizations that depend largely upon unskilled and skilled labor for their production, the school must attempt to get professional service. In other words, the school must depend upon the fact that the majority of its teachers will grow in effectiveness as a result of their own efforts: thus, there is need to understand the conditions under which growth takes place and to make appropriate provisions for them. Research in this field permits us to suggest that the following conditions are conducive to, and probably necessary to, professional growth:

1. Creativity, experimentation, and expression of individual skill and talent are encouraged by school leaders.
2. Help is readily available and, when requested, does not automatically carry the connotation of weakness.

3. Teachers have the assurance that administrators will support them against unjustifiable criticism.

4. The emergence of leadership from within the ranks is not only encouraged but made essential to organizational solidarity.

5. The central office operates more in the facilitating, servicing, and co-ordinating functions than as an agency of control.

The implications of this summary of observations is that the expectation of and confidence in the high-quality achievement of the staff are essential elements of the climate for growth. The leader brings out the best in people by searching for individual talents and finding ways to make use of them in improving institutional productivity. We cannot hope to make great progress toward professionalism in teaching until teachers know that they are counted upon to become partners of those in administrative and supervisory positions to chart the course of education and to help solve problems of teaching. Perhaps one of the outstanding deterrents to professionalism pertinent to this discussion is that in too many instances administrators and supervisory personnel have acted as if they knew better than teachers how to teach. We suspect that greater progress toward professionalism would result if status people, along with teachers, entered seriously into a study of perplexing teaching and learning problems.

Supply Adequate Resources and Services

It may appear to some people that little leadership is necessary to supply appropriate resources and services to facilitate teaching and learning. Supply, however, is not merely the simple task of exploring what services are needed or of delegating to a subordinate the job of making them available where needed. It is because administrators have viewed the problem in just this routine manner that it is being discussed here.

We have never seriously set about the task of determining what resources add substantially to the learning situation and in what ways. It is true that as new learning media and approaches become available—radio, television, teaching machines, team-teaching—we buy as much as we can afford. But merely to be among the first to make use of such media or to employ the newest approach to teaching is not to exercise the leadership for which educators should be held responsible. There can be little doubt about the fact that in the future people will be required to give a more substantial part of themselves and their material resources to the cause of education. Leadership is needed to convince the public of the need for a greater investment of both human and material resources in children and youth. Real commitment to such a cause requires that schools do everything in their power to seek this investment. It should, of course, be recognized that as the investment goes higher and higher, the disposition to accept mediocrity diminishes. Evidences of expertness in educational know-how and skill are being demanded on every hand. The problem is twofold: (1) to make the best use that we can of the intelligence that can be brought to bear on the problems of teaching and learning; and (2) so to work with the supporting public that their confidence in such expertness is built and maintained.

Such a responsibility seems to demand of administrative personnel the ability to project both to the staff within the school and to the supporting public of the school those propositions necessary to improve the work of the school. Such a course may require the employment of specialized personnel with limited spheres of expertness who can consider at depth various problems which the school faces. Some of these people will be experts in teaching and guidance, some in communication and human relations, some in organization, some in the utilization of specific devices invented to improve learning, some in buildings and their utilization, other in finance and business management. But above all, the conceptual skill of the administrator who works with these specialists in the framing of propositions to be tested on the local scene will be most in demand.

DETERRENTS TO EDUCATIONAL LEADERSHIP

Leadership has been described and illustrated in many ways throughout this discourse. Essentially we have said that it is the function of the interaction of persons. A person is said to have exhibited leadership behavior when he has influenced people to move in the direction of a goal that becomes increasingly acceptable to the members of the groups affected. There are many ways by which this is done. Some leaders use force. Others, through the sheer charm of personality, gain a group of followers. We would hope that in the schools an increasing amount of leadership results from the acceptance of the leader's proposals as intelligently conceived, appropriate to the group and situation, and feasible under the circumstances in which the school operates. The proposals are influential because they make sense to those who are to be involved in their realization. Why do we not get more of this kind of leadership?

HIERARCHICAL STRUCTURE CONFUSED WITH AUTHORITARIANISM

Intentionally or not, education has copied much of the traditional organizational and administrative forms of government, the military, church, business, and industry. An assumption common to these organizations is that hierarchical structure automatically places higher priority upon commanding than upon leading. In fact, in many instances these terms are looked upon as practically synonymous; that is, unless the occupant of a status position has the authority to command his subordinates, he loses his effectiveness as a leader.

In Chapter 5, where we dealt more fully with process in educational administration, we pointed out that such terms as *commanding* and *controlling* are giving way to *decision-making, influencing,* and *evaluating.* The trend is not necessarily, however, away from control. Our interpretation of the meaning which students of process wish to convey is that control is located less in persons than in the organizational structure. The person who exercises the control knows that he is actually the spokesman for the members of the organization. Practice, however, has not kept pace with the changing theory. We still find many who confuse hierarchical structure with authoritarianism.

CONFUSED CONCEPTS OF DEMOCRACY

Many discussions of democracy in administration imply that democratic action lies on a continuum about halfway between autocratic behavior and anarchy. This impression is in error, because it assumes that all three forms of behavior can be explained on the basis of a common set of premises. Autocratic behavior results when a person assumes that the authority for his behavior resides outside the organization of which he is a part. Democracy, on the other hand, is a concept which implies that in any organization decisions are "of, by, and for the people." Those who confuse democracy with a "hands-off" policy, or with anarchy, do not understand the meaning of these words, either. Democracy implies responsible and controlled behavior, whereas anarchy implies irresponsibility. Democratic leadership cannot be characterized by laissez-faire behavior. An institution is not democratic when the members may do as they please, without regard for organization, regulation, and control.

When an administrator asks, somewhat in despair, "How democratic can we get?" he is frustrated by his mistaken belief that democratic leadership is identical with no leadership at all. When he implies that to keep the educational ship on an even keel he must make the decisions, issue the orders, and enforce them, he is substituting autocratic control for that control which is exercised through agreement on organizational goals and procedures.

FAILURE TO SOLVE THE AUTHORITY PROBLEM

In our confusion about the meaning of democracy, could we have failed to solve the authority problem? Certainly, schools cannot operate effectively when no one has authority. Neither do we get efficient operation when every person is his own authority, or even when groups of people attempt to administer. In an organization, policy, rules, and regulations are necessary, along with someone assigned to the executive function of administering them.

What the administrator needs to remember is that he really does not have the authority which he assumes is vested in him by his board of education unless his staff and the people of the community also agree. The status leader is as much interested in the extent to which the people with whom he works understand and make laws as he is in how these laws are enforced.

INADEQUATE SELECTION PROCEDURE

People are still placed in status positions for reasons other than their competence for the job to be done. This situation is partly due to the practice of the spoils system, where position is obtained by "pull" or by knowing "the right people." While irresponsible behavior such as this may be expected to continue (on a diminishing scale, we hope), it has never been seriously proposed as a way to select educational leaders.

A variety of the trait approach to leadership, however, has been operating in the selection of administrators for many years. School boards responsible for appointment of superintendents of schools are often guilty of selection because "he looks like a superintendent," "he was successful as a principal," "he has good recommendations," "he has a good academic record," or "he possesses the traits which other people say make a good superintendent." We now know that there are many people who possess the traits of the administrator stereotype. Not all of these people are good administrators, nor if they succeed in one situation can it be guaranteed that they will succeed in others. Some more reliable means of selection is needed to provide greater assurance that we are placing in administrative positions men who can lead.

There are some encouraging practices that are based on our knowledge of leadership behavior. In addition to the usual credentials supplied by placement bureaus, some schools are seeking evidence of *capacity*, including verbal facility and judgment; *achievement,* including scholarship and knowledge; *responsibility*, including dependability, self-confidence, and ambition; *participation,* namely adaptability, sociability, and activity; and former *status.* Such information is sought not only through the usual testing procedures, but by observation of the behavior of the candidate when he is called upon to perform administrative tasks similar to those required in the position which he seeks. Demonstrated competence in a variety of situations where the demands upon the candidate have been similar to those of the position he seeks adds much to the reliability of the judgment that he should be employed.

This careful approach to the selection of administrators, however, is by no means commonplace. Until those who are selecting school administrators know better what the job requires of the man, and until the man has demonstrated his competence for the job, leadership in status positions will continue to be largely a game of chance.

STATUS IS NOT ENOUGH

The school administrator may or may not be a leader. The chances are against upward mobility in his profession, however, if he does not exercise leadership behavior in a variety of situations. He is not the only leader; members of his staff and patrons of the school may be important educational leaders also. The wise administrator recognizes and rewards such leadership.

Research evidence indicates that the best way to identify leadership behavior is to observe it in action. Leaders must influence people. How they do this reveals their leadership style.

Within a democratic framework leaders tend to identify with the people whom they are leading. They recognize that the productivity of an organization is dependent both upon how they structure the work to be done and upon their regard for the workers. Stogdill has developed a partial theory for explaining how leadership affects achievement in a group situation. It is one of a number of models which the student of leadership might use to examine his own behavior.

There are many leadership responsibilities that must be accepted by school administrators. Deterrents to success in these areas include the persistence of the authoritarian way, confusion about the meaning of democracy, failure to solve the authority problem, and poor selection procedures. One of the problems which any leader must decide for himself is where to concentrate his efforts and when to guard against the dissipation of his energy in many activities that may be interesting and, indeed, useful but low on the priority list for him. The three chapters that follow should help the status leader solve this problem.

SUGGESTED ACTIVITIES

1. Read Selznick's discussion on "routine" and "critical" decisions (see bibliography). Make a list of the decisions in school administration which you consider to fall into each of these two classes.
2. From Stogdill's model (read his Chapter 1; see bibliography) develop a list of hypotheses which you think might be tested in the school setting.

3. Observe the behavior of a group (your own staff in faculty meetings, for example). Identify leadership acts. Tell what the acts are and what evidence you observe that causes you to believe them leadership acts.
4. Compare the leadership behavior of a status person and an informal leader in your faculty. What similarities and differences do you notice?
5. Plan a technique for getting a point across in your group. Try it out. Note carefully what happened at each step along the way. Evaluate the result.

SELECTED READINGS

Association for Supervision and Curriculum Development. *Leadership for Improving Instruction.* 1960 Yearbook. Washington, D.C.: N.E.A.

BASS, BERNARD M. *Leadership, Psychology, and Organizational Behavior.* New York: Harper & Brothers, 1960.

BRICKELL, H. M. *Organizing New York State for Educational Change.* Albany, New York: Department of Education, 1961.

BROWNE, C. G., and COHN, THOMAS S. *The Study of Leadership.* Danville, Illinois: The Interstate, 1958.

CULBERTSON, JACK and HENCLEY, S. P. (eds.). *Preparing Administrators: New Perspectives.* Columbus, Ohio: The University Council for Educational Administration, 1962.

HALPIN, ANDREW H. *The Leadership Behavior of School Superintendents* (2nd ed.). Chicago: Midwest Administration Center, The University of Chicago, 1959.

JENNINGS, EUGENE E. *An Anatomy of Leadership.* New York: Harper & Brothers, 1960.

MILES, MATTHEW (ed.). *Innovation in Education.* New York: Bureau of Publications, Teachers College, Columbia University, 1964.

National Society for the Study of Education. *Behavioral Science and Educational Administration.* Chicago: 63rd Yearbook, Part II, The Society, 1964.

SELZNICK, PHILLIP. *Leadership in Administration.* White Plains, New York: Row, Peterson, & Company, 1957.

SHARTLE, CARROLL L. *Executive Performance and Leadership.* Englewood Cliffs, N.J.: Prentice-Hall, Inc., 1956.

STOGDILL, RALPH M. *Individual Behavior and Group Achievement.* New York: Oxford University Press, 1959.

TANNENBAUM, ROBERT, WECHSLER, IRVING R., AND MASSARICK, FRED. *Leadership and Organization.* New York: McGraw-Hill Book Company, 1961.

7

The School

as a Social System

WE HAVE VIEWED ADMINISTRATION FROM THE STANDPOINT OF ITS PURPOSE, its tasks, its process, and in terms of the leadership behavior of its status leaders. We shall now look at administration in the setting of the school as a social system. This is perhaps our most theoretically oriented approach to administration. We shall present the theoretical framework of administration as a social process, examine some of the studies which such a framework has generated, note the limitations and extensions of this formulation, and then suggest some implications for practice growing out of such an approach.

THE CONCEPTUAL WORK

The formulation of the concept of administration as a social process was essentially the work of Getzels and Guba.[1] Our description of this concept follows closely part of a paper given by Getzels at a seminar on administra-

[1] Jacob W. Getzels and Egon G. Guba, "Social Behavior and the Administrative Process," *School Review*, 65 (Winter 1957), pp. 423–41.

tive theory sponsored by the University Council for Educational Administration and the Midwest Administration Center.[2]

To comprehend the model described in the next few pages requires some knowledge of concepts found in sociology and psychology. For many students, however, careful reading of these pages and some of the material mentioned in the footnotes will be found rewarding.

Getzels suggests that administration may be conceived structurally as the hierarchy of subordinate-superordinate relationships within a social system. Functionally, this hierarchy of relationships is the locus for allocating and integrating roles and facilities in order to achieve the goals of the social system. It is in these relationships that the assignment of positions, the provision of facilities, the organization of procedures, the regulation of activity, and the evaluation of performance take place.

While the functions named above are the responsibility of the superordinate member of the hierarchy, each function becomes effective only as it "takes" with the subordinate members. This interpersonal or social relationship is the crucial factor in administration as a social process.

The model or concept begins with a consideration of the most general context of interpersonal or social behavior, i.e., a given social system. The term "social system" is of course conceptual rather than descriptive and must not be confused with society or state, or thought of as applicable only to large aggregates of human interaction. Within this framework, for one purpose, a community may be considered a social system, with the school a particular organization within the more general social system. For another purpose, the school itself or even a single class within the school may be considered a social system in its own right. The model proposed here is applicable regardless of the level or size of the unit under consideration.

The social system is conceived as involving two classes of phenomena that may be thought of as independent but, in an actual situation, are interactive. There are, first, the institutions characterized by certain roles and expectations in keeping with the goals of the system. And there are, second, the individuals with certain personalities and dispositions inhabiting the system. The social behavior found in this system may be understood as a function of two major elements: institution, role, and expectation, which together constitute the nomothetic or *organizational* dimension of activity in a social system; and individual, personality, and need-disposition, which together constitute the idiographic or *personal* dimension of activity in a social system.

---

[2] Jacob W. Getzels, "Administration as a Social Process," in A. W. Halpin (ed.), *Administrative Theory in Education* (Chicago: Midwest Administration Center, University of Chicago, 1958), pp. 150–65.

THE ORGANIZATIONAL DIMENSION

To understand the nature of observed behavior—and to be able to predict and control it—the nature and relationships of these elements must be understood. Certain key terms need further elaboration.

The term "institution" has received a variety of definitions which cannot be reviewed here. It is sufficient to point out that all social systems have certain imperative functions that come in time to be carried out in certain routinized ways. These functions—such as governing, educating, policing within the state—may be said to have become "institutionalized," and the agencies established to carry out these institutionalized functions for the social system as a whole may be termed "institutions." Thus, the school is the institution devoted to educating.

An important part of the institution is the role. Roles are, to use Linton's terminology, the "dynamic aspects" of the positions, offices, and statuses within an institution, and they define the behavior of the role incumbents or actors.[3] In the school these incumbents are superintendents, principals, teachers, and other workers.

Roles are defined in terms of role expectations. A role has certain normative obligations and responsibilities, which may be termed "role expectations," and when the role incumbent puts these obligations and responsibilities into effect, he is said to be performing his role. For instance, the role expectations for the third grade teacher, the guidance counselor, and the principal are quite different. The expectations define for the actor, whoever he may be, what he should or should not do as long as he is the incumbent of the particular role.

Roles are complementary—interdependent in that each role derives its meaning from other related roles in the organization. In a sense, a role is a prescription not only for the given role incumbent but also for the incumbents of other roles within the organization, so that in a hierarchical setting the expectations of one role may to some extent also form the sanctions for a second interlocking role. Thus, for example, the role of sergeant and the role of private in the army, or of principal and teacher in a school, cannot really be defined or implemented except in relation to each other. It is this quality of complementarity which fuses two or more roles into a coherent, interactive unit and which makes it possible for us to conceive of an organization as having a characteristic structure.

The elements constituting the nomothetic or organizational aspects of social behavior have been examined. At this level of analysis, it was sufficient to conceive of the role incumbents as "actors," devoid of personalistic

[3] Ralph Linton, *The Study of Man* (New York: Appleton-Century-Crofts, Inc., 1936), p. 14.

or other individualizing characteristics—as if all incumbents were exactly alike and as if they implemented a given role in exactly the same way. This permits certain gross understandings and prediction of behavior in an organization. For example, if the roles in a given educational institution are known, some rather accurate predictions of what the people in these organizations do without ever observing the actual people involved can be made.

THE PERSONAL DIMENSION

But roles are of course occupied by real individuals, and no two individuals are alike. Each individual stamps the particular role he occupies with the unique style of his own characteristic pattern of behavior. Even in the case of the relatively inflexible role of sergeant and private, no two individual sergeants and no two individual privates fulfill their roles in exactly the same way. To understand the observed behavior of specific sergeants and specific privates, it is not enough to know the nature of the roles and expectations—although, to be sure, their behavior cannot be understood apart from these—but the nature of the individuals inhabiting the roles and reacting to the expectations must also be known. That is, in addition to the nomothetic or organizational aspects, the idiographic or personal aspects of social behavior must also be considered. Both the sociological level of analysis and the psychological level of analysis must be included.

Just as it was possible to analyze the organizational dimension into the component elements of role and expectation, so it is possible, in a parallel manner, to analyze the individual dimension into the component elements of personality and need-disposition. We may turn to a brief consideration of these two terms.

The concept "personality," like the role of institution, has been given a variety of meanings. Personality is defined by Getzels as the dynamic organization within the individual of those need-dispositions that govern his unique reactions to the environment. The central analytic elements of personality are the need-dispositions, which we can define with Parsons and Shils as "individual tendencies to orient and act with respect to objects in certain manners and to expect certain consequences from these actions." [4]

Returning to the example of the sergeant and the private, an essential distinction can now be made between two sergeants, one of whom has a high need-disposition for "submission" and the other a high need disposition for "ascendance," and a similar distinction between two privates, one with a high need-disposition for "submission" and the other for "ascendance," in the fulfillment of their respective roles, and for the sergeant-private interaction. In short, to understand the behavior of specific role-

---

[4] Talcott Parsons and Edward A. Shils, *Toward A General Theory of Action* (Cambridge, Mass.: Harvard University Press, 1951), p. 114.

incumbents in an institution, we must know both the role-expectations and the need-dispositions. Indeed, both needs and expectations may be thought of as motives for behavior, the one deriving from organizational obligations and requirements, the other from personalistic sets and propensities.

One troublesome facet of the model, to which insufficient attention has been given, is the problem of the dynamics of the interaction between these organizationally defined expectations and the personally determined needs. To put the problem concretely, one may ask: How is it, for example, that some sergeants and privates—or to generalize the case, some complementary role-incumbents—understand and agree at once on their mutual obligations and responsibilities, while others take a long time in reaching such agreement and quite frequently do not come to terms either with their roles or with each other?

The essential relevant concept Getzels proposes here is selective interpersonal perception; people see what their own backgrounds permit them to see. In a sense, the prescribed organizational or normative relationships of two complementary role-incumbents may be conceived as being very different. On the one hand, there is the prescribed relationship as perceived by the first organization member in terms of *his* needs, dispositions, and goals. On the other hand, there is the same prescribed relationship as perceived by the second organization member in terms of *his* needs, dispositions, and goals. These private perceptions are related through those aspects of public objects, symbols, values, and expectations which have to some extent a counterpart in the perceptions of both individuals.[5]

When it is said that two role-incumbents—for example, a subordinate and a superordinate—understand each other, it means that their perceptions and their own organization of the prescribed complementary expectations are congruent; when it is said that they misunderstand each other, it means that their perceptions and their own organization of the prescribed complementary expectations are incongruent. The functioning of the social system depends not only on a clear statement of the public expectations, but on the degree of overlap in the perception and individual organization of the expectations by the specific role incumbents. As will be shown, the relevant research suggests that when participants evaluate an interaction, the congruence of the perception of expectations often takes priority over actual observed behavior or even accomplishment.

THE MODEL

By way of summarizing the argument so far, the general model is pictured in Figure 7.1.

[5] See Jacob W. Getzels, "A Psycho-sociological Framework for the Study of Educational Administration," *Harvard Educational Review*, XXII (Fall 1952), pp. 235–46.

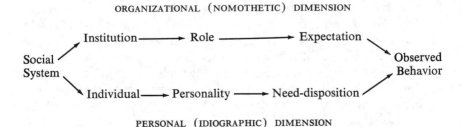

ORGANIZATIONAL (NOMOTHETIC) DIMENSION

PERSONAL (IDIOGRAPHIC) DIMENSION

Figure 7.1 General Model Showing the Organizational and Personal Dimensions of Social Behavior (from Getzels and Guba)

The organizational axis, shown at the top of the diagram, consists of institution, role, and expectation, each term being the analytic unit for the term preceding it. Thus the social system is defined by its institutions, each institution by its constituent roles, each role by the expectations attaching to it. Similarly, the personal axis is shown at the lower portion of the diagram and consists of individual, personality, and need-disposition, each term again serving as the analytic unit for the term preceding it.

A given act is conceived as deriving simultaneously from both the organizational and personal dimensions. That is to say, social behavior results as the individual attempts to cope with an environment composed of patterns of expectations for his behavior in ways consistent with his own independent pattern of needs. Thus, one may say that behavior in an organization is a function of a given institutional role defined by the expectations attaching to it, and the personality of the particular role incumbent defined by his need-dispositions.

The proportion of role and personality factors determining behavior will of course vary with the specific act, the specific role, and the specific personality involved. The nature of the interaction can be understood from another graphic representation, as indicated in Figure 7.2.

A given behavioral act may be conceived as occurring at a position represented by the dotted line through the role and personality possibilities represented by the rectangle. At the left, the proportion of the act dictated by considerations of role-expectations is relatively large, while the proportion of the act dictated by considerations of personality is relatively small. At the right, the proportions are reversed, and considerations of personality become greater than those of role-expectation. In these terms one may, for example, have on the one hand the behavior of an army private conforming almost entirely to role demands and on the other the behavior of a free-lance artist deriving almost entirely from personality dispositions. Most schools are probably somewhere between these extremes. In a given setting, administration always deals with proportions of both these components.

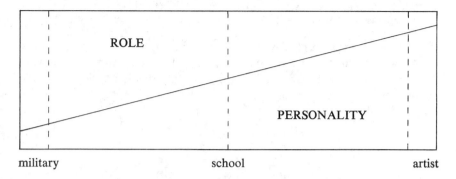

Figure 7.2   The Interplay Between Role and Personality in a Behavioral Act (from Getzels and Guba)

In any case, whether the proportion tends toward one end or the other, behavior insofar as it is social remains a function of both role and personality, although in different degree. When role is maximized, behavior still retains some personal aspect, because no role is ever so closely defined as to eliminate all individual latitude. When personality is maximized, social behavior still cannot be free from some role prescription. Indeed, the individual who divorces himself from such prescription is said to be autistic, and he ceases to communicate with his fellows.

Some critics of the social process model have maintained that it lacks a dynamic quality. Abbott[6] has recently suggested some intervening variables between the organizational and personal dimensions and some feedback mechanisms which may help answer this criticism. He summarizes his argument as follows:

. . . a formal organization may be viewed as a specific social system in which role expectations become formalized and institutionalized. Such expectations constitute a codified behavior system, which is more or less explicit but which is generally understood by all employees. As specific individuals, with their own patterns of organizationally relevant needs, are socialized in respect to the organization's codified behavior system, they achieve a cognitive orientation to roles and they respond affectively to this orientation. Thus, behavior in a formal organization is conceived as deriving simultaneously from an individual's cognitive orientation to roles and his affective responses to roles.

Both the cognitive orientation to roles and affective responses to roles are modified over time, largely as a function of the operation of two feedback

[6] Max G. Abbott, "Intervening Variables in Variables in Organizational Behavior," *Educational Administration Quarterly,* 1 (winter 1965) pp. 1–14.

mechanisms within the organization: the reward system and the reference-group norms. Feedback, in this sense, is a perceptual process in which the cognitive orientation is monitored in terms of its congruence with the "real" situation.[7]

The relevance of the general model for administrative theory and practice becomes apparent when it is seen that administration inevitably deals with fulfillment of both organizational and personal requirements within the context of a particular social system, and that these requirements may be modified over time.

SOME EMPIRICAL STUDIES

A theory, as we suggested in Chapter 3, should, among other things, generate hypotheses that can be tested. The theory described above has been the source of a number of hypotheses which have become the bases for empirical studies, some of which will now be reported. These reports should be read not only for their findings, but also to illustrate the way by which studies may be derived from a theoretical framework.

SELECTIVE PERCEPTION

One of the early studies dealt with selective interpersonal perception. To Ferneau the theory suggested that when two or more persons come in contact with each other over a sufficient length of time, each begins to have certain expectations as to how the other will act or behave.[8] He wished to examine the expectations of superintendents of schools and consultants from state departments of education as they worked together on curriculum problems.

He reasoned that expectations become generalized; for example, while the contact may have been with only two or three consultants, the school administrator begins to expect much the same behavior from all consultants. In turn, the consultant working with a few administrators begins to have certain expectations as to how all administrators will behave. Expectations on the part of either the administrator or the consultant are not completely rigid. There is what is termed a "range of permissiveness"; either may exhibit a variety of behavior within certain limits and still stay within the expectations of the other. However, when the actions of one fall outside this range, the other rejects such behavior. This situation results in a lack of

[7] *Ibid.,* pp. 12–13.

[8] Elmer F. Ferneau, "Which Consultant?" *Administrator's Notebook,* 2 (April 1954), No. 8.

rapport, in one or both becoming defensive or aggressive, or in some other attitude which makes their contacts useless.

Ferneau was able to describe three possible roles for consultants: the expert, the resource person, and the process person. He then developed a check list of sixty items which required respondents to choose for each item the preferred behavior of the consultant. One hundred thirty-two superintendents in the states of Kansas, Michigan, Nebraska, and Wisconsin who had recently used consultants from their respective state departments of education responded to the instrument. These same superintendents, in another study, had previously given an evaluation of these consultant services. In these same states forty-three consultants who had given these services to the superintendents also completed the check list and evaluated the effectiveness of the services as they viewed them.

With these data available, it was possible to match the replies of the consultants with those of the administrators whom they had attempted to help. It was possible also to determine the behavior the administrators had expected the consultants to exhibit and what the consultants had expected of the administrators. Then it was possible to compare the administrator's evaluations of the consultations in which both administrator and consultant behaved as the other expected him to behave and when the behavior of one differed from that which the other expected.

In responding to the various statements used in the questionnaire, the respondents rated each behavior on a six-point scale with regard to its appropriateness. When a consultant and an administrator disagreed by as much as an average of two points in evaluating each statement, nineteen out of twenty times the consultation in which they were involved was rated as of low value by one or both. This finding was tested in three ways; each test gave the same result. Consultants and administrators must perceive each other as functioning in the manner expected if the consultation is to be effective.

Within each of the four states included in the study there was much greater agreement between consultants and administrators as to the behavior that they expected of each other than there was among the consultants and administrators in the states as a group. For example, in one state both administrators and consultants ranked first among the four states in the number of times they expressed preference for behavior classified as the "expert" approach. In another state, both groups ranked last in the number of times they expressed such a preference.

This study seems to support the idea that expectations have more to do with the judged effectiveness of consultant services than the nature of the service itself. There is at least the suggestion that in any interaction between two people the congruence of expectation of behavior may be most important.

ROLE-PERSONALITY CONFLICT

One of the most definitive studies on the model was done by Merton Campbell, who examined the degree of self-role conflict (the amount of spread between the two dimensions of the model) existing among teachers and the relationships between such conflict and satisfaction, effectiveness, and confidence in leadership.[9] Included in the study were fifteen schools and 284 teachers. Appropriate instruments were developed to test the variables being studied.

Four of the hypotheses developed by Campbell were from the standpoint of an outside observer, as suggested by "A" in Figure 7.3. It was hypothe-

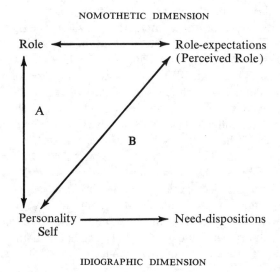

NOMOTHETIC DIMENSION

IDIOGRAPHIC DIMENSION

Figure 7.3   Partial Social Process Model Showing Variables Tested

sized that teachers with a low degree of self-role conflict in the teaching situation will (1) rate themselves higher in teaching satisfaction, (2) rate themselves higher in teaching effectiveness, (3) be rated by the principal as more effective teachers, and (4) express greater confidence in the leadership of the principal than will those teachers with a high degree of conflict.

Hypotheses 1, 3, and 4 were confirmed. Teachers with a low degree of

[9] Merton V. Campbell, "Self-Role Conflict Among Teachers and Its Relationship to Satisfaction, Effectiveness, and Confidence in Leadership" (unpublished Ph.D. dissertation, Dept. of Education, University of Chicago, 1958).

self-role conflict expressed greater satisfaction in teaching than did high-conflict teachers. Low-conflict teachers were rated as more effective by their principals than were high-conflict teachers. Low-conflict teachers expressed greater confidence in the leadership of their principal than did high-conflict teachers. Hypothesis 2 did not hold: low-conflict and high-conflict teachers were not differentiated on the basis of their own ratings of effectiveness.

Another set of four hypotheses was developed from the standpoint of the teacher (the actor), suggested by B in Figure 7.3. It was hypothesized that teachers with a low degree of conflict between self and *perceived* role will (1) rate themselves higher in teaching satisfaction, (2) rate themselves higher in teaching effectiveness, (3) be rated by the principal as more effective teachers, and (4) express greater confidence in the leadership of the principal than will those teachers with a high degree of conflict.

Again, hypotheses 1, 3, and 4 held. With respect to the conflict between self and perceived role, the low-conflict teachers expressed greater satisfaction than high-conflict teachers. Principals rated the low-conflict teachers as more effective than the high-conflict teachers. Low-conflict teachers expressed greater confidence in the leadership of their principals than did high-conflict teachers. As before, however, low-conflict and high-conflict teachers did not differ significantly on the basis of their self-ratings of effectiveness.

These findings led the investigator to conclude:

Teachers do differ from each other in respect to the degree of self-role conflict and the degree of conflict between self and perceived-role. It is possible to order the teachers on each of these two indexes. This tends to substantiate the theoretical framework of this study, that role and personality (self) are two important constructs to be considered when studying the administration of a social system such as the school. This study provides an empirical link with the conceptual creation of a social system, by using an on-going real life setting to test the theoretically contrived hypotheses.[10]

ROLE CONFLICT

Moyer[11] did a study of the principal's leadership role, the attitudes of teachers and principals toward the role, and the relationship between these attitudes and teacher satisfaction. His hypothesis was as follows: close correspondence between teachers' and principals' attitudes toward leadership will be associated with a high degree of teacher satisfaction.

[10] *Ibid.*, pp. 140–41.

[11] Donald C. Moyer, "Teachers' Attitudes Toward Leadership as They Relate to Teacher Satisfaction" (unpublished Ph.D. dissertation, Department of Education, University of Chicago, 1954).

Two styles of leadership—leader-centered and group-centered—were defined, and Q-sort statements were developed to permit teachers and principals to choose items which would describe their ideal principal. A rating scale for teacher satisfaction was also developed. These instruments were administered to the principals and teachers of seven schools—four elementary and three secondary. In the analysis, the responses from the principal and teachers of each school, from 12 to 15 in number, were treated separately.

Some of the major findings follow: (1) the closer the correspondence of attitudes and needs toward leadership within a teaching group (group solidarity), the higher the overall satisfaction of the teachers in the group; (2) the closer the members of a teaching group correspond in group-centered attitudes toward leadership, the higher the level of teacher satisfaction in the group; (3) the extent to which a principal defines his ideal principal as one who encourages teachers to be less dependent on him and more interdependent, the higher the overall satisfaction of the teachers in his group.

While Moyer may have been more preoccupied with teacher satisfaction than with role definition and role conflict, his findings do suggest the importance of role perception on the part of both teachers and principals. Moreover, conflict in how the principal's role is perceived does affect the satisfaction and presumably the productivity of members of the organization.

PERSONALITY CONFLICT

The third type of conflict suggested by the model lies within the idiographic or personal dimension. Getzels and Guba did some work at Maxwell Air Force Base in which this aspect of the theory, among other things, was tested.[12] The setting was Air University, an advanced training center for higher echelon officers in the Air Force. At the time the research was undertaken, the university consisted of what they called nine "courses" but which we may call "schools." The institution was staffed by officers, chiefly of field rank, and the study was initiated because of certain strains in the institution and dissatisfaction among the personnel. An analysis of the existing social system in the terms of the model revealed that each officer-instructor occupied two roles which were in fundamental conflict along a number of dimensions. On the one hand, there was the officer role with certain military expectations, and, on the other hand, the instructor role with certain opposing educational expectations. In addition to stimulat-

---

[12] Jacob W. Getzels and Egon G. Guba, "Role, Role Conflict, and Effectiveness: An Empirical Study," *American Sociological Review,* XIX (April 1954), pp. 164–75; "Role Conflict and Personality," *Journal of Personality,* XXIV (Sept. 1955), pp. 74–85.

ing the overall study, the model suggested hypotheses for testing both role conflict and personality conflict.

We shall report here only the part of the study relating to personality conflict. With respect to individual differences among the faculty in felt conflict, it was hypothesized that the intensity of such conflict would vary as a function of certain emotional characteristics. For example, officer-instructors who were "rigid," "defensive," "extrapunitive," and so on, would be more conflicting than other officer-instructors. Personality data were obtained by three standard instruments: the Guilford-Martin Inventory GAMIN and STDCR, the California E and F Scales, and the Rosenzweig Picture—Frustration Study.

To test the hypothesis having to do with differences in personality conflict among instructors, the quarter of officer-instructors scoring highest in felt conflict was compared with the quarter scoring lowest in felt conflict on each of the personality variables provided by the three experimental instruments. Significant differences were found on seven of the ten factors of the Guilford-Martin, on both the E and F sections of the California Scale, and on five of the six variables of the Rosenzweig; and in each case, the results were in the direction predicted by the model. For example, those high in felt conflict were found on the Guilford-Martin to have a greater "feeling of inferiority," to be more "nervous," "introverted," "depressive," and "cyclical in temperament"; on the California E-F Scale to be more "rigid" and "stereotyped"; and on the Rosenzweig to be more "extrapunitive" and "defensive."

LEADERSHIP STYLE

The model suggests that some leaders may be more nomothetic in their behavior and some more idiographic in their behavior. Moser was able to use these ideas and define three styles of leadership as follows:[13]

1. The nomothetic style is characterized by behavior which stresses goal accomplishment, rules and regulations, and centralized authority at the expense of the individual. Effectiveness is rated in terms of behavior toward accomplishing the school's objectives.

2. The idiographic style is characterized by behavior which stresses the individuality of people, minimum rules and regulations, decentralized authority, and highly individualistic relationships with subordinates. The primary objective is to keep subordinates happy and contented.

3. The transactional style is characterized by behavior which stresses goal accomplishment, but which also makes provision for individual need fulfill-

[13] Robert F. Moser, "The Leadership Patterns of School Superintendents and School Principals," *Administrator's Notebook*, 6 (September 1957), No. 1.

ment. The transactional leader balances nomothetic and idiographic behavior and thus judiciously utilizes each style as the occasion demands.

Moser undertook to examine the relationships between the behavior of superintendents and principals in the performance of their different, yet complementary, roles. He also undertook to assess the relationship between the leader-follower leadership styles of superintendents and principals and their effectiveness ratings, confidence in leadership, and job satisfaction.

Twelve superintendents and twenty-four principals in twelve school systems participated as subjects in the study. The superintendents and principals answered interview questions designed to stimulate subjective responses concerning perceptions of their own and the others' leadership style, their major problems as leaders, and their relationships to each other. In addition, each participant responded to a series of instruments designed to permit analysis which would produce indices related to the following variables: leadership style, agreement or disagreement on role definition, ratings of effectiveness, confidence in leadership, and satisfaction.

In relating the perceived and professed leadership styles of principals and superintendents to the relationships that exist among them, Moser found the following points significant:

1. Superintendents express highest confidence in and give the highest effectiveness ratings to those principals whom they perceive as exhibiting transactional behavior. Superintendents express less confidence in and give the lowest effectiveness ratings to principals whom they perceive as exhibiting idiographic behavior.

2. Superintendents express the highest confidence in and give the highest effectiveness ratings to principals who profess to be nomothetic.

3. Superintendents who profess nomothetic behavior are given the highest effectiveness ratings by principals and enjoy the confidence of principals.

4. Superintendents expect principals to be transactional, with emphasis upon the nomothetic. Likewise, principals expect superintendents to be transactional-nomothetic. Principals want positive leadership from superintendents, and superintendents want principals who are positive leaders.

5. Principals tend to emphasize idiographic behavior in dealing with teachers and nomothetic behavior in their relations with the superintendent. This indicates that the principal is subjected to different expectations from his superintendent than from his teachers and that the principal behaves differently with his superiors than with his subordinates.

6. The principal's rating of the superintendent's effectiveness is a function of the agreement between the superintendent and the principal on the expectations held for the principal role. On the other hand, the superintendent's rating of principal effectiveness depends upon the superintendent's and principal's agreement on the definition of both roles.

7. High mutual ratings of effectiveness and confidence by superintendents and principals are accompanied by similarities in leadership style, feelings of

security, general satisfaction with the relationships, desire to consult with one another on important matters, and clear delineation of duties and authority of decision making.

This short review of some of the studies generated by the social-process model should demonstrate that the model has been useful in suggesting research. The findings of a single study, however, should be accepted with considerable caution. One should recognize that the population included, the nature of the instruments used, the limited variables being tested, and other factors will often limit the generalizations that may be drawn from a single study. We shall have more to say about the implications of these and related studies later.

LIMITATIONS AND EXTENSIONS OF THE THEORY

The social process view of administration appears to be a most useful way of looking at the in-organization relationships of a school or school system. It seems to serve less well as a way of viewing the out-organization relationships of a school or school system. As we shall show later, implications for personnel selection and supervision, for instance, are readily apparent. On the other hand, implications for the relationships between the school organization and the larger society of which the school is a part are not so readily apparent. The theory does little, for instance, to explain operating-levy elections in a community.

Every administrator is aware that he has many out-organization relationships as well as in-organization relationships. One of us participated in a study in which the interactions of four superintendents over an extended period of time were observed and described.[14] In this study 515 of the interactions of the four superintendents, observed a half-day each week over a six-month period, were with organizational members, but 256 of the interactions were with the board of education, community groups, and professional groups. Community groups included governmental agencies at local, state, and national levels, and nongovernmental organizations and individuals of many kinds. The reality of these out-organization relationships is illustrated in the following description of one incident from the study:

The newspaper reporter pulled a chair up to the front of the superintendent's desk, moved the name plate and calendar to one side, and started taking notes. After several questions the reporter said, "Now about that budget hearing this

[14] Midwest Administration Center, "Observation of Administrator Behavior" (Chicago: The Center, University of Chicago, 1959), 188 pp.

week, I think I ought to tell you that the industrial group is going to be down at County Seat to fight the budget you have proposed, along with the Tax Committee of the industrial group, though I don't know why."

The superintendent replied, "Well, I'm a little surprised at that, as I thought they were on our side."

The reporter then asked who all would represent the schools at the hearing, and he added, "I suspect it will be a knock-down, drag-out affair."

The superintendent told him that the director of finance, the attorney, the principals, the PTA president, the representatives of the teachers' union, the representatives of the labor organization in industry, the voters' organizations, the legal organizations, and certain civic groups would represent the schools. In addition, he said, "It may be that the president of one of the big industries will be there, also, to say that they do not go along with the members of the opposition group." Then the superintendent laughed and said, "Now don't go list all of this, or you will really stir up the opposition." The reporter added that we would not, but he said, "We'll have someone down covering the hearing by telephone, and I'll be writing the story at the *Herald,* so all of this background helps. Hell, I wouldn't have told you about who was planning to oppose this unless I had a little judgment, although this bit about their industry people jumping the traces is really 'hot' and would break the opposition right into two camps."

"That's exactly what we hope to do," replied the superintendent.

"That's fine for now; we'll see you tonight at the meeting," the reporter concluded.[15]

Getzels and Thelen, recognizing the limitations of the social process model, have developed a new dimension designed to picture more adequately the reality of the school in the larger society.[16] Just as one is able to think of organizations in sociological terms, one may also think of them in cultural terms, for the organization is embedded in a culture with certain mores and values. The expectations of the roles must in some way be related to the ethos or cultural values. This relationship, however, is by no means clear. Parsons and Shils, for example, view cultural elements as a highly complex constellation of elements that tend to become organized into systems.[17] Yet this system is not viewed as a motivated system, but as patterned symbols and value-orientations which may become embodied either in institutionalized role-expectations or in the superego structure of the personality.

Perhaps just as one can analyze the sociological dimension utilizing the central analytic elements of role-expectations, one can also focus on values

[15] *Ibid.,* p. 85.

[16] Jacob W. Getzels and Herbert A. Thelen, "The Classroom Group as a Unique Social System," in National Society for the Study of Education, *The Dynamics of Instructional Groups* (Chicago: The University of Chicago Press, 1960), Chapter 4.

[17] Parsons and Shils, *op. cit.,* p. 21.

as analytic elements of the cultural or anthropological dimension. The term value, like that of role, has been used in many different ways and in many different contexts.

An entirely new concept of values was suggested by Spindler when he said, "Conflicts between groups centering on issues of educational relevance, and confusions within the rank and file of educators, can be understood best, I believe, in the perspective of the transformation of American culture that proceeds without regard for personal fortune or institutional survival." [18] Spindler defines values as objects of possession, conditions of existence, personality or characterological features, and states of mind that are conceived as desirable and act as motivating determinants of behavior. He has characterized values as traditional or emergent.

The rationale of Spindler has been elaborated by Getzels to distinguish between *sacred* and *secular* values.[19] The sacred values—which we all tend to accept—were seen as democracy, individualism, equality, and human perfectability. The traditional secular values—the operating, down-to-earth beliefs—were seen as the work-success ethic, future-time orientation, independence or the autonomous self, and puritan morality. Getzels suggested that the sacred values have remained stable, but that the secular values are liable to the strains and cleavages of regionalism, rural-urban differences, social class, and social change. Encroaching upon the traditional secular values are the emergent values of sociability, conformity, relativism and present-time orientation.

In analyzing the relationship between the anthropological and the sociological dimensions, one must recognize that the two dimensions are not necessarily parallel to each other. However, the relationship may be represented schematically according to the diagram shown in Figure 7.4.

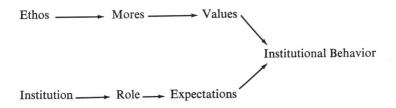

Figure 7.4 The Relationship of the Anthropological and Social Dimensions of Social Behavior (from Getzels and Thelen)

[18] George Spindler, "Education in a Transforming American Culture," *Harvard Educational Review,* XXV, No. 3 (Summer, 1955), p. 156.

[19] Jacob W. Getzels, "Changing Values Challenge the Schools," *The School Review,* LXV (Spring, 1957), 92–102.

The model with three rather than two dimensions is shown in Figure 7.5.

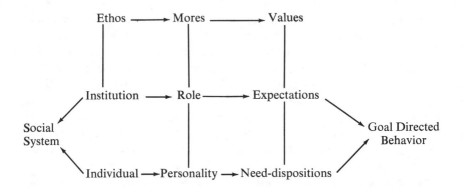

Figure 7.5   Extended Model Showing a Third or Cultural Dimension of Social Behavior (from Getzels and Thelen)

This model permits one to posit some relationships between cultural values and institutional expectations, a possibility which stimulated Abbott to undertake a study of the influence of values upon the superintendent–school board relationships.[20] The central thesis of the investigation was that difficulties in interpersonal relationships may be expected to arise, not so much from complexities and differences in values that are in the open and understood, as from complexities and differences that are underground and misunderstood.

Two hypotheses were formulated, based on prior theoretical and empirical work in the general area of values: first, an individual's own values were expected to influence his perceptions of the values held by others; second, both an individual's values and his value-perceptions were expected to influence his relationships with others.

The following questions provided the focus for the investigation:

1. What is the relationship between superintendents' value-orientations and their perceptions of the values held by individual board members? Conversely, what is the relationship between board members' perceptions of superintendents' values and their own value-orientations?

2. What is the relationship between the confidence that board members evince in their superintendents' leadership and (a) congruence in value-orientations, (b) accuracy of perception of value-orientations, and (c) perceived similarity in value-orientations?

[20] Max G. Abbott, "Values and Value-Perceptions in Superintendent-School Board Relationships," *Administrator's Notebook,* 9 (December 1960), No. 4.

A values inventory was used to obtain from board members and super-intendents responses to a series of items that represented a traditional–emergent value dichotomy. From the responses that were obtained, both self-scores of respondents and their perceptual scores of others were derived. A confidence-in-leadership scale was used to ascertain board members' confidence in their superintendents.

Thirty-seven superintendents and 213 board members from 27 ele-mentary districts, 5 high school districts, and 8 unit districts, all located in the Midwest, made up the sample.

Interpersonal relationships were indeed influenced by the values people held and by the way in which those values were perceived. An individual's own values had an important influence upon his perceptions of the values held by others. Persons who held emergent values tended to view others as being emergent, while those who held traditional values tended to view others as being traditional. Moreover, these patterns of perception were unrelated to the actual values of those whose values were being perceived.

The values held by individuals had an important influence upon kinds of perceptual errors made. When the values of the perceiver and the per-ceived were similar, errors tended to be random. When the values of the perceiver and the perceived were dissimilar, errors followed a systematic pattern and tended to move in the direction of the perceiver's own value position with a frequency that was significantly greater than would have been expected to occur by chance.

The hypothesis concerning the relationship between confidence-in-leader-ship and agreement on values was substantiated. Board members whose values were most similar to those of their superintendents expressed slightly higher confidence to those superintendents than did board members whose values were least similar.

There was a relationship also between confidence-in-leadership and the accurate perception of values. Board members who were most accurate in perceiving their superintendents' values expressed significantly higher con-fidence in their superintendents than did board members who were least accurate.

A strong relationship was found between confidence-in-leadership and perceived similarity in values. Board members who perceived their super-intendents to be most similar to themselves in values, regardless of actual similarity, expressed significantly higher confidence in their superintendents than did board members who perceived their superintendents to be least similar to themselves.

In general, it may be said that confidence was related positively to the accuracy with which board members understood their superintendents' value positions. Confidence was also related positively to the extent that board members assumed that they themselves were in agreement with their superintendents on basic issues. Whether or not this presumed agreement actually existed appeared to be relatively unimportant.

The concept of selective interpersonal perception is, therefore, important in understanding administrative relationships. In a sense, each person may be said to function in a world of his own making. His attitudes and values serve as a perceptual screen; he interprets his environment according to the way he perceives it; and he reacts to that environment in accordance with his interpretations. Thus, in analyzing the superintendent–school board relationship, it is not sufficient merely to determine whether or not superintendents and board members are in agreement on basic issues. It is necessary also to know how each member of the relationship perceives the positions of other members, since it is these perceptions which influence largely the action that will be taken. The findings of this investigation suggest that harmonious interpersonal relationships can be maintained despite differences in basic value positions, provided the differences are assessed accurately.

The extension of the social process model illustrates another characteristic of theory: it has within it the seeds of its own destruction and reconstitution. In other words, if the theory does not depict reality accurately, the testing of the hypotheses generated by the theory will reveal the shortage and will call for revision of the original formulation. With its new dimension the social process model describes a larger segment of administrative behavior—whether large enough remains to be seen.

IMPLICATIONS FOR PRACTICE

A theory of administration should suggest implications for practice as surely as it does hypotheses for research. Let us see if the social-process theory can meet such a demand.

IN-ORGANIZATION MEDIATOR

Within the organization it seems clear that the theory we have been discussing makes the administrator a mediator between the organizational and the personal dimensions. At one point as organizational spokesman he will find it essential to explain, to reinforce, to emphasize the school's objectives and procedures. At another point he will find it desirable to listen to members of the organization, to ascertain their feelings about certain school practices, and to diagnose as best he can why they take the positions they do. When and under what circumstances he does either is part of the art of administration. Clearly, there are no recipes as to when the administrator behaves nomothetically or idiographically, but his judgment regarding such matters may be sharpened if he knows that both kinds of behavior are appropriate for the administrator. Some examples may help clarify this point.

The capacity of the administrator to play both nomothetic and idiographic roles is illustrated in the employment of personnel. Such a process is critical both for the school and the person, and thus the interests of both should be thoroughly explored in the employment process. The administrator should do his best to make clear the goals, program, and characteristics of the school and the expectations held for the prospective staff member. At the same time, every effort should be made to understand the aspirations, the values, the motivations, and the strengths of the person being considered. Such a process can do much to insure some congruence between organizational expectations and personal dispositions should the candidate become a staff member, a condition necessary to best school operation.

A similar demand pertains in terms of the assignment of personnel. If the administrator emphasizes only his nomothetic role, he will tend to look upon staff members as cogs in the organizational machine, each somewhat alike and replaceable by the other. On the other hand, if the administrator becomes completely idiographic, he will strive to make assignments conform to individual whim with little or no regard for the total program of the organization. Clearly, neither extreme is acceptable; few administrators act completely one way or the other. It may help, however, to recognize that at times even unpopular assignments have to be made if the total program is to be served. At the same time, it should be clear that people tend to be more productive if at least part of the time they are doing those things they enjoy and for which they have competence.

Perhaps in the supervision of personnel the two dimensions of the model are even more suggestive. The aim of supervision is the improved performance of personnel, which in a school system means enhancement of the teaching-learning process. Both in the diagnosis of any difficulties a teacher may be having and in developing ways for overcoming such difficulties, the two dimensions of the model seem pertinent. The difficulty may lie, for instance, in a misunderstanding of what the school expects, or it may lie in unrealistic aspirations on the part of a teacher. Such diagnosis suggests the remedial measures: clarification of school goals in one instance, and modification of individual standards in the other.

Guba has extended the model by way of suggesting the actuating force or power of an administrator in an organization. His concept is shown in Figure 7.6. The administrator is seen as having two kinds of power: status and authority, which reside at the role or nomothetic dimension; and

Figure 7.6   The Power Relationships of the Administrator[21]

prestige and influence, which reside at the person or idiographic dimension. The first kind of power resides in the office and is delegated to the administrator. The second kind of power must be earned by the administrator. Clearly, an effective administrator has and exercises both kinds of power.

Conflict between institutional expectations and personal dispositions are seen as alienating forces in an organization. For instance, a school may establish ability groups in mathematics or English. Some of these groups will be composed of slow learners but, even so, they must have teachers. If assigned to teach one of these groups, a teacher who has no patience with slow learners will probably resent the task and may actually sabotage the program. In any case, the lack of congruence between institutional expectations and personal dispositions is clear.

The alienating force of this conflict may be reduced by employing goals and values as integrating forces. Thus, in our illustration the forming of ability groups may be seen as one way of differentiating instruction for pupils who have a wide range of capacity. Moreover, the desirability of giving even slow learners an opportunity to do their best may be seen as consonant with the values of schools within a democratic society. This

[21] Egon G. Guba, "Research in Internal Administration—Is It Relevant?" in R. F. Campbell and J. M. Lipham (eds.), *Administrative Theory as a Guide to Action* (Chicago: Midwest Administration Center, University of Chicago, 1960), Chapter 7.

kind of exploration may make teaching a group of slow learners more rational and possibly more palatable. If at the same time such an assignment can be coupled with teaching a fast-learning group, more in keeping with the personal dispositions of the teacher, the total assignment may become quite acceptable.

THE ADMINISTRATOR IN THE MIDDLE

Another implication of the model, particularly if the cultural dimension is included, places the administrator squarely in the middle of a number of reference groups. There is the community with its many publics, the board of education with some lay and some professional understandings and convictions, the school system itself with its own set of social arrangements, and the impingement of the larger world at both lay and professional levels. Within this welter of forces there are many conflicting expectations and demands.

Conflicts within some of the reference groups have been very well documented. Ordinarily, the people of a community are not of one mind. One public, for instance, may wish the school to provide a program of released time for religious education, while another public opposes any such idea. One public may advocate extensive provisions for vocational education, while another public would leave all such efforts to industry. One public may place great stress upon the intellectual purposes of the school, while another public would give almost equal emphasis to social purposes.[22] These conflicts may become so sharp that they furnish the battleground for conflicts between competing leadership groups in the community.

Within the school itself there may also be sharp conflicts. In a study of 77 school administrators and 1065 teachers, Seeman found that teachers differ appreciably in their expectations of administrators.[23] For instance, teachers were almost evenly divided on the question of whether or not a superintendent should invite teachers to his home for social occasions.

In many school systems a number of other conflicts may be observed. Elementary and secondary school teachers differ in their viewpoints on many questions. Elementary school principals are seldom accorded the same status as secondary school principals. Some secondary school teachers believe that the high school should be a selective institution, whereas others think it should serve all youth. Although some teachers want almost com-

---

[22] Lawrence W. Downey, *The Task of Public Education* (Chicago: Midwest Administration Center, University of Chicago, 1960).

[23] Melvin Seeman, "Role Conflict and Ambivalence in Leadership," *American Sociological Review,* 18 (August 1953), pp. 373–80.

plete freedom in their work, others have great need for direction from administrative and supervisory personnel.

Boards of education ordinarily talk out their conflicts until they reach agreement, but this should not obscure the fact that board members too have different expectations of administrators. One board member may think that the superintendent should be a "strong" leader, while another may believe he should consult freely with his staff. Still another may value above all else careful financial management and be opposed to all expansions of program regardless of need. Or current issues, such as changes in attendance area boundaries to further integrate Negroes, or shared time between public and nonpublic schools, may divide board members just as they do citizens at large.

Even the influences of the larger world upon the administration of a school district are not of one voice. School practices in other communities may be quite diverse. Programs at the state or federal level may actually seem unacceptable to the people of a local school district. Witness, for instance, state programs of school district reorganization which are seen as undue meddling with local operation. Or note the number of school districts that have difficulty with the implementation of some of the federal programs.

Alas, even the professional voices heard by the administrator are not in complete unity. The teachers may be urging that since he knows good school practice, he should proceed to institute it in his school district. Some of his colleagues, on the other hand, perhaps as a result of bitter experience, urge caution. He may find in his professional magazines descriptions of opposing school practices, each of which is reputed to be professionally sanctioned.

Each of the reference groups to which we have alluded—the community, the board of education, the school system itself, and the larger environment —may have in a particular school community some common expectations for school administrators, but within each group there appear to be many real or potential conflicts. The administrator must chart a program despite these conflicts.

Perhaps even more significant to school administration than the differences within the various reference groups, as noted above, are the differences among these groups. Halpin found, for instance, that school staff members and board members usually agreed within their respective groups in describing the leadership behavior of superintendents, but that the two groups did not agree with each other.[24] In companion studies Buffington[25]

---

[24] Andrew W. Halpin, *The Leadership Behavior of School Superintendents* (2nd ed.). (Chicago: Midwest Administration Center, University of Chicago, 1959).

[25] Reed L. Buffington, "The Job of the Elementary School Principal as Viewed by Parents," Stanford University *Dissertation Abstracts,* 14 (1954), pp. 943–44.

and Medsker[26] attempted to identify the job of the elementary principal from the standpoint of the parents and teachers, respectively. In many respects the perceptions of these two groups were far apart. For example, the parents tended to see the principal's first duty as that of developing relationships with parents and other groups in the community. The teachers, on the other hand, perceived the principal's first duty as that of providing leadership for them.

In a sense these conflicting expectations among reference groups place the school administrator squarely in the middle. In order for the principal to meet the expectations of the parents, he may not be able to meet the expectations of the teachers, or vice versa. In like manner a superintendent may find his board of education holding one set of expectations for him, while his staff holds another. This is not merely a theoretical matter; it is one which has been documented time and again in practice. Consider the expectations each group holds for the superintendent on the question of salary negotiations. Or reflect upon the superintendent's dilemma when a board of education is anxious to improve the physical plant of the district and the teachers are in great need of an improved salary scale. Or think of the school administrator who gets caught in a school district reorganization hassle, with his local community resisting any change and the state department of education and other professionals urging a larger district and combination of high schools.

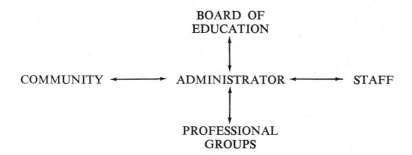

Figure 7.7   The Administrator and Some of His Major Reference Groups

The dilemma of the administrator as the man in the middle is shown in Figure 7.7. Each major group holds expectations for the administrator, and there is often conflict among these expectations. Within each of these groups there may also be conflict in terms of what is expected of the admin-

[26] Leland L. Medsker, "The Job of the Elementary Principal as Viewed by Teachers," Stanford University *Dissertation Abstracts,* 14 (1954), pp. 946–47.

istrator. We might conclude, after noting the conflicting expectations facing administrators both within and among the various reference groups, that the only alternative is to do nothing. Actually, it is not that simple; to do nothing is in a sense a program and some groups will, after a time, object even to that program. The administrator is thus faced with the development of the best program that can be devised within the limits of the situation.

Despite the many limitations which characterize most situations, there is on most questions some flexibility, or an "area of tolerance." Although the board of education, for instance, may not believe in citizens' advisory committees in general, it may be willing to try out a citizens' advisory committee organized around a particular task, such as a bond campaign. Or teachers may be dead set against a merit factor in a salary schedule, but they may be willing that a program designed to evaluate teaching be developed for instructional improvement purposes only. It is within these areas of tolerance that a school administrator may be able to resolve at least some of the conflicts which seem to exist both within and among major reference groups.

The limits discussed above also suggest the real challenge to educational administration; most of the limits have a time dimension. A position taken by a community, a board, or a faculty today need not hold forever. We need only to look at a few of the positions taken by such groups a decade or two ago to find how true this is.

But the administrator cannot be content merely to wait in hopes that time will alter the situation. He needs some way of getting at the dynamics of the situation. The questions become: Under what circumstances do people have a chance of changing their minds? How and to what extent may I bring these circumstances about?

While the answers to these questions are by no means complete, one prerequisite to bringing some harmony out of disagreement seems to be face-to-face communication. School boards and faculties usually find more in common when they have many opportunities to talk together. In like manner teachers and parents find the grounds of agreement broader when they confer frequently with each other. The administrator can facilitate the kinds of communication alluded to above.

Another element in the process of change appears to be complete information. To be sure, some people are like the chap who said, "My mind is made up; don't confuse me with the facts," but most people are willing to give some attention to the facts that are relevent to a problem. Often these facts include a description of what is being done elsewhere. While this proves nothing, the example of others is a powerful argument to many people. Again an administrator can facilitate the processes of fact-gathering and presentation.

Complete integrity on the part of the administrator is also necessary if people are to be willing to make compromises or arrive at new positions. This situation may mean that no group comes to love the administrator, but all groups come to respect him. Seldom can the educational leader take a position completely to the liking of a particular reference group, but his reasons for not doing so should be clear, and he should be seen as serving a larger constituency. Difficult as this role may appear, it is only leadership of this kind which will help the school fill its unique place in our society.

In the great dilemma about which we have been speaking lies the real challenge to administrative leadership. If areas of tolerance are to be extended, if members of reference groups are to understand how the school must stand above the welfare of a particular group in order to serve all groups, if change is to be seen as a way of life, the leadership of the administrator must help all groups understand the viewpoints of other groups and the administrator's position as a competent adjudicator.

SUGGESTED ACTIVITIES

1. Describe the similarities and differences between the initial Getzels-Guba model and the major concept of Argyris or the two dimensions suggested by Cartwright and Zander.
2. Formulate a few simple questions pertaining to some issues affecting the public schools of your community, and use these questions to interview a number of citizens. Note the similarity and diversity of their opinions.
3. As one of your questions above, ask each citizen to name the three most influential people in the community. To what extent do you get a duplication of names? Determine to what extent incumbent school board members are numbered among the community leaders named by citizens.
4. Interview a number of teachers in a particular school or school system, and ask them what they consider the important duties of the principal to be. Interview a number of parents of pupils in the same school or school system, and ask them what they consider the important duties of the school principal to be. Note similarities and differences in the responses.

SELECTED READINGS

ARGYRIS, CHRIS. *Integrating the Individual and the Organization.* New York: John Wiley & Sons, 1964.

CAMPBELL, ROALD F. and GREGG, RUSSELL T. (eds.). *Administrative Behavior in Education*. New York: Harper & Brothers, 1957, Chapter 7.

CARTWRIGHT, DORWIN and ZANDER, ALVIN. *Group Dynamics: Research and Theory*, 2nd ed. Evanston, Ill.: Row, Peterson & Co., 1960 pp. 496–99.

DOWNEY, LAWRENCE W. *The Task of Public Education*. Chicago: Midwest Administration Center, University of Chicago, 1960.

GETZELS, J. W., LIPHAM, J. M., and CAMPBELL, R. F. *Administration as a Social Process: Theory, Research, and Practice*. Forthcoming.

GROSS, NEAL, MASON, WARD S., and McEACHERN, ALEXANDER W. *Explorations in Role Analysis: Studies of the School Superintendent Role*. New York: John Wiley & Sons, Inc., 1958.

GUBA, EGON G. "Research in Internal Administration—What Do We Know?" in Campbell, R. F., and Lipham, J. M. (eds.). *Administrative Theory as a Guide to Action*. Chicago: Midwest Administration Center, University of Chicago, 1960, Chapter 7.

HALPIN, ANDREW W. *The Leadership Behavior of School Superintendents*, (2nd ed.). Chicago: Midwest Administration Center, University of Chicago, 1959.

HEMPHILL, JOHN K. *Situational Factors in Leadership*. Columbus, Ohio: The Ohio State University, 1949.

LIPHAM, JAMES M. "Organizational Character of Education: Administrative Behavior," *Review of Educational Research*, 34 (October 1964), pp. 435–454.

8

Roles of School Personnel

in Administration

IF, INDEED, THE SCHOOL ADMINISTRATOR IS A LEADER among the various reference groups with which he works, and if the school operates as a social system in the manner previously described, many people participate in the educational enterprise, with the administrative head giving direction to and co-ordinating their involvement. This chapter deals with the implications of theory and experience for a co-operative working relationship among school employees. For the most part, this discussion will be confined to the internal operation of the school. We shall not attempt to give a comprehensive list here of all the duties of all school personnel. Rather, our purpose in this chapter is to highlight those roles of superintendents, members of the central office staff, principals, teachers, and other school employees which are synchronized to provide a co-ordinated organizational effort.

THE ROLE OF THE SUPERINTENDENT

The superintendent of schools accepts final responsibility for the operation of the schools. The accountability of the total staff to the public is usually marked by pressure upon the superintendent. While in many school systems the superintendent delegates authority and some degree of responsibility to assistant superintendents, business managers, directors, co-ordinators and supervisors, principals, teachers, and other personnel, he cannot delegate final accountability for the tasks which they perform. This dilemma in delegation may govern the degree of the superintendent's direct involvement in the activity assigned to other persons, and his understanding and perception of his and others' roles in the performances of administrative tasks. Delegation is also dependent upon the understanding which other staff members have of their roles, and their readiness to accept the roles.

We spoke previously of various leader behavior styles or patterns. These patterns are observable in the working relationships between the superintendent and his staff members. One superintendent may delegate so completely that he participates very little in the proposing, planning, conducting, and evaluating of programs. Another superintendent may work with members of his staff in such a way as to enhance the leadership performance of those individuals directly responsible to him. Still another superintendent might keep a tight rein on all activities conducted by his associates.

While, conceivably, in the variety of situations that exist, superintendents may operate successfully at any point within the range of practices just described, the latter practice of "being in on everything" becomes less and less tenable as the size of school districts becomes larger. One fact is clearly established: the course of action that the superintendent chooses to take must be generally acceptable to the board of education and to his staff. The wise superintendent makes clear his perception of his role and seeks general agreement from these two important reference groups to operate in accordance with this perception.

A GENERALIST

As the number of school districts is reduced and the size of each is increased, it seems reasonable to expect that the superintendent will, more and more, assume the role of a generalist rather than that of a specialist in a particular phase of school operation. That is, the trend is in the direction of establishing an administrative team, including a number of specialists whose work he must co-ordinate. It is he whose responsibility it is to view the entire enterprise in broad perspective.

In a recent publication Miller describes the superintendent as a perceptive generalist:

The perceptive generalist must know enough of the general field and enough of the nature and problems of the specialists so that he can communicate with them with understanding, comprehensible among the specialists as a collective group and meaningful between specialists and the general public. He will miss the detail of many of the specialties but he sees all of them in wider configuration than do the specialists.[1]

The superintendent's expertness lies in his conceptualization of the tasks to be performed, in his inventiveness and genius in organization, and in his ability to work with people. His is an overall or *general* perspective, which he utilizes in charting the course that the school is to take. Although his staff assists him in achieving this perspective, he must articulate it, and he must have the power to use it as a guide for action.

A STAFF LEADER

It is often said that the strength of a superintendent can be measured by the competence of his staff—a statement which does not mean that a strong staff has no need of a strong superintendent. We hope that we have made it clear that staff strength is dependent upon leadership strength. The leader and his staff are dependent upon one another; the strength of one enhances the strength of the other.

As a consequence of the acceptance of this point of view, much is done to build up staff strength. Assessment and appraisal are common activities used to find the most competent teachers. Recruitment, selection, and orientation of new teachers have taken on added importance as administrative functions in recent years. In-service education and individualized help in instruction have become increasingly important.

Griffiths and his co-authors describe the growing importance and complexity of the superintendent's staff leadership role as follows:

> The personnel function of the superintendent is assuming larger and larger proportions. Due to such factors as increased size of school districts, increased professional preparation of teachers, the teacher shortage, increases in salaries of professional educators, and the general change in employer-employee relationships in the country, the superintendent of today faces many more problems than did his predecessors. Some of these factors are of the superintendent's own making. He exercises no control, however, over most of the factors, but must cope with them nevertheless.[2]

Not only are the better superintendents of schools alert to the sources of competent personnel; they devise ways of improving the competence of the personnel already on the job. They find ways of deploying the services of

---

[1] Van Miller, "The Superintendent of Schools," in D. J. Leu and H. C. Rudman, eds., *Preparation Programs for School Administrators* (East Lansing, Michigan: Michigan State University, 1963), Chapter 5.

[2] Daniel E. Griffiths, *et al., Organizing Schools for Effective Education* (Danville, Illinois: The Interstate Printers & Publishers, Inc., 1962), p. 165.

their staff members to accomplish the tasks of the school as effectively and efficiently as possible. If necessary, they separate the incompetents from the school system. The tasks involved in personnel development have become so important and so complicated that specialists in personnel and instruction have been employed with assignments in their particular fields.

A SYMBOL

In spite of much talk in our society about equalizing the status of the leader and the members of his group, in the school at least it is still a fact that the status of the superintendent permits him to establish, in marked degree, the behavior pattern of the staff. "Businesslike procedures," "good communication," "courage to act," "kindness with firmness," "vision and foresight," "a good organizer" are typical of terms used by staff members to denote the tone set by superintendents whom they respect. On the other hand, lack of respect for superintendents is shown by such terms as "careless business practices," "lack of integrity," "favoritism among staff members," "failure to communicate," "poor organization," and "lack of vision."

Reference has been made to the fact that students of leadership and of administrative behavior agree that staff morale is as much a function of staff accomplishment as of warm human relationships. Whether the superintendent wishes it or not, he becomes the symbol of his school; in turn, perhaps to a somewhat lesser degree, the school tends to be described in the same terms as those applied to the superintendent. Therefore, regardless of the number of helpers he has or their disposition toward the tasks to which they have been assigned, the superintendent is the head of the school system and cannot escape the role of setting the stage for staff participation.

THE ROLES OF CENTRAL OFFICE PERSONNEL

With the growth in the size and complexity of school systems, we witness a corresponding growth in the number and complexity of the functions of the central administrative office. These new demands upon the central office have created a need for the development of new and more efficient ways of conceptualizing school district organization and structure. Systems analysis and research as it is applied to educational institutions seems to offer a powerful means by which educational leaders can analyze, and adapt to, the changing role which the central office must play.[3] Hencley uses a form of systems analysis when he writes:

[3] See D. E. Griffiths, "The Nature and Meaning of Theory," in National Society for the Study of Education *Behavioral Science and Educational Administration*, 63rd Yearbook, Part II, 1964, pp. 116–118.

The need for developing goal-centered and implementation-centered policies, and the parallel need for integrating, formalizing, and unifying workflow patterns in organizations requires members of administrative performance systems to be sophisticated in various administrative processes. Functional order in organization, adjustments in organizational workflow patterns, and maintenance and improvement of the organizational environmental exchange system are achieved through administrative processes such as communication, decision-making, change, and morale maintenance. The need for competence in such processes is not restricted to intraorganizational settings. As figure 10 indicates, the administrative performance system is an open system which interacts and exchanges information with its environment. Thus sophistication in the use of administrative processes is necessary in several kinds of settings: intraorganizational, extraorganizational and interstitial.

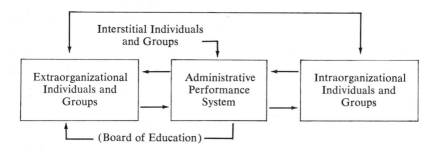

FIGURE 10. The Administrative Performance System as an Open System (from Leu and Rudman)[4]

. . . Perhaps the most important point brought out by study of figure 10 is that all members of the administrative performance system require some sophistication in the process area of administration. However, the degree of sophistication required is determined by the level and function of the various positions and by the number, type, and complexity of social and organizational variables confronting administrators in these positions.[5]

While it is not our purpose here to elaborate on all of these functions and processes, we call attention to the fact that the growth of the central office staff of a school system comes about, in general, in response to the need for greater specialization in various aspects of school administration, better co-ordination of the separate but related phases of the school program, and increased services to the several operating units of the systems. We shall discuss the roles of central office personnel in terms of these functions.

[4] S. P. Hencley, "Functional Interrelationships Within Administrative Performance Systems," in D. J. Leu and H. C. Rudman, eds., *Preparation Programs for School Administrators* (East Lansing, Michigan: Michigan State University, 1963), p. 82.

[5] *Ibid.,* p. 89.

SPECIALIZATION

The role of some persons on the central office staff is that of providing special expertness in certain phases of school operation. Assistant superintendents are examples of people who assume such a role. They may be placed in charge of instruction, staff personnel, pupil personnel, business or other functions. While each assistant superintendent is responsible to the superintendent, he has been employed because of his expertness in his particular field of specialization. The employment of an assistant superintendent of schools is based upon the assumption that his special expertness will be directed to that limited sphere of school operation designated by his assignment.

Other specialists are often needed in the school. They may have various titles depending upon where they work and the manner in which their specialty is used. The title of administrative assistant or assistant to another administrator connotes a *staff* rather than a *line* responsibility. *Staff* personnel carry out specific assignments for their superior officer, while *line* officers direct the work of a number of other people. The superintendent may employ a *general* administrative assistant who performs a variety of tasks assigned to him. In contrast to this, a research assistant or an assistant in communications may have a *specific* function.

Specialists may be assigned to work at almost any level of the administrative hierarchy and with either staff or line responsibilities. To bring special expertness to the instructional program, for example, an assistant superintendent in this area may decide that he needs *directors* of elementary and secondary education, each of whom can center attention upon that part of the program for which he is responsible. In turn, the director of elementary education may assign a specialist in reading to serve as a supervisor, consultant, advisor, or teacher helper in the several elementary schools of the system.

Griffiths has made an interesting distinction between various kinds of staff officers. He writes that:

Staff officers may be classified as either coordinative or advisory. Coordinative staff officers assist the chief administrator in the discharge of many detailed functions of his position and aid him in the general coordination of school affairs. Any authority they may exercise is derived from the chief school administrator and exercised in a specific situation. For example, staff officers are not assigned authority to handle an area of school operation or given responsibility for that area. This type of staff officer must, however, be a generalist skilled in working with people.

. . . .

Advisory staff officers are specialists who supply expert assistance upon request. They have no authority except that which comes from their specialized knowledge in an area. An example of such a position in the public schools would be the subject-matter consultant or helping teacher. On a higher authority level, an assistant superintendent for business affairs or instruction might be placed in such a position. He would have hierarchical authority over those persons connected directly with his central office staff, but none over building principals or teachers.[6]

There is a growing trend in larger school systems toward a decentralized organizational structure. Decentralization in a school system requires, in most cases, the assumption of greater line authority by building heads or principals and the increased specialization of staff personnel at the central office. Under a decentralized arrangement most of the central office personnel will be either coordinative or advisory staff officers.

The increased size and complexity of many modern school systems have created a need for the central office to make proper use of innovations such as data processing systems, computer information systems, and centralized purchasing-accounting systems. These innovations have created the need for a different breed of specialization. For example, a school system utilizing computer-based data processing will need both technicians to operate and program the machines, and research-oriented analysts to provide questions and research frameworks for the machines.

The reader should recognize that the practice of discussing organization in terms of line and staff positions has some limitations. A clear dichotomy between *line* (denoting authority) and *staff* (denoting a consultive or co-ordinating role) should not be made. Experience has shown that such a dichotomy is inadequate for describing precisely how people function in a school system and how jobs get done.

Thus, the function of providing greater expertness through specialization can be accomplished through the services of a number of different kinds of personnel working at different levels and in various ways throughout the school system. Their competence supplements and complements that of other specialists—the superintendent, the principal, and the teacher. Increased specialization in the central office should make it possible both to intensify and diversify the educational effort of the school system.

CO-ORDINATION

The assistant superintendent of instruction must give his attention to planning and co-ordinating instruction throughout the school system. Thus, while he serves as a specialist in instruction, in contrast to specialists in staff personnel and business, he also serves the school in the capacity of a co-ordinator. Assistant superintendents must view their co-ordinating role in at least two ways. One of these we have just mentioned, namely the

[7] Daniel E. Griffiths, *et al., Organizing Schools for Effective Education* (Danville, Illinois: The Interstate Printers & Publishers, Inc., 1962), pp. 23–24.

system-wide co-ordination within his sphere of school operation. Another essential view, however, concerns the co-ordination of efforts among the several task areas of administration. That is, business, staff personnel, instruction, and other functions must be worked out together.

There are other levels at which co-ordination plays an important part in the operation of the school. Co-ordinators of elementary education, of pupil personnel, and of audio-visual education all have responsibilities for system-wide co-ordination within their functional areas as well as for seeing that pupil personnel services and the facilities of the audio-visual instructional department are used to facilitate instruction in the various elementary schools of the system. This example clearly illustrates our point that personnel in the central office do have a co-ordinating role and that co-ordination is important both within and among divisions of school operation.

SERVICE

Many schools employ a number of persons whose primary function is that of service to the several building units.

Resource People

Supervisors, consultants, and resource persons may be classed primarily as service personnel. Their function is to help teachers or other school workers carry out their specific assignments. True, they are specialists who may have particular competence in diagnosing difficulties and improving upon the means generally used to overcome them. However, their usefulness to the school system is demonstrated by their acceptance as helpers rather than by the authority of the status position that they hold.

In a certain sense all central office personnel perform a service role. They are employed to carry out those functions that facilitate teaching and learning. The effectiveness of the central office operation depends, in large measure, upon the acceptance and utilization of its services in the several school units in the system.

Other Service Personnel

In addition to the members of the professional staff, there are other employees whose work contributes to the system-wide effort. Many of them are associated in some way with school management. Among such employees are the school clerk who keeps the official records of the board of education; various clerical workers, such as secretaries, filing clerks, typists and stenographers, and bookkeepers; custodians, bus drivers, cafeteria managers and cooks.

Although most of these people do not expect to take an active part in making the professional decisions with which our previous discussion has been concerned, nevertheless they are an integral part of the school system.

Their effectiveness is dependent both upon how well they understand the roles they play and the degree to which they feel that they truly belong to the school system.

Job descriptions are often useful in clarifying assignments. In-service education meetings to discuss improvements in procedures and the improvement of skills can also be very helpful. Often, training programs are provided at the state, regional, or university level for the up-grading of the services of such personnel. The advantage of the utilization of such means to the improvement of services cannot be overstressed.

The Role of the Principal

The individual school is the center for all teaching and learning. In any given neighborhood the effectiveness of the local school may be the criterion by which people judge the effectiveness of the entire school system. Hence the principal is a key person in the administrative organization. He performs administrative tasks similar to those of a superintendent of schools, but he does so within the policy limits of the system. Instructional leadership, community relationships, staff personnel, pupil personnel, facilities, finance and business management, and organization are all areas in which tasks must be performed at the school-building level as well as the level of central-office administration.

The nature of the responsibilities differs somewhat among elementary schools and junior and senior high schools. High schools, for example, tend to recognize more managerial responsibilities than do elementary schools. The size and complexity of the schools are factors that affect the nature of these responsibilities also. Ordinarily we transport high school youth greater distances than we do elementary school children. Enrollments in high schools are usually larger than in elementary schools. The curriculum of the comprehensive high school is extensive and complex. The role of the junior high school in the American school system is not as clear as that of the elementary and high schools. Thus, not only are the functions of administration at the building level as varied as those for the entire system, but in addition they are complicated by circumstances that require treatment unique to each school.

AN ORGANIZER

While in smaller school systems principals are expected to perform all of the tasks associated with the office, this expectation results from a lack of appreciation for the scope and comprehension of the job. In larger school systems, where the complexity of the work of the principal is more apparent, specialized personnel either are assigned as regular assistants to the principal or are supplied by the central office. Both practices are common in our better school systems.

Whether or not the principal himself performs all of the tasks associated with his office, he must organize his school in such a way that the tasks are accomplished. True, the basic administrative unit of which the principal's school is a part determines the financial structure for the system. It provides the building and furnishings. The financial resources of the total school system provide for the operating expenses of the school, including the teachers' salaries. As indicated previously, the central office provides for many resources. But these provisions supplied in such manner do not make a school. The principal must understand how to weld these resources—those of his teachers, of the neighborhood which his school serves, of special personnel, and of the students—into a school community that has a character of its own.

A COMMUNICATOR

Another reason why the principal holds such a key position in the organizational structure of a school system is that he stands in an intermediate position between the central office and his teachers, and between the people of his local school neighborhood and the citizens of the entire attendance unit. It is not enough that his school take on a unique character indigenous to the particular circumstances immediately surrounding it. The individual school is also a part of a system. The principal is the chief interpreter of official policy of the system for his staff and for the school community. It is also largely through him that certain special contributions of the individual school become incorporated as integral parts of the total system. Thus, his understanding of the decision-making process and his ability to communicate to staff and community and to central administrative officers are one measure of his competence.

AN INSTRUCTIONAL LEADER

Important as it is for the principal to play the roles of organizer and communicator well, they are inadequate to explain the common reference to his as a *key* administrator. Like the superintendent of schools, he holds a position of high visibility in his community. He must not only be articulate about the purposes which his school is to serve, but he must demonstrate that under his leadership the school is achieving them in reasonable degree. He is at once a diagnostician of the problems that his school needs to solve and a synthesizer of the forces that must be brought together to solve them.

If he fulfills this expectation, he develops a congenial working relationship among his staff members; he encourages their creativity by seeking out the special talents of individual members and encouraging their innovation and experimentation; he assesses the need for the use of resource personnel and deploys them to spots where they may be effective; he appraises the effectiveness of the instructional program and takes the steps necessary to improve it.

A LINE OFFICER

The principal is, in most forms of administrative organization, the line authority in his building. His authority devolves from the laws of the state and, through the superintendent, from the board of education and the people of the community. This devolved authority is the principal's legal-traditional source of power. However, to operate successfully within his school, the principal must possess another kind of authority—authority based on *competence*.

Griffiths has recognized four types of functions in which all principals must be competent:

1. Improving the educational program.
2. Selecting and developing personnel.
3. Working with the community.
4. Managing the school.[7]

THE TEACHER'S PLACE IN THE ORGANIZATION

The teacher derives considerable satisfaction from the recognition of the importance of his task. The satisfactions resulting from a successful experience in the classroom are among the enduring benefits of the teaching profession. However, as schools have become larger and an organizational effort is required to do the total job of the school, the need for identification with the total organization has increased. The teacher of the one-room school knew how he fared in the school enterprise, because there were no intermediaries between him and the school board on the one hand, and the children and the parents on the other. Furthermore, this teacher taught all of the children in all grades. He determined the standard of achievement at all grade levels.

[7] Griffiths, *op. cit.*, p. 172.

INTERDEPENDENCE OF TEACHERS

In the school of today each teacher is a contributor to the total educational endeavor; he cannot carry out his assignment alone. He works in a co-operative enterprise in which the educational process is a team affair. This interdependence among contributors to the educational process is a phenomenon of the multiple-teacher school. The larger and more complex the school or school system, the more important this phenomenon becomes as a factor in organization and administration.

It is now common to speak of the ungraded primary divisions of the elementary school, team teaching, the utilization of master teachers either within the school system or by television, and various forms of grouping of pupils; and of teaching machines, the teacher's helper, and other novel ways of organizing the school and combining various forms of instruction to meet differentiated learning needs of pupils.

The modern school system is an intricate network of varied activities and services carried on by personnel who assume a variety of responsibilities for the teaching-learning process. Teachers are aware that the organizational achievement is more than the sum of their individual efforts. Their satisfaction must be derived from the knowledge that their individual and collective efforts have contributed both to the formulation and to the achievement of the school's goals. Teachers who gain these satisfactions feel an identification with the organization, its purposes, and its methods of achieving these purposes.

THE TEACHER'S POSITION IN THE HIERARCHY

Teachers and administrators should strive to understand the working relationship among those who have responsibility for the day-by-day operation of the school. One method of accomplishing this purpose is to supply school personnel with a handbook of policies, regulations, job specifications, and diagrams showing working relationships thought to be instrumental in achieving the goals of the school. Organization charts shown in such handbooks describe line and staff organizations which illustrate the functional relationship between citizens of the community, the board of education, the superintendent of schools and the central office staff, the principals, the teachers, and the pupils.

A very careful explanation of such a chart should contribute to the teachers' understanding of their places in the total organization. The diagram shows that the teachers are members of the organization. It suggests, too, that the teachers are responsible *to* the principal and *for* the pupils. It identifies a line of authority. It indicates that there is a functional relationship between certain staff and line personnel. All of the variations in the understandings and the misunderstandings of the faculty concerning the administration of a school cannot be diagrammed, however. Administrative organization will actually be understood only when it becomes a legitimate subject for study by the faculty.

An administrative problem of particular concern to teachers involves the hierarchical levels on which personnel are classified. Some administrators fear that teacher participation in decision-making jeopardizes the exercise of their authority. Teachers, on the other hand, accuse administrators of being too authoritarian. Is there a master-servant relationship that must be maintained? Does the administrator have more or less authority than the teacher? What is the source of authority? Does authority flow down from the top through the administrative line? Or could it flow in the opposite direction also ?

These are difficult questions to answer, and the administrator who attempts to be democratic by including the faculty and other reference groups in decision-making often becomes discouraged when he finds that he must accept responsibility for a decision with which he does not agree. The obvious consequence is that, losing faith in broad participation in the making of decisions, he resorts to the more comfortable autocratic procedure which he previously abandoned. With this reversal of action the teachers see the administrator becoming more dictatorial and their own importance in the organization diminishing.

Cabot and Kahl, in discussing the social theory of organization, describe the problem this way:

The existence of hierarchy within an organization implies that those with lower status in the organization will not completely share the values of those with higher status. Hence, the lower-status individuals are "under-privileged" in terms of the values of those of higher status, since these latter values are mostly related to the over-all purpose of the organization.[8]

The administrator of a school system has a responsibility to see that the decisions which are made contribute to the accomplishment of the overall purpose of the organization. He may feel that teachers or any other single group of people associated with the school are not in a position to see this total purpose. He may think that their participation in decision-making reflects the bias that results from the limited perspective with which they view the problem.

On the other hand, teachers who would like to participate in making important decisions about school practices must find a way to gain the

[8] Hugh Cabot and Joseph A. Kahl, *Human Relations* (Cambridge: Harvard University Press, 1953), Vol. I, p. 232.

perspective of other groups which have a stake in the decisions that are made. The opportunity to make decisions also carries with it the responsibility for them. Neither teachers nor administrators have found a satisfactory means for sharing the responsibility for many decisions which they have made together. It must be remembered that even though an administrative procedure has been developed from faculty thinking, it is often the administrator whom the board of education and the people of the community hold responsible for the decision.

While we would not argue that the administrator's judgment and wisdom are necessarily any better than the judgment and wisdom of his teachers, the administrator does occupy a position that requires him to look at problems in terms of the interests of all groups affected by the school—the pupils, the citizens of the local community, the teachers and other school employees, the board of education, the state, the schools and education at large, and the total profession. This is what makes the participation of special-interest groups so very difficult. If administrators have been wary of teacher participation in the past, it may have been largely because they had not yet found a satisfactory means by which teachers could perceive the total problem without spending so much of their time on it that their effectiveness in the classroom was jeopardized.

The problem with which we are faced is one of reducing the master-servant feeling while at the same time maintaining such an organizational arrangement as permits an efficient system of decision-making, respected by all for its fair treatment of everyone's interests. The method of solving the problem has been to increase the amount of participation of those groups concerned. The solution has not been easy. Parsey and Chase, reporting on studies of teacher participation, comment, "Some people talk as if it were easy for all teachers in the system to share in the making of all kinds of policies. Yet, even the best school systems have had only partial success in enabling teachers to take an active part in educational planning." [9]

The modern concept of administration rejects the idea that the administrator is "the boss" who makes decisions for the group, and it will not condone the paternalistic attitude of the administrator who, through his kindly and fatherly wisdom and maturity, makes decisions for the welfare of the group. But this modern viewpoint rejects also the notion that the administrator simply leaves decisions up to the group. It espouses a participative structure that recognizes the administrator as the person who, through his leadership or by the authority granted him by the group, leads his teachers toward the achievement of a goal that has come to be accepted as desirable. The realization of such a concept will be achieved neither by teacher demand

[9] John M. Parsey and Francis S. Chase, "The Teacher and Policy Making," *The Administrator's Notebook,* 1 (May 1952), 1.

nor by administrative compromise. Both teachers and administrators need to work at the problem together. A little success from small beginnings will open the door to new ventures in co-operative decision-making.

THE TEACHER AND ADMINISTRATIVE AUTHORITY

A second factor that has in many instances served as a serious deterrent to good working relationships among teachers and administrators has been confusion concerning the nature and the extent of the authority of the administrator. Here again, although there is considerable precedent upon which we may draw in arriving at a satisfactory understanding, teachers and administrators within a given school system need to arrive at their own understandings of how and where authority is to operate in the organization that has been built to accomplish their purposes.

Actually, there may be a number of sources of authority. Certainly the state, charged with the responsibility for the public school system, has powers that are vested in it by the authority of law. The community has certain authority which it exercises through local option. The teachers have authority in their own classrooms. Much of this kind of authority is legal in character. It can be tested in the courts. It can be described by a chain of relationships leading from the state, through the local school organization, to the pupil.

The state has delegated certain of its powers to the board of education of the local school district. This delegation of powers gives the board the authority to exercise these powers. The citizens of the school district by vote and moral support add to the authority of the local school board. In turn, an administrative organization is developed to execute those functions of the board which deal with school operation. The administrator of the school is charged with responsibility for the effective operation of this organization to accomplish the purposes for which the school exists. Administrators differ in the manner in which they carry out this responsibility. Those who abuse their authority in discharging their responsibilities are misusing the powers of their office.

There is another kind of authority that must be recognized if the school is to accomplish its purposes. This is the authority derived from the philosophy and science of education. It emanates from the theory of how children learn and from the values that people hold for education. This source of authority, while alluded to in the professional literature and in our professional associations, has not been given consideration equal to that of legal authority in designing administrative organization. In reality, this source of authority cannot be used effectively in determining organizational structure unless the teachers play an active role both in the accumulation of new knowledge about education and in the assessment of values which people hold for education. The teachers have very real responsibility for the interpretation of the implications of this knowledge and these values for organizational structure. By virtue of their knowledge and competency, teachers have a right to some degree of authority in the administration of schools. However, the teaching profession seems to have encountered a major problem in getting their right to authority recognized and legitimatized in the legal-traditional channels of the American educational system. The existence of this "problem" may explain, in part, the trend toward increased formal professional organization of teachers into teachers' unions or associations.

Many attempts have been made to picture a type of organization built out of a consideration of these two kinds of authority. The object of such a representation is to show that important considerations flow in both directions along the line—from the bottom to the top as well as from the top down. As one administrator has so aptly stated, "Authority bubbles up as well as trickles down." The two-way flow of authority in the line concept of administration may be pictured as follows:

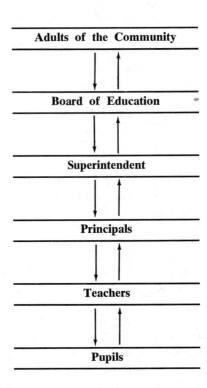

| Adults of the Community |
| Board of Education |
| Superintendent |
| Principals |
| Teachers |
| Pupils |

In deciding matters of some consequence to the school, the administrator, before exercising the authority vested in him by the board of education, usually seeks the counsel of those who are most directly affected by the decision. Often he asks that a study be made by professional people whose competence in such matters can be respected. The administrator's recommendation to the board of education is based upon this study. Most school systems, for example, accept the judgment of teachers as the most authoritative source of information on the selection of textbooks and other instructional materials. For all practical purposes the teachers make the decision, even though their decision must be acted upon by the board of education.

This means, then, that the functions of the participants in the organization are established on a rational basis, giving due consideration to the kinds of influences that have a bearing on these functions. The effective educational administrator knows that the organization succeeds insofar as there is mutual acceptance of these functions and the relationships that are established and maintained between the participants who must carry out these functions. This mutual understanding and acceptance of the working arrangement that is to exist is what we have chosen to call *organizational authority*. It is that type of authority which Dubin says is "based on rational grounds." [10]

According to this concept, it is conceivable that an administrator may make decisions for the organization because it makes sense for him to do so, rather than because he has traditionally been given the power to do so, or because he possesses an unusual or superior wisdom. He simply occupies a position where, if he is competent, the purposes of the organization are best achieved this way. The rules established for the operation of the organization determine the authority structure. The administrator derives his authority from them. It is from this same set of rules that the teacher, too, obtains organizational authority, and thus group approval, to carry on those functions assigned to him. We hope, of course, that a process of interaction can be established whereby the mutuality of understanding of the organizational structure is maintained among the administrators and the reference groups who have a stake in the educational enterprise.

THE TEACHER'S PART IN DECISION-MAKING

Teachers do not want to participate in all decisions that administrators need to make; in fact, they chafe at some of the decision-making in which

---

[10] Robert Dubin, ed., *Human Relations in Administration* (Englewood Cliffs, N.J.: Prentice-Hall, Inc., 1951), pp. 196–97.

they are asked to take part. Sometimes their reluctance is justified, because the decisions are of so little consequence that the time used on them is an utter waste of human resources. Faculty meetings often deal with routine matters that were previously settled and are being announced in a group meeting. Such administrative behavior is not conducive to further staff participation. On the other hand, administrators have a justifiable criticism of teachers who are unwilling to spend the time or accept the responsibility for shared decisions. Since in the great majority of our schools both administrators and teachers have to learn how to share in decision-making, it seems appropriate at this time to discuss those areas in which teacher participation has the most promise of success.

DETERMINING GOALS AND OBJECTIVES

While cultural values and the community's interpretation of the implications of these values have much to do with the determination of goals and objectives to be achieved by the schools, the teacher feels that he has a stake in this important decision-making process. Certainly there is no group in the school community that has had more opportunity than the professional staff to study the role of the school in American society. If we accept the proposition that the professional knowledge of the staff is essential to intelligent decision-making in this area, we have established a very important responsibility for the teachers in the school. According to this proposition, the teachers of the school, because of their insight into the educational alternatives open and the implications of each alternative for society, should take positions of leadership in helping the citizens determine the kind of educational program which they can actively support.

It is a mistake for the administrator, either superintendent or principal, to assume that he can obtain an effective community understanding of the purposes of the schools by "going it alone." Kimbrough's work on the power structure of communities provides ample evidence to support the position that lay leadership is effective in influencing people's decisions about school and other important matters.[11] Pierce and his colleagues, in reporting upon studies conducted in the southern states, point out the need for understanding the leadership patterns and forces of the community as a basis for bringing about changes in education.[12] The research of the Ohio Center for the Co-operative Program in Educational Administration suggests that there are nine critical areas of administrative behavior. They

[11] Ralph B. Kimbrough, *Political Power and Educational Decision-Making* (Chicago: Rand McNally & Company, 1964).

[12] Truman M. Pierce, *et al.*, *Community Leadership for Public Education* (Englewood Cliffs, N.J.: Prentice-Hall, Inc., 1955).

are (1) setting goals, (2) making policy, (3) determining roles, (4) appraising effectiveness, (5) co-ordinating administrative functions and structure, (6) working with community leadership to promote improvement in education, (7) using the educational resources of the community, (8) involving people, and (9) communicating. One implication of the research is that the quality of administrative behavior in these areas depends not only upon the role played by the administrator but also by the reference groups with whom he works.[13] *How* decisions are made seems to be just as important as a determiner of group action as *what* decisions are made. For purposes of this discussion, then, the people involved in determining goals and the way goals are set are crucial factors in bringing about their achievement. A mutual understanding of goals derived by faculty and citizen co-operation is urged as the really effective means by which community support for the school is derived and maintained.

POLICY-MAKING

As suggested above, another kind of decision-making in which teachers can participate effectively is in the area of policy-making at both the school building and the system levels. The National Education Association was so convinced of this that in 1958 it distributed widely among its membership a folder designed and produced by its Committee on Tenure and Academic Freedom to assist schools in developing adequate personnel policies.[14] While the booklet provides specific assistance in the development of policy in one branch of administration only, the attitude of the Commission on who should participate in policy-making is that policies should be made by those who will be expected to live and work according to them.[15] This principle has been accepted not only by observers of human relations among

---

[13] John A. Ramseyer, *et. al.*, *Factors Affecting Educational Administration*, SCDS Monograph No. 2 (Columbus, Ohio: The Ohio State University, 1955). See also the following doctoral dissertations designed to test hypotheses suggested in the above publications:

Dean Clark, "Critical Areas in the Administrative Behavior of High School Principals" (unpublished doctoral dissertation, The Ohio State University, 1956).

John E. Hartzler, "Critical Areas of Administrative Behavior of City School Superintendents" (unpublished doctoral dissertation, The Ohio State University, 1956).

Odean L. Hess, "Critical Areas of Administrative Behavior of Elementary School Principals" (unpublished doctoral dissertation, The Ohio State University, 1955).

David S. Rosenberger, "Critical Areas of Administrative Behavior of Local School Executives" (unpublished doctoral dissertation, The Ohio State University, 1956).

[14] Committee on Tenure and Academic Freedom, *Developing Personnel Policies* (Washington, D.C.: N.E.A., 1958).

[15] *Ibid.,* Section 1.

public school employees, but also by those who have studied the problems of human relations in business and industry as well.

A policy statement is a working agreement. Once understood and accepted, it clarifies the manner in which school employees, the board of education, the administrators, the pupils, and the citizens of the community relate themselves to each other to meet the goals and objectives to which they have subscribed. The problem in the incident related in Chapter 1, entitled "Jimmy Is Promoted," centers in the school. It appears from the facts presented that the policy in operation, which as a written policy had the official approval of the board of education, had, in part, been formulated by personnel who had left the school. Even the superintendent of schools was not fully committed to the policy and thus supported it halfheartedly. Making, maintaining, and improving policy are parts of a continuous process. Staff changes, changes in point of view, and the assessment of the effectiveness of certain policies are factors that constantly affect policy.

Teachers are interested not only in those policies which affect teacher personnel practices, but they have much to do—and, hence, to say—about daily school procedures relating to marks, promotion, reporting to parents, attendance, the punctuality of pupils, discipline, grade placement of pupils, use and distribution of resources, selection of textbooks, standards of achievement, and many other school operations. However, some administrators and teachers act as if they must actively participate in each of the myriad *decisions* that must be made about matters of every kind in the course of a school year even if the matters do not directly concern them. How much better it is to arrive at *policy* agreements, which give to the individuals most directly concerned the *authority of the organization* to act without having to get a decision from an entire staff each time an action becomes necessary.

APPRAISING THE EDUCATIONAL PROGRAM

Much of the responsibility for achieving the objectives of the school rests with the teachers. Both their individual efforts as classroom teachers and the total organizational effort to which they contribute are important factors in the school's achievement. Hence the school cannot really take stock of its efforts without involving its teachers. But what are the measures of a good school program? How should these measures be applied and by whom?

The critics who decry the ineffectiveness of our schools on the basis that our young people have not mastered the 3 R's suggest one criterion for appraisal. Those who think that the schools should prepare youth to meet successfully the highly competitive challenges of industrialized society suggest more emphasis on a program designed to meet the needs of the gifted child. Some people are concerned about the youth who leave school earlier than is normal. Does a high drop-out rate in a school suggest that the program is not meeting the needs of students? What are the students' needs, and what are the needs of society that the schools must try to meet? These and other questions that could be raised relate to the objectives of the school. Even these are difficult to answer. A school has established some basis for an appraisal program when it has answered for itself these and similar questions that have been at issue in the district in which it operates. The co-operation of the teachers is essential in creating such understanding in the community.

Measurement of the effectiveness of the school in achieving these objectives is still a problem. Available measuring instruments are crude. If their limitations are recognized, however, they can serve a useful purpose. It is not the measure of the pupils' achievement that causes the great difficulty. Crude as the instruments may be, they do provide us with meaningful information concerning the pupils' growth. However, once we know that pupils are or are not achieving, how do we detect the positive and negative influences of the school? Can these be traced to the influences of poor, average, or superior teachers?

PROVIDING FOR IN-SERVICE EDUCATION

The need for the professional improvement of school personnel is practically taken for granted as an essential part of a staff personnel program. The rapidly increasing school enrollment; the increase in the numbers of teachers needed; the rapid turnover of school personnel; the large number of temporarily certificated teachers; the new knowledge that is accumulating concerning the learning process, human relations, and administrative behavior; and the rapidly changing industrial, political, and social character of our society amply prove that acquiring the knowledge necessary to become and continue to be a good teacher or educational leader is a lifetime endeavor. The four- and five-year teacher education programs do not adequately prepare prospective teachers for their careers. All that can be claimed for them is that they provide the prospective teacher with the basic knowledge and skill which he must use to continue to develop his competence throughout his career. Part of the continuance takes place in graduate programs of education. Much of it is done through in-service education.

In those schools where in-service education programs are proving to be successful, teachers participate in planning, organizing, and evaluating them. Programs planned for the teachers solely by the administrators are doomed to failure before they begin. Teachers as well as administrators must be in on the process of growing. An adequate program provides growth opportunities for both.

The American Association of School Administrators and the National Society for the Study of Education thought this subject so timely that they devoted their 1957 yearbooks to an extensive treatment of it.[16, 17] Both publications stress the importance of the involvement of personnel affected at all stages in the program from planning to evaluation. Both recognize the importance of the status leader in creating an appropriate climate for growth. Together they give credence to the concept that in a growth situation, leadership from within the group emerges, and that when this happens the opportunity for shared responsibility is enhanced. Parker, writing in the NSSE Yearbook, discusses twelve guidelines that he recommends for in-service education programs. They are listed here to reflect the nature of thinking of the writers of this yearbook concerning the participative structure that should characterize in-service education of school personnel:

1. People work as individuals and as members of groups on problems that are significant to them.

2. The same people who work on problems formulate goals and plan how they will work.

3. Many opportunities are developed for people to relate themselves to each other.

4. Continuous attention is given to individual and to group problem-solving processes.

5. Atmosphere is created that is conducive to building mutual respect, support, permissiveness, and creativeness.

6. Multiple and rich resources are made available and are used.

7. The simplest possible means are developed to move through decisions to actions.

8. Constant encouragement is present to test and to try new ideas and plans in real situations.

9. Appraisal is made an integral part of in-service activities.

10. Continuous attention is given to the interrelationship of different groups.

---

[16] American Association of School Administrators, *The Superintendent as Instructional Leader* (Washington: AASA, 1957).

[17] National Society for the Study of Education, *In-Service Education,* Part I (Chicago: University of Chicago Press, 1957).

11. The facts of individual differences among members of each group are accepted and utilized.

12. Activities are related to pertinent aspects of the current educational, cultural, political, and economic scene.[18]

CHANGING THE CURRICULUM

The dynamics of curriculum change have been suggested in the previous discussion of teacher responsibility in decision-making. If teachers participate in the determination of goals and objectives, policy-making, the appraisal of effectiveness, and in-service growth activities, they have gone a long way toward curriculum planning and change. The important principle to keep in mind here is that curriculum change is dependent upon the changes that take place in people. For purposes of this discussion, the changes in teachers' beliefs about the role of education in our society, their understandings about how learning takes place, their interpretations of the needs of children and youth, their interpretation of the impact which the demands of society should make upon the program, their increased knowledge about the world in which we live, and their development of skills in working with pupils, parents, and others who have an effect upon learning are some of the factors that change the learning activities provided and the way teachers relate themselves to the teaching-learning process.

Change, however, must be of two kinds—change in individual staff members and institutional change. The teachers' changing conceptions of what and how to teach must add up to orderly program changes. Some program decisions must be made for the school, the school district of which each school is a part, and for the state. The suggestion made here is that program changes for the total institution emanate from changes in individuals, largely changes in the understandings of teachers; but some effort needs to be made to group these changes in meaningful and related learning experiences for pupils. Leadership and co-ordination on the part of administrators should provide not only the climate for change to occur, but the procedures by which changes in individuals can add up to system-wide or institutional changes.

In discussing the theory of institutional change, Coffey and Golden take the position that

. . . the central problem of institutional change is the development of those conditions in which institutional goals and means can be reassessed for the purpose not only of adapting to change going on within the social system but also of assuming responsibility for exerting influence on the various alternatives of change which may be open to the society.[19]

[18] J. Cecil Parker, "Guidelines for In-Service Education," *ibid.*, pp. 103–28.

[19] Hubert S. Coffey and William P. Golden, Jr., "Psychology of Change within an Institution," *ibid.*, pp. 67–102.

What the teacher wants to accomplish through his participation in decision-making is to exert an influence on the educational program. He is not satisfied with his own individual growth nor the improvements that he makes in his own teaching. He wants to have a part in molding the educational program. This is his *professional* stake in the business of education. The teacher's competence as a professional educator, as contrasted to that of a skilled craftsman, comes to fruition when this competence is used to make improvements in what is being taught, in the services the schools render, in the size of classes, the grouping of pupils, the instructional materials to be used, the classroom environment and the resources to be used in teaching, and in the nature of the agreements among the schools within the system on these and related matters.

Teachers and administrators must keep in mind that the major purpose of this participation is not merely the maintenance of good morale, however necessary that may be. Staff participation in decision-making must be justified not merely because of what it does for teachers, but because experience and research show it to be the most effective means available to accomplish the purposes for which the schools are organized. The challenge for the administrators is to get and maintain the kinds of participation discussed here among an increasing number of teachers in the kind of organization that leads to accomplishments mutually satisfying to school personnel and their clients—the children and the adults of the community. The challenge to teachers is to keep the objectives of the school foremost, to improve their own teaching, and to build those team relationships which enhance the effectiveness of the organization of which they are a part.

Planned Staff Participation

Effective staff participation does not just happen. It must be nurtured. The assumption that there is a democratic working relationship when each employee is permitted to go his own way has led not only to individual stagnation but to lack of organizational achievement as well. Fortunately, studies of teacher participation indicate that both teachers and administrators desire an organizational pattern in which there is some structure to guide their behavior. The most effective teacher-administrator relationship, from the standpoint of both morale and productivity, is a participative one. That is, a condition must exist whereby both administrators and teachers call upon each other to define the structure that increases their productivity in achieving the ends desired by their organization, the school. Teachers need to know that, with the help of their administrative leaders, they are working on vital educational matters. They need to know that when they give time, energy, and interest to the consideration of crucial matters, their ideas or proposals for action make a difference to those who have the power to make final decisions.

In developing an organizational structure which optimizes staff participation in decision-making, the administrator must remember that his purpose is not one of concession to others. The school is operated to educate effectively its children and youth. The wise administrator knows that he must capitalize on the creativity of all his staff members in building a structure that places a premium upon the co-operative effort required to do this job. In other words, the co-operative method is better than any other yet devised.

BUILDING SOUND PERSONNEL POLICY

The interests of staff members in personnel policy are broad and varied. Sometimes they are criticized because their interests in what appear to be matters of their personal welfare overshadow their concern for the solution of other professional problems. Those who are active in programs for the welfare improvement of staff personnel take the position, however, that this is an integral part of a broad program of professional improvement. In other words, sound personnel policies form a foundation upon which to build sound programs for professional advancement.

Personnel policy statements with which we are familiar include such topics as these:

1. Absence
2. Assignments and transfers
3. Benefits and services
4. Contractual status
5. Discharge
6. Suspension
7. Employee–group relationship
8. Ethics
9. Evaluation
10. Exchange teaching
11. Extra duties and compensation
12. Grievances
13. Health and safety
14. In-service growth
15. Leave of absence
16. Official communications
17. Orientation
18. Outside employment
19. Overtime
20. Pay procedures
21. Probation
22. Professional meetings
23. Promotions and demotions
24. Re-employment
25. Resignations
26. Responsibilities
27. Definition of positions
28. Retirement
29. Salary schedules
30. Selection
31. Seniority
32. Sick leave
33. Substitute teachers
34. Vacations
35. Workmen's compensation
36. Work schedules, daily and yearly

Any complete textbook on staff personnel gives an even more comprehensive list of personnel concerns with which the school administrator must deal. His problem is to provide leadership in determining who should make what decisions. It is generally agreed that to develop satisfactory personnel policies for a school system, it is necessary to involve those who are affected by such policies. We know, also, that all school employees respect the fact that their welfare is conditioned by organizational agreements other than their own personal interests. Studies of teacher participation have shown that teachers differ widely in their opinions about the degree to which they should participate in decisions concerning themselves and those who are soon to join their ranks. For example, not all of them are agreed that they should participate in the actual selection of new teachers, in promotions, or in the evaluation of the effectiveness of their colleagues. On the other hand, a great many teachers do have definite opinions concerning the criteria to be used for their selection, promotion, and evaluation.

In some schools, teachers are ready to assist in the formulation of procedures to be applied in carrying out a given policy. In most school systems teachers insist on having some voice in the determination of salary schedules, teaching assignments, work schedules, and benefits to be derived in the form of compensation for extra duties and extra preparation for teaching. Some schools are finding teachers willing to consider salary schedules based upon a rating of teaching effectiveness.

Throughout the country, perhaps the greatest weakness that has been recognized in attempts to solve staff personnel problems is that, for too long a time, administrators and staff members have not been thinking together. Books have been written for school administrators telling them what they should do in the area of staff personnel. Teachers and other employees have been meeting in their local associations and unions to do their own thinking about these problems. Co-operative action does not result when two groups who have been thinking separately begin to make demands upon each other. Under these conditions, each group may yield certain concessions to the other, but the working relationship that results from such behavior seldom leads to co-operation.

Prospective administrators would do well, therefore, to be alert to the personnel concerns of their employees and prepare to assume the leadership for a co-operative solution of such problems. The thinking of all groups involved should certainly be included in policy decisions. In many schools decisions about the procedures to be used to implement policy can be shared with a high level of satisfaction to all concerned. The results from the experience of thinking together on the policy level furnish a reliable basis for ascertaining what further co-operation is necessary or desirable. One principle of action that may be followed with reliability is that as long as there is a breach between administrators and other personnel on policy governing staff welfare, there is further work to be done.

PATTERNS OF STAFF PARTICIPATION

Various attempts have been made to involve the staff of the school in decision-making. Not all of them are successful; examples of unsuccessful faculty meetings are legion. Yet we suspect that the faculty meeting called by the superintendent of the district or by the principal of the building is the only formal means by which many teachers have an opportunity to participate, even passively, in matters pertaining to the entire school. Often these meetings are nonparticipative; their agenda are not planned with the purpose of engaging the faculty in a consideration of matters that make a difference in the operation of the school. The following organizational patterns, which have been tried for the purpose of improving instruction, show promise for improvement in other aspects of the school also.

Central Office Planned Participation

Some school systems, in an effort to improve the education of children and youth, have greatly enlarged their central office staff to include personnel to plan teacher involvement, particularly in the area of improvement of instruction. With the increasingly large numbers of temporarily certificated teachers and the mobility of teachers from one school system to another, the need for acquainting them with procedures employed in the local system has been greatly emphasized. Conferences and workshops are planned to assist in instructional improvement. Orientation programs are planned to acquaint new teachers with the local school program. Committees of teachers assist in selecting textbooks, in planning courses of study for each of the several grade levels, and in solving a number of problems which are defined by the central office personnel.

This pattern of organization is based on the belief that improvement programs should be determined, planned, initiated, and carried out by central office personnel who call upon the teachers for assistance and advice. Often it is a program organized *for* the teachers rather than *by* the teachers.

It has the advantage of being easily controlled. Originating in the central office, it can be as narrow or as broad in scope as the central staff wishes. Plans can be put into operation quickly. New techniques or methods to be employed can be defined by relatively few people and brought to the attention of teachers by direct communication from the central office. There can be little question about the fact that recommendations have the support of the administration and therefore carry the weight of administrative authority. Its greatest advantage is that it focuses upon the problems of the entire school system rather than upon those which seem important in a particular school only or to a few individuals.

In recent years, schools that operate in this pattern of organization have greatly broadened their opportunity for teacher participation. Many teachers become involved in getting the work done. Often a wide range of resources is used in meaningful ways to solve school problems. Curriculum leaders, special supervisors, and special service personnel have been added to the central office staff to assist teachers in improving learning.

In some situations, however, participation planned and conducted by central office people does not accomplish its purpose. Teachers participate, but fail to identify themselves with the problems on which they are working. There is no real involvement, because teachers are called upon to work on problems that were originally identified not by them but by their superiors. No matter how sincere administrators may be in wanting to serve the school's purpose through such an organizational pattern, those who fail in its application do so largely because they have not succeeded in imbuing the entire staff with their own faith in the co-operative process.

School-building Autonomy in Planning

In contrast to this highly centralized system, some school administrators and educational theorists have advocated great decentralization in programs for school improvement. Under such a system, the building principal becomes the administrator who is charged with the responsibility of giving leadership to the improvement of the educational program in his building.

The effectiveness of this plan depends to a great extent upon the ability of the individual principals to work with their teachers. Some principals are prepared neither to institute an improvement program of their own design nor to involve their teachers in building a co-operative plan for improvement. But where principals are capable of good leadership, effective results are obtained from improvement programs in individual buildings.[20]

It is obvious that one of the purposes to be achieved by the administrator's decision to use a decentralized plan of attack on the problems of the school system is to obtain greater involvement of school personnel. Hence, the principal who is autocratic in his dealings with faculty, or who is inept in teacher involvement, defeats the plan at its inception.

An advantage of the decentralized system is that the focus is upon the work to be done at the place where the need is felt most keenly. If the teachers are given an opportunity to define the problems of the school, and if the principal is authorized to take action upon the recommendations that they make for solving these problems, much can be accomplished. Thus, school programs can be adjusted to the particular needs of the

[20] David H. Jenkins and Charles A. Blackman, *Antecedents and Effects of Administrator Behavior,* SCDS Monograph No. 3 (Columbus, Ohio: The Ohio State University, 1956).

residential area which the school serves. Often such an adjustment causes no system-wide problem. On the other hand, where the instructional problem is complex, where services in the several schools of the district differ, or where practices in dealing with the public vary from school to school, questions may be raised concerning the equality of the educational opportunity afforded by the several schools.

The flexibility of decentralized planning lends itself to adaptation to the needs of particular schools. The planning and the program for improvement, however, may be as different as the several staffs who engage in it. Without some leadership from the central office, there is no guarantee that individual schools within a school district will continue to improve simply upon the initiative of the local staff. It is important to raise the question of how much and what kind of flexibility or uniformity is necessary in a school system to provide equal educational opportunity.

Central Office Co-ordinated Planning

This plan incorporates certain features of both the centralized and decentralized plans described above. Both the faculty of each building and the personnel of the central office are involved in the planning. Ideas for improvement originate with the teacher, the principals, and the central office personnel. (Sometimes this includes pupils, parents, and other community representatives, also. It is not implied that these groups are unimportant; since this chapter deals with teacher participation, these groups are omitted.) By a system of representation from each of the several groups involved, a co-ordinating council is organized. This body receives ideas, sorts them in terms of urgency or need, establishes its best judgment concerning the wishes of the people whom it represents, and finally emerges with recommendations for administrative action.

After receiving administrative approval, the plan of action is generally executed through the usual line and staff organization. To the extent that the plan involves individual buildings, the principals are called upon for leadership. Teacher representatives who have been active on the co-ordinating council furnish excellent assistance. However, the major interest of teachers is that their ideas get to the administration and that they have some voice in determining what should be done about them. They are not vitally concerned that they have an active role in executing these ideas. If, on the other hand, the administration fails to take any action, the co-ordinating council reports this matter to its group members, who may decide to use the force of their numbers to apply pressure on the administration. The employment of the centrally co-ordinated plan of participation implies that the chief administrator believes in action and that this action is most effective when it grows out of the intelligent thinking of the groups who are affected by it.

One school system that has been using central office co-ordination with real success began by asking the teachers, the officers of the Parent-Teachers Association, and the members of the board of education to list the major needs of the school. The superintendent of schools enlisted the co-operation of each of the building principals in securing the initial list of these needs which, incidentally, contained more than 500 items. A temporary committee consisting of three teachers, a principal, a P.T.A. officer, and a representative of the central office staff sorted the items and ranked them according to the frequency with which each was mentioned. The committee also suggested a classification of items which made possible the grouping of related problems.

The next step taken by the committee was to check this classification and ranking of items with all of the groups that had participated in preparing the original list. With this portion of the work approved, the committee then suggested immediate action for certain improvements which the responses to the check list showed to be the most urgent. This suggestion was accepted by the superintendent of schools. From his study of the list of needs, the superintendent discovered several problems that he believed could be solved almost immediately with a minimum of study, time, materials, and expense. He informed the members of the committee that he was ready to act on these matters. He further instructed them to devise a plan for studying some of the more intricate problems to which the teachers, parents, and board members had given a high priority.

This administrative act proved to be a great morale builder for the teachers. In fact, a number of teachers who had expressed a lack of enthusiasm for the project originally were pleasantly surprised to find that the administrator meant business. This was not a "talking game," an expression they used to describe previous in-service and improvement projects.

In the course of the two years during which this project was observed, it was not possible to make changes as rapidly as some people would have liked. What was evident, however, was that during this brief period there was a growing confidence in the leadership of the superintendent of schools; the co-ordinating council (an outgrowth of the temporary committee that acted in this capacity) had gained in status; and the morale and productivity of the teachers had steadily improved. Many of the little annoyances—such as leaking faucets in the rest rooms, failure of janitors to sweep adequately, and torn window shades—were quickly corrected. Program changes came more slowly. Differences in points of view among teachers concerning standards of achievement at the several grade levels were still apparent, but one observable accomplishment was that even the teachers agreed that there was no simple answer to this problem. Teachers found that they could discuss the matter calmly as a problem to be solved rather than in terms of emotionally charged biases. Furthermore, after two years of co-operative effort, the staff showed a readiness to agree that many of the most important problems which they listed required intensive study before action should be taken. Many of these problems have become subjects for study by faculty and community groups, to whom resource persons from neighboring schools and universities have been found to be of great assistance.

In a discussion with the members of the co-ordinating council, at least two principles of action emerged as being of real importance for administration. They are (1) that teachers (and representatives of all participating groups) must believe that their ideas are wanted by the administrator and that their ideas will have an effect upon the actions that the administrator recommends, sanctions, or makes himself; and (2) that some action on matters of prime importance to teachers should be initiated by the administrator and vigorously supported on the basis of the evidence available. The members of this particular co-ordinating council did not feel that the administrator needed to be always in agreement with his teachers. It was their judgment, however, that if an administrator fails to approve a group decision or if he recommends an action contrary to that approved by the group, he should report the same and give his reasons.

No generalizations concerning the relative merits of these three patterns of organization can be drawn from one incident. It merely illustrates that teacher participation can be meaningful or not according to the insight and skill of the administrator. There is no gainsaying the fact that teachers need to grow, that they learn by doing just as surely as do the children, and that helping to solve the problems of the school is probably more meaningful to them than many simulated growing experiences that are created for them.

COLLECTIVE ACTION BY TEACHERS

Teacher participation in policy development has, in the past, resulted from the board of education's voluntary cooperation with the teachers involved. Behind this action has been the belief that those who would be affected by changes of policy should, after all, have some voice in these changes. However, since boards of education have had the legal right to control their relationships with teachers, it cannot be said that these relationships were fully bilateral.

Now, as the result of many complicated, frequently misunderstood, and interrelated forces, American teachers are requesting, or even demanding, the right to play a stronger role in the formulation of educational policy. The *New York Times* of January 16, 1964, said:

A resurgence of militancy among the nation's public school teachers marked the year of 1963. There was mounting evidence that teachers are no longer content to rule only in the classroom to which they are assigned. They want a hand in the assignment and a voice in the policy that controls their professional lives. They are not asking to run the schools, but they want their views heard and heeded.

This new militancy has continued to mount. Numerous school districts have held elections among teachers to determine who would be the exclusive representative for negotiating with the board of education. In addition to such elections, there have been strikes, boycotts, or sanctions in several cities and in two states—Utah and Oklahoma.

In Utah, where the Utah Education Association imposed a form of professional sanction against all the public schools of the state, the teachers of the UEA voted 7,785 to 189 to interrupt all contract negotiations for the 1963–64 school year "until the present financial impasse has been satisfactorily resolved." [21] In their report of an investigation[22] of the Utah situation the National Commission on Professional Rights and Responsibilities of the NEA found, in part, that:

1. Very little evidence was presented to show an increase in classrooms, instructors, supervisors, administrators, services, supplies, and equipment which was proportional to the increase in the total number of pupils in the 20 Utah school districts which were studied.

2. One of the weakest areas of the school program in Utah was that of special educational programs for exceptional children.

3. In the schools studied, 53 percent of the elementary classes had 30 or more pupils in them. Less than one-third of the classes in the high schools were of a satisfactory size for the most effective instruction.

4. The beginning pay for many custodians was higher than the beginning pay for teachers.

5. The tardiness and reluctance with which the state and the school districts had proceeded with necessary improvements in buildings, grounds, and equipment for the schools has had a damaging effect on the educational program.

6. The quality of the educational program in Utah is threatened by many inadequacies. At the elementary level, it is threatened by large classes, lack of special services, and inadequate equipment. Together with insufficient supervision at the high school level, it is threatened by a narrow curriculum offering, inadequate vocational opportunities, and insufficient counseling, library, and other special services.

[21] National Commission on Professional Rights and Responsibilities, *Utah: A State-wide Study of School Conditions* (Washington: The NEA, March 1964), p. 9.

[22] *Ibid.*

7. Teacher salary levels in Utah are not yet adequate to meet prevailing costs of living, nor do they offer sufficient compensation for the increasingly high degree of training and ability required of today's teachers.

State-wide sanctions were applied in Oklahoma by the National Education Association in May 1965. In a report by the National Commission on Professional Rights and Responsibilities of the NEA, issued in February 1965, the following statement appears:

The heated meetings of Oklahoma teachers in November 1964 were not merely the result of isolated incidents or of the recent failures of referendums to improve educational conditions. They were the result of prolonged resentment of neglect of the educational welfare of children by responsible state officials and agencies and of accelerating determination by conscientious educators that the children of Oklahoma should have better educational opportunities and that the teaching profession should be given the respect and compensation commensurate with its basic importance to the well-being of American communities, states, and the nation.[23]

In another section of the report, this statement appears:

It is unfortunate that Oklahoma's teachers have not demanded improvement in school conditions earlier. The subminimal conditions in many Oklahoma schools did not suddenly develop in the fall of 1964; they have been developing steadily over a period of years.[24]

These two statements have been cited to illustrate some of the basic factors that may be responsible for the so-called increased militancy of the teaching profession. Obviously, many of the problems found in Utah and Oklahoma public education are of such magnitude that *individual* boards of education and administrators are unable to resolve them to any significant degree.

Among the problems and issues most relevant to the role of school personnel in administration is the question of teacher representation in policy formulation: who should represent teachers and what are the effects of designating a single teachers' association as the sole representative for the entire staff? Other highly visible issues include:

1. Should negotiation procedures become part of the policy of the board of education, and if so what should be the nature of these procedures?

2. What matters in the internal affairs of public education are negotiable?

[23] National Commission on Professional Rights and Responsibilities, *Oklahoma: A State-wide Study of Conditions Detrimental to an Effective Public Educational Program* (Washington: The NEA, February 1965), p. 31.

[24] *Ibid.*, p. 25.

3. What should be done if and when negotiations result in an impasse?

4. What is the role of the superintendent in board-teacher negotiation arrangements?

5. What action can and should be taken at the state level? By whom?

Unfortunately, there are no sharply defined answers to these questions; in fact, at the present time there are very few reliable guidelines for action in this area. Perhaps the best that the administrator can do is to spend time studying current conditions and tracing the factors that have led to the existence of these conditions.

At this time there is no reliable quantitative measure of the bargaining or negotiating relationships that exist between teachers' groups and school boards. But, according to Wildman, we do know that:

In many localities NEA affiliated groups as well as AFT locals conduct some manner of consultation or negotiation with school boards, sometimes incorporating agreements in written documents. Examination of such teacher-board "contracts" discloses extreme variability in terms and general coverage, with little pattern emerging. The forms taken by teacher collective action *vis-à-vis* local school administrations and boards encompass an entire range of possibilities from (1) wholly informal solicitation of teacher views, either through the administration or by the board directly to (2) an "advisory" sort of negotiation conducted by the school board, meeting with representatives of teacher groups in the system, possibly accompanied by a legally innocuous "memorandum of understanding" incorporating any agreement reached to (3) a formal relationship between a majority representative union and the board marked by "hard" bargaining in the traditional labor sense, and the execution of a complete collective bargaining agreement. Also, strong teacher organizations in many of our larger metropolitan areas can and do exert a significant degree of effective power over the school administration and board on matters concerning the employment relationship without any formal "bargaining," grievance, or consultive procedures whatsoever.[25]

Obviously, there is no longer any question regarding the right of teachers to join a formal organization for the purpose of taking collective action to engage in bargaining and/or negotiation with boards and administrations. The important question today is: What direction will this movement toward a formal system of collective action take in the future? Another question might be: What direction *should* it take for the good of American public education? There are four major organizations involved in attempting to resolve these and related questions at the national level. They are the National School Boards Association (NSBA), the American Association of School Administrators (AASA), the National Education (NEA),

[25] W. A. Wildman, "Collective Action by Public School Teachers: An Emerging Issue," *Administrator's Notebook,* Vol. XI, No. 6 (February 1963).

and the American Federation of Teachers (AFT). In a recent article, Steffensen stated that:

The Policy of the NSBA firmly opposes legislation condoning bargaining or mandating mediation with the teacher groups. The NEA and AFT, while in agreement on many important aspects of collective negotiation and on what they see as the need for such legislation, disagree upon certain points. They disagree, for example, on the role of the superintendent; they also disagree on the wisdom of affiliation with groups external to education. The AASA, representative of the "man in the middle," is naturally deeply concerned over the matter, including any possible diminution of the superintendent's role in the total area of board-staff relationships.[26]

It would appear, then, that as we move toward a formal system of collective action and representation for teachers, a resolution of some powerful organizational forces at the national, state, and local levels will be necessary. These forces will be created by actions of the four organizations mentioned above and by state legislatures, local communities, the courts, and other interest groups.

The problem of deepest concern to school administrators is defining the role of administrators, especially the superintendent, in the formal teacher-board negotiating situation. One facet of this problem involves the question of how the administration relates to that portion of the staff which is represented by, but not a member of, the association with the sole right to represent the teaching staff. Traditionally, the superintendent represented both the board of education and the teachers; but in a situation where a teachers' organization has sole representation rights, the superintendent's position becomes unclear. Who, for example, represents individual teachers or groups of teachers who do not accept, or are not satisfied with, the representation provided by the majority organization? In theory, situations such as this are not supposed to occur—all matters of concern to teachers are to be handled through duly elected, representative teachers' association channels. In practice, however, this arrangement does not often work in just this way. This is especially true when the election to determine the majority representative was hard fought and fairly close. The defeated organization (or the independent teachers) does not just give up and merge with the victorious organization.

A second facet of the formal negotiation problem is determining the role of the superintendent and other administrators in the negotiation and bargaining procedures. In his study of the Alberta, Canada, Teachers' Association, Kratzmann found that:

If highly organized bargaining situations come into being between teachers and school boards, the participation of the school superintendent in board

---

[26] James P. Steffensen, "Board-Staff Negotiations," *School Life*, Vol. 47, No. 1 (October 1964), p. 6.

decision-making may be diminished. In Alberta, where teachers and trustees alike are active at the provincial level, and where both groups have access to out-of-district agents in times of disputes, the superintendent's role has been reduced to that of providing information to both parties.[27]

Most proposals currently being made for formal arrangements between teachers' associations and boards either state or imply that the two active parties in negotiation procedures will be the teachers and their boards. Steffensen found that:

. . . both teacher organizations [AFT and NEA] call for direct face-to-face communications with the board of education. The AFT, as a proponent of collective bargaining, regards the superintendent as the employer at a negotiating session. The NEA position on professional negotiation views the superintendent in a dual role—executive officer of the board and professional leader of the professional staff.

The development of a definition which recognizes both the dual role of the superintendent and the need for direct communication with the board offers a challenge. The superintendent's role needs to be defined just as concisely and clearly for the board as it is for the teachers—and for the superintendent.[28]

We believe that, more than any other individual within a school community, the superintendent is deeply involved in decisions between the teachers and their boards. To bypass the superintendent or to make him a mere provider of information for the teachers and the board is to misuse and/or waste the talent, skill, and knowledge of the one person who is, or who should be, most aware of the needs, problems, and resources of the community, the school system, the teachers, and the pupils.

Although he does not provide the details for a solution to this problem, Wildman does provide a guideline for approaching the problem when he suggests that:

If a person of authority in an organization sees a dilution of that authority imminent as the inevitable result of a process he decides he is unable to forestall, and abdicates or is unable to gain control over responsibility for the new bargaining relationship which is threatening his prerogatives, his effectiveness and leadership potential within the organization is likely to be diminished; if, on the other hand, the administrator, despite the necessity to share through bargaining some measure of previously unilaterally exercised authority, is ultimately responsible for representing his and the organization's interests in the new relationship and plays an indispensable role within the nego-

[27] Arthur Kratzmann, "The Alberta Teachers' Association: A Prototype for the American Scene?" *Administrator's Notebook,* Vol. XII, No. 2 (October 1963), p. 4.

[28] Steffensen, *op. cit.,* p. 8.

tiating mechanism through which power is to be shared, his status and functional potential within the organization is more likely to be enhanced than eroded.[29]

NO PLAN IS A PANACEA

In developing the teamwork approach to the solution of problems in the school, the administrator must remember that no plan is a panacea. Three possible approaches have been explained very briefly to provide the administrator with suggestions upon which he may build a program suited to the needs of the school in which he has such a responsibility. Other writers have pointed out the advantages and disadvantages of each of these plans.[30] The authors of the Thirty-fifth Yearbook of the American Association of School Administrators tend to favor the central office co-ordinated plan as a means for the improvement of instruction.[31] Berge, Russell, and Walden, in a questionnaire including 145 school systems, found 83, or 57 percent, favoring this plan. Of the rest, 25 percent strongly favored the central office planning, and 18 percent preferred the decentralization of planning to building units.[32] In this study, however, participation was limited to in-service education projects.

None of the three approaches discussed in the first part of this section included suggestions on handling the changes brought about by the introduction of formal negotiation procedures into the school's organizational structure. Certainly the introduction of such procedures will create different conditions in the internal organization of school districts, although it is still too early to recognize and evaluate all of them. However, the administrator should recognize that most of the policies and practices that serve to increase staff participation in planning and administration are viable in school districts with formal provisions for staff representation as well as in those which do not have such provisions.

The implication is indeed clear that the administrator of the modern school should be more a leader of people than a manipulator of things. The accomplishment of the school's task requires a teamwork approach. Teachers and other school employees are a significant part of this team. It is essential, therefore, that an administrator be able to understand and

[29] Wesley A Wildman, "Implications of Teacher Bargaining for School Administration," *Phi Delta Kappan*, Vol. XLVI, No. 4 (December 1964).

[30] Ronald C. Doll *et al., Organizing for Curriculum Improvement* (New York: Teachers College, Columbia University, 1953).

[31] American Association of School Administrators, *op. cit.*, pp. 172–73.

[32] NSSE, *op. cit.*, p. 221.

work with his staff. The plan he will use must be built upon a profound insight into human relations and a sound set of principles of co-operative action.

Trend Toward Functional Staff Participation

There is a definite trend toward more functional staff participation in making important decisions for the school. Much of this trend is evidenced by the emergence of an organizational structure that encourages teamwork among all employees. The roles of various staff members are being defined in terms of the kinds of expertness which they can bring to bear in facilitating the teaching-learning process.

To obtain meaningful involvement of the staff, an organizational structure is needed, and staff participation must be planned. Teachers do not expect to participate in all decisions, but they believe they have a professional stake in the decisions that involve program planning and execution. Means have been found to involve central office personnel, principals, and teachers so that all groups can make meaningful contributions in crucial decision-making areas. Such practices are not universal, but the trend is definitely in this direction. The administrator should note that this trend may be leading toward a seeming paradox. According to Wildman:

. . . there may be a seeming paradox in the fact that widespread adoption of the current best thinking and practice regarding democratic or consultative administration has been accompanied by an apparent increase in the desire of teachers to organize. On this interesting subject, let me simply observe that to consult with subordinates and to encourage them, in the best of faith, to formulate opinions and judgments outside their sphere of ultimate responsibility and control, and to encourage them to voice dissatisfaction when it is felt, may lead inevitably to a desire to have some actual power over the decision making process, and may give rise to a desire for an impartial adjudication of disputes. It appears at least conceivable that in some situations democratic administration of any enterprise may actually hasten the process of organization and power accumulation. There are indications that where democratic administration is practiced, participation of subordinates is often an uncertain privilege and that unless the right is guaranteed, it tends to be withdrawn; strong desire may exist within homogeneous employee groups to convert privilege to right.[33]

Neither theory, practice, nor the opinions of staff members suggest that all staff personnel should participate in making all important decisions. The problem to be solved in educational administration, as in the admin-

[33] Wildman, *Phi Delta Kappan, op. cit.*

istration of other institutions, is to bring expertness, wherever it is to be found, to bear on the making of crucial decisions at the time and place where such decisions will be to the benefit of the greatest number of people.

SUGGESTED ACTIVITIES

1. Study the organizational structure of the school in which you work. Describe the role of teachers in this organizational pattern.
2. Visit a neighboring school system and, by observation and interview, determine the organizational structure. Draw a diagram of the administrative organization, and describe briefly how it works in making curriculum changes. Check your description with the superintendent, the principal, and a group of teachers.
3. Obtain a copy of a formal agreement between a board of education and a teachers organization. Apply the agreement to your school system, or to a system with which you are familiar. Acting under the terms of this agreement, how would the role of teachers differ from that which they now play in decision-making? What are the potential advantages and disadvantages of operating under the terms of a formal agreement with the board of education?
4. Attend a state meeting of a professional organization. Prior to your attendance set up criteria for effectiveness. After attendance write your evaluation of the meeting based on your established criteria.
5. Write a critique of the chapter on "The Faculty Meeting" in Griffiths' *Human Relations in School Administration.*
6. Examine the minutes of the board of education in your school district. List the personnel policies which you find recorded there. Add to this list the areas in which you think there is further need for policy.

SELECTED READINGS

Administrator's Notebook, "The Teacher and Policy Making" 1 (May 1952); "My Teachers Are Not Interested," 1 (November 1952); "What's Wrong with Faculty Meetings," I (December 1952); "What Are Your State Associations Accomplishing?" 3 (December 1954); "Who Should Make What Decisions?" 3 (April 1955); "Some Causes of Conflict and Tensions Among Teachers," 4 (March 1956); "What About Improving Instruction?" 5 (January 1957); "Administrative Procedure in Curriculum Revision," 5 (February 1957); "The Leadership Patterns of School Superintendents and School Principals," 6 (September 1957); "Administrative Behavior and Staff Relations," 6 (October 1957); "The Superintendent of

Schools: Officer or Employee?" 6 (November 1957); "The Process of Educational Policy Development," 7 (January 1959); "A New Concept of Staff Relations," 8 (March 1960); "Bureaucracy and Teachers' Sense of Power," 11 (November 1962); "Collective Action by Public School Teachers," 11 (February 1963); "The Alberta Teachers' Association: A Prototype for the American Scene?" 12 (October 1963); "Teacher Participation in Decision Making," 12 (May 1964).

American Association of School Administrators, *Roles, Responsibilities, Relationships of the School Board, Superintendent, and Staff.* Washington, D. C.: The Association, 1963.

CASTETTER, WM. B. *Administering the School Personnel Program.* New York: The Macmillan Co., 1962.

CORBALLY, JOHN E., JR., JENSON, T. J., and STAUB, W. FREDERICK. *Educational Administration: The Secondary School.* Second Edition. Boston: Allyn & Bacon, Inc., 1965.

GRIFFITHS, DANIEL E. *Human Relations in School Administration.* New York: Appleton-Century-Crofts, Inc., 1956.

LEU, D. J. and RUDMAN, H. C. *Preparation Programs for School Administrators: Common and Specialized Learnings.* East Lansing, Michigan: Michigan State University Press, 1963.

MILLER, VAN. *The Public Administration of American School Systems.* New York: The Macmillan Co., 1965.

National Society for the Study of Education, *In-Service Education,* Part I. Chicago: University of Chicago Press, 1957.

9

Policy Formation

in Education

MANY VIEWS OF EDUCATIONAL ADMINISTRATION, including some presented in this book, deal inadequately with the policy-making aspects of education. While some hold that policy evolves from the practices and procedures followed in an institution, such an approach leads to inconsistent practices and procedures and to an inability to evaluate the effectiveness of the institution. Policy must underlie practices and procedures. We are using the term policy to mean the expression of the broad goals or purposes of education. We look upon policy decisions as essentially lay decisions, made, we hope, after information and judgments have been provided by the professionals. We suspect that many laymen and a fair proportion of their professional advisers do not appreciate the complexities of the policy-making process in a free society, and we hope to help clarify that process in this chapter.

Parsons, as we have noted in Chapter 3, does give a cue to this understanding when he suggests that organizations have three levels: the technical, the managerial, and the institutional. It is chiefly at the institutional level that policy-making or legitimation, to use Parson's term, goes on. The entire community, the board of education, and the chief administrator of the school system seem to us to be very directly involved with policy formation.

We shall first describe the process by which policy evolves,[1] then report an actual case in which a board of education sustains a policy decision, and finally suggest a few implications for the school administrator growing out of such an analysis.

How Policy Evolves

BASIC FORCES

Schools, like other institutions in our culture, are affected by basic social, economic, political, and technological developments. The amount of schooling of the adults of a community, for instance, is significantly related to the aspirations which that community holds for schools. Economic resources determine, in part, the level of program which a school may establish. For example, the relationship of the cold war to the establishment of the National Science Foundation is clear. Policies for education begin with the basic movements in society.

At the moment, these forces include international tensions, economic interdependence of all people, population mobility, widespread communication, technological advancement generally, the growth of knowledge, and the push for self-determination on the part of people everywhere. Moon shots and other events serve to dramatize the effervescence of the present day.

These basic social forces are not local in character; they are national and world-wide in scope. Yet they impinge upon every local school community in the land. Every school budget is affected by the fact that defense needs require a $50 billion expenditure per year. Employment conditions in industrialized communities are not localized in their results. The movement of hundreds of Negroes each month from the farms of the South to the city slums of the North is not merely a local problem. The thrust for self-determination in Ghana is not an event which we can ignore in our diplomatic maneuvers.

Let us look at a specific case. In 1957 the Russians inaugurated the Sputnik era. The Congress, heretofore loath to face up directly to the question of national policy for education, found this force too strong to resist, and in 1958 passed the National Defense Education Act. Early in its oper-

---

[1] Some of the ideas expressed in this chapter first appeared in Roald F. Campbell, "Process of Policy Making Within Structures of Educational Government as Viewed by the Educator," in Wm. P. McLure and Van Miller (eds.), *Government of Public Education for Adequate Policy Making* (Urbana: Bureau of Educational Research, University of Illinois, 1960), pp. 59–76.

ation the act was implemented in a number of ways. Congress appropriated millions of dollars for loans and fellowships for college students; for projects in science, mathematics, and modern languages; and for other programs. During the initial year of operation of the Act, state education departments also did much to implement the new law. Nearly all of the fifty-five states and territories had plans approved for new guidance programs and almost as many states had plans approved for the improvement of their statistical services.

But the story does not end there. In hundreds of school districts steps to implement the Act were also taken. Some of these steps included augmented testing programs to identify gifted students, the establishment of language laboratories, reconstruction of the mathematics and science programs, and the employment of additional guidance personnel.

To be sure, local implementation of the Act was subject to nominal approval of local boards of education and school officers. But has any local community really been free to examine the merits of statistics in the mathematics program? Have not the impingements of national policy and money and, in turn, the pressures of state officials really called the tune? In this instance and many more that could be cited, such as the civil rights movement, basic social forces, nation-wide and sometimes world-wide in scope, finally affected educational policy in many school districts.

ANTECEDENT MOVEMENTS

Movements designed to change educational policy are born in response to basic social forces. These movements may be nonofficial, such as the National Merit Scholarship Program, the Conant studies of high schools and teacher education, and the Rockefeller report on education; or they may be official, such as the White House Conference on Education, the President's Committee on Education Beyond the High School, and President Johnson's task force study on education.

It should be noted that these movements tend to be nation-wide in character. Funds for National Merit Scholarships included an initial grant of $18 million from the Ford Foundation and subsequent sums from over a hundred other donors. The President's Committee on Education Beyond the High School had a membership of thirty-eight, among whom were college presidents of both public and private institutions and a number of well-known industrialists. The report was aimed at the demand and need of education beyond the high school in the nation as a whole.

Significant in this connection is the way the press, television, and other media reinforce the national impact of such influences as noted above. Sponsors of the nonofficial movements, particularly, are often skilled, or have ready access to those who are skilled, in mass media. These movements are good copy, hence releases by their sponsors are used widely by the newspapers of the nation.

Nor do the official movements lack communication reinforcement. The 1955 White House Conference on Education was made up of 2,000 delegates from every state and territory, two-thirds of them lay citizens. In many communities and in most states there were White House Conferences preliminary to the main event. All of these activities were thoroughly publicized. Following the conference a prominent novelist was engaged to write the report, excerpts from which continue to be included in speeches of lay and professional leaders in education.

The role of the philanthropic foundations in supporting the antecedent movements that often culminate in policy should be noted. For instance, foundations underwrote the National Manpower Council, the National Merit Scholarship Program, the Rockefeller report, and the Conant studies. The relationship between some of the major foundations and the Executive Office of the President has tended to be a close one. All of these activities seem to be antecedents to educational policy.

We have noted that the forces which provoke educational policy are national and world-wide in scope, that the antecedents to policy may be official and nonofficial. These movements are often financed by the foundations. Moreover, the activities of the principals in these movements are given extensive reinforcement through the press, TV, and platform. Let us now examine another step in the evolution of educational policy.

POLITICAL ACTION

The antecedents and the resulting proposals provoke political activity in and out of government. One aspect of this activity is the debate that goes on among educators and among lay citizens, and between the two groups. Among educators these proposals are often met by opposition and defensiveness. For instance, the National Association of Secondary School Principals once advocated the banning of *Life* Magazine from high school libraries, in response to the series, "Crisis in Education," which appeared in that periodical. The series included a report of the Conant study on high schools and advocated programs for the gifted, ideas now actively espoused by the principals' organization.

There may be good reasons for resistance on the part of school people. Often these movements have ignored the educational fraternity, and non-educator enthusiasm may never have been tempered with the realities which school workers know reside in the situation.

Despite initial reluctance, however, educators usually respond by making studies of the problems related to the antecedent movements. Special provision for the education of the gifted is a case in point. The urgency of the social needs to make better use of our manpower or to produce more scientists clearly prods school people toward making such an examination. The individual development of students has, by comparison, been a weak but perhaps a growing stimulation. In any case, studies of the gifted have mushroomed. Some of these studies are being made by competent investigators, others by opportunists who do not wish to miss the bandwagon.

These studies by educators may come at the local, state, or national level. They may have official or semiofficial status, or they may be done by voluntary organizations such as state and national education associations. More and more, however, it appears that resources to conduct such studies are available at the national level. Again it should be noted that the foundations supply each year about $850 million for various purposes, a large part for the study of education.[2]

The studies and reports engaged in by the educators often result in the endorsement of the original movement or some modification of it. Many educators, for instance, were not too comfortable with Mr. Conant's announcement that he proposed to study the schools of this country. His approach to the problem, however, proved to be reassuring; and his recommendations, although at first resisted in some quarters, have now become almost canons to many educators.

The antecedent movements to policy also stimulate lay citizens to action. Debate is aroused by such questions as, do our schools teach the 3 R's? Are our schools too soft? Do our bright kids just loaf? Discussion of this sort appears to have been particularly lively over the last decade. Analysis of the views of citizens on education reveals some of them to be basic and probing, some opportunistic and irresponsible. Perhaps we are coming into a period characterized by a little more sound inquiry into educational problems.

Newspapers, magazines, books, TV, and other media aid and abet this debate. The record of this debate has become so voluminous that anthologies are required even to sample it.[3]

As one might expect, debate and discussion, in the minds of some people, tend to crystallize positions. These people individually and through their organizations demand that local boards of education, state legislatures, and the Congress take action to rectify what they term weaknesses in our educational system. For instance, many school boards, particularly in Northern cities, have been pushed to eliminate de facto segregation, and

[2] Ann D. Walton, and Marianna O. Lewis (eds.) et al., The Foundation Directory (New York: Russell Sage Foundation, 1964).

[3] See C. W. Scott, S. M. Hill and H. W. Burns, The Great Debate: Our Schools in Crisis (Englewood Cliffs, N.J.: Prentice-Hall, Inc., 1959).

many state legislatures have been confronted with pressures to abolish education courses required for the certification of teachers.

Again the local-state-national interrelationships of these debates, their wide publicity, and the subsequent demands on official bodies should be noted. The local post of the American Legion, for instance, may base its whole campaign for more Americanism in the schools upon the report of one of its national committees published in the Legion magazine. Or the argument to strip state boards of education of fiscal powers may emanate from the studies of the National Council of State Governments. Most local organizations are part of state and national networks. To assume that most problems are purely local in nature is sheer nonsense.

The activities of educators and lay citizens with respect to proposed educational policy may be reflected in the platforms of the political parties at state and national levels. Activities of citizens may also lead to studies and hearings on the part of government. A board of education may commission outside experts to study the extent of segregation in the schools. A state legislature may refer to a legislative reference bureau problems dealing with the foundation program or the tax structure of the state. At the national level the Hoover reports on the reorganization of government, as authorized by the Congress, are well known. The device of holding hearings is used broadly by local, state, and national policy-making groups.

Devices for study and investigation are a recognized part of the governmental process. It should be noted, however, that these are ordinarily employed *after* issues have been raised, debated, investigated, and perhaps polarized by lay citizens and educators. Seldom does government initiate. Ordinarily, governmental studies merely formalize what vigorous proponents have already said. Nor are politicians adverse to settling for a study of an issue in place of action upon it.

FORMAL ENACTMENT

This process—change in basic social conditions, the organization of nation-wide antecedent movements, and political activity in and out of government—often culminates in policy. Usually policy requires some kind of legal formulation, an action that may be taken by local, state, or national governments. At any of these levels, particularly at state and national levels, the policy may be formalized by legislative, administrative, or judicial bodies.

At the local level, policy most frequently is formalized by the board of education and in some cases the city council. Many boards of education, however, give their superintendents leeway in formulating administrative regulations which also serve as guides to action and thus constitute policy statements.

Policy formalization for education at the state level is perhaps more complex. In the American scheme of things the state legislature is clearly the chief policy-making agency in education. Each state has a formidable body of school law which sets the formal limits within which all agencies can act. Literally hundreds of bills affecting education are introduced at each legislative session in most states, and these bills reflect the temper of the times and the antecedent movements to which we have referred. When "Americanism" rides high, we get bills, and some laws, requiring teachers to take oaths of allegiance. When education for the gifted is in fashion, we get bills, and some laws, establishing merit scholarship programs. But policy for education also emanates from state boards of education, special state commissions, state superintendents, state auditing agencies, state building boards, and the state courts.

Even though education is generally thought to be a state function, policy for education is also formed at the national level. The Congress cannot evade such questions as the need for scientists and mathematicians, the lack of research, the shortage of schoolhouses, and state differentials in the capacity to provide financial support for education. Deliberation on some of these questions led to the establishment of the National Science Foundation in 1950,[4] and to the passage of the National Defense Education Act in 1958,[5] both major policy enactments.

Educational policy also stems from the executive branch of the national government. The U.S. Office of Education is charged with the administration of the National Defense Education Act, to implement which more than two hundred administrators were added to the Office staff. The administrative regulations formulated by this group far exceed in wordage the Act itself, and in many instances these regulations are policy interpretations. Much of this wordage is the product of the attorneys who in their endeavors to interpret policy actually become policy makers. In the Bureau of the Budget another set of policy makers is at work. What may have seemed to be a simple enactment on the part of the Congress becomes a veritable maze in the hands of administrators, attorneys, and budget controllers, all part of the executive branch of government.

By now it seems abundantly clear that the federal courts also make policy for education. Actually, the U.S. Supreme Court alone has made over fifty major decisions, of which the Brown case is but one, on educational issues.[6] These decisions cover such questions as the legality of private schools, public provision of textbooks to parochial pupils, public trans-

[4] Public Law 81:507.

[5] Public Law 85:864.

[6] Clark Spurlock, *Education and the Supreme Court* (Urbana: University of Illinois Press, 1955).

portation of parochial pupils, released time for religious education, teachers and subversive organizations, and Negro-white integration.

A FLOW CHART

In summary, may we note that educational policy has its genesis in basic social change; its generation in nation-wide antecedent movements; its promotion by educators and lay citizens in and out of government; and its formalization in legal expression by local, state, or national government. This process is depicted in Figure 9.1.

Because basic social changes are usually nation-wide in scope, and the antecedent movements also often nation-wide efforts, inevitably these forces tend to shift the major policy foci from local to state and to federal levels. Only the Congress can provide for education in terms of national survival. Usually, states talk of minimum foundation programs. Despite our tradition of localism, local boards of education find themselves ever more working within and restricted by the frameworks of state and national policy for education.

The flow chart in Figure 9.1 enlarges our concept of the policy-making process. We can no longer be concerned chiefly with the formal, legal expression of policy. Somehow we must give more attention to political action, to antecedent movements, and to basic social forces. In this task we have natural allies; the economist, the political scientist, and the sociologist have been at work on these matters for some time. With their help, our conception of this process can be further clarified.

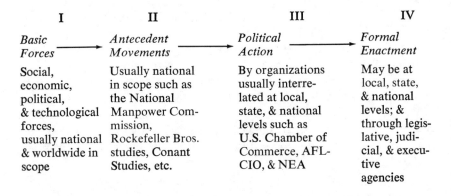

I	II	III	IV
Basic Forces	*Antecedent Movements*	*Political Action*	*Formal Enactment*
Social, economic, political, & technological forces, usually national & worldwide in scope	Usually national in scope such as the National Manpower Commission, Rockefeller Bros. studies, Conant Studies, etc.	By organizations usually interrelated at local, state, & national levels such as U.S. Chamber of Commerce, AFL-CIO, & NEA	May be at local, state, & national levels; & through legislative, judicial, & executive agencies

Figure 9.1   A Flow Chart on Policy Formation in Education

Let us turn next to an actual case that illustrates the many forces playing upon a local board of education as it attempts to establish or re-establish policy.

A Case: Book-burning in Daleview[7]

Daleview is a long-established suburban community of moderate size and rather favored circumstances, and is in a county that has been "Republican since McKinley." The present population of the high school district of about 30,000 includes many who live in newly developed sections, but the growth of the district, while rapid in recent years, has not been wholesale and uncontrolled. The district has a tradition of strong, well-educated boards of education, benefiting from the high professional level of many of the residents.

Dr. Charles Shields, the district superintendent, has held his position for seventeen years, and has a great respect for his community. The community returns the respect—or so we infer if supporting some twenty bond issues or tax rate increases during Dr. Shields' term means anything. Mr. Carl Priestly, the president of the board of education, is typical of the type of leadership to which Daleview has become accustomed. He was a Phi Beta Kappa and an athlete in his college days, and is now a senior partner in a prominent law firm in Metropolis. He is popular in his community for his vigor and forthright manner.

DEVELOPMENT OF THE PROBLEM

Recently the social studies department of the Daleview High School developed, and received board approval for, a four-semester sequence of courses in American History to be taken by selected juniors and seniors. One of the three electives that could be taken as the fourth semester of this sequence was to be called "Contemporary American Civilization." This course went into operation in the spring semester following approval of the program.

As it developed, the talented young teacher of the course, Mrs. Shirley Harnet, distributed to the twenty-three seniors in her class a course outline containing the following statement:

The basic text for the course will be Max Lerner's *America as a Civilization* and we will follow primarily his table of contents as our outline.

[7] The initial report of this case was written by Robert A. Bunnell.

It was this use of the term, text, that was later to result in serious misunderstanding. The school code in this state required that a text must be adopted by the board of education and reported to state and county authorities. In fact, Lerner's book was one of thirty-three on the reading list of the course, and had never been adopted as a text in the legal sense, but was to be used as a reference in the course. In the debate that developed, the resolution of this question of fact was never fully reported—nor understood, it would seem—by the groups attacking the book.

With no advance notice of discontent in the community, the president of the board of education received a lengthy letter of protest from the Daleview post of the American Legion, dated February 10 of that year. The letter stated in part:

It has come to our attention that the book entitled *America as a Civilization*, by Max Lerner, is currently being used as a textbook in one of the advanced history courses in the Daleview High School.

We, of Daleview Post #52, The American Legion, feel that the selection of this particular book, written by Mr. Lerner, was indeed an unfortunate one. We respectfully wish to state our reasons for this belief and request that this matter be brought to the attention of the school board at your next meeting. . . . Please realize that we bring this matter to your attention without rancor and that we are seeking only to take a firm stand in regard to a matter which is of great concern to us. . . .

Our objections to this book may be briefly summarized under three main headings: the writer's background, the book itself, and the effect of this book on the students.

Under the first heading were listed seven Communist front organizations with the "evidence" that Lerner had been a member of importance in all of them. The next section objected to the book itself by noting that:

Again . . . we disagree with Lerner as he develops the false notion that we live in a "democracy" rather than a "republic." The motives he ascribes to those who would call our government by its proper name, "republic," rather than his "constitutional democracy," we believe grossly misrepresent their position and should not be stated as historical fact but as his personal opinion. As a result, we feel quite certain that no student having studied this text, will ever gain the clear conception and fundamental truth that the United States of America, governmentally, is not a "democracy," but a "republic."

. . . . That he holds the Legion and VFW in contempt is obvious from his writings in his chapter entitled "The Joiners." It is indeed unfortunate, however, that the only contribution this scholar makes to the young people regarding the Legion and VFW is one of slander and vilification.

The final objection raised an issue of morals in addition to the problem of subversion:

We hope also, that the student will not be unduly influenced by the writer when he asserts that "sexual revolt in America has asserted three freedoms: the freedom to break the formal codes; the freedom to diverge from the majority sexual patterns *into deviant behavior* [emphasis supplied by the letter writers]; the freedom to lead a fully expressive sexual life in the pursuit of happiness. It is a . . . revolt for a healthy, expressive life" (p. 687). Should the suggestions made in this chapter be taken seriously by the student . . . and coupled with the problem of teen-age drinking . . . we suggest that only further impairment of teen-age morals can logically result.

We urge that another book be substituted as speedily as possible as a text in this course which will satisfy the standards of objectivity and integrity deserved by our students.

Following the receipt of the letter from the Legion, the teacher and department head involved prepared memoranda on the subject. Mrs. Harnet wrote that continued use of the book should be made because:

I. The class is made up of students of high academic ability. . . .

II. . . . Lerner's book acts as a stimulating and comprehensive outline. . . .

III. . . . We also have a full stock of books on all phases of American history (as a means of providing a contrast to Lerner).

IV. The role of the instructor is to remain objective and stimulating.

V. Many words can be said about academic freedom, but let it suffice to say that accepting pressure for censorship from any non-representative community group destroys the idea of public education.

The memorandum prepared by the department head dealt with the same problems and strongly recommended retention of the book:

There is no "basic" text for the course. The decision to use the book was based primarily on the fact that the department believes it to contain the best compendium synthesis of material upon the subject available. Hence, the structure of the course has been patterned on Lerner's table of contents.

In our opinion Lerner's book is not even controversial.

The author, it might be interesting to note, was mildly berated by *Time*—a publication hardly of the left-wing stripe—as having no point of view whatsoever. We heartily disagree, then, that Lerner is advocating anything—except understanding.

The fact remains, however, that Lerner's past record is absolutely irrelevant *unless* it can be demonstrated that this record is reflected *in the book*.

We recognize that the Legion is earnestly striving—as we all are—to keep America Free. It would seem that one way *not* to accomplish this aim would be to join the throng on *Unter den Linden* watching SS Troops burning books. . . .

The department strongly urges the Board of Education to permit continued use of the book.

The Legion letter was considered at the regular board meeting of February 27. At that time, the above memoranda were presented, though the fact was not noted in the board minutes, and the board proceeded to act as follows:

Mr. Priestly read excerpts from a letter from the American Legion, Daleview post, received by all Board members requesting removal of the book *America as a Civilization*, by Max Lerner, from use as supplementary text in the social studies department. Following discussion Dr. Karton moved that the board thank the American Legion for its thoughtfulness in calling this matter to the attention of the board, but decline to withdraw it from use as reference book in the class. Mrs. Bussee seconded the motion. On the roll call, voting "aye" were President Priestly, Mrs. Long, Mrs. Bussee, Messrs. Oak and Karton; "nay" Mr. Dyer. The President declared the motion carried.

The board then went on to its regular business and adjourned. Another phase of the problem was stirred by a letter published in the *Daleview Record*.

The *Daleview Record* has given extensive coverage to the Daleview High School Senior Prom situation. [A decision by the board to discontinue proms on the grounds that parents had provided pre-dance cocktail parties; which decision was later reversed.] May I review the following in our defense.

[Here the letter writer quotes Lerner's analysis of freedom in sex already quoted above in the Legion letter.]

It seems to me that the very officials who are decrying the lack of parental responsibility are providing textbooks guaranteed to undermine the morals of our students in areas far beyond one yearly senior prom.

Mr. Vallencall, the department head, became increasingly concerned over this turn in the emphasis in the controversy, especially as the comment in the community became directed at the personality of the teacher, Mrs. Harnet. The board, in pursuing the resolution of the problem, had suggested that Mr. Vallencall not become involved as one who answered such criticisms as noted above, but rather that he serve the function of providing the board with appropriate information necessary to facilitate the board's continuing to work toward a solution. Consequently, Mr. Vallencall prepared a memorandum, which said in part:

I feel there is a compelling need to clarify one particular theme that has turned up repeatedly in the anti-Lerner crusade.

1. Lerner is not advocating sexual revolt . . . .

2. It is an attempt to classify and categorize without any personal recommendation . . . .

Mrs. Harnet concurs that this distortion of Lerner seems so vicious that it would be helpful to have our reactions on this point a matter of record.

On March 4, Mrs. Harnet received a letter from the author of the disputed book in reply to one that she had written to him.

I would very much appreciate your writing to me and sending a copy of the [Legion] letter to Mr. Priestly . . . .

. . . I would like to state, for the record, that I never was a Communist, and no sane person has ever dared make such an accusation.

I, too, am amazed at these outbursts, and can only attribute them to the tensions of the nuclear age, and of the recent Presidential campaign.

Mr. Lerner also wrote to the publisher of the *American Legion Magazine* in which he asked that ". . . some perspective be given to the Daleview Legion."

The continuing controversy over the book in the local, and finally in the Metropolis, papers and the national wire services, prompted Superintendent Shields and President Priestly to call in a good friend and head of a well-known public relations firm to assist them in the preparation of an open letter to the Legion. It was hoped, in the superintendent's words, that such a letter would "put out the fire." Pertinent portions of the carefully constructed three-page letter follow:

In view of your interest and that of the community at large, I am glad to make clear the position of the Board on this matter . . . The book, *America as a Civilization*, is a major reference work used in that course. There are a number of other source books recommended to the class, including *Democracy in America* by de Tocqueville, *The Public Philosophy* by Walter Lippmann, and *The Conscience of a Conservative* by Barry Goldwater.

The course was described in the school catalogue as part of the enriched social studies program. The catalogue states, "The program is designed to challenge the superior student to develop the technique of critical thinking regarding recurring issues in history; . . . to relate issues and events to present day situations."

The need for such courses was recently expressed by Dr. Conant in his report on *The American High School Today*, in which he urged that "Free discussions of controversial issues should be encouraged. This approach is one significant way in which our schools can distinguish themselves from those in totalitarian nations."

The book by Max Lerner, a Yale graduate and former faculty member at Harvard and Williams, is not designed as a text book and is not so used at Daleview. More than 1000 pages in length, it has extensive references to source material and cites the research of many earlier scholars in the field.

It might interest you to know that yesterday I talked on the telephone to James F. O'Neill, publisher of the *American Legion Magazine*, who said, "In my opinion Max Lerner is not pro-communist and is not subversive." Mr. O'Neill has agreed to send me a letter stating his views on this subject.

The letter then went on to quote liberally from reviews of the questioned book which appeared in national magazines such as *Time* and *Newsweek,* and in the *New York Times.* At the suggestion of the head of the department, Mr. Vallencall, the letter also dealt with the side issue of Lerner's treatment of sex:

Reactions to a few observations in the book on sexual morality in the United States will naturally vary. Since the author comments as a reporter, not as an advocate, we are confident that, with proper guidance, students taking this course have the maturity to evaluate it as objective social commentary, not as personal doctrine.

The letter also offered support to Mrs. Harnet when it stated:

Our students . . . will continually come into contact with a wide range of reading materials and varying points of view on all the controversial issues of our times. We believe that students are much more likely to react intelligently, critically, and objectively if they are introduced to such subjects under the direction of a skillful teacher.

The closing paragraph then made a plea for objectivity:

This [objectivity] we believe is a basic part of the American ideal of liberty. Many years ago Jefferson said, "Here we are not afraid to follow truth wherever it may lead, nor to tolerate error so long as reason is left to combat it." More than one hundred years later Justice Holmes said, "The best test of truth is the power of the thought to get itself accepted in the competition of the market." And only a few years ago President Eisenhower reiterated this philosophy when he told a graduating class at Dartmouth, "Don't think you are going to conceal faults by concealing evidence that they ever existed. Don't be afraid to go into your library and read every book . . . . How will we defeat Communism unless we know what it is?"

On March 10, a resolution over the signatures of all members of the social studies department was transmitted to the board requesting,

. . . the Administration and Board to issue a statement specifically in the defense of Mrs. Harnet. The current controversy has degenerated into personal attack upon the character of a member of the teaching profession . . . . Such a situation warrants a strong statement from the Administration and Board supporting Mrs. Harnet and the department.

In the ensuing weeks no such specific statement was forthcoming, probably due to the board policy of not adding fuel to the fire by making statements that opponents would feel obliged to counter.

March 13 may be noted as the climax and conclusion, for all practical purposes, of the crisis. The minutes of the board meeting tersely summarize the story:

In view of the large number of visitors, the meeting was immediately recessed to convene at 7:45 P.M. in the speech lab of the high school.

In addition to all members of the Board, the Director of Curriculum and the Business Manager were present. Absent: Secretary of the Board, Superintendent Shields.

The President welcomed the visitors to the meeting. Mr. Priestly stated that the Board at its last regular meeting had voted not to remove the book (*America as a Civilization*) from class use, and read in full the letter dated March 7.

The President next stated that visitors would be allowed to address the Board to present their views on the subject. The President first recognized Mr. H. R. Nash, Americanism Chairman of the Daleview Legion; Mr. Nash read his letter of February 10 and read another statement from the Legion to the Board.

There followed general discussion with fifteen people participating.

At 9:00 P.M., the President terminated the discussion and recessed the Board to reconvene in the board room to conduct the regular business of the Board.

The additional statement by the Legion, five pages in length, reiterated in some detail the earlier letter and went on to say:

Our position has been badly distorted by some who perhaps have not been fully informed on the subject.

The statement went on to request that the department head's statement and the teacher's statement, as well as Priestly's letter and all the Legion letters, be given wide publicity. The statement continued:

In conclusion, we respectfully suggest that there surely must be better tools than books of this type to stimulate the young mind.

Once again we suggest the publication of the statements and letters previously referred to.

We remain firm in our objections to the use of this book as a text and urge that you review your decision.

The decision quite naturally and properly rests with you.

One aspect of the meeting which the minutes noted only briefly was the absence of the superintendent. The explanation was that a previously scheduled speaking engagement, out of town, happened to fall on that day. In line with the policy of minimizing these events, it was felt that the cancellation of such an engagement would be an error, in that it could be picked up by the press as evidence that the administration was "running scared." With the superintendent *not* present, the board's leadership in the fight was clearly noted, and the importance of the whole matter appeared diminished. The director of curriculum was present, and did in fact participate in gathering materials and dealing with some questions in the general discussion.

During the time that had elapsed since the first salvo of the Legion letter, Metropolis newspapers had from time to time published letters related to the controversy. On the day of the well-attended board meeting an interesting contrast in the views of two of the papers was noted. One carried an editorial that supported the stand the board had taken on February 27. The title of the editorial was "The Unburned Book":

. . . True, the overview is undeniably Lerner's view. The book is not the same selection of facts that a de Tocqueville, a Lippmann or Goldwater would put into his overview. We presume that is why Goldwater's, Lippmann's, and de Tocqueville's books are included in the same course.

It seems to us that this combination of viewpoints, far from tending to undermine the mind or morals, is about what a group of intellectually promising eighteen-year-olds ought to be digesting.

Meanwhile, another paper carried a by-lined story headlined: "Daleview Mothers Carry School Book Fight to Teachers." This article described a town where all the mothers would be going out that night on a "mother's march." The story went on:

The battle lines are drawn . . . .

The school is on the defense . . . .

Divided also is the class of advanced students applying [sic] for enrollment in the course.

The protesting mothers will march to the school tonight armed with copies of the prospectus which lists Lerner as the basic text.

Meanwhile, State Senator, Mrs. Abby Winter, was contacted by the mothers. The Senator said, "Books like Lerner's contribute to juvenile delinquency."

And on that note, the news story ended.

Both papers carried stories the following day, including pictures taken at the open meeting. The *Metropolis News* headlined its story, "Daleview Debates a Textbook"; the *Metropolis Citizen* headed its story, "That Book to Stay in Daleview School." Both papers carried statements of persons at the meeting, with the former reporting affirmative comment, "Our daughter is now doing some thinking," while the latter reported negative comment, "I'm wondering if the social studies department is going too far left." The two papers agreed when they reported that the board had pretty well made up its mind. Mr. Priestly was quoted as saying, "We already have had a full discussion of the subject. The issue is closed." And, except for a few parting shots from the other side, that was probably true.

While all this was going on in Daleview, interested persons favoring both sides were watching the events from outside the community. When the decision of the board was announced in the Metropolis papers and carried by the wire services, the superintendent and board began to receive calls and mail. Superintendent Shields has two lasting impressions of these communications:

I was amazed at the vigor of the letters from *both* sides. You know, some thought the Legion was a little rough, but some of those liberals wrote some pretty strong letters. Both sides—the ones that wrote anyway—were real strong in their positions.

Another thing that, well, didn't surprise me, but I found it gratifying, was that about 9 out of 10 calls and letters were complimentary. "Hooray for Daleview" and that sort of thing. They wrote from all over the country.

Some of the more surprising letters in the superintendent's file on this case came from persons of considerable prominence in Metropolis. Others were from teachers and students who praised the action in the name of academic freedom. Many local citizens also contributed their support in the form of congratulatory letters. Two interesting exceptions were to be found. In one letter, it was suggested that the board and social studies faculty were "dupes" of the Communists and were to be pitied and encouraged to read competent authorities to help them out of their misunderstanding. The valedictorian of a previous year's class at Daleview High, then a student in an Eastern college, was shocked at the board's failure to adhere to patriotic ideals. She felt that only at the college level could a person encounter strange ideas, and be able to evaluate them in terms of a good and sound American philosophy of life. Additional organized opposition in the form of letters came also from the Legion posts and VFW groups in surrounding communities.

IMPACT ON SCHOOL POLICY

Two changes were effected in the policies of Daleview High School as a result of the controversy over this book. First, the administration and board of education, in co-operation with the heads of departments, worked out a detailed plan for the approval of books used in the school. A category called "On approval for possible adoption" was created to include books that might not be desired on a five-year basis as the law requires of the legally approved "textbook." All supplementary paperback books were to be ordered through the school bookstore, which makes monthly reports to the board of titles in use. No censorship was implied in this system, but rather the board preferred to know exactly what was being used to avoid being suddenly embarrassed by another "revelation" from the community.

The other change came in the staffing of the course. In the following semester, the course was to be continued, but due to the resignation of Mrs. Harnet, whose husband moved from the community, the course was to be taught by the head of the department. This step may be viewed as a concession to the community in that, although the adequacy of the teacher was never doubted by the school, the school was willing to adopt the view of the community that the course should be taught by a mature individual, "familiar with the attitudes and background of the community."

Whether the community will again engage in this kind of reaction to the school is a moot point. The critical groups remain, the need to teach the controversial issues persists, and possibility of disagreement is undoubtedly present.

Some Implications

We shall first note some of the ways in which the case just presented illustrates the flow chart on policy-making presented earlier in this chapter. Then we shall suggest some of the more general implications for the administrator growing out of such a concept of policy formation.

REFLECTIONS ON DALEVIEW

The basic social-political force operating in Daleview at the time of the attempted book-burning was undoubtedly concerned with the growth of international Communism. The values of Communism and of the Western world are in many ways diametrically opposed. This conflict is reflected almost daily in tension spots over the world, in protracted but often useless attempts at negotiation, and in the use by both sides of many of the same words but with widely disparate meanings. The American Legion of Daleview was reacting to a world-wide movement.

A second political force also seemed to be operating in Daleview at the time of the Lerner affair; a hard fought and closely contested national election had just been concluded. The state in which Daleview is located was a key state in that election, and the results were so close as to be uncertain for several days. Finally, the opposition candidate, as far as Daleview was concerned, was found to have carried the state. This prompted accusations of fraud at the polls in nearby Metropolis. These circumstances led members of the Legion post and other citizens to view with considerable bitterness an author who seemed to have political views somewhat different from their own. Both national and world-wide movements were affecting the local serenity of Daleview.

The antecedent movements were also present in the case. The national emphasis on a more rigorous educational program had undoubtedly influenced Daleview school people to create an "honors group" in high school social studies and to bring to that group the writings of mature students of the social scene. Conant's studies of the secondary schools were known and were alluded to in the letter the board of education released to the public.

The local-state-national interrelatedness of those movements was illustrated in several ways. The whole controversy was covered in the local press, in the papers of Metropolis, and in the wire services that served the entire nation. The local post of the American Legion was not permitted autonomy; the national office of the Legion was brought into the picture. When the board of education took definitive action on the case, letters poured in from "all over the country." The issue in Daleview had more than local interest and import.

Political action was also illustrated in the Lerner affair. The local post of the American Legion, acting as a bona fide interest group, objected to the school program and attempted to have the program changed. The educators in the schools were requested by the board of education to stay out of the fight but to prepare memoranda for the use of the board as it weighed the problem. Mr. Lippmann and Mr. Goldwater, both political figures of considerable stature, were invoked in the controversy. The board, after exchange of letters with the Legion and considerable newspaper publicity, held an open meeting where some fifteen citizens expressed their views. All of this is political action in the best tradition of democratic societies. As with the other steps in policy-making, local political action has its overtones in the national arena.

Finally, we note that the Daleview Board of Education did formally enact some policy decisions. Most important, the disputed book was retained on the reading list. But two safeguards were provided: the status of the book was clarified, and the board was to be kept informed about supplemental books as well as textbooks used in the school. Possibly, the circumstance that permitted reassignment of the course to a more mature teacher who was "familiar with the attitudes and background of the community" was also in the nature of a policy decision.

In a sense this case had a happy ending. The freedom of students to read divergent views on controversial questions was sanctioned, even if under a somewhat greater prescription of conditions. But what might have happened in a community where the Legion had less restraint, where the board of education was less able, where the chairman of the board was less influential, where the professionals were less competent? Any one or more of these conditions could have altered the outcome.

Daleview dealt with policy-making at the local level, but the forces of the larger world were evident at every step of the process. The implications to which we now turn would seem to apply to policy-making at local, state, and national levels.

UNDERSTAND POLITICS

First, we think it is important that administrators understand the realities of politics. Contrary to what many have written (and perhaps more have wished), public education is squarely within the political realm. James has stated the matter succinctly in a recent research report on school finance:

All but negligible portions of their revenues are allocated through the voting mechanism, either at the state or at the local level. Three conditions are therefore essential to public school support. The first is that the expectations for service from the institution be sufficiently pervasive within a voting unit to receive majority support. The second is a system of voting that allows the voters to express preferences on the alternatives for allocating available resources between the public and the private sectors of the economy, among competing institutional components of the public sector, and among alternative services within the educational institution. The third condition is, of course, availability of resources.[8]

If the resources of our society are to be allocated among various institutions, including those in education, and if this allocation is dependent upon the voting preferences of people, and if these preferences are dependent on the expectations or values people hold, schools are inevitably in the business of creating expectations and of influencing voters. This is political action.

Nor is this political action limited to the local school district. Such action goes on at the state level, as school people attempt to influence the state legislature and other state policy-making bodies. Bailey has described this process as attempts were made to secure state foundation programs in the eight Northeast states.[9] Recent sessions of Congress have furnished abundant proof that education is involved in political action at the national level.

[8] H. Thomas James, "School Revenue Systems in Five States." Co-operative Research Project No. 803, School of Education, Stanford University, 1961, pp. 2–3.

[9] Stephen K. Bailey et al., Schoolmen and Politics (Syracuse: Syracuse University Press, 1962).

The people and the organizations that attempt to influence educational policy are numerous and persistent. A board of education may find that an election to consider an operating levy or a bond issue is greatly influenced by spokesmen who represent the local chamber of commerce, the farm bureau, or the labor union; or, as a board of education attempts to operate schools within the decisions made at the polls, it may find that the views of the local teachers' organization and of the local chapter of the John Birch Society have to be taken into account. But these influences come from more than local sources. Teacher selection is limited by state certification requirements. A school supply firm insists that it has an indispensable teaching machine. The physical science program emanating from work done at the Massachusetts Institute of Technology under the auspices of the National Science Foundation becomes a most persuasive innovation. The momentum of the National Merit Scholarship program with over a half-million high school students taking the examinations in a single year, and other forms of external testing, can not be ignored.

At the state level Blanke found that in the judgment of chief state school officers, agriculture, business, labor, and professional educators were most effective in gaining access to state legislatures on educational issues.[10] Of these, in terms of techniques employed to gain access to the legislature, agriculture provided useful information often prepared by the land-grant colleges, organized effectively at the local level, and marshalled partisan political power. Educational groups supplied useful information and organized effectively at the local level, but were loath to employ partisan political power. Business seemed to be most effective in supplying information, and labor in utilizing partisan political power.

Clearly a part of the reality of politics is a recognition of the many influences that play upon boards of education, state legislatures, and other policy-making bodies. Moreover, an understanding of the nature of these influences and the methods employed by the groups that exert influence is also a part of the reality of which we speak.

In the public realm a review of the concept of federalism under which our government was organized may also be helpful to the administrator. As Grodzins has pointed out, federalism from the beginning has been a device for dividing the decisions and functions of government.[11] There has never been a time when it was possible to make neat divisions of federal, state, and local functions. Our system of government is really not a "layer cake"; it is more aptly described as a "marble cake."

[10] Virgil E. Blanke, "Educational Policy Formulation at the State Level as Viewed by Chief State School Officers." Unpublished Ph.D. dissertation, Department of Education, University of Chicago, 1961.

[11] Morton Grodzins, "The Federal System," in Report of the President's Commission on National Goals, *Goals for Americans* (New York: Prentice-Hall, Inc.), pp. 265–82.

No function of government is strictly local. Even a city police department, if it is to do its job, is dependent upon state crime laboratories, the Federal Bureau of Investigation, and other nonlocal agencies. In similar fashion most local school districts are greatly affected by actions of state legislatures, state boards of education, and other state agencies. The influence of the Congress and the federal courts has already been noted. Our point is simply that federalism is also a reality in our local scheme of things.

While government, be it local, state, or national, often becomes the arena within which decisions about education are made, one must look at the private realm to see those groups which bring pressure on government. This is illustrated by a conversation one of us recently had with a secretary of a state chamber of commerce. The secretary had just attended a meeting of secretaries of chambers of commerce from midwestern states, called by the U.S. Chamber of Commerce. When asked if the U.S. Chamber had definitive positions on political issues that it had urged on the meeting, the answer was in the affirmative. "Did these positions receive support from the state secretaries?" the secretary was asked.

"Yes, they did," was the answer.

"And what do you expect to do about these matters in your state?" was the next question.

"I expect to hold meetings with every local chamber of commerce and work like everything to get them to endorse the positions we took at the meeting," he replied.

We think this little interchange illustrates not only what goes on in business organizations but also the process employed in agriculture, labor, education, and many other groups. In brief, we are suggesting that in the private realm there are numerous organizations with interlocking relationships at local, state, and national levels. Such arrangements permit pressure to be mobilized and applied where needed.[12] This phenomenon also appears to be a part of the reality of politics.

Both federalism in the public realm, and interlocking chains of influence in the private, reduce the amount of discretion left to a local board of education and alter the nature of that discretion. Burke, who has recently examined this question for each of the fifty states, concluded that the trend in recent decades has been toward increased state control.[13] The trend seemed particularly marked in the areas of personnel and teacher certification, for instance, and in finance.

[12] For extension of this point, see Roald F. Campbell, Luvern L. Cunningham, and Roderick F. McPhee, *The Organization and Control of American Schools* (Columbus: Charles E. Merrill Books, Inc., 1965), Chapter 17.

[13] Arvid J. Burke, "Fifty State School Systems" (Albany: New York State Teachers Association, 1961). Mimeographed.

This brief discussion of the need of the school administrator to understand the reality of politics suggests that in his program of preparation major attention should be given to the concepts and research of the social sciences where political behavior has been systematically analyzed. There is also the need to extend these concepts from the campus to the real world, for the administrator is a man of action, not merely one of contemplation.

CLARIFY VALUES

But it is not enough that we see the political process in the clear light of reality. We must also ask what values we hold for that process. The ones we shall enumerate have their origin in our basic political documents. Some of our political leaders use these values as "liberal rhetoric" and resist any attempt to spell them out in terms of political action. We take the position, however, that they can and must be made operational if the policy-making process is to operate effectively. Some such value orientation as that discussed briefly below seems necessary.

We think that the individual is primary, the state secondary. This means that all people are important, and that all people are to have opportunity for individual development. It means that associations, organizations, and even governments are formed to help individuals achieve their utmost development, and that when these organizations no longer perform that function, they should be altered or destroyed.

While individual development to us is the ultimate goal, individuals live in a complex society, and in such a society there must be co-operation for the common good. This fact suggests that no individual has freedom to harm or restrain other individuals. The best society is one that protects the right of the most people to pursue their own purposes without subverting the purposes of others. Freedom then is relative, but it is also widespread.

We think that men, when adequately informed, make rational decisions. This statement presumes a belief that all men have some capacity to think and that the method of inquiry is an appropriate one. It assumes, moreover, that there are ways of providing relevant information so that the rational process may go forward. It does not deny the individual differences found in people nor the affective influences on decision-making, but it does place the emphasis on rational problem-solving.

Since capacity is widespread among men and opportunity is to be provided generally, it follows, we believe, that a mobile society is a better one. This belief suggests that any elite, except one of competence, is a dangerous one. Barriers to prevent upward mobility of the competent, or downward mobility of the incompetent, are to be removed. It follows that leaders in a society should be those who know more or who can apply knowledge more effectively.

While we accept the position that policy decisions by their very nature are public decisions, we also think that such decisions should take into account the specialized knowledge of the professional. Only by this kind of interaction can the alternative decisions be freely explored or the consequences of a particular decision ascertained. Such a procedure requires an enlightened lay leadership for education and competence on the part of those who speak as professionals.

The desirability that school administrators clarify their own values suggests a second body of knowledge which should be utilized in the preparation of administrators. We refer to the humanities. Surely those who would discern and influence educational policy should know and appreciate the values that have come to epitomize what we call Western civilization.

ACCEPT THE POLITICAL ROLE

As a final implication, we suggest that school administrators accept the fact that they are political functionaries. We do not imply that this is the only role of the administrator, but we do insist that when a status official is in the business of seeking the best agreements he can get from people within an institution and those without the institution who have some control over it, he is engaged in a political role. Unless the administrator can accept the political role, he will have few satisfactions and much discouragement.

For anybody who serves in a political role in our country, it is well to recognize that we live in a pluralistic society. While we may have a core of national values, with respect to many questions Americans have divergent views. Often these views are represented in a single school district. And it is with such divergent views that the school administrator must work.

The pluralism of our society, as well as the availability of resources and other factors, points to the necessity for each administrator to assess his situation as carefully as possible. While situations may have many things in common, each probably has a few unique characteristics. These common and unique characteristics may be found in the demographic, the physical, the financial, the cultural, or the attitudinal realm. As a wise politician the administrator comes to understand the circumstances in each realm.

But understanding is only a means to an end. The administrator is concerned with getting the best agreements possible in a particular situation at a particular time. People may approach these agreements from different philosophical bases and from varying motivations. The administrator is not basically concerned with philosophy, nor with motivation; he is concerned with operational agreements. He may, for instance, get people with much and with little schooling to agree that both academic and vocational programs are essential in the high school.

For each such agreement the administrator may be able to establish an "area of tolerance." Within such an area, people of divergent views will probably be willing to accept the programs and the direction given by the professionals. If the professionals exceed the "area of tolerance," dominant lay groups who can influence school policy will take steps to change school programs. Recent insistence on the part of some lay groups that schools provide for more integration is a case in point.

We should note, however, that the school may actually have exceeded the "area of tolerance," or it may have merely been perceived as doing so. Ethically, the administrator can not ignore the actual situation; practically, he can not ignore the perception of the situation. In the first instance, the professional staff must somehow come to understand what the "area of tolerance" is and be willing to work within it. In the second instance, the communication between school and community must be sufficiently complete and appropriate so that misperceptions and suspicions are kept at a minimum.

All of this may suggest that we seek a generation of administrators who are milquetoasts. Such is not the case. Just as we would have administrators determine what the area of tolerance is, we would also insist that the real challenge to administration is the enlargement or the extension of the area of tolerance. We advocate that administrators live dangerously. But to insist upon a program regardless of its acceptance in a particular situation at a particular time would probably mean the firing of the administrator. There are times when even this outcome may be good for a school organization. The dramatic events leading up to the firing might do much to crystallize difficulties in the organization or the community, and might lead to forthright steps designed to correct such difficulties.

More frequently, however, we think administrators must get their satisfactions from accurate assessment of a situation, from helping people see what can be done in that situation now, and from leading professionals and laymen to improve that which now exists. Such a plan may require the administrator to compromise at the level of program; it does not require him to compromise his goals.

SUGGESTED ACTIVITIES

1. Ascertain what revenues were received from the federal government by your school district during the past year. Determine what controls, if any, accompanied this money.
2. What school bill was debated vigorously in the last meeting of your state legislature? Why?

3. Determine how many teachers on the faculty of a city or county school district attended graduate school during the past summer on fellowships provided by some agency of the national government.
4. Check on the high schools of your county for the number of students who took the National Merit Scholarship qualifying test, the number of semi-finalists, and the number of merit scholars.
5. Find out how many high schools in your county are using curricular materials developed in the national curriculum programs in mathematics, physical science, biological science, chemistry, English, and social studies.
6. What do the findings for questions 3, 4, and 5 suggest?

SELECTED READINGS

BAILEY, STEPHEN K. *et al. Schoolmen and Politics.* Syracuse: Syracuse University Press, 1962.

CAMPBELL, ROALD F., CUNNINGHAM, LUVERN L., and McPHEE, RODERICK A. *The Organization and Control of American Schools.* Columbus: Charles E. Merrill Books, Inc., 1965.

EDWARDS, NEWTON. *The Courts and the Public Schools.* Chicago: The University of Chicago Press, 1955.

KIMBROUGH, RALPH B. *Political Power and Educational Decision-Making.* Chicago: Rand McNally & Co., 1964.

MASTERS, NICHOLAS A., SALISBURG, ROBERT H., and ELIOT, THOMAS H. *State Politics and the Public Schools.* New York: Alfred A. Knopf, 1964.

National Society for the Study of Education Yearbook, *Social Forces Influencing American Education.* Chicago: University of Chicago Press, 1961.

QUATTLEBAUM, CHARLES A. *Federal Educational Policies, Programs and Proposals.* Part II, "Survey of Federal Educational Activities." Washington, D.C.: U.S. Government Printing Office, 1960.

Report of the President's Commission on National Goals, *Goals for Americans.* Englewood Cliffs, N.J.: Prentice-Hall, Inc., 1960. (Particularly Chapter 3 by John W. Gardner and Chapter 12 by Morton Grodzins.)

Part Two

The Man

THE PURPOSE OF PART TWO IS TO DISCUSS the educational administrator as an individual. A book of this sort, the authors believe, should help the student examine himself as a prospective administrator. In addition to referring to the research relating personal characteristics to administrative behavior, we have assembled some common-sense knowledge in this area to stimulate the student to further investigation. We have approached this subject with a discussion in Chapter 10 of personal motivations for administrator behavior. Chapter 11 helps the student to assess his own potential as an administrator in terms of the competencies required of an educational administrator. Chapter 12 suggests ways of planning and preparing for a career in educational administration and the importance of continued professional development.

10

Personal Motivations

for Administrator Behavior

ADMINISTRATORS, LIKE ALL HUMAN BEINGS, act in an environment in which the conditions are never completely known. Psychologists tell us that even the physical conditions which surround us have an effect upon behavior; the comfort of working conditions, the color of the room, the adequacy of the lighting, and the relative humidity of the atmosphere—all have their effect upon what people do. When the environment contains people who react differently to these and other existing conditions, and to each other, the problem of explaining behavior· becomes exceedingly difficult. Indeed, when we consider the fact that one's reaction to one's surroundings is a function of conditions within the person as well as those without him, the intricacy of the science of human behavior is obvious.

FACTORS AFFECTING BEHAVIOR

In this chapter we shall not attempt to assume the role of psychologists or psychiatrists in explaining or dealing with the problems of human behavior. Nevertheless, since the administrator's stock in trade is human relationships, his behavior should have a sound psychological base. The most generalized principle provided him as a guide to understanding the basis for his actions is that *behavior is dependent upon the interaction of the conditions within the person and those which surround him.* Allport describes a field theory of personality in much the same way that the physical scientist speaks of the "field" in the atomic theory of matter. As he says, "Roughly speaking, the field theory of personality regards the total environmental setting as well as the inner structure of the person as decisive in the shaping of conduct." [1] Allport's field theory is similar to what many psychologists refer to as an "open system" in which one's own fund of understandings form the basis for his understanding of the world around him. In turn, what he perceives in the outside world affects his inner self. A transaction between his inner and outer worlds is constantly changing both of them.[2]

Thus, psychologists provide us with a clue for thinking about human behavior. To understand it we must know something about the nature of the "field" in which behavior is exhibited. Yet the characteristics of the field are not directly observable. They must be inferred from the observations of people who, themselves, are a part of this field. To illustrate this in educational administration, let us take the case of two administrators who at different times held the same administrative position. For one of them, the position presented the challenge through which he successfully developed his leadership potential. The other found the position uninteresting and exceedingly limited in the opportunity it gave him to do those things that he felt compelled to do as an administrator.

Apparently *the man in the situation* made the difference. Conditions in the situation elicited different responses in each of the two men. In turn, the two men had different effects upon the situation. Forces, reactions, circumstances, and relationships among things and people were altered by the exchange of the two administrators. Observing these two administrators, one would find it difficult to attribute differences in their behavior merely to the observable conditions in the school district in question. Part of the cause must be attributed to what Allport has referred to as "the inner structure" of the persons involved.

Careful observers of human behavior find it difficult to attribute a specific behavior to a particular cause. Rather, they agree that the behavior of individuals is due to a combination of causes difficult to unscramble. There is, therefore, a reluctance among these observers to establish a cause and effect relationship between specific behaviors and the elements of the

[1] Gordon W. Allport, *Personality: A Psychological Interpretation* (New York: Holt, Rinehart and Winston, Inc., 1937), p. 364.

[2] For a brief review of pertinent literature, see Daniel E. Griffiths, Lawrence Iannaccone, and James Ramey, *Perception: Its Relation to Administration* (New York: University Council for Educational Administration, 1961), p. 11.

situation merely on the basis of observational evidence. At the present stage in the development of the science of human behavior, it is probably more meaningful to speak, not of causes of behavior, but of factors that affect behavior. We shall deal primarily with those factors which may be altered by educational processes, namely, one's understandings, beliefs, values, attitudes, sentiments, motivations, perceptions, and skills. We shall assume, too, that education which results in behavioral changes has, in some way, altered one or more of these factors. The major purpose of this chapter, then, is to help the prospective administrator begin his assessment of himself by briefly recalling concepts and principles of behavior which, although previously cited, pertain to the development of himself both as a person and as an administrator.

LACK OF AWARENESS OF FACTORS

It cannot be assumed that, because a person has had a college education or because he has been prepared by all of the conventional means to become a school administrator, he has given sufficient thought to factors that affect his behavior or to the effect his behavior has upon those with whom he works. Indeed, he may have given very little thought to what causes him or his associates to behave as they do. If the behavior of an administrator corresponds favorably with the expectation of his teachers, he is, undoubtedly, getting along quite well with them. It is probable, however, that there will be clashes in behavior between administrators and other school personnel if the expectations of each for the other differ to any appreciable degree.

Halpin's study of the leadership behavior of fifty superintendents of schools reveals the expectations and perceptions of this behavior as seen by members of the staff, the board of education, and the superintendents themselves. It is significant that he found differences among the three groups both as to what was expected of the superintendent and how his performance was perceived.[3] An obvious conclusion of the Halpin study is that administrators do not see themselves as others see them. Bidwell engaged 195 teachers in five school systems in a study of desired and actual behavior of administrators. He found a group of dissatisfied teachers who reported administrator behavior in terms quite different from those used by teachers who had expressed satisfaction in their jobs.[4] Conflict and ambiguity in the teacher's perception of the role of the administrator

[3] Andrew W. Halpin, *The Leadership Behavior of School Superintendents,* SCDS Monograph No. 4 (Columbus, Ohio: The Ohio State University, 1956).

[4] Charles E. Bidwell, "The Administrative Role and Satisfaction in Teaching," *Journal of Educational Sociology,* 24 (September 1955), pp. 41–47.

is reported also by Seeman.[5] Jenkins and Blackman found a discrepancy between the administrator's description of his role in improvement of instruction and the descriptions given by some teachers.[6] All of these studies lead one to infer that there is yet much to be learned about administrative behavior and what lies behind it.

Few researchers have attempted to identify and classify the various factors in one's environment that affect his behavior. However, if human behavior is explained by the "open system," where one's inner self and the environment in which one lives constantly play one upon the other, persons must develop some awareness of the operation of this process in their own lives. One attempt to assist the administrator with this problem was made by a group of observers at The Ohio State University. They identified thirty-seven factors that seemed to affect the behavior of people as they participated in administrative decisions about the schools. These factors were classified in the following categories: (1) beliefs and attitudes, (2) intellectual processes used, (3) social-psychological factors, (4) community expectations and traditions, and (5) community characteristics.[7]

The research team responsible for the identification and classification of these factors made no pretense of showing that all of these factors were involved in each administrative act. They recognized that people and situations differ, but it was quite obvious to them that conditions within and among people as well as those outside of their interpersonal relationships were affecting administrator behavior without sufficient awareness on the part of administrators that this was so.

PROBLEMS IN CHANGING BEHAVIOR

Lest we be misunderstood, we remind the reader that, for the most part, the behavior patterns with which we are concerned fit well within the normal range. It should be clearly understood that any mention we make of changing behavior is within the behavior patterns of normal people. Therapy intended to bring abnormal behavior patterns into the normal range requires the professional assistance of qualified psychologists and psychiatrists; such changes are not discussed here. What we are referring to are those changes which may be made through a preparatory

[5] Melvin Seeman, "Role Conflict and Ambivalence in Leadership," *American Sociological Review,* 18 (August 1953), pp. 373–80.

[6] David H. Jenkins and Charles A. Blackman, *Antecedents and Effects of Administrator Behavior,* SCDS Monograph No. 3 (Columbus, Ohio: The Ohio State University, 1956).

[7] John A. Ramseyer et al., *Factors Affecting Educational Administration,* SCDS Monograph No. 2 (Columbus, Ohio: The Ohio State University, 1955), pp. 57–59.

program for educational administrators. By this we mean those changes that are willfully made by an individual because of his new insights into, and understanding of, the conditions that prompt him to act.

It is easy to talk about doing things differently from the routine manner in which they have been done. But how is the routine broken and a new pattern of behavior instituted? Curriculum experts have been telling us for many years that, to change what is being taught and how it is being taught, changes must take place in the teachers. It is because of changed insights into the role of the school; changed understandings of the processes of learning; changed skills in handling relationships among the teachers, children, and youth, and the learning material and environment, that new learning patterns emerge. For most teachers the mere act of reading about what other people have done is insufficient, in and of itself, to produce changes in their own teaching habits. Mere discussion about changes that should be made may be equally ineffective as a single change medium. Most authorities on the improvement of instruction agree that, along with study and exchange of ideas among colleagues, there must be some action, some trying out of new ideas and approaches to the teaching-learning situation. The teacher who, through various learning procedures, develops a new orientation to his task changes his teaching practices. Change by any other method is artificial and, in the long run, ineffective.

The competent administrator knows this; instead of dictating certain changes, or exhorting teachers to change their existing behavior, he provides experiences through which understandings, beliefs, attitudes, and skills have some likelihood of change. Improvement in administrative practices and in the patterns of administrative behavior come about by a similar process. Much has already been said about situational factors and how these affect what can be accomplished in the schools. Reference has been made to the power structure of the community and the decision-making patterns that exist and that must be considered in effecting changes in the schools. We have discussed how organizational relationships may be altered to bring about desirable change, what experience has taught us about procedure, and what tasks need to be co-ordinated to make administration effectively serve the school's purposes.

UNDERSTANDING ONESELF

This chapter focuses attention on those insights and understandings of themselves which administrators should have. Long ago, Socrates called attention to the importance of "knowing thyself." One of the implications of this bit of wisdom is that if a person understands himself, he has excellent chances for accepting himself and for gaining the acceptance of others. Many people have had the experience of being incapable of giving a rational explanation for certain of their actions. It is known, too, that some people rationalize behaviors that are considered by others to be unreasonable. An administrator's behavior should have a rational basis. Therefore, the questions, "What prompts me to do what I do?" and "What prompts me to do it in the manner that I do?" are good questions for each administrator to ask himself.

Obviously, too, there is a point beyond which it becomes unhealthy to question one's own behavior. Overemphasis on introspection may result in blocking desirable action. What is there, then, about oneself and one's behavior that should be known and can be learned with profit to oneself and to others?

Administrators should, at least, be able to assess the range within which they can work and relate themselves to others with reasonable comfort. They should be particularly interested in those aspects of their personality which constitute limitations and potentialities for marshaling people and things to get a job done. In Chapter 11 we shall provide information about a battery of tests as well as about some informal means by which competence may be estimated. In general, these measures may be used to assist the administrator in assessing: (1) his capacity to understand and conceptualize the administrative problems with which he will be confronted; (2) his understanding of people and his skill in the leadership role he must play; and (3) the technical knowledge and skill he has at his command to perform the tasks for which he must assume responsibility.

The remainder of this chapter will deal with five areas of consideration which our experience has shown to be worth every administrator's time. By taking stock of (1) his values and beliefs; (2) his perception of himself; (3) his perception of others; (4) the work patterns that he finds to be rewarding; and (5) his concept of success, the administrator can learn much about his likelihood for satisfaction in the field of educational administration.

Values and Beliefs

The value we place on things is dependent upon what part they play in satisfying our basic drives and urges. We are motivated by these basic drives or needs to seek those things which satisfy them. The things we value furnish the incentives by which we are motivated. Since, in this country, food, shelter, and clothing are reasonably assured, many of our drives are somewhat secondary in nature. Better food, better shelter, and better clothing have their values too. Often one's desire to improve his standard of living impels him to change his occupational status.

Some people say they want to be administrators because they *need* the money to buy the things needed by their families. What they really mean is that they wish for themselves and their families a standard of living better than that which is possible on a teacher's salary. The incentive, in this case, is the belief that a higher standard may be attained as school administrators.

Beliefs are closely akin to understandings. When one has gained a certain understanding about how children learn, he establishes a belief, or faith, in the methods implied by his knowledge. Some beliefs are held on presumed knowledge and understanding; often these are the beliefs that are held most rigidly and are least subject to change. Let us discuss those areas in which an administrator's values and beliefs make a difference in his behavior.

AUTHORITY AND RESPONSIBILITY

One can be motivated to enter the field of administration because of an insatiable desire for power or the importance of having great responsibility. Such people illustrate what Jennings typifies as the Machiavellian "prince." [8] Hitler is an example taken from contemporary times. To a person so motivated, power and responsibility satisfy an inner drive which, possibly, even he cannot explain. Such a person is in time likely to exercise this authority in ways that are undesirable to his subordinates. Some teachers hold the opinion that it is only this kind of person who seeks an administrative post. For them, authority has an evil connotation, and they abhor the air of importance that the administrator attaches to his responsibility.

A point of view we have held throughout this book is that in every organization there must be authority and responsibility. No responsibility can be assumed successfully without the authority to do so. The legal authority flowing from the state and community through the board of education, combined with the authority of the profession—that of competently trained personnel—makes it possible to establish an organizational authority that makes sense to all concerned. This is a new concept, however, for most administrators. Their experience has taught them that final responsibility rests with them. Consequently they have come to believe that authority must rest with them also.

The person who has attained his position as administrator because of his demonstrated leadership behavior usually does not need to worry about having sufficient authority to carry out his responsibilities. It is granted to him by members of the organization. His approach to the problem is first to seek agreement on the responsibilities that the organizational task

---

[8] Eugene E. Jennings, *An Anatomy of Leadership* (New York: Harper & Brothers, 1960), Chapters 3 and 4.

requires of each of its members. His next concern is to determine what agreements are necessary to give each member of the organization the authority to carry out his responsibility. This is a rational approach that necessitates the acquisition of new understandings and new beliefs that may temper one's desire to be seen as an authority figure.

ROLE OF THE SCHOOL

The concepts that people have of education differ greatly. For some it is the means of preparing people for the vocation they will use to earn a livelihood in adult life. For others it is an experience to be endured while in childhood. Still others have found it to be the ladder to a new social level; children of unskilled workers have risen to the status of professional workers. Some see in education the hope for freedom and the realization of the democratic ideal upon which this country was founded. Many other concepts could be cited. The way the administrator deals with them makes a difference in the kind of leadership which he gives in developing the school program.

For example, in one community the school calendar of extracurricular events, including such activities as scholastic contests, dramatic plays, school parties, and club activities, is worked out in co-operation with the leaders of churches, scouting organizations, the 4-H Club leaders, and other groups that occupy the time of school children. In a neighboring school district, such school events come first; all other community agencies must fit into the pattern established by the school. In some school districts, the school is used as a center for many community-sponsored activities. In others, the use of school buildings is restricted to school projects. Some schools concern themselves with the problems and issues that arise in the community of which they are a part. Other schools leave these problems strictly alone.

What makes the difference? Some administrators report that increasing the number of community relationships just increases the number of headaches for the administration and the board of education. Others report that such relationships form a tighter bond of co-operation between the schools and other community agencies. The net effect of these relationships, according to the latter group, is one of increasing rather than diminishing satisfaction in the job. Could this difference be attributed to the differences in the values held by these groups or to the beliefs which they hold about the role of education in our society?

What should the administrator do when his teachers tell him that a certain percentage of the children cannot learn? Should he approve a policy to dismiss them from school at the earliest possible age? Or should he lead a campaign to adapt the program, the facilities, and the teaching methods to the varying learning capacities of all the children of school age? What about the incorrigibles? Does society have agencies better able than the schools to mold them into prospective useful citizens? Or does their incorrigibility deny them the right to further education and, incidentally, gain for them the privilege of taking their places outside of school as responsible adults? In these instances again, what the administrator thinks about the role of the school will have much to do with his course of action.

Another issue that weighs heavily upon the shoulders of school administrators is whether or not the children and youth of our land should have equal access to public education. If so, how is this to be attained? Does this mean more state equalization in financing? larger administrative units? more federal aid to education? some federal controls? The school administrator cannot escape the issue. The problem is pressing hard upon us as a nation, and the people are seeking leadership to resolve it.

What is actually done about these matters rests largely with the people. On the other hand, what the people do about such matters depends largely upon the statesmanship of their educational leaders. Some school administrators have been dismissed from their positions because they dared to take a stand for what they believed to be right in matters of this kind. Some, even against great odds, have weathered a stormy career while they successfully led the people to greater insight and understanding, and the building of a stronger educational program. Doubtless there are many who have succeeded in a similar way and have kept the general good will of the people in doing so. There are still others, few in number we hope, who have kept their positions, added little new educational insight, straddled the controversial issues, and retired from the profession leaving education decades behind the times.

In returning to our principle that what a man does is prompted both from within and without, we must agree that the situation in which he finds himself is partially responsible for what he does. A pertinent point, however, is that the situation changed when he entered it. What he is, believes, and values is part of the situation as soon as he enters it. Therefore, these aspects of his life must also be partial determiners of the behavior he exhibits.

ROLE OF EDUCATIONAL ADMINISTRATION

Recently a man was overheard to remark that he had served his apprenticeship as a teacher and that he thought he deserved "to get a little of the gravy in the school business." What does he mean? Is it the higher salary that he covets? Or does he regard administration as a "softer" job? Maybe it is the prestige of the office, the swivel chair, and the luncheons with the men downtown that appeal to him. The remark raises the interesting question as to when one "deserves" to be an administrator.

It is probably true that any good teacher deserves a higher salary and more prestige than he now enjoys. It does not surprise us that both of these incentives have rather high value to teachers. The concern here, however, is whether the holding of these values qualifies one to be an administrator. How much has the man referred to above thought about the responsibilities of administration and his competence to meet such responsibilities?

Often we hear that men have entered the field of educational administration because it pays more money than teaching. How often is this the primary incentive? Or is it usually the primary one? Maybe there are other incentives in administration about which the person is not articulate. In conversations with graduate students who are interested in preparing themselves for educational administration, one of the authors found that he usually got a number of different answers to the query, "Why do you want to become an administrator?" Higher salary and more prestige were mentioned very often but always in combination with other incentives. Usually the candidate proceeded to explain that he had been given opportunities for administrative responsibility and enjoyed the experience, that he had often been elected to leadership posts and offices by fellow teachers, that he found himself working in an organizing capacity in various community groups, that his employers had encouraged him to enter the field of administration, or that he saw opportunities to provide leadership in the educational program and believed that he had the ability and the desire to be such a leader.

We submit the proposition that a person usually enters the field of administration for a complex of reasons, some of which reflect an interest in the material benefits that might accrue to him and some of which demonstrate a faith in his ability to be of greater service in the capacity of administrator. In a study designed to determine the effect of value differences held by individuals and groups upon relationships within the school, Prince has shown that:

> . . . the extent of agreement in values between teachers and principals has a significant relationship to the teacher's rating of the principal's effectiveness and to the teacher's confidence in the principal's leadership. At the same time, the extent of agreement in values seems to have little effect upon either individual satisfaction or the principal's ratings of teacher effectiveness. Studies of administrative behavior have previously shown that the major reference groups in the school perceive the administrator in different ways. Studies of value differences may suggest one clue as to why this is so.[9]

[9] Richard Prince, "Individual Values and Administrative Effectiveness," *Administrator's Notebook,* Vol. VI, No. 4 (December 1957).

We suspect that those who see the job as primarily routine will do quite a different job from those who view administration as a developmental task providing an opportunity to give leadership to people who are seeing and approaching new educational horizons.

In Chapter 3, the opportunity was provided to study the purpose of educational administration. Here we are saying that no matter what one has concluded from his consideration of this subject, the values he holds for administration still affect his beliefs, and these in turn his behavior. In Chapter 11 we shall present an examination and an assessment of values, and show how such an assessment can be used to affect one's action.

In the above discussion we mentioned that administrators may not see themselves as others see them. This seems a little harsh on administrators at first glance, but when we stop to think about it, we must conclude that no one really sees himself as others see him. Every suitation and every person in it will be seen differently by each person doing the looking. Furthermore, each person may assume that what he sees is real—which, in a certain sense, is true. A color-blind person may view all of his world in terms of black, white, and various shades of the two colors; this is the way he sees it. Experiencing color has no meaning for him. We say he does not see the real thing. Yet all that we can do for him may not help him to see objects as we do.

When we are dealing with perceptions, we must recognize that each person sees through his own eyes and interprets what he sees in terms of his own experiences and his own fund of meanings. Therefore we must warn the reader that what is as clear as the nose on your face to one person may be as clear as mud to another. For a theoretical discussion of perception we refer the reader to Ittleson and Cantril.[10] Suffice it to say for this discussion that if people are to see alike, they must see a situation from similar vantage points, with similar backgrounds for viewing it, and with a common fund of meanings for its interpretation.

AS A PERSON

With this brief background, let us consider the administrator's conception of himself, not in any specific professional role but just as a person. When he looks in a mirror, what does he see? Does he see a well-adjusted person, one who enjoys living, accepts responsibility with enthusiasm, is energetic, sociable, willing to prepare himself adequately for the tasks that lie ahead of him? Or does he see a person who is discontent with what teaching has done for him, is looking for the easy way out, withdraws from

[10] William H. Ittleson and Hadley Cantril, *Perception* (New York: Random House Inc., 1954).

associations with people, and is frustrated by decisions that he cannot make?

The next question is, "Is he willing to face up to what he sees?" Undoubtedly, as he makes out his ledger, he will find both assets and liabilities. Can he live with them? Does he have sufficient confidence so that even though he is aware of some weaknesses in the picture, he believes he is the man for the job? Can he face up to the fact that when the weaknesses overbalance the strengths, he should bow out graciously?

As a person, does he worry about what other people think of him? Sometimes it is argued that those who seek executive positions are egotistical, that they feed on favorable publicity, and that they are unwilling to accept criticism. The administrator lives in a world of controversy. He must make frequent decisions and he will make many unpopular ones. What will this do to him and to his family? Can he maintain his balance even though he knows that he is disliked by some?

What about his ability? The ability to help people make decisions by which they are willing to live is of a high order. The prospective administrator should be able to approach his first position with some confidence that he has this ability. He should assume leadership roles in his school system or the community in which he works. He can discover much about his ability by testing himself in semi-administrative roles to which he may be assigned by his principal or superintendent.

His position is like that of the batter in a baseball game. He may strike out once in a while. He will not always be the long ball hitter. But he must reach first base fairly often. The good hitter bats about .300 or above. He has confidence when he steps up to the plate. So it is with the school administrator. He tests himself until he has sufficient confidence that he can maintain an appropriate batting average—which, by the way, should be considerably higher than that required for baseball. The next two chapters will provide some help in achieving this goal.

AS AN ADMINISTRATOR

Although looking at oneself as an administrator may be a difficult assignment, there are a number of vantage points from which views may be had. One way for the administrator to look at himself, with considerable profit we think, is from the standpoint of purposes. Let him ask himself whether his primary purpose is to facilitate the development of goals, policies, and programs, or whether he prefers to control, manipulate, and manage their development. His real purposes will be reflected in his actions more than in any verbal expression he may make concerning them. A careful examination of one's behavior might reveal that it is difficult for the administrator to behave purely one way or the other. Does this mean that there is a conflict in his purposes, that he holds dual purposes, or that the two purposes are ends of a continuum along which his action shifts from time to time according to the circumstances? Or could an examination of his behavior reveal the fact that his purposes, after all, have not been clearly established?

This also raises the question of whether or not the administrator must see himself primarily as the chief "doer," or as the man who organizes so that things get done. We often speak of administrators as action men. So much emphasis can be placed on this concept that administrators feel compelled to engage in every activity carried on by the school. Principals need to examine their behavior, for example, to determine whether they should be the chief disciplinarians of the school or whether they should be spending their time helping teachers develop experiences, techniques, and programs that promote controlled pupil behavior. Superintendents may need to check themselves to determine whether they are carrying on the proper activities to provide the architect with appropriate educational specifications for building planning or whether they are actually trying to be architects. Here again, the critic could raise the question of the advisability of "either-or" thinking, that is, seeing things as black or white without recognizing the middle ground. For purposes of examination, at least, we think that this kind of thinking is advisable. An administrator cannot do everything. He must make choices. The educational leader does not have the time to be involved in all the minutiae of the operation of the school district.

Some administrators say that it is impossible in days of building and teacher shortages to give the educational program top priority. For them, what time is spent on the performance of one task is lost to another. The reason they feel this way is that they have made all of the administrative tasks competitive to each other. There is another way to look at this problem; when the problems in one task area are solved well, all other tasks are made easier. Hence, worthwhile contributions in one task area make a contribution to the solution of problems in all others.

An administrator ought to be well aware of the balance of his strengths and weaknesses and be able to check these against the reaction that he is getting from his constituents. Returning now to the labels mentioned in Chapter 1, what behavior do people see which causes them to label an administrator a dictator, a boss, a co-ordinator, or a leader? What set of labels would be preferable? Jenkins and Blackman, in their study of elementary principals, make the following observation:

One group of principals was judged to approach problems primarily through *relations-building*, getting the relevant people together to work the problem out. Another group was primarily *administration-centered*, the administrator making the decisions and taking whatever action he deemed necessary.[11]

[11] Jenkins and Blackman, *op. cit.*, p. 45.

Further analysis is necessary, however, to attach real meaning to the names given to these two groups. One is likely to make the assumption, as these researchers did, that the *relations-building* group was the more "democratic" of the two, and hence would be the group preferred by the teachers. However, the following paragraph taken from the study indicates that such an assumption was not warranted:

Originally it was expected that the relations-building category would represent a "democratic" approach; the principal would show a high degree of concern about his staff members and their relations to himself and each other. It was expected also that he would believe it important to take action to build more satisfying relationships among his staff members. In contrast, the administration-centered approach was believed to represent a disregard of the staff members as individuals and the assumption of decision making by the administrator, who would attempt to put his decisions into effect with despatch. From this orientation it was assumed that the teachers would express greater satisfaction from the relations-building approach. This did not prove to be the case. . . .[12]

Actually, as a result of their investigation, Jenkins and Blackman found that those administrators who could balance "relations-building" and "administration-centered" activity were preferred by teachers and were more successful in promoting staff productivity.

Halpin makes the case that morale is not enough. His dimensions of administrator behavior, initiating structure in interaction, and consideration referred to in Chapter 6, and shown in this four-quadrant diagram,[13] are interesting for purposes of the analysis of perceptions and expectations of administrator behavior. While his study was not intended to produce

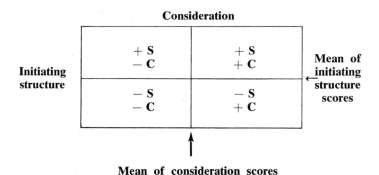

Figure 10.1   Initiating Structure and Consideration as Co-ordinate Dimensions of Administrator Behavior

[12] *Ibid.*

[13] Halpin, *op. cit.,* p. 10.

a measure of the effectiveness of administrators, Halpin does provide evidence that effective administrators are those whose behavior reflects both initiation of structure and consideration. The purposes of the school must be achieved at the same time that staff morale and co-operative effort are maintained.

In view of the research cited, the administrator would be well advised to view his behavior in terms of the two dimensions—consideration and initiating structure—suggested above. He should contemplate, for example, what is likely to result when he emphasizes one of these dimensions rather than the other, as is indicated by behavior represented by the plus and minus symbols in the upper left-hand and the lower right-hand quadrants of the above figure; and what happens to a staff and to the program of the school when the administrator's behavior is weak in both dimensions, as shown by the two negative symbols in the lower left-hand quadrant. The figure provides the administrator with a device for classifying perceptions of his behavior as measured by consideration and initiating structure.

Another way of viewing one's self as an administrator is by attempting to define one's primary responsibility as an administrator. In a study conducted by Sweitzer,[14] five general categories of perceived primary responsibility were identified. They were:

Authority-centered. The authority-centered administrator sees his primary responsibility as achieving purposes through clarifying and carrying out the official policy adopted by the school board.

Inner-directed. The inner-directed administrator conceives his primary responsibility to be modifying, improving, and interpreting policy and proceeding along lines he thinks will best meet the educational needs of the community.

Work-group-oriented. The work-group-oriented administrator considers his primary responsibility to be facilitating the cooperative development of group standards and procedures that tend to meet identified local needs.

Individual-centered. The individual-centered administrator conceives his primary responsibility to be enabling individuals and groups to carry out their tasks, largely self-appointed and self-defined, with as little interference as possible.

Other-directed. The other-directed administrator conceives his primary responsibility to be knowing as best he can the wishes of the people served, and seeing to it that the goals and procedures felt to be most worthwhile are officially adopted and then achieved.

Sweitzer's study indicated that superintendents, principals, and teachers viewed the relative desirability of each of the five categories in the same order of rank. In order of most-to-least-desirable, these three groups ranked the role categories in the following order:

[14] R. E. Sweitzer, "The Superintendent's Role in Improving Instruction," *Administrator's Notebook,* Vol. VI, No. 8 (April 1958).

1. Work-group-centered

2. Other-directed

3. Individual-centered

4. Authority-centered

5. Inner-directed

With regard to these findings, Sweitzer states, in part, that:

There was a high level of agreement among the role-perceptions of a given reference group. Data indicated that group membership may have been a more crucial factor in determining role-perceptions than was membership in a particular school system. Less common agreement existed among the groups regarding role-perceptions than was apparent in the case of role-expectations.[15]

AS A RESOLVER OF CONFLICT

Research in the field of perceptions, expectations, and climate of opinion indicates that there are bound to be differences in points of view among those with whom the administrator works. An administrator cannot hope to have the unchallenged support of his teachers or the constituents of his school district throughout his career. It is more probable that during his tenure in any school district there are some who will support him wholeheartedly, a larger group who will be somewhat uninformed and apathetic about school matters, and still another small group of disgruntled and dissatisfied citizens. The composition of these groups may change from time to time or from issue to issue.

The implication is that the administrator who expects to have smooth sailing all of the time is due to have a severe shock. Most important decisions are going to take hard work; the bulk of this work lies in getting sufficient agreement among people to carry the decisions into action. Much of the life of an educational administrator is spent giving leadership to a group (students, faculty, board of education, constituents of the school district) who must make decisions and act upon them.

PERCEPTION OF OTHERS

How an administrator works with people is partially dependent upon his assessment of himself, but it is determined also in part by his faith in

---

[15] *Ibid.*

others. The democrat and the autocrat do not see eye to eye on this matter. Decisions of, by, and for the people is a concept espoused by democratic nations. Does it apply equally well to schools that foster the democratic ideal? And if it does, what does it mean for the relationship between the educational administrator and all others who are involved in the decision-making process? We shall approach the problem from the administrator's point of view. Let us look at the administrator's assessment of people, his concept of group interaction, the formal and informal relationships which he deems important, and finally the role he sees for the reference groups with which he works.

ASSESSMENT OF PEOPLE

While we believe in co-operative processes of decision-making, we cannot condone the pooling of ignorance. A second and equally important tenet of democracy is that, as people make decisions, intelligence, not ignorance, must be brought to bear in sound problem-solving procedures. What the administrator needs to assess, then, is the probability that the methods which are employed for problem-solving will utilize the intelligence available. Some faculties are not accustomed to solving their own problems. In such a case it is likely that a certain ineptness will be detected when they are given such responsibilities. The administrator will have to make judgments as to how far he can go in this direction and still get intelligent behavior.

The same situation prevails with the board of education or with other groups in the community with whom the administrator works. Groups that have experienced the need for responsible group behavior may be able to participate wisely in group decision-making processes. Groups lacking such experience may need to approach the problem of shared decision-making more gradually.

Another kind of assessment that must be made when numbers of people are involved requires determining who should make a given decision. Are there some decisions that can be made more appropriately by laymen than professionals? And would the converse also be true? Who is likely to have the knowledge that is required for a given decision? Deciding how much people should be told, helped, or allowed to make decisions for themselves is a responsibility of no mean proportions. Making sure that decisions are in the hands of groups qualified to make them is equally difficult. How an administrator makes the assessment, however, and the outcome of his assessments, may be determined in large measure by his own attitudes toward co-operative decision-making processes.

GROUP INTERACTION

In Chapter 6 we had much to say about how administrators relate them-selves to groups. Their approaches to group activity are determined by their understanding of the dynamics of group involvement. Some adminis-trators stay aloof from the group, as is suggested in Diagram 1 of Figure 10.2. "A" represents the administrator; the circle is the group. Such administrators would attempt to exert their leadership by efforts to attract the group to them and to their way of thinking. According to this concept the administrator pulls on the group in an attempt to overcome group pressures that are exerted in the opposite direction. Another way to look at leadership is illustrated by Diagram 2 of Figure 10.2, where the leader is accepted as a member of the group. Thus his influence is from within rather than from without the group. He affects group decisions, but they are nonetheless *group* decisions—not leader decisions having group approval. Diagram 3 of Figure 10.2 is not wholly different from Diagram 2 except that it is intended to point out a situation in which the leader may recognize that within a given group there is a nucleus of power that must be dealt with in order to get group action. When the power group has given

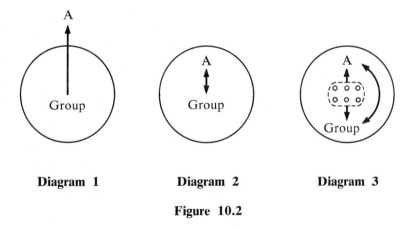

Diagram 1   Diagram 2   Diagram 3

Figure 10.2

its approval, the group is ready to act also. In this case the leader has the alternative of obtaining approval of the power group or of bypassing it in his relationships with other members of the group. The decision to take either alternative is a delicate one. The understandings of leadership behavior developed in Chapter 6 should be of some help to the administrator in deciding how his effectiveness as a leader is affected by his relationship to the group.

There are at least three groups with whom the administrator works very closely. If he is a superintendent of schools, these groups are the voting populace of the community, the board of education, and the staff. In

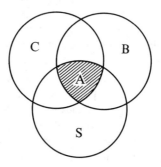

Diagram 4

Figure 10.3

Diagram 4 (Figure 10.3), the circle designated as C represents the people of the community, circle B represents the board of education, and circle S represents the staff. Note that A, the administrator, sees himself as a member of each of these three groups. The shaded area indicates the extent of agreement among the three groups. It is obvious that as the centers of these circles move closer together, the shaded area becomes increasingly larger. An administrator would like to view his activity as an influence that makes for a large shaded area, hence a large core of common agreement. On the other hand, it is obvious that as the circles move farther apart, the area of common agreement decreases, thus diminishing the effectiveness of the administrator.

FORMAL AND INFORMAL RELATIONSHIPS

Some administrators ask whether it is a good idea to have informal social relationships with certain members of the faculty. Principals have reported, for example, that jealousy results when they entertain in their homes or visit with certain teachers more than others. Superintendents are reported to be lonely people. Teachers are afraid to entertain them because such behavior may give the impression that they are seeking favors.

Moore tells us that the school administrator is a stranger in the school districts in which he serves.[16] He is a stranger in the sense that "there are certain factors in American culture which tend to deny him a full participation in the life of the community in which he lives and which he serves." [17] School administrators thus find themselves working in formal relationships with people throughout the community and on the staff, but may discover that informal relationships are difficult to establish. It is generally conceded that a superintendent of schools may develop a social relationship with members of his board of education and other executives of business or industry in his community more easily than with members of his staff. The principals have a somewhat easier time in making social contacts within the school system, perhaps due merely to the fact that in many school systems there are a number of principals who can associate with one another.

What happens to administrators because of this restriction of informal contacts we do not know. We know, of course, that social relationships do exist throughout the groups with which administrators work, and that other informal arrangements and agreements are constantly being made within them. Many of these informal relationships contribute to good working conditions both within the school and between the school and the community. Certainly most administrators are not isolates in the sense of being denied involvement in social affairs or informal arrangements. Nevertheless, if a barrier exists, the initiative in breaking it down generally lies with the administrator. The administrator's problem, then, is to see how formal and informal relationships contribute both to the achievement of educational objectives and to job satisfaction, for himself and for his staff.

ROLE OF REFERENCE GROUPS

Chapters 7 and 8 dealt at length with the problem of reference groups. Now the administrator must assess his own perception of the role that people play in the administrative process. In what areas do the people with whom he works actually make the decisions? What people make what decisions? Are any decisions reserved solely to administrators? What criteria should be used to answer such questions?

Does not the answer depend in large measure upon whether the administrator has a preconceived notion of how the schools should be run and is trying to get people to conform to his pattern, or whether he is giving

[16] Harry Estill Moore, *Nine Help Themselves* (Austin: The University of Texas, Southwestern Co-operative Program in Educational Administration, 1955), pp. 56–57.

[17] *Ibid.*, p. 66.

guidance and leadership to a group that is constantly growing and realizing a greater measure of their potential in the development of a sound educational pattern? The people do not take over; the leader does not abdicate. Rather, an orderly process of improvement in thinking and in the development of techniques is achieved through wide participation of all reference groups in a plan co-ordinated and directed by an accepted status leader.

REWARDING WORK PATTERNS

Another factor that affects administrative behavior is the kind of work pattern that produces satisfaction. For example, some people get satisfaction from a job in which they are told specifically what to do and how to do it. Possessing the skill to carry out this operation well assures them of the job they want. Little thinking is required. Few decisions are to be made. The important factor in achievement is skill. The reward is good pay and little cause for worry.

Some people like to work with things; others like to work with people. Working with inanimate objects can become a complex operation demanding not only skill but understanding of a complex body of knowledge and insight into intricate processes. The accountant and the chemist are examples of professional people whose work is mainly with things.

Some administrators believe that when they leave the classroom they will no longer be bothered with pupils about whom decisions have to be made. Actually, the work of which they speak is clerical, not administrative. Perhaps there are many people who mistakenly seek administrative positions because they think that their duties will be largely clerical. This may be one of the reasons why many administrators spend more time on clerical responsibilities than on other duties to which they are assigned.

One of the authors worked for a year with a number of principals of elementary schools in a metropolitan area. All of the principals agreed that they spent over one half of their time on clerical duties such as making out student records, answering the telephone, writing reports for the superintendent, opening and answering mail, and greeting people who came to the office. The same principals agreed that although some of this was necessary, it should not consume such a large portion of their time. When asked what they wanted to do with their time, all replied that they would like to give more time to the leadership of a program for the improvement of instruction. If they really wanted to do this, why did they not change their own patterns of behavior?

To be fair to these administrators, it must be reported that the activity in which they were engaged was what was expected of them both by their superintendents and by their teachers. Another reason why they behaved as they did was that they had fallen into the habit of doing clerical tasks, and the habit produced some satisfactions. All the principals admitted that while they were trying to change their behavior, they had many periods of anguish in which they honestly wished they could return to their former, more comfortable jobs.

So the prospective administrator must not only ask himself whether or not he wishes to accept the responsibilities of an assigned leadership role, but he should try it for size. While preparing for an administrative position, before he is actually certificated, he often has opportunities to work with his colleagues in a leadership capacity.

SATISFYING ACTIVITIES

People who find administration rewarding undoubtedly find many activities in which they engage satisfying to them. We believe that in this pattern of satisfaction there will be at least two activities that will prove especially rewarding. They are (1) working through the decision-making process with other people and (2) carrying out the executive function in terms of established policy. The former activity is essential to the latter. However, once policy is clearly established, implications for action are set forth.

The big job in finance is neither making out the budget nor spending the money that is available. Rather it is seeing that the budget makes sufficient sense to the people so that they will provide the necessary revenue to pay the bills incurred. Again, in building the school plant, the real job is providing the people with the information necessary to prove to them that there is an educational need of such urgency that immediate action is imperative. Administrators everywhere agree that it is this kind of work that separates the men from the boys.

SATISFYING AND DISSATISFYING SITUATIONS

Men of action often wish to achieve goals more rapidly than is possible in many communities. The pressure to move faster than the community is willing to go and the resultant resistance on the part of the community can be frustrating to all concerned. Situations can be cited where a superintendent of schools became so dissatisfied with the community's failure to act that his only recourse was to move to a new school district in the hope that conditions there would be different. In some instances, boards of education, being receptive to the community pattern of action, have forced the superintendent to move.

A similar situation could be cited within the school itself. The failure of the principal or the superintendent and the faculty to see goals alike may cause them to work at cross purposes or to move toward their achievement at different rates of speed. Dissatisfaction on the part of both administrators and teachers is bound to occur. Is it possible to synchronize the methods of achieving goals so that they are completely satisfactory to all concerned? Probably the answer is no.

Of course, we must entertain the possibility that there are situations, too, where teachers and the people of the community are chafing at the bit and the administrators are holding a tight rein. We would hope that this would be for some intelligent reason. Nevertheless, the situation is one in which tensions mount to proportions equal to those developed when the administrator feels that the people are blocking progress.

Does this suggest that administrative situations are never calm and serene? Must somebody be unhappy all the time? No, but administrative situations are always in a state of flux. They are dynamic. They are action situations. This is something to which the administrator must become accustomed. Sitting on the lid while the pot is boiling is dangerous administrative strategy.

Let us return to Figure 10.3, which illustrates the fact that the major decision-making groups are probably never in complete agreement. The effective administrator is satisfied to have an area of agreement sufficiently large to accomplish certain goals which his constituents see in common. The areas of disagreement (portions of the circles that do not overlap) are challenges too. What can be done to help people who see school matters somewhat differently to understand each other better? If anything positive can be done in answer to this question, the area of agreement can be extended, and new accomplishments become possible. The creative administrator knows the purposes to be achieved by further agreement in objectives, and he knows, too, what authority for action is granted when this happens.

Thus he does not expect to have people see goals and objectives alike without a great deal of effort on his part. The administrator revels in his opportunity to foster agreement by degrees. Long-term goals he may have for the schools, or which he hopes the people will have for their schools, are achieved by a series of short practical gains, each of which brings those satisfactions that make people ready for the next one.

In short, if a person gets satisfaction from working with other people in dynamic, fluid situations such as those described above, he may have an aptitude for administration. If, on the one hand, such activity and such situations wear him out and cause undue frustration and fear, he will undoubtedly shrink away from his responsibility as leader. On the other hand, the administrative staff for a school district, especially in our larger school systems, have need for personnel who perform specialized tasks requiring specific knowledge and skills. Staff positions usually do not require as much skill in working with people as do line positions. A person interested in school administration should investigate positions of both kinds and assess himself, his abilities, and his interests to determine the kind of administrative position in which he is likely to gain his greatest satisfactions.

Concept of Success

What is success? This is an age-old question, the meaning of which each generation in turn struggles to discover. Those who gave up the relative security of their homes to found a new nation in America seemed to prize freedom above security. Those who keep on the cutting edge of a frontier seem to prize the forward movement of the frontier more than any personal or material gain or security. One criticism that has been leveled at people of this day and age is that they are so preoccupied with security for themselves that they fail to recognize the fronts upon which social progress can be made. Whatever one's attitude toward this issue may be, it is generally recognized that there is within each of us an urge to succeed. This urge has its effect upon what we do. It is imperative, therefore, that an administrator give some thought to the concept of success which motivates his activity.

Ambition to Better One's Self

The young man to whom reference was made because he thought he deserved some of the "gravy" in the teaching profession must have placed personal gain very high on his scale of values. Is he successful when he moves progressively from one administrative position to larger and more lucrative positions? Or are his chances for success greater when he remains in the same position for a relatively long period of time, expecting by so doing to grow with the system? In which case is he likely to obtain a higher salary? In which of the two does he have greater opportunity to improve the educational program?

Some administrators get the reputation of being professional nomads, always moving to situations where the pasture seems to them to be greener. Others become stereotyped as unambitious individuals satisfied to stay in relatively small school systems. If one is inclined to climb the professional ladder to positions of greater and greater responsibility, what must one do to obtain sufficient renown to be seen favorably as a candidate for the next higher position? If a person feels that he can realize his personal and professional goals by remaining in one position for a relatively long period, how does he avoid the stamp of failure?

Probably there are few administrators regarded as successful by the profession who have no personal ambition to better themselves. On the other hand, there are few who would get the opportunity to better themselves unless they had demonstrated their ability to make contributions to school improvement. There are exceptions, of course, and the number of boards of education that have established adequate criteria for the selection of school administrators is few. Nevertheless, we can be reasonably assured that people who place personal gain either in dollars, prestige, or status over and above responsibility for educational leadership do not succeed in school administration. It may be possible, too, that a man will do an excellent job in school improvement in his own school district or in the school building in which he is principal without this leadership coming to the attention of those who are in a position to promote him.

SUCCESS IS A CONSTELLATION CONCEPT

Many factors join together to form a pattern that is called success. Baker, in a study of the selection of superintendents of schools, reports that there are fourteen personal characteristics of superintendents which school board members list as being important in selection. These, together with the percentage of school board members mentioning each, are:

Personal appearance (89.1); agreeableness and friendliness (87.8); ability to work democratically with staff (87.3); personal integrity and fairness (87.0); ability to supervise instruction (81.2); experience as a superintendent of schools (80.8); range of professional experience (80.0); aggressive leadership in improving school program (80.0); ability to discipline students and teachers (79.0); length of service in previous position (75.0); personal habits (72.9); skill in financial matters (71.3); skill in working with parent groups and the public (71.3); and health (69.6).[18]

There is little in this set of characteristics to suggest that an administrator's point of view—what he believes about the role of the school—makes any difference in his selection.

Any set of criteria used for either the preparation or the selection of administrators betrays the concept of success used by the training institu-

[18] Thomas R. Bowman and William W. Savage, "Selecting a Superintendent," *Administrator's Notebook* (February 1956), 3, in which among other studies the authors report the findings of an unpublished doctoral dissertation by John E. Baker, "The Selection of Superintendents of Schools by Boards of Education," Department of Education, University of Chicago, 1952.

tion or the school that is doing the selecting. Mention has already been made of competencies that educational institutions have adopted as a basis for preparing school administrators. A more adequate opportunity to consider these competencies is provided in Chapter 11. The appearance of these lists suggests that thought is being given to the development of more adequate criteria for the success of school administrators.

Recently, the American Association of School Administrators published a statement which emphasizes that the selection of a chief school administrator should be a well-considered, systematic procedure. The pamphlet also stresses the point that searching for a highly qualified school administrator takes time, and the decisions relative to this process should not be made hastily. The selection procedure suggested by the association is as follows:

1. Know what you want (develop a job description and a list of qualifications).

2. Determine evaluative procedures (credentials evaluation, interview evaluation, and visitation evaluation).

3. Announce the vacancy (make it public).

4. Examine local candidates (in terms of qualifications).

5. Develop a list (outside candidates with appropriate qualifications).

6. Narrow the field (ten or fewer qualified candidates).

7. Interview the best (determine values, conceptual skills, operational skills).

8. Visit the candidate's community (validate impressions in terms of demonstrated performance).

9. Make a choice (judgment based on data collected in steps 1–8).

10. Work with the press, television, and radio (articulate confidence in person selected).[19]

The joint committee of the American Association of School Administrators and the National School Boards Association, which prepared this publication, expressed its belief that the success of the superintendent is based not upon a single criterion, but upon a constellation of factors determined systematically by the series of steps just enumerated.

In his study to determine which personal variables are related to administrative effectiveness, Lipham hypothesized:

. . . effective principals would tend to rank higher than ineffective principals on the following measurable, relevant personality variables:

1. *Activity drive:* to move forward purposefully; to direct strong mental or physical effort toward the solution of problems.

[19] American Association of School Administrators, *On Selecting a Superintendent of Schools* (Washington: AASA, 1962), p. 6.

2. *Achievement drive:* to do one's best; to improve one's competencies through general and specialized study.

3. *Mobility drive:* to become a leader of groups; to operate in a position of prestige, power, and authority.

4. *Social ability:* to associate successfully with others in the solution of problems; to participate in friendly groups.

5. *Feelings of security:* to view family relationships with pride and satisfaction; to view authority figures as serving constructive purposes.

6. *Emotional control:* to assess environmental conditions objectively and realistically; to adjust well to irritations, frustrations, confusion, and criticism.[20]

As evidence to support his hypothesis, Lipham could present contrasting pictures of the effective and ineffective principal. In summary, he portrayed the effective principal as a person inclined to engage in strong and purposeful activity, concerned with achieving success and positions of higher status, able to relate well to others, secure in interpersonal relationships, and stable in the face of highly affective stimuli.[21] The ineffective principal was described as deliberate and preoccupied with speculative reasoning, accepting with a meek and servile attitude his present level of achievement and status, lacking the skills essential for working with adults but anxious to give assistance and consolation to children, highly dependent upon others for support, and likely to exhibit strong emotional reactions in upsetting situations.[22]

In recent years there has been a trend toward identifying the differences in the behavior of successful and unsuccessful administrators, rather than toward determining what the characteristics of the successful ones are. One of the most extensive and outstanding studies of this type was conducted by Hemphill, Griffiths, and Frederiksen.[23] They were aware of the effect of different field situations on experimental results. Consequently, Hemphill and his colleagues introduced 232 elementary principals to one simulated school[24] and had them react in writing to a standardized set of

[20] James M. Lipham, "Personal Variables of Effective Administrators," *Administrator's Notebook,* Vol. IX, No. 1 (September 1960).

[21] *Ibid.*

[22] *Ibid.*

[23] John K. Hemphill, *et al., Administrative Performance and Personality.* (New York: Bureau of Publications, Teachers College, Columbia University, 1962).

[24] The simulated school in-basket items and other instructional aids developed in this study are now available for use in training administrators. They may be ordered from the University Council for Educational Administration, 65 South Oval Drive, Columbus, Ohio, 43210.

in-basket items, kinescopes, film strips, tape recordings, and other background materials. After being scored and analyzed, the simulated items were correlated with test data regarding the abilities, knowledge, skills, interests, and personalities of the test subjects. From these data, the experimenters distilled eight first-order and two second-order factors, which they believe describe the important differences in principals' behavior. The factors are:

A. Exchanging information

B. Discussing before acting

C. Complying with suggestions

D. Analyzing the situation

E. Maintaining relationships

F. Organizing work

G. Responding to outsiders

H. Directing others

X. Preparation for decision

Y. Amount of work[25]

While these factors are not in themselves evaluative, they serve as a basis for contrasting superintendents' and teachers' perceptions of appropriate principal behavior, and are useful categories for describing administrative performance. Although definitions of the "good" principal vary widely in this study, the researchers indicate there is evidence that the respondents to their inquiry favor the principal with high verbal ability and high professional knowledge.[26] Another conclusion is that the "best" principals are those who tend to make definite preparation for decision-making.[27]

These reports show that the successful administrator is perceived somewhat differently by different investigators; but none of them is presented as the last word in thinking about success as an incentive. All illustrate the fact that criteria for success, whether established by professionals or laymen, come in clusters. Measuring up to one criterion indicates some degree of positive behavior on other criteria as well. It is probably unrealistic to assume that the beginning administrator can think solely in terms of a list of criteria such as those suggested by researchers in educational administration; the impressions of boards of education constitute a factor too strong to permit this. An expectation for the near future, how-

[25] Hemphill, *ibid.*

[26] *Ibid.*

[27] *Ibid.*

ever, is that additional study in this area will bring professional educators, practitioners, and laymen to greater common agreement on what constitutes success in educational administration.

EXAMINE FACTORS AFFECTING BEHAVIOR

In essence, we have said that there are many factors, both within and without the person, which affect behavior. Administrators, like all educated people, attempt to use education to improve upon what they do and how they do it. Preparation programs for educational administrators are designed with increasing emphasis upon knowledge about the factors that affect administrator behavior.

It has seemed to the authors of this book that the research in this field suggests that much improvement can be made in administration by a careful examination of these factors. Some which the administrator can explore with profit are (1) his beliefs and values about authority and responsibility, the role of the school, and the role of educational administration; (2) his perception of himself as a person, an administrator, and a resolver of conflict; (3) his perception of others—his assessment of people, his concept of group interaction, his use of formal and informal relationships, and the role that he sees for the reference groups with whom he works; (4) the work patterns that he finds rewarding, including satisfying activities and satisfying situations in which to work; and (5) the administrator's concept of success. Most of these factors deal with the "inner structure" of the administrator's personality. However, it is not sufficient for the prospective administrator merely to know himself. Knowledge about him should suggest both to him and to others that he can acquire the competence necessary for administration. Chapter 11 provides some of the means by which such knowledge may be attained. The conscientious student of administration will continue his personal assessment while on the job and take the initiative in adjusting his role in administration in terms of the competence that he demonstrates.

SUGGESTED ACTIVITIES

1. Read one of Chapters 2, 3, 4, 5, or 6 in Griffiths' *Human Relations in School Administration* (see selected readings), and write a brief analysis of the implications of the chapter for administrative behavior.

2. Visit an administrator whom you regard as successful, and get his viewpoint concerning the drives which motivate him to exert the energy he does to improving education in his school district.

3. Go with an administrator (principal, supervisor, or superintendent), and observe his behavior in all of the activities in which he is engaged in fulfilling his professional responsibilities for the day. Try to analyze his behavior in terms of causes that may have prompted him to behave as he did.

4. Observe an administrator in a staff meeting, a meeting of the board of education, or a meeting of his administrative advisory council. From what he does, interpret his perception of his role and that of the others in the group. Give reasons for your interpretation.

5. Think of an instance in which you have disagreed with the action of the administrator of your school. Describe the situation briefly, tell what the administrator did, tell what you would have done, and try to explain what you think lies behind the two different kinds of behavior.

SELECTED READINGS

ALLPORT, GORDON. *Personality: A Psychological Interpretation*. New York: Holt, Rinehart and Winston, Inc., 1937. Chapter 7.

CAMPBELL, ROALD and GREGG, RUSSELL, eds. *Administrative Behavior in Education*. New York: Harper & Brothers, 1957.

DUBIN, ROBERT, ed. *Human Relations in Administration*. Englewood Cliffs, N.J.: Prentice-Hall, Inc., 1951. Pages 188–98.

GRIFFITHS, DANIEL E. *Human Relations in School Administration*. New York: Appleton-Century-Crofts, Inc., 1956. Chapters 2–6.

HEMPHILL, J. K., GRIFFITHS, D. E., and FREDERIKSEN, N. *Administrative Performance and Personality*. New York: Bureau of Publications, Teachers College, Columbia University, 1962.

ITTLESON, WILLIAM H. and CANTRIL, HADLEY. *Perception*. New York: Random House, 1954.

11

Competencies

and Potential

THE PLATITUDE SOMETIMES OFFERED TO A CHILD that "you can be anything you want to be" is, unfortunately, only partially true. It becomes even less true if the idea of effectiveness is introduced. It may be that anyone with persistence can become some kind of administrator, but it is not possible for anyone or everyone to make himself an effective educational administrator.

It is equally true that it is now and probably always will be impossible to present a test, or an interview schedule, or any combination of measuring devices that will predict without fail that Mr. X can be and Mr. Y cannot be an effective administrator. There is, however, increasing evidence that one person with certain characteristics and abilities has a better chance of succeeding as an administrator than others without these characteristics and abilities.

A person gains more happiness and success from a life's work for which he is suited than he does by attempting to succeed where he is not well suited. It is the purpose of this chapter to describe what is known about the competencies required of a school administrator and to indicate some of the ways in which a person can determine the degree to which he possesses these competencies. The chapter will also describe ways in which competencies can be improved if improvement is required.

THE NATURE OF COMPETENCIES

THE TRAIT APPROACH

It was once quite generally believed that a person who possessed a certain number of characteristics or traits of a particular kind would be qualified to perform a given task. Thus, it was sometimes stated that a man who was tall, of above-average intelligence (but not too far above), with a good and resonant speaking voice, with personal characteristics of tact and honesty, and with a certain amount of ambition, could become a successful administrator because of the possession of these traits. It was recognized that there were exceptions, but these merely served to prove the rule.

Stogdill found that the various traits suggested as important for leaders could be grouped under five main headings: *capacity,* including such things as intelligence, verbal facility, and judgment; *achievement,* including scholarship and knowledge; *responsibility,* including dependability, self-confidence, and ambition; *participation,* meaning sociability, adaptability, and activity; and *status,* or socio-economic position and popularity.[1] It can be seen that it would be sufficient, if the trait approach were completely accurate, to devote major efforts in choosing administrators to the development of instruments that would measure a man's traits and classify him in terms of his administrative potential. But, fortunately or unfortunately, other elements keep entering the picture.

TRAITS AND COMPETENCIES

The administrator does not work in a vacuum. He works with many people and in many varying situations. There are many kinds of administrative positions—each of which has certain characteristics of its own in spite of many similarities with other positions. Because of the great influence of the situation, including the co-workers, on the ways in which an administrator can operate effectively, it has become obvious that the trait approach is not sufficient in and of itself for the identification of potential administrators. A number of studies have revealed that successful leaders in different situations possessed strikingly different traits.[2] Some of these findings are obvious; for example, leaders in athletic situations must have certain physical characteristics completely unimportant for a leader in a

---

[1] R. M. Stogdill, "Personal Factors Associated with Leadership: A Survey of the Literature," *Journal of Psychology,* 25 (January 1948), p. 64.

[2] For example see W. H. Cowley, "Three Distinctions in the Study of Leaders," *Journal of Abnormal and Social Psychology,* 23 (July-September 1928), pp. 144–57; Otis W. Caldwell and Beth Wellman, "Characteristics of School Leaders," *Journal of Educational Research,* 14 (June 1926), pp. 1–13; or C. W. Crannell and W. G. Mollenkopf, "Combat Leadership," *Psychological Research on Problems of Redistribution* (Washington: U.S. Government Printing Office, 1947).

social club. The ethical and personal requirements for a leadership position such as that held by gangster Al Capone differ from those required of a spiritual leader such as Gandhi—although both were extremely successful leaders. In some cases, such as leadership in civic groups, extroverts seemed to excel, while in others, such as leadership in a school science club, extroversion seems to be a handicap. It becomes apparent, then, that something more than the possession of a prescribed set of traits characterizes the leader.

This fact led students of administration to consider leadership behavior —the ways in which a leader or administrator (and we hope that these terms are synonymous) uses the traits and abilities he has. In turn, this has led to an emphasis on competencies rather than on traits. A competency is related to the ability to do something; in the case of the administrator, it is the ability to behave in a way which research and our value criteria show is effective administrative behavior. It is very likely that the possession of certain traits will make it possible for one person to behave in certain ways more readily than others. Intelligence, for example, is a trait that is vital to effective administrator behavior. Good physical appearance will facilitate personal relations with colleagues. A resonant speaking voice may aid in communication. However, these and other traits can be used in many ways. Intelligence can become diabolical, good physical appearance may aid the confidence man, and the resonant voice may utter resonant nonsense. It is behavior—the way in which the traits are used—rather than the mere possession of the traits, which becomes crucial.

While the trait approach has not been discredited and abandoned, it has become clear that this approach in and of itself is not enough. Various traits overlap, are difficult to measure, may result in differing kinds of behavior, or may have different importance in different situations. For these reasons and others, the trait approach has given way to the competency approach but has at the same time been included as a part of the competency approach.

A competency, as used here, is a factor that can be shown to contribute to or to be an integral part of effective administrative behavior. Competencies may include personal attributes, knowledge, understanding, or skills, but to be classified as a competency for an educational administrator, each of these attributes must be shown to be related to behavior that is considered effective administrative behavior.

HOW COMPETENCIES GET ON THE REQUIRED LIST

It is not enough to say that there are competencies which are required of a successful school administrator. The next question is, of course, how to discover the competencies that belong on this required list. An early study of this problem provided an excellent statement of the criteria used by the researchers in developing such a required list.[3] First they considered the *purpose* of educational administration. What is it all for, anyway? Secondly, the question of *quality* was considered. What are desirable ways of meeting the purpose? Finally, *specific abilities* were isolated. What does it take to do a quality performance in educational administration?

It can be seen that the first two of these points require some philosophical consideration. Purpose and quality can be stated only after certain value judgments have been made. Once the questions of purpose and quality are answered, the more objective consideration of the abilities that are necessary to meet these requirements can be undertaken.

Earlier chapters have indicated our judgments of the purpose of educational administration and have given some indication of our feelings regarding "good" administration. These judgments are not ours alone; they represent the results of thinking and study on the part of many people. The competencies to be presented here are those which research and our best judgment show to be important in meeting the purposes and the quality criteria discussed earlier. This research includes job analysis studies,[4] observations of administrators in action,[5] introspective analyses by practicing administrators,[6] and combinations of several such methods.[7] Job analysis studies involve having a number of people watch others perform a job and make reports concerning what they consider the job to consist of and what they judge to be especially effective or ineffective ways of performing the job. The observational approach is similar to this, except that usually a single researcher observes a number of administrators and gathers data from his observations. Introspective analysis is really a high-sounding term for "armchair research," in which the person who performs a job thinks about and analyzes his own performance to arrive at conclusions about the job. All of these methods have added considerably to our knowledge of competencies of educational administrators, but there is still a need for

[3] Reported in Orin B. Graff and C. M. Street, *Improving Competence in Educational Administration* (New York: Harper & Brothers, 1956).

[4] For example, see Robert E. Sternloff, "The Critical Requirements for School Administrators Based upon an Analysis of Critical Incidents" (unpublished doctoral dissertation, University of Wisconsin, 1953).

[5] For example, see John Hemphill *et al., Administrative Performance and Personality* (New York: Bureau of Publications, Teachers College, Columbia University, 1962).

[6] For example, see John A. Ramseyer *et al., Factors Affecting Educational Administration,* SCDS Monograph No. 2 (Columbus, Ohio: The Ohio State University, 1955), pp. 134–41.

[7] For example, see Graff and Street, *op. cit.*

hunches—the best insights of those who have devoted time and study to educational administration. The educated guess, while it must be carefully labeled as such, has a place in putting competencies on the required list.

One final word should be said while discussing a required list of competencies. The research cited above and many other studies show that it is less correct to think of each competency in isolation than to think of a pattern of competencies. The successful administrator should have a balance of many of the competencies; extreme high points and extreme low points are likely to be handicaps. Even though trait studies have shown that a very plump man is less apt to be a leader than a more slender person, in terms of competencies, a somewhat well-rounded man is the goal.

BORN—OR MADE?

"Leaders are born, not made" or "Every man who can follow can also lead." These sayings illustrate two opposite poles of the question posed here. It is likely that every man does have the potential to be a leader in some situation. Wars reveal the ways in which the unsung common man can reach heights of leadership. However, the leadership considered here must be restricted to the area of leadership as an educational administrator.

Actually, the answer to the question, "Born or made?" is "Neither!" Certainly, some people will be born with some leadership advantages. On the other hand, various personal qualities and abilities can be learned by an individual. Thus a leader is both born and made. One person may have a congenital advantage in some competencies and a congenital deficiency in others. The factors of motivation, of the situation, and of preparation may all combine, however, to make a good educational administrator in spite of some real lacks in the raw material. For some others, however, these deficiencies plus other environmental factors may add up to difficulties that cannot be overcome.

At the present time it can be said that some people will, at birth, have a better chance to become educational administrators than will others; yet, with certain exceptions, it cannot be said that an educational administrator must be born and cannot be made.

COMPETENCIES AND SITUATIONAL CONDITIONS

Everyone knows at least one person who has been an exceptional leader in one situation and an average or below-average leader in another. If should be recognized that various communities, schools, and positions may impose requirements peculiar to their settings; the situations can affect the requirements of the administrator. It follows that a competent administrator may be less competent in some situations than in others.

For example, the successful superintendent in a small, isolated, rural village will need certain skills or competencies which will differ from those required of a superintendent of schools in a larger industrial city. The rural man may not need to be so skilled in establishing and maintaining a complex administrative structure. He may need great skill in informal personal relations on a face-to-face basis and less in the techniques of meeting with large formal groups. It may be important that the rural man have an excellent memory for names and family ties, and less important that he understand the complexities of the power structure in a city. It may be helpful if the rural superintendent has a background of farm experience, but too much rural experience may be harmful to the city superintendent. Other examples of differences could be given, but it should be remembered that even in these examples there is some danger of implying that every rural situation or every urban situation is the same. Such factors as tradition, economic conditions, or nationality can cause differences to exist where similarities might be expected.[8]

The potential administrator should remember, then, that there is a wide variety of administrative positions in a wide variety of situations. Although many of the competencies to be mentioned here are basic to administration in any situation, each position and each situation may require certain minor changes in its competency pattern. Thus the ability to assess a situation and to judge the particular skills that it may require are, in themselves, competencies that an administrator should possess.

MEASURING POTENTIAL

As soon as measuring potential is mentioned, two basic questions arise. The first concerns what is meant by the term "measurement," and the second concerns the meaning of the term "potential." Before attempting to consider the actual assessment of potential, some clarification of these terms is necessary.

PROBLEMS OF MEASUREMENT

Some years ago Harold Rugg provided a searching analysis of scientific measurement in education in his *Foundations for American Education*, and

[8] Excellent summaries of studies reinforcing this point are found in William C. Schutz *et al.*, *Procedures for Identifying Persons with Potential for Public School Administrative Positions*, Cooperative Research Project No. 677 (Berkeley: University of California, 1961), and in Edgar L. Morphet and William Schutz, *Procedures for Identifying Potential School Administrators*, Cooperative Research Project No. 1076 (Berkeley: University of California), undated.

much of what he said is still of real value for one preparing to measure one's potential for success in any undertaking.[9] He stated that in the measurement of a dimension of a person, we are able to measure on three scales—performance, ability, and capacity.[10] Obviously, performance is the thing that is actually measured. When a person is subjected to a reading comprehension test, for example, we are actually measuring how well this person performs in answering specific questions about a specific passage which he has read at a specific point in time. From this measurement of performance, a measure of ability can be inferred. The inference is drawn from studying the performance scores of a number of different people who have answered the same questions dealing with the same passage, thus establishing norms for the reading comprehension test. The inference of ability will be as good or bad as the methods used in establishing the norms that are its basis. Thus, we measure performance, and from this measurement we infer a measure of ability. But what about capacity or potential? Are there any means by which they may be measured?

The measurement of capacity or potential is even more an estimate than is the measurement of ability. Actually, the measurement of capacity is an estimate derived from the inferred measure of ability. Rugg points out that various factors—a less than perfect environment, the individual's internal conditions at the time of measurement, failure of the individual's environment in the past, or inadequacies in the test itself—are capable of distorting estimates of capacity.[11]

All this does not mean that estimates of potential are not worthwhile. It merely means that they must be used with understanding and judgment. It means that the weaknesses of measurements of potential should be recognized, but that the strengths should not be overlooked. Measurement techniques improve steadily, and, if used with care in the light of their shortcomings, they can help a person answer many questions about his potential.

MEANING OF POTENTIAL

We have just pointed out that potential is difficult to measure, a consideration that leads to the question, "What do we mean by potential?" Actually, the word has a sense of the future to it. It is a description not so much of where a person is at present, as of where he might hope to be in the future. The present is represented by "ability"; the future, by "potential."

---

[9] Harold Rugg, *Foundations for American Education* (Yonkers, N.Y.: World Book Company, 1947), pp. 719–805.

[10] *Ibid.*, p. 744.

[11] *Ibid.*, p. 745.

Thus when one speaks of his or of another's potential, he is making assumptions about the future. He is assuming that the environment will be favorable rather than unfavorable to the realization of potential. He is assuming that other personal characteristics or abilities or environmental factors will not interfere with potential in a given field. For example, we have all read murder cases in which everyone says, "The murderer would have had a brilliant future, but . . ." The same thing might also be said of the murdered person. In both cases, other factors rendered an estimate of potential useless.

Another basic assumption made when discussing potential is that the person with the capacity will want to develop his potential to the full and is willing to work to do this. A swift-flowing stream has great potential as a producer of electrical power, but we all know that the stream itself does nothing to realize this possibility. It is also true of a person; the mere possession of some potential does not guarantee achieving a desired objective. The person must develop to his capacity, or he will merely flow along digging a deeper river bed—or rut, as it might be called.

It is necessary, then, that the reader understand the meaning of the measurement of his potential. This measurement is an estimate of what can be done, but it does not mean that the person with potential can sit passively and wait for it to come to the surface. The possession of potential is an indication that if one works hard, one has a good chance of success in a chosen field.

Personal Attributes

We defined a competency as a factor that can be shown to contribute to or to be an integral part of effective administrative behavior. It is apparent that most personal attributes are competencies because they contribute to effective administrative behavior. Remembering that there are few hard and fast rules and that patterns rather than isolated characteristics are to be sought, we shall in this section consider personal attributes as a part of the competency pattern for educational administration.

PHYSICAL CHARACTERISTICS

It is obvious that good health is a prerequisite to success in almost any endeavor. This fact holds true in educational administration. To the basic factor of good health should be added physical energy. The educational administrator needs to be able to enjoy a wide variety of activities and must have the physical energy to stand a demanding scope of such activities.

Days that begin at 8:00 A.M. or earlier and end after midnight are not uncommon. The forty-hour week is a goal which, at present, seems unrealistic for the administrator. Much of the work of the educational administrator requires that he work with groups of people, a type of activity that requires the expenditure of much more physical energy than is often realized. Good health and above-average physical energy, then, are two personal attributes of the effective school administrator.

Physical appearance also plays a role in the success of an educational administrator. While it is no longer felt that a certain height and a particular weight are criteria of administrative success, it can be said that extreme deviations from what is considered normal appearance create difficulties for the potential administrator. In securing a position, in working with teacher and community groups, in working with colleagues, and in working with children, such deviations cause real problems. They are not insurmountable, but they need to be recognized. A normal physical appearance is another personal attribute which leads to effectiveness in educational administration.

MENTAL ATTRIBUTES

A number of studies have been made of the intellectual abilities of leaders. In almost every case, it has been shown that there is a definite and positive relationship between intelligence and leadership. The educational administrator works with a group of generally above-average intelligence. For this reason, it is not easy to say that the school administrator will generally be of superior intelligence in relation to the group with which he works. It is apparent that the type of leadership which we have been discussing requires intelligence on the part of the leader.

A gross I.Q. score is not especially meaningful as a measure of actual intellectual ability. Psychologists refer more and more to intelligences or factors of intelligence. Mental ability tests that deal with many factors and in which scores in each factor assume importance are much more the rule than are tests that provide but a single score. Some of the factors now considered to be components of intelligence are verbal facility, computational skill, reasoning ability, memory, spatial judgment, judgmental capacity, and observational skill. Many people feel, and preliminary studies indicate, that verbal reasoning, judgmental, and observational factors are of particular importance in this field. However, we do not know that all of the factors of intelligence have been discovered, and this aspect of intelligence is still under study.

It may be of interest to note that a number of studies have shown the effectiveness of a leader to be minimized if he is a great deal more intelligent than the group he is to lead. If the intelligence gap becomes too great, the leader may not be accepted by the group, and his communication with it may become difficult. For example, he may falsely assume that certain ideas which he can grasp easily are as readily grasped by the group members. He may leave gaps in his communication because he makes wrong assumptions regarding the knowledge possessed by the group. He may become impatient with the necessity of making explanations that seem unnecessary to him. On the other hand, group members may feel that the leader is purposely talking over their heads or is making things unnecessarily complicated. Thus there may be an upper limit of intelligence as well as a lower limit for the administrator. The determining factor here would, of course, be the group with which the administrator is to work.

Insight is a mental attribute that has been studied in relation to leadership. Unfortunately there is a wide disagreement as to the exact meaning of the term. Many feel that it is a component of intelligence. Perhaps an acceptable definition of insight is that it is the ability to see beyond the surface, in relation both to people and to problems, and thus to understand and deal with implications not readily apparent. For example, if the townspeople repeatedly reject a school tax levy, a person with insight should be able to probe beyond their apparent miserly attitude to a more basic cause of the defeats. Interestingly enough, regardless of the several definitions used for insight, every study made of it indicates that it is an important attribute of a leader.

Philip Smith made a study in which he attempted to relate certain aspects of critical thinking to administrative effectiveness.[12] He discovered that certain patterns of what he called "philosophic-mindedness" on the part of the educational administrator are related to such things as staff morale, communication, and the successful fulfillment of certain administrative tasks. The dimensions of philosophic-mindedness seem clearly related to intellectual ability and may well represent at least a partial summary of the mental attributes that help make up the competency pattern of the educational administrator. These dimensions are:

Comprehensiveness
  Viewing particulars in relation to a large field.
  Relating immediate problems to long-range goals.
  Utilizing the power of generalization.
  Maintaining tolerance for theoretical considerations.

Penetration
  Questioning what is taken for granted or is self-evident.
  Seeking for and formulating fundamentals.

[12] Philip G. Smith, *Philosophic-Mindedness in Educational Administration,* SCDS Monograph No. 5 (Columbus, Ohio: The Ohio State University, 1956).

Utilizing a sensitivity for implication and relevance.
Basing expectations on an abductive-deductive process.

Flexibility

Being free from psychological rigidity.
Evaluating ideas apart from their source.
Seeing issues as many-sided and developing alternate hypotheses, viewpoints, explanations, etc.
Maintaining a tolerance for tentativeness and suspended judgment.[13]

SOCIAL PERSONALITY ATTRIBUTES

In the field of personality, one finds great difficulty in determining the meaning of terms and their use. Even the term *personality* is subject to a wide variety of definitions. In general, however, the definitions of personality have a point of similarity in that they refer to the reactions or reaction patterns of a person in social situations. These patterns, which we will call a man's social personality, are, of course, influenced by all the other attributes which have been and will be discussed here. As these and other attributes create a reaction pattern to the social scene, it is said that one's social personality is revealed.

Although a number of social-personality attributes have been found to be related to effective administrator behavior, these individual attributes must be present in a person in a balanced proportion. In general, research does show that a serious deficiency in any of these attributes can be a distinct handicap for an educational administrator. It should be remembered, on the other hand, that a distinct oversupply of one or more personality attributes might also be a definite handicap.

Introversion–extroversion

The general overall personality description of introversion or extroversion has been studied with leaders in many situations. While it would seem logical to suppose that a person who tends toward introversion would avoid leadership roles, surprisingly enough there are no clear-cut findings which show that one or the other is most closely related to effective leadership. In general, extreme behavior at either end of the introversion-extroversion scale is a handicap, and the particular administrative situation plays a dominant role in determining whether a tendency toward one or the other is more effective. Apparently this factor is more important in determining whether one enters administration in the first place than it is in determining administrative effectiveness.

[13] *Ibid.*, pp. 30–31.

Adaptability and Originality

Adaptability is an attribute that has been found to be significant in the behavior of a leader. The person who cannot adjust to a variety of situations has real difficulty in administration. This seems logical as a requirement for a position in which a man may work for an hour with parents of elementary school children, the next hour with chamber of commerce leaders, the next hour with a group of science teachers, and then hurry off to address a meeting of the local council of labor unions. An educational administrator requires adaptability both to situations and to ideas. The inflexible person will find it difficult to meet the behavioral competencies required of an educational administrator.

Some writers treat originality as a separate personality attribute, whereas others include it as a part of adaptability. Regardless of how it is classified, it is definitely related to effective administrator behavior. The person who can react to social situations without constantly resorting to stereotyped solutions is much more likely to be effective in administration than is one who can do only what he has done before or what he has heard that others have done.

Initiative, Persistence, and Ambition

It has also been shown in a number of studies that the personality attributes of initiative, persistence, and ambition contribute to effective leadership. Not only do these attributes play an important role in helping a person reach an administrative position, but their possession, according to some evidence, helps the administrator become effective once the position is attained. As a matter of fact, it is unlikely that many people aspire to administration unless they possess these attributes.

Disposition

There have been very few studies attempting to relate such things as sense of humor or other aspects of disposition to effective leader behavior. Observation and good judgment, however, lead to the surmise that in any endeavor that involves working with people, an even disposition and a sense of humor are distinct advantages. The person who is subject to temper flare-ups or moodiness, or who cannot laugh at many things—including himself—will find himself much more subject to ulcers in a leadership position than will one without these personality attributes. Thus, while there is no distinct evidence to relate disposition and sense of humor to leadership behavior, experience does show them to be related to personal satisfaction and happiness for the administrator.

Dominance

One rather incongruous note is that a person who likes to dominate a situation is not necessarily best suited to be a leader in that situation. The emphasis in educational administration is on creative leadership—leadership in which the abilities of all are recognized, utilized, and encouraged. Therefore the so-called dominant personality may serve as a handicap to the educational administrator. Much depends upon the specific situation and administrative position in making a final judgment of the role of dominance, but it is safe to say that dominance as an attribute is not shown to be a prerequisite to effective administrator behavior.

Other Attributes

Several other personality attributes have been shown by some studies to be valuable for the educational administrator. Confidence and self-assurance, if not carried to extremes of egotism, are helpful characteristics. A person who does not find it difficult to gain popularity with his peers has certain advantages, but here again, this popularity must not be gained at the expense of others or through ignoring other attributes of personality and character. The sociable or gregarious person has certain advantages, primarily related to the fact that educational administration involves working with people. Finally, for a lack of any better place to mention it, it has been found that if a person's socio-economic status is neither lower than nor too far above that of the group he is to lead, he has certain leadership advantages.

Although they are not restricted to a requirement for educational administrators, brief mention should be made of the necessity of habits of personal cleanliness and neatness. As a leader in both a school system and, it is hoped, a community, the educational administrator ought to look the part. This same requirement, of course, holds true for any profession and needs no amplification here.

Summary

It can be seen that there is a great deal of uncertainty connected with this discussion of personality attributes as they relate to competency in educational administration. In brief—and to summarize—it should be recognized that educational administration is primarily concerned with working with a wide variety of people. Those personality attributes which are seen by most people to be "normal," plus a few more which mark him as a person with some drive, are the ones that an administrator should possess.

CHARACTER ATTRIBUTES

Many psychologists find it difficult to distinguish between character and personality. In general, however, those personal attributes which are commonly subject to value judgments of "goodness" or "badness" are ordinarily classified as character attributes, while those not subject to such judgments are considered to be personality attributes. For example, it is not usually considered to be "right" or "wrong" for a person to have a sense of humor, but it is a definite matter of "right" or "wrong" for a person to be honest. Therefore, the attribute to which value judgments are assigned —in this case, honesty—is a character attribute, whereas a sense of humor remains a matter of personality. It should be recognized that people differ in their perceptions of behavior and that it is impossible to state with certainty which attributes will or will not be subject to value judgments. We have attempted here to describe as character attributes those characteristics which seem to be more often subject to classification as "right" or "wrong" ways to behave.

Needless to say, an educational administrator is expected to be a person of excellent character. Many character attributes cannot be directly related to effective leadership behavior, but they are strongly related to the degree to which an administrator will be accepted by his staff and his community and, consequently, are directly related to his chances for tenure in his position.

It does not seem necessary to discuss in detail what is considered to be "good" character. Such things as honesty, integrity, tact, loyalty, and morality are aspects of character with which everyone is familiar. What is important to the competency pattern of an educational administrator is that he have a value system to which he can subscribe. It is not enough for an administrator to think that he possesses good character traits; he must be aware of the conceptual framework that makes these attributes "good." In other words, an administrator needs to know what he believes to be right and why he holds these beliefs. While the word frightens many people, this means that a person needs a philosophy of life. Without such a philosophy, such words as "honesty" or "morality" cannot be defined adequately. The lack of a basic philosophy of life may lead to inconsistency in behavior and can lead to indecision and confusion. These conditions reduce the effectiveness of the administrator.

POTENTIAL IN TERMS OF PERSONAL ATTRIBUTES

A number of the personal attributes that are part of the competency pattern for educational administration are rather easily measured; others present difficulties in measurement which can scarcely be solved. Health and physical energy are examples of the former, while social personality factors are among the latter. As the reader considers his potential in terms of personal attributes, he should remember that there is some question regarding the extent to which certain personal characteristics can be trained and developed. This fact means that if the present status of a person with regard to the possession of some characteristic is difficult to measure, the potential is even more difficult to assess.

PHYSICAL ATTRIBUTES

Good health and above-average physical energy are important attributes of the administrator. The student should have little difficulty assessing the degree to which he possesses these attributes, although if he finds them lacking, it would be wise to seek out causes. We could also mention that some people never do extend themselves sufficiently to determine the amount of physical energy which they possess. Such a lack of activity could lead to either of two false assumptions: that the person has an untapped, but extensive, resource of physical energy; or that the person is deficient in physical energy. This would seem to indicate that the prospective administrator needs to put himself to the test and to engage in activities sufficient to assess his physical energy potential.

As a teacher, for example, the prospective administrator could make such a test by taking an active role in the local teachers' association, affiliating with an active church or other community group, plus continuing a graduate education program. If these activities lead to extreme weariness, to inefficiency on the job, or to severe mental stress, there is a strong possibility that the physical rigors of educational administration would prove to be too burdensome for the teacher. This generalization would be particularly true with reference to top-level administrative positions, such as a superintendency or a principalship.

In addition, the prospective administrator should follow a program of regular medical check-ups. Indeed, this advice is pertinent for everyone, regardless of profession or age. Generally, a health or physical problem that is detected and treated in the early stages creates far fewer difficulties than one that is detected only when it becomes serious. Thus, part of the self-evaluation procedure of both a pre-service and an in-service educational program should be regular medical examinations.

The matter of physical appearance was also discussed as having a part in the competency pattern of an educational administrator. While we do not wish to go on record as favoring plastic surgery, we do think it important that a prospective administrator consider his personal appearance and take reasonable steps to remedy difficulties. If, for example, a person is short and stout, he can take steps to remove some weight and to choose a wardrobe appropriate to his physical stature. The person with a very poor complexion should recognize this as a possible handicap and take appropriate steps to make what improvement is possible. The key idea is that the prospective administrator should view himself in a mirror and see what a board of education would see if he were to appear for a job interview. If the mirror image is not pleasant, something can and should be done to lead to improvements.

In the case of physical attributes, potential is measured largely in terms of judgment. The following questions seem typical of those which need to be asked:

Is my health generally good?

Do I have a fairly high energy level?

Do I take some pains with my appearance?

Do I wake up each day refreshed and "raring to go"?

If the self-evaluator finds that he can answer most of these questions positively, it would seem to be a good judgment that his physical attributes enhance his potential as an educational administrator.

MENTAL ATTRIBUTES

General Intelligence

The first thought which comes to mind in considering mental attributes is the I.Q. or intelligence quotient. We have stated, however, that a gross I.Q. score is not particularly meaningful in assessing administrative potential, especially in discovering the more subtle aspects of mental potential. However, there is evidence that an above-average I.Q., regardless of the specific meaning of this score, does correlate with success in educational administration.

Current literature is replete with "quickie" intelligence tests. Such popular magazines as *Changing Times* and *The Reader's Digest* have from time to time presented short quizzes designed to help the reader discover whether he is of "superior," "very good," or "average" intelligence. These are actually of some value in providing at least an indicator of general intelligence. The prospective administrator who took such quizzes and consistently scored below average or even average might well ponder the state of his mental equipment. However, lack of careful validation of these tests does mean that they should be considered only as indicators. The careful self-evaluator of potential will want to seek better measuring instruments.

A number of mental ability tests do have carefully constructed norms for adults. Also, the person considering administration might be able to secure from his high school or university a record of his past performances on mental ability tests. If a new test is desired, any one of the following will provide useful information related to general mental ability:

Army General Classification Test: 1st Civilian Edition (AGCT). Science Research Associates, 57 West Grand Avenue, Chicago 10, Illinois.

California Short Form Test of Mental Maturity. Advanced Form. California Test Bureau, 5916 Hollywood Blvd., Los Angeles, California.

Ohio State University Psychological Examination (OSPE). Form 21. Ohio State University Press, Columbus, Ohio.

The prospective administrator might well attempt to take such a test at a testing or counseling center located on a university campus or as part of a public school system. In terms of potential for educational administration, various studies have indicated that the median I.Q. of school administrators was about 127 and that the range was from 109 to 133. These figures provide some insight into the meaning of the reader's score as related to his potential as an educational administrator.

Factors of Intelligence

A number of efforts have been made to determine ways to measure factors of intelligence that seem to be closely related to success in educational administration. Careful analyses of test results as compared with other ratings of administrative potential have been made by a number of students of educational administration since the early days of the Kellogg-sponsored Cooperative Project in Educational Administration. Both because of difficulties involved in measuring success in any absolute way and because of the lack of well-documented longitudinal studies covering complete administrative careers of individuals, it is impossible to cite any test or tests as infallible indicators of potential. Much attention has been centered on three tests—the *Miller Analogies*,[14] the *Cooperative English C2*,[15] and the *Watson-Glaser Critical Thinking Appraisal.*[16]

Each of these three tests is designed to measure more than the possession of mental attributes. The *Miller Analogies Test* is, essentially, a high-level

---

[14] *Miller Analogies Test.* Psychological Corporation, 522 Fifth Avenue, New York, N.Y.

[15] *Cooperative English Test, Form C2.* Cooperative Test Division, Educational Testing Service, Princeton, N.J.

[16] *Watson-Glaser Critical Thinking Appraisal.* World Book Company, Yonkers, N.Y.

scholastic aptitude test designed to provide a measure of aptitude for work at the graduate level. It emphasizes measurement of the ability to reason and to draw inferences and consequently provides information regarding the attributes of insight and reasoning ability.

The *Cooperative English Test* is of particular value in assessing such components of reading comprehension as understanding of mood and purpose in written material. Thus, while this is an excellent instrument for the measurement of the usual components of reading comprehension, it too provides a valid indication of the reasoning ability and insight of the prospective administrator.

The third instrument, the *Watson-Glaser Critical Thinking Appraisal*, is particularly designed to give information regarding the attribute of "philosophic-mindedness." This test provides problems and situations which require the application of critical thinking abilities. The norms are constructed to provide data concerning the present status of one's critical thinking apparatus as well as to give information concerning one's potential to develop critical thinking ability.

While it would be inaccurate to state that these tests can predict administrative success, unpublished studies at The Ohio State University Center for Educational Administration do reveal that the latter two tests are fairly good predictors of success in graduate programs in educational administration. Certainly, results from these tests provide excellent tools for self-analysis as one considers one's potential for educational administration. Because of the complexities involved in the measurement of intellectual factors, the best instruments for such measurement are standardized instruments such as those cited above. There are, however, certain questions which anyone can ask of himself; honest, frank answers to these questions can help that person assess his intellectual potential for administration:

To what extent do you work in terms of long-range goals?

To what extent are you able to develop short-term goals that lead toward the attainment of a long-range goal?

When you attack a problem, to what extent are you aware of a theoretical basis for your method of attack?

When you hear an action proposal, to what extent can you visualize the future implications of the proposal?

When you are a member of a group that faces a problem, to what extent can you distinguish between relevant and irrelevant proposals for the solution of the problem?

For a given problem, to what extent can you consider proposed solutions that differ markedly from solutions you would propose?

To what extent can you understand the basic factors that create various problems you face?

To what extent are you unwilling to act on a major problem until you can gather what seem to be basic facts regarding the problem?

To what extent are you able to evaluate the degree to which a course of action is meeting the objectives it was designed to serve?

Positive answers to these questions indicate the presence of the mental attributes of comprehension, penetration, and flexibility.

SOCIAL PERSONALITY ATTRIBUTES

The measurement of social personality attributes is a difficult task. For the most part, it involves the use of some kind of inventory, which is a device to formalize self-appraisal. Thus, the score any person receives on a social adjustment or other personality inventory is influenced to a great extent by the degree to which this person is frank in answering the questions and how well he is able to recognize his real feelings about certain questions. If, for example, we are asked to respond to the statement, "I am aware of my social shortcomings," with some indication of the extent to which this is a true statement, we must first be willing to admit that it is possible that we do have such deficiencies, and we must then be competent to know what a social shortcoming really is.

Another problem in the use of such inventories is the widespread lack of the ability to see ourselves as others see us. We may, for example, be aware of what we consider to be our social shortcomings; our friends and associates may have quite different perceptions of us. They may consider what we call a shortcoming to be a strength and may think of other attributes as shortcomings in us. We can only guess, then, how our social personality attributes affect and are perceived by others. The obvious way to overcome this problem is to ask our friends to assist in the evaluation of social personality attributes. As difficult as this may seem, if it is objectively and frankly done, it can be a great help in the evaluation of our social reaction patterns.

In spite of the criticisms that can be leveled at the devices used to measure social personality attributes, these instruments do have real value. Once again, they are primarily indicative rather than definitive. However, the indications which one can gain through the use of these instruments are of help as one attempts to measure potential for educational administration.

Standardized Instruments

Several published inventories or scales with standardized norms have been found to have some predictive value in measuring social personality attributes that influence leadership potential. Of even greater importance, however, is the fact that these instruments can be used for diagnostic purposes. Thus, the devices may not actually measure potential as we have defined it, but they do measure one's present social personality "condition" and indicate areas where improvement should be sought.

In describing such instruments, it should be noted that no easy categorization of tests under certain social personality factors seems possible. In most cases, each instrument yields descriptions of social personality in terms of those dimensions which seemed to be most valuable from the viewpoint of the designers of the instrument. Thus, in using these devices, the user must make sure that he understands the meaning of his scores, and this will often require consultation with a qualified counselor.

The *Guilford-Zimmerman Personality Inventory* appears to provide excellent insight into administrator potential.[17] These inventories are designed to provide information about the areas of social personality generally described as introversion-extroversion, activity-nervousness, masculinity-femininity, ascendance-submission, and inferiority. In terms of specific factors, this study revealed that those rated by other means to be high in administrator potential scored consistently high in the areas of sociability, freedom from depression, masculinity, freedom from inferiority feelings, freedom from nervousness, objectivity, and cooperativeness. This inventory, then, would appear to offer excellent diagnostic opportunities.

Another instrument used in the study of administrative potential is the *Allport-Vernon-Lindzey Study of Values.*[18] This device is used to measure certain value attributes which are purported to be extremely important in shaping and revealing social personality characteristics. In a sense, the most valuable contribution which this instrument can make in self-evaluation is to enable a person to assess his value framework and to discover—sometimes to his surprise—what values he holds.

Gibb reports a number of studies that have used the *Bernreuter Scale*[19] in research with leaders and nonleaders.[20] While there are certain exceptions, it can be said that leaders generally scored higher than nonleaders

[17] *Guilford-Zimmerman Personality Inventory.* Sheridan Supply Company, Post Office Box 837, Beverly Hills, California.

[18] *Allport-Vernon-Lindzey Study of Values,* rev. ed. Houghton Mifflin Company, Boston, Massachusetts.

[19] *Personality Inventory* (Bernreuter). Stanford University Press, Stanford, California. Distributed by C. H. Stoelting Company, 424 North Homan Avenue, Chicago 24, Illinois.

[20] Cecil A. Gibb, "Leadership," in Gardner Lindzey, ed., *Handbook of Social Psychology,* Vol. II (Cambridge, Mass.: Addison-Wesley Publishing Co., 1954), pp. 886–88.

on the *Bernreuter Scale* in the areas of self-confidence, sociability, and dominance, and lower in the area of introversion.

Another standardized instrument valuable in measuring administrative potential in terms of personal attributes is the *Kuder Preference Record—Personal*.[21] This instrument appraises a person's attitude toward various life situations. Five areas are scored: being active in groups, working with ideas, directing others, being in familiar and stable situations, and avoiding conflict. It seems that relatively high scores in the first three areas and relatively low scores in the last two are appropriate for the prospective administrator.

Nonstandardized Instruments

In the measurement of social personality attributes it may be necessary for the self-evaluator to consider some less formal means than those described above. Here again, it is likely that a number of questions can be framed, which, if frankly answered, provide insight into the state of one's social personality attributes as related to potential for educational administration.

It will be recalled that a number of specific social personality attributes that are related to administrative competency were described earlier. An examination of each of the attributes mentioned will reveal the possibility of posing certain common-sense questions whose answers can help one assess the degree to which one's own social personality make-up seems to enhance one's potential for educational administration. It could even be said that the person with the insight required of an administrator would find it fairly easy to conduct a self-examination of his social personality characteristics.

Some of the questions which seem to us to be appropriate for such a self-examination will be presented here. By no means exhaustive of all the possibilities, they are primarily indicative in nature. In general, there are no "perfect" answers to these questions. However, the demands of educational administration as we have discussed it indicate that many of the questions presented below do have preferred answers. The technique to follow in considering these questions is to respond to each, first, in terms of "what is." Then it would seem advisable for the evaluator to consider each question in terms of "what ought to be." These two considerations could then become the basis for discussion with colleagues, classmates, and instructors and for future planning as one prepares for educational administration.

---

[21] *Kuder Preference Record—Personal*. Science Research Associates, 57 West Grand Avenue, Chicago 11, Illinois.

Introversion

The general aim in this aspect of one's social personality make-up is balance. The following questions are typical of those which could be asked to determine the balance that does exist in the prospective administrator in the introversion-extroversion area:

Do I enjoy working on a group project as well as I enjoy working by myself?

Do I enjoy entering new social situations?

If someone criticizes my ideas am I willing to discuss this criticism with him?

Adaptability

Adaptability is strongly desired in an educational administrator, and answers to questions such as the following tend to provide insight into one's adaptability and to indicate potential as an educational administrator:

When a completely new problem or situation faces me, can I meet it fairly effectively rather than being thrown for a complete loss?

Am I willing to try things which I have never done before?

When I am leading a group and it becomes obvious that my plan of action is not effective, can I change my action rather than carry on to the bitter end with my original plans?

Originality

Originality is another desirable attribute and is closely akin to adaptability. The key difference between the two seems to be in the nature of the adaptation which one makes to the various situations one faces. Questions such as the following are designed to stimulate self-evaluation in the matter of originality:

Do I tend to enjoy and consider new ideas rather than to reject them immediately?

If I were asked to plan a meeting, would I tend to think of my own ideas rather than turn immediately to a "How to Do It" manual?

Have I ever received some group disapproval because my ideas seemed "too radical" to the group?

Initiative

Initiative is another attribute that some studies have found to be present more in leaders than in nonleaders. Like all the other social personality attributes, initiative needs to be tempered with wisdom.

If I see a situation in which many things need to be done, do I tend to start doing something about it?

Would I try to solve a problem rather than wait for someone else whom I consider an expert to start action?

Do people sometimes come to me and ask if I would help get a program or an activity started? Would I accept and enjoy such an assignment?

Persistence

The attribute of persistence might well be called "intelligent stubbornness." It is sometimes difficult to tell when one is being wisely persistent and when one is a seeker after lost causes. The following questions tend to provide insight into the extent of one's persistence as related to potential for educational administration:

Am I willing to support an idea I believe is good even though I seem to be in the definite minority?

If one approach to solving a problem fails, do I try new approaches rather than avoid attacking the problem?

Am I able to tell the difference between basic principles, which are not subject to compromise, and subordinate ideas, which may be altered without compromising basic principles?

Ambition

Ambition seems to be another prerequisite for effective educational administration. It should be remembered, however, that ambition must be coupled with character and morality. There is no room in educational administration for the person with so-called ruthless ambition. While there may be an extremely rare exception, we believe that no effective administrator can reach the top level in his profession over the bodies of his colleagues.

Do I feel a certain basic discontent with what I am doing and with the extent of my knowledge which leads me to strive for self-improvement?

Do I sometimes do things I don't particularly enjoy because I feel that they will further me professionally?

Even Disposition

The talk about balance in social personality attributes should not lead one to the idea that we seek lack of color. In the matter of disposition, this is particularly true. A sense of humor is almost a necessity and a little righteous anger is expected of almost any administrator. However, extremes of disposition which make a person difficult to work with do represent handicaps for the administrator.

Do I enjoy the give and take of informal social gatherings even if I become the victim of teasing or joking from time to time?

Can I control my temper so that it does not cause me problems?

Am I rarely, if ever, moody?

Self-confidence

A somewhat fine line divides self-confidence from egotism. The first prerequisite of self-confidence is, of course, something about which to be confident. Self-confidence does not mean that one feels able to "go it alone" or that one is superior in every respect. It does imply that a person feels he can do his job and that, with the help of those who share the mission with him, the job will be done in a superior fashion.

Do I start any task I undertake with an expectation of success?

If I had to choose a group to work with me on a problem, would I choose very able people rather than people who would not "show me up"?

Do I find that I am not very worried about problems of tenure or security?

Sociability

This attribute is another that researchers have found to be closely associated with leaders. In a sense, most of the attributes discussed earlier play a role in determining one's sociability. However, questions such as the following provide insight into the specific ways in which these attributes contribute to one's sociability:

Do I make an effort to meet and to know people?

Am I fairly comfortable and at ease in almost any social situation?

Using Test Results

Whether one takes a series of standardized tests, asks oneself questions such as those listed above, or both, the matter of what to do with the results will arise. It is hoped that the prospective administrator will be able to discover through these means those aspects of his social personality make-up which seem to represent definite strengths and definite weaknesses in his competency pattern. This discovery should then lead to attempts to re-inforce strengths and to alleviate weaknesses. Some weaknesses may prove impossible or extremely difficult to remove. In such cases, the prospective administrator must learn to work around these weaknesses; or, if similar weaknesses appear in other competency areas, he may have to consider seriously the wisdom of his choice of career.

CHARACTER ATTRIBUTES

In order to re-emphasize what we mean by character, another source might be cited. Thorndike and Hagen indicate that "character traits are aspects of individual behavior to which a definite social value has been attached." [22] This definition points out one major difficulty in measuring character attributes—the task of keeping abreast of social values. Twenty years ago, for example, a teacher who smoked was considered morally unfit in many communities. Even today, the expectations and perceptions of communities vary widely in the matter of what constitutes acceptable behavior.

As one evaluates one's character, however, certain rather obvious things can be pointed out. Honesty, integrity, and loyalty are well-understood concepts and a person can ordinarily assess the degree to which he possesses them. In some of the more debatable areas of morality, common sense does dictate certain standards. Alcohol and tobacco, for example, if used at all, certainly need to be used with moderation and judgment. One's social life should not deviate in an extreme way from the social life of other respected members of a community. If such a statement seems too restrictive to the prospective administrator, it is a clear indication that educational administration will offer problems he will find difficult to overcome.

Equally as important as the possession of desirable character attributes for the educational administrator is the possession of a value framework upon which these attributes are based. Counts proposes that the major sources of American values are found in the Hebraic-Christian ethic, the humanistic spirit, the scientific method, faith in the rule of law, and faith in democracy. [23] While these headings are subject to interpretation and judgment, an educational administrator should know what each heading means and should have a conscious value system which he has developed through his own interpretation and judgment. A value system should be reflected in the administrator's life. In other words, as a prospective administrator, one should have or should feel impelled to develop a conscious value system and should be able to translate this system into action as one faces the many moral and ethical decisions that will occur both on and off the job.

[22] R. L. Thorndike and E. Hagen, *Measurement and Evaluation in Psychology and Education* (New York: John Wiley & Sons, Inc., 1955), p. 22.

[23] George S. Counts, *Education and American Civilization* (New York: Bureau of Publications, Teachers College, Columbia University, 1952), pp. 207–91.

In brief, then, we have said here that as a person attempts to assess his potential for educational administration in terms of his character attributes, he should ask himself such questions as:

Do I understand, in general, the social values that have been placed on certain kinds of moral and ethical behavior?

Would I be willing to make certain adjustments in my behavior in order to avoid a serious conflict with the mores of the community in which I might work?

Do I have a basic value framework that underlies my action?

Do I test actions I may take or proposed decisions I may make against my value framework?

Educational Background

It has been pointed out that educational administrators do not have to be born to the position. One of the major factors in the making of an educational administrator is his educational background.

BEFORE COLLEGE

It cannot be said that one particular kind of educational background will automatically provide a person with the necessary prerequisites for educational administration. It can be said, however, that certain educational patterns will prove more helpful than others.

In high school, the student who participates in activities that provide him with leadership possibilities or with opportunities to observe various leaders will find these experiences an aid to becoming an administrator. If the student is fortunate enough to have had several courses in which he begins to gain understanding of the American culture, social problems and possibilities, and the historical background of American public education, he will find himself better able to profit from future education and experience.

It is also to be hoped that the high school student will have increasing opportunities to begin to know himself. Through guidance programs, or through certain courses, or both, the high school student should begin to know what lies behind his own behavior.

For the majority of educational administrators, it is probably during the high school years that an interest in teaching is formed and that certain subject matter begins to stand out as possible teaching subjects. As a young man or woman leaves high school to enter a college or university, his or her competency pattern as a potential educational administrator will be enhanced if he has a genuine interest in teaching as a career, if he has started to know himself and his culture, and if he has had a wide variety of experiences and subject matter, which will provide meaning for the experiences and subject matter to follow.

UNDERGRADUATE BACKGROUND

A part of the competency pattern of an educational administrator consists of learned knowledge and skills. It is in the teacher education program that appropriate knowledge and skills begin to be specifically taught and, we hope, learned. Several statements defining the competencies felt to be required of educational administrators describe the understandings and skills that are a part of these competencies. Although certain of these are a part of the graduate program for school administrators, others cannot be delayed until a student enters graduate school. Those which we think are most readily acquired during the undergraduate program of the potential educational administrator include knowledge about:

1. Child growth and development.
2. Methods of teaching.
3. Curriculum plans.
4. Group processes.
5. Community youth programs.
6. Teaching aids.
7. Counseling and guidance programs.
8. Community health and sanitation problems.
9. Tests and other instruments of measurement.
10. Other professions and occupations.
11. The aims of education.
12. Family living.
13. Social forces in a community.
14. Social values and beliefs.
15. Democratic values, goals, and processes.
16. Human behavior.
17. Governmental structure in the United States.
18. Economic systems with particular emphasis on capitalism in the United States.
19. Past and present economic trends in the United States.
20. The general legal structure in the United States.

In addition, there are a number of understandings which are essential for an educational administrator. Many of these should also begin to be developed during the undergraduate studies of the potential educational administrator. These would include:

1. The nature of individual and group life.

2. Democracy as a way of life.

3. Objectives, methods, and place of education in American society.

4. Operational beliefs in the area of curriculum and instruction.

5. The importance of planning.

6. The methods and importance of communication.

7. The nature and methods of critical thinking.

A statement developed at The Ohio State University concerning competencies needed by school administrators included several whose development should be well started during the undergraduate program of the administrator.

1. Understandings, attitudes, and skills resulting from an adequate general education.

2. An understanding of the role of the school in the social order.

3. An understanding of the instructional program and the administrator's role in its improvement.

4. An understanding of the processes of human growth and learning.

In addition to these somewhat general understandings, the potential administrator will devote a major portion of his undergraduate days to preparing to teach. While there is no strong evidence to show that one must be an excellent teacher to be a good administrator, there does seem to be some agreement that a poor teacher will not make a good administrator. Stogdill's review of studies of leadership also shows that when academic grades are related with leadership potential, leaders are found to make better grades than do nonleaders.[24] Consequently, the undergraduate academic record of the potential administrator provides some insight into his administrative potential.

As in the high school experience of the student, undergraduate activities add experiences and understanding of value in developing administrative

[24] Stogdill, *op. cit.*, p. 46.

competency. This is particularly true when such activities provide leadership experiences.

It can be seen, then, that the undergraduate experience of the potential administrator is most valuable if it provides a broad, general educational background, preparation adequate for the development of a good teacher, and experiences which enable a person to know more about himself and the ways in which he reacts to group situations.

GRADUATE EDUCATION

When his decision has been made and the student enters a graduate program to begin his formal preparation for educational administration, it is to be hoped that many of the required competencies are already at least partially developed. The graduate program should enhance and continue this development. There are, in addition, a number of technical skills and understandings peculiar to educational administration which need to be developed during the graduate program. While it has been noted that certain physical and personal attributes contribute to competency in educational administration, a profession also requires that its practitioners possess a body of basic knowledge and pertinent skills.

It should be noted that graduate work as a prerequisite for educational administration has long been recognized in the certification requirements of most states. In recent years, emphasis upon this prerequisite has been given by the profession itself through the adoption by the American Association of School Administrators of membership requirements which include two years of graduate work in educational administration in an accredited university program. This recognition by the profession of the need for advanced educational preparation for its practitioners is clear evidence of the growing significance and complexity of the field of educational administration.

Graduate programs for the preparation of educational administrators are almost without exception started after the student has had teaching experience. During the first years of such a graduate program, usually leading to a master's degree, a state administrator's certificate, or both, the emphasis is generally on developing breadth in the potential administrator rather than leading him down a narrow trail of specialization. Stress is on courses that provide more understanding of American culture, of the role of the public school in this setting, of child and adult behavior, and of methods of teaching and curriculum development. In addition, emphasis begins to be placed on the related areas of critical thinking, problem-solving, and research. Finally, the beginning graduate student in educational administration is introduced to some concepts of administration which will lead to understandings about the meaning of administration, the variety of administrative positions in education, the role of an administrator, and the administrative process.

As the graduate program continues—perhaps toward a doctorate or toward some other degree or certificate above the master's level—increased attention is given to the specifics of educational administration. Chapter 4 has outlined the tasks in educational administration. Each of these requires specific knowledge, skills, and techniques which may become the content of graduate courses in educational administration. At the same time, the development of competency in educational administration requires that isolated learning be constantly interrelated and that this interrelated learning be linked with the broader general learning that has been stressed throughout the earlier educational experience of the student.

It is not enough that the graduate program teach a student about administration; he must begin to experience administrative behavior. For this reason, internships, field relationships, observations, simulated administrative experiences, and various other attempts to relate theory and practice are becoming standard parts of graduate programs in school administration.

From his graduate education program, then, the student should be expected to develop competency in the technical aspects of school administration, in the use of sound problem-solving or research procedures in dealing with administrative concerns, and in the process of administration itself. In addition, competencies that have been developing prior to the graduate program should be reinforced and further developed through formal class work and through experience. Finally, the potential administrator needs to gain through his graduate program a conviction that he wants to be an educational administrator and that this desire is based on a well-founded analysis of his own strengths and weaknesses.

EXPERIENCE AS EDUCATIONAL BACKGROUND

Fortunately, one's learning is not restricted to formal classroom activities. A rich background of experience forms a valuable part of the competency pattern of an educational administrator. The greater the variety of experience, the more ability an administrator may have to understand and to work with a variety of people in a variety of situations.

There are no studies which purport to tell exactly what kinds of experiences are most fruitful in developing administrative competency. Common sense, however, seems to indicate that travel, work experiences at a variety of levels, and experiences in a variety of social and civic organizations will enhance many of the competencies mentioned here.

There is not as yet much evidence from research to indicate what sort of teaching experience is most conducive to administrative effectiveness. Here again, the person with experience at several levels of the school program has an advantage in understanding the total program. On the other hand, the person who has had all of his experience in high schools and has rarely been in an elementary school since his own school days will need to take special pains to develop an understanding of elementary education.

The major difficulty in using experience to gain competency is insuring that one really learns from experience. The old comparison between "twenty years of experience" and "one year of experience twenty times" is extremely significant. Experience leads to increased competency only if conscious efforts are made to produce this result. Competency is what counts, and though experience can increase competency, the relationship is not an automatic one.

Experience can lead to competency too only through mental activity. One's experiences should be related to past experiences and to knowledge gained from reading and reflective thought. Generalizations need to be drawn from experience and these generalizations need to be tested. A single experience should not be considered sufficient to prove that some relationship is forever true.

Dewey detailed certain dangers of assuming too much about the value of experience when he stated that:

. . . experience and education cannot be directly equated to each other. For some experiences are mis-educative. Any experience is mis-educative that has the effect of arresting or distorting the growth of further experience. An experience may be such as to engender callousness; it may produce lack of sensitivity and responsiveness . . . a given experience may increase a person's automatic skill in a particular direction and yet tend to land him in a groove or rut. . . . Again, experiences may be so disconnected from one another that, while each is agreeable or even exciting in itself, they are not linked cumulatively to one another. Energy is then dissipated and a person becomes scatterbrained.[25]

Certainly these comments indicate that if one's experience is to aid one in the development of competency as an educational administrator, this development must be consciously sought.

POTENTIAL IN TERMS OF EDUCATIONAL BACKGROUND

In general, the school administrator is first a school teacher. Regardless of this, a successful administrator needs to understand the teaching-learning

[25] John Dewey, *Experience and Education* (New York: The Macmillan Company, 1938), pp. 13–14.

process, the aims of public education, and other learnings required of a successful teacher. From this it follows that certain instruments designed to measure teacher potential will be of help in assessing administrator potential.

EVALUATION OF EDUCATIONAL BACKGROUND

Probably the most widely known tests to measure certain aspects of teaching potential are the *National Teacher Examinations*.[26] They are particularly helpful in that they provide a measure of the extent of one's professional and general cultural information. In addition, a series of examinations has been prepared as a part of this battery to measure knowledge of methods and subject matter in specific fields—elementary school, social studies, industrial arts education, etc. It should be remembered that these tests can measure what one *knows*, but not what one will *do*. Thus the examinations can do only part of the job in the identification of potentially successful teachers—a fact that is clearly acknowledged by the originators and publishers of the battery.

An instrument that is more specifically aimed at measuring understanding of the psychological foundations of education is the *Kelly-Perkins How I Teach Inventory*.[27] While the instrument is designed primarily to measure understanding of principles of child and adolescent psychology, it is clear that many of these principles are important to the group work which will be required of an educational administrator.

One final examination will be mentioned which provides insight into general knowledge and thus helps appraise potential for educational administration. The *Graduate Record Examinations*,[28] while somewhat awe-inspiring, are excellent sources of information about the all-around knowledge of a college graduate as compared with the knowledge of his peers. These examinations measure knowledge in a wide variety of fields from fine arts to chemistry and are extremely helpful for diagnostic purposes. The prospective administrator who virtually draws a blank in an area or areas is made aware of his own needs for further study.

ACADEMIC ACHIEVEMENT AND SELF-EVALUATION

We cannot state categorically that the successful administrator must be a Phi Beta Kappa or a *summa cum laude* graduate. As a matter of fact,

[26] *National Teacher Examinations*. Educational Testing Service, Princeton, N.J.

[27] *Kelly-Perkins How I Teach Inventory*. Educational Test Bureau, 720 Washington Avenue, S.E., Minneapolis, Minnesota.

[28] *Graduate Record Examinations*. Educational Testing Service, Princeton, N.J.

the great variety of activities in which a potential administrator might participate while in college could hinder such achievement. However, certain facts do apply. It is obvious that the undergraduate record must be sufficiently good to permit entrance to a graduate school which is accredited to prepare educational administrators. The graduate school achievement must be of a caliber that permits regular standing, often a minimum grade average of "B."

In addition, the record of university achievement, particularly in graduate courses, becomes a source of data for school boards as they select administrators. While grades are admittedly not everything, the potential administrator should realize that they are an important part of his record and that he should take them seriously. The undergraduate record should indicate general academic success, and the graduate record should provide evidence of better than average performance. For some people, this warning may come too late, and these people should realize that their poor academic record either indicates that they should reconsider their professional choice or that they must recognize that they have a definite handicap to overcome.

EVALUATION OF PROFESSIONAL KNOWLEDGE

It is not expected that the new student in educational administration will bring with him a complete body of skills and knowledge in the operational areas of educational administration or in the administrative process. Gaining such knowledge and skill is one of the purposes which he hopes to achieve in his program of preparation. It seems important, however, that the prospective administrator should take some pains to insure that he has a record of his progress in acquiring these necessities of administrative life.

The Check List Approach

In Chapter 4 we listed and described what we consider to be the six operational areas of educational administration as follows:

1. School–community relationships.
2. Curriculum and instruction.
3. Pupil personnel.
4. Staff personnel.
5. Physical facilities.
6. Finance and business management.

Each prospective administrator should develop for himself a check list upon which he can record his progress in learning the requirements of the tasks in these operational areas. In addition, he needs to make certain that he is gaining experience in the administrative processes as he studies each operational area. A check list might well include spaces for recording, for each area, reference material that has been studied, course work taken, experiences that have contributed to learning about the area, and plans for future activities to meet needs as yet unmet. Table 11.1 illustrates a possible format for such a check list. Notice that the table has been developed for only one of the six operational areas we described. The prospective administrator should develop a form similar to this for each of the other operational areas, in order to check his progress.

TABLE 11.1

PROGRESS IN GAINING PROFESSIONAL KNOWLEDGE AND SKILL IN EDUCATIONAL ADMINISTRATION

Operational area: *school–community relationships*

Major tasks:	Have studied	Have observed	Have participated
Studying community characteristics Assessing community opinion Providing information Co-ordinating educational activities Working with community agencies Working with community leaders			

Pertinent reference material:

Plans for improving knowledge and skill in this area:

The Administrative "Game"

The ideal way to measure a person's professional potential would be to place him in an administrative position at the level to which he aspires and observe him in action. For a number of reasons, this ideal is impracticable. However, such simulated situation devices as the Link Trainer for pilots and various so-called "management games" for business executives are now being adapted to educational administration.

The best-known procedure that uses simulated situations for educational administration is the one developed under the auspices of the University Council for Educational Administration with the co-operation of the Educational Testing Service.[29] In this procedure, a group of potential administrators are introduced to a mythical school district and a specific school in this district through the use of a film, film strips, printed material, and recordings. After this introduction, the students receive envelopes which represent the in-basket on the desk of the principal of the simulated school. They must then decide the order in which they would act on the material, the additional data they would need, and the actions they would take. Choices are recorded in various ways and the reaction of each candidate to the in-basket can then be evaluated.

Although this adaptation of the management game is still in the developmental stage, it shows promise of becoming an excellent device for gaining insight into certain aspects of the professional potential of a prospective administrator. How one acts in a simulated situation differs subtly from patterns in real life, but this technique is an excellent one for providing an additional assessment of the administrative candidate.

EVALUATION OF EXPERIENCE

We have stated that the gross of one's experience does not necessarily equal net educational gain. Much of one's background experience will be reflected in the results of the tests mentioned above and in one's academic achievement. It is necessary, however, to go one more step and consider experience specifically.

Experience can be categorized somewhat loosely under three headings— work, school and community activities, and travel. Each of these groups should receive attention in self-evaluation.

Work Experience

Work experience for most administrators-to-be will include both teaching and nonteaching experience. The ideal—but seldom realized—teaching background for an administrator would include teaching at both the secondary and elementary school levels plus teaching in both large and small schools. Usually, some of this experience must be gained vicariously. Anyone analyzing his own teaching background should ask himself such questions as:

[29] John Hemphill *et al., Administrative Performance and Personality* (New York: Bureau of Publications, Teachers College, Columbia University, 1962).

Do I have a general and a direct knowledge of problems in both the secondary and elementary schools?

Has my teaching experience permitted me to observe several administrators in action?

Do I have a general and a direct knowledge of the differences that are found among large and small schools?

Have I had opportunities to direct and participate in nonclassroom teaching activities, such as student interest groups or professional teacher organization activities?

Have I observed a board of education in action under various circumstances?

Have I taught different classes that have brought me into contact with a variety of children?

Has my teaching experience included a number of contacts with parents?

Have I been able to use or to observe the use of services of such special personnel as school psychologists, supervisors, guidance counselors, or social workers?

Have I had some semi-administrative experiences, such as positions as department head or committee chairman?

Nonteaching work experience is also valuable for the educational administrator. A variety of jobs undertaken during high school and university work or during a period of time away from school provides many insights not otherwise gained. The educational administrator must work with all kinds of community groups and individuals; and work experiences can create valuable understanding to improve the quality of these contacts. We think that it is important that the prospective educational administrator consider questions such as the following:

Have I experienced or observed sufficient kinds of work to gain respect for the many skills required of workers in any given field?

Have I experienced unskilled or manual labor so that I appreciate the problems involved in such work?

Have I developed a feeling of self-confidence through general success in a variety of jobs?

Experience in School and Community Activities

Activities are another source of useful experience for prospective administrators. Participation in activities usually accomplishes at least three things: it provides a background of experience, it provides a testing ground for social personality attributes, and it provides an opportunity for practice in budgeting time. This last point is particularly important. The prospective administrator whose self-evaluation reveals a shortcoming in academic achievement cannot excuse this by citing a long list of activity accomplishments. Under most circumstances, this imbalance reveals a lack of ability to budget time or to put first things first. Therefore we would stress that activities need to be evaluated in terms of the total scope of the educational and experiential background of the prospective administrator.

As one attempts to assess one's experience in terms of participation in activities, one might well consider questions such as these:

Have I participated successfully in activities as both a leader and a follower?

Does my history of participation show some range of activities?

Have I ever helped to organize a school or community activity group, or participated as a member of such a group during its first year of existence?

Have I been able to be a successful participant in an activity group at the same time that I had rather heavy demands from a job or from school?

Have I been somewhat active in community or church groups as well as in activities connected with my school experience?

Have I engaged in certain activities on an exploratory basis in addition to engaging in activities in which I already had a keen interest and a known ability?

Travel Experience

The old expression that "travel is broadening" is an advertising phrase with many elements of truth in it. Travel, however, has an unusual ability —it may either broaden a person's outlook or make him more provincial than he was at the outset. To gain from travel, one must attempt to understand and to appreciate differences rather than look down on customs and conditions that differ from the ones at home.

In evaluating one's travel background as part of one's competency pattern for educational administration, many difficulties arise. Problems of time, finance, and general circumstances often make extensive travel impossible. While some young men and women have had world-wide travel opportunities due to war which have provided much insight into world conditions, others have not left the confines of a county or state because of equally pressing circumstances. It is important, however, that every school administrator make an effort to visit at least one region in the United States which differs from his home territory. The New Englander might see what the Plains States are like, and the Middle Westerner might explore the Rocky Mountain country. The cosmopolite from New York, Chicago, or San Francisco could profit from a tour through the rural country of the South. In return, the rural Southerner could learn much of value by visiting Los Angeles or Philadelphia. We have indicated earlier that many major problems in education are international in scope. Foreign travel opportunities are becoming increasingly abundant and reasonably priced, and such opportunities should be taken advantage of by the potential administrator. The future educational leader must have some concept of the cultural and geographical context in which the problems that must be met, at least in part, by education will arise.

In addition to foreign travel, there are increasing opportunities for educational service in foreign countries. Many teachers have taught in military-dependent schools overseas, and, although they teach American students, such experiences permit first-hand acquaintance with foreign countries. Finally, such opportunities as the projects sponsored by the Agency for International Development and the Peace Corps offer work experiences in a variety of countries.

If a prospective educational administrator who asks himself where he has been and what he has seen must admit that the answer is "nowhere and nothing," it is time to improve the situation. However, the self-evaluator must be sure that he has both "been" and "seen." If he has only "been," he should retrace his steps and discover the many things to be seen and to be learned through travel.

Working with People

Administration implies the activities of a person as he plays a leadership role in a group that is striving to reach a goal. For this reason, an important part of the competency pattern of an educational administrator consists of his knowledge and skill in the area of human relations.

WORKING WITH INDIVIDUALS

In an earlier chapter, the motivations behind administrative behavior were discussed in detail. It is important that the administrator understand that all people are motivated to act by things which are often not easily apparent. Even though the present discussion cannot attempt to be even a partial treatise on the psychology of human behavior, it seems important to describe a few key concepts that should be understood by the educational administrator as he works with individuals.

Self-respect

Psychologists and psychiatrists name a loss of self-respect as among the most dangerous of human ills. The administrator must be aware of its importance and of the possibilities of his work for strengthening or weakening the self-respect of those with whom he works. Every person constantly builds and defends his self-respect. Acts by administrators which tend to attack this "citadel" are vigorously resisted. Often such administrative acts are completely unintentional and unnoticed by the administrator, who would deny ever attacking a staff member's self-respect. Little things, such as an imagined snub, an off-hand remark at a staff meeting, or a harsh word can be magnified until major problems in human relations result. The administrator needs an awareness of this problem, and perceptiveness and tactfulness to enable him to avoid making remarks that could unnecessarily offend the person with whom he is dealing.

Irrational Behavior

Every administrator will have to deal from time to time with behavior he considers irrational. It is important to remember that everyone has a reason for doing whatever he does and that this reason is rational to the actor. In understanding and working with individuals, the administrator is often faced with the necessity of assessing reasons for behavior. To assume that certain individual behavior occurs for no reason at all is a false assumption that can, in fact, be dangerous.

Goals

There is often such a strong tendency in education to stress society's goals, community goals, or the goals of the school that the goals of the individual can be forgotten. The stress on individual differences usually emphasizes differences in ability and aptitudes as individuals strive to reach group goals. The administrator needs to understand that individuals, too, have goals and that these individual goals are important forces in meeting group goals.

These are but a few of the understandings of the individual which an administrator needs. The important fact is that in these days of group dynamics, group management, and group decisions, the competent administrator will understand the individual as well as he understands the group. He will know the techniques and skills of face-to-face human relations as well as he knows the equally important area of group relations. He will feel that it is as important to be able to work with and communicate with individuals as it is to work with groups. He will respect the individual problem as much as he respects the group problem. In short, to borrow from chemistry, he will realize that the group is not the basic element of human relations, but rather that it is most like a mixture in which the elements are individuals—each different, each important, and each a key determinant of the nature and the properties of the group. The chemist will instantly see errors in this analogy. In a mixture, each element retains its own properties, while in a group each individual becomes a different person because of his group affiliation. Neither is the group like a compound in which properties of elements become lost and completely new molecules are formed. The administrator cannot afford to ignore the individuals in a group with which he deals nor can he assume that a given group, once formed, will always respond in the same way to the same stimuli. Dealing as he does with individuals and with groups of individuals, he needs to keep a clear focus on the individual as well as on the group.

WORKING WITH SMALL GROUPS

Much of the work of the administrator is with small groups of from five to twenty people. Some of these groups are permanent parts of the structure of a school or community with fairly well-defined duties and responsibilities. Others are the product of a current need or problem with less clearly defined goals and with no expectation of permanence.

A great deal has been written dealing with group leadership, group dynamics, group action, "human engineering," brain-storming, and other techniques of working with groups. This type of activity is a process that occupies a considerable amount of administrative time and in which the administrator needs real competence. In spite of many discussions of the ways in which leadership grows from a group, it must be remembered that an administrator is a status or appointed leader and in a majority of cases is expected to assume a leadership role in groups with which he works. It does not follow that he will stifle leadership in the group, but rather that his leadership will encourage that of others.

In working with small groups, the administrator may find himself in one of two different positions. At times he will be asking a group to perform a definite function whose fulfillment is his responsibility. In these cases, the goals of the group are defined by the demands of the organization as exemplified by the superintendent, the board of education, or some other administrative officer in the line of the organization. While the group may have some flexibility in ways of working, it is expected to meet a definite and assigned responsibility. At other times, the administrator will find himself working with groups in which group goals are not assigned from any position in the administrative hierarchy. In such cases, the group itself will play a major role in developing statements of goals.

WORKING WITH LARGE GROUPS

The educational administrator will work with many large groups. Here again it is wise to recall that any group, regardless of size, is composed of individuals. It is often easy to hear a group opinion, particularly from a large group, and yet know very little about the real opinions of those who make up the group.

In working with any group, the competent administrator must be an able communicator.[30] With the smaller group, much of this communication will be rather informal in nature—face-to-face contacts in which communication is relatively free and easy. With the large group, the more formal means of communication will be utilized to a great extent. These consist of such things as bulletins, booklets, or formal speeches. The flow of communication and the ability to detect the way in which it is being received will be difficult to assess at times. This implies that both the administrator's sending and receiving apparatus must be in good working order. Many times, it is more important for an administrator to be able to listen well than to speak well. In discussing some of the requirements of good listening, Dale stresses that the good listener needs to develop an ability to like to listen as much as he likes to talk; to listen actively so that he knows exactly what was said; and to frame pertinent questions about what he hears so that he can gain clarification of the meaning of what was said.[31]

The "sending" side of communication requires ability in speaking and writing fluently and clearly. When dealing with a large group it is difficult to tell whether or not communication is being understood as it is meant to be. In order to minimize the possibilities of misunderstanding, the communication should be brief, to the point, and complete. The competent educational administrator must be able to speak and write in a well-organized manner, and with an absence of high-sounding but generally meaningless words.

The other competencies needed in working with large groups vary little from previously outlined competencies. Special mention might be made here of the need for insight in this phase of administrative work. What are the goals of the large group? What does it expect of its leader? Why these goals and expectations? These questions are key ones and the ability to find correct answers is an important part of the competency pattern of an educational administrator.

GENERAL THOUGHTS ON WORKING WITH PEOPLE

The administrator plays an important leadership role in his school and community. A number of studies have indicated that school or community

[30] For an excellent discussion of communication in administration, see Theodore L. Reller, Jack A. Culbertson, and Paul B. Jacobson, *Administrative Relationships: A Case Book* (Englewood Cliffs, N.J.: Prentice-Hall, Inc., 1960), Chapter 5, pp. 380–413.

[31] Edgar Dale, "Why Don't We Listen," *The Newsletter,* 22 (February 1957), pp. 1–4.

morale is high when people in the school or community hold expectations of the role of the administrator that coincide to a great extent with the administrator's perception of his role. While high morale is a hoped-for condition in any organization, the administrator has to consider more than morale, for there is a danger that high morale can be a result of mutually low expectations. While great dreams of "what is possible" are not the exclusive property of administrators, the competent administrator should be one who can dream such dreams and who can help the groups with which he works see the reality of such dreams and become interested in capturing this reality. In addition, he should be able to recognize a "big idea" when one is presented by a staff member. This is perhaps the greatest challenge facing the administrator as he works with a wide variety of people. It is a challenge that requires a belief in and a knowledge of the possibilities of public education in America, a philosophy of life and of education, and an understanding of the cultural and social setting in which public education in America operates.

POTENTIAL IN TERMS OF WORKING WITH PEOPLE

In almost any administrative activity, the end result is attained only as the administrator works with people. Many, if not all, of the attributes and other competencies discussed previously contribute to or detract from one's ability to work with people. In one sense, much of the evaluation up to this point has included some assessment of such an ability. It is possible, however, to help the prospective administrator organize his self-evaluation to provide insight into this ability and to suggest certain instruments to aid in this specific part of his evaluation.

In some cases, we feel that tests or other instruments designed for several purposes are most helpful in appraising one's effectiveness in working with people. Such an instrument is the *Valenti-Nelson Survey of Teaching Practices*.[32] It describes a number of situations that may face a teacher and provides alternative ways of meeting them. Of the 102 situations presented (actually seventeen situations with six different pairs of alternatives) at least two-thirds of them involve relationships with people. A careful interpretation of scores made in this survey will, then, provide insight into one's patterns of behavior in dealing with people.

The problems and processes of communication also are involved when the administrator works with people. Many universities and colleges provide

---

[32] *Valenti-Nelson Survey of Teaching Practices.* Science Research Associates, 57 West Grand Avenue, Chicago, Illinois.

speech tests as part of the teacher-training program. The administrator-to-be should review his speaking ability and should take steps to insure that his manner of speaking is an asset rather than a handicap. Another obvious need is the ability to use the English language acceptably in both oral and written form. The prospective administrator can examine papers and projects which he has submitted as part of his university work to gather data on the adequacy of his English usage. The ability to understand and to construct visual materials such as graphs and charts is another easily assessed aspect of communication skill.

More difficult to assess is one's ability to communicate ideas and to have these ideas understood and acted upon. It is also difficult to determine if one's "receiving" apparatus is of a type to permit easy communication *with* as well as *from*. At the present time, we think that these evaluations for a prospective administrator are forced to be extremely subjective. However, subjectivity, or informed self-judgment, has a definite value and should be considered as a necessary and important part of any evaluation. A person might ask himself such questions as the following to attempt to gain some insight into his ability as an effective communicator:

Do I understand the meaning of the process of communication?

Am I generally understood when I try to give directions or instructions to someone?

In my teaching, do my students understand my assignments and act accordingly?

When I hear a speech, can I detect the purpose and major arguments of the speaker?

Do I critically appraise books or articles that I read?

When in a discussion group, do I listen when others are speaking and relate my remarks to the general flow of the discussion?

The final test of one's ability to work with people is what happens when one works with people. Most of the evaluative questions dealing with activity participation also can be applied to this area. If the prospective administrator has found that he can and does maintain good human relationships with his close friends, with social and professional colleagues, with his teachers, with people met only occasionally, and with his students, the chances are good that he has some mastery of the techniques of working with people. In addition to working with people, the educational administrator is expected to be a leader of people. Here again, the final test is what happens as one tries to lead. If the prospective administrator has found that he has emerged as a leader in several groups and has been able to fulfill a leadership role successfully, he has evidence that among his techniques of working with people is the important ability to be a leader.

COMPETENCY IN A PROFESSION

To summarize our discussion of competencies, it can be said that several areas of competency have been presented—many of which are particularly pertinent to educational administration, many pertinent to any profession, and many pertinent to a successful life regardless of occupation. The good administrator must first of all know himself—his beliefs, his values, his aims and goals. He must then understand other people and must have skill in working with other people.

The man himself must bring certain personal attributes to his work as an educational administrator. Important attributes discussed include:

Physical attributes
 Good health
 Above-average energy
 Normal physical appearance

Mental attributes
 Above-average intelligence
 Insight
 Comprehensiveness
 Penetration
 Flexibility

Social personality attributes
 Balance
 Adaptability
 Originality
 Initiative
 Persistence
 Ambition
 Even disposition
 Self-confidence
 Sociability
 Personal cleanliness and neatness

Character attributes
 "Good" character (honesty, morality, loyalty, integrity . . .)

The educational administrator, through his education and experience, must come to understand the purposes and methods of public education in America. He must understand the child—the basic consumer of public education. It then becomes necessary for him to understand the specifics of his profession—educational administration. He needs to know what it is, what its processes are, and what it is supposed to accomplish. In addition, he must understand and have skill in a number of specific techniques involved in educational administration.

A profession also requires that its members possess a basic dissatisfaction with their performance in it. This dissatisfaction leads to a constant drive for self-improvement based on self-analysis, and a drive for the improvement of the profession. It is likely that a person who is easily satisfied will be less competent in a professional career than one who is continually seeking something better. Such a search leads to creativity, to a mind which can envision what the "something better" might be.

Finally, a basic requirement is the desire to be competent. Possessing competencies and using them effectively are two different things. Aesop's hare was competent to win a footrace against the tortoise, but the inclination to use these competencies was lacking. A person who possesses most of the competencies required of an educational administrator, but does not really want to be an effective administrator, will undoubtedly not be effective. A person who lacks some competencies, but has a burning desire to be an effective administrator, will take some steps to remove these deficiencies and may well become an effective administrator. Without this basic desire, the possession of the other competencies means little.

The Overall View of Potential

In any evaluative procedure, the time always arrives when it is necessary to ask, "What does all this mean?" If the prospective administrator has reached the point where he has taken a number of tests and has examined himself in terms of a number of questions, what next? In the first place, the general question of one's desire to be an administrator has not yet been considered. This question must not be answered too quickly or glibly. The answer will greatly influence the interpretation of one's self-evaluation. The desire to be an administrator may not seem to be strong, or it may be based only upon consideration of finance or prestige. In this case, any handicaps discovered through self-evaluation will be more difficult to overcome than if the desire is based on a sincere conviction that educational administration offers a professional challenge and opportunity for growth too great to be ignored. The question of desire must then be reveiwed as one prepares to consolidate one's self-evaluation.

Secondly, steps must be taken to gather the results of the various steps in the evaluative process into a meaningful summary. Here again a written record will be of help. The following form has proved useful in some university programs for the preparation of administrators. It will be noted that the categories of competencies are different from those used in this chapter, but that the specific competencies are similar to those discussed here.

AREAS OF COMPETENCE

For each area of competence place a check mark at the position on the scale which most nearly represents your judgment of your own competence. Your present competence should be considered in relation to the competence required of an effective educational administrator. Use the following scale:

> 5—Superior
> 4—Somewhat above average
> 3—Average
> 2—Somewhat below average
> 1—Very low

Below the scale, in the space provided, indicate plans for improving your competence. These plans might include teaching or other experience, university course work, and considerations of certification and advanced degree requirements.

A. Personal Characteristics

1. Possession of a reasonable degree of appropriate personal attributes and a disposition to improve them.

5	4	3	2	1

Plan_____

_____

_____

2. An ability and a disposition to apply sound problem-solving procedures to school concerns.

5	4	3	2	1

Plan_____

_____

_____

3. An inclination to act in terms of conscious value judgments.

5	4	3	2	1

Plan_____

_____

_____

B. General Educational Background

4. Understandings, attitudes, and skill resulting from an adequate general education.

5	4	3	2	1

Plan_____

_____

_____

5. An understanding of the role of the school in the social order.

5	4	3	2	1

Plan _____

_____

6. An understanding of the instructional program and the administrator's role in its improvement.

5	4	3	2	1

Plan _____

_____

7. An understanding of the processes of human growth and learning.

5	4	3	2	1

Plan _____

_____

C. Conceptual Skills

8. An ability to comprehend and make articulate the role of the school in the social order.

5	4	3	2	1

Plan _____

_____

9. An ability to comprehend the impact of the many forces and agencies upon the school and to seek an equilibrium among them in building and maintaining an adequate educational program.

5	4	3	2	1

Plan _____

_____

10. An ability to comprehend the many contributions of the various parts of the school and effect an organizational structure that is instrumental in their co-ordination to achieve the school's goals and objectives.

5	4	3	2	1

Plan _____

_____

D. Human Relations

11. A disposition and an ability to work with people in planning, executing, and evaluating courses of action.

| | | | | |
|5|4|3|2|1|

Plan_____

_____

_____

12. An inclination and an ability to understand one's own motivations for action and how they affect one's way of working with people.

| | | | | |
|5|4|3|2|1|

Plan_____

_____

_____

13. A disposition and an ability to lead lay and professional people in considering the continuing improvement of the school and community; the ability to discover and promote such leadership in others.

| | | | | |
|5|4|3|2|1|

Plan_____

_____

_____

E. Technical Skills

14. Understandings and skills in the technical aspects of the phases of ad-administration in which one works.

| | | | | |
|5|4|3|2|1|

Plan_____

_____

_____

15. An understanding of and skills in the use of administrative processes.

| | | | | |
|5|4|3|2|1|

Plan_____

_____

_____

F. Change

16. The ability and disposition to take one's place as a leader in the initiation and assessment of change.

| | | | | |
|5|4|3|2|1|

Plan_____

_____

_____

17. The ability and discipline required to continue professional growth throughout one's career.

Plan_____

_____

_____

Whether this form or some other is used, it is necessary to organize the evaluation to permit moving on to the next step in the process.

The third step, which is implied by the form presented above, is, of course, planning. An evaluation must lead to some kind of action, and it should be planned action. Perhaps the evaluation will reveal so many limitations that it seems best to plan not to enter educational administration. This means that some alternative plans need to be made. In what ways, for example, can a person fulfill a certain leadership role as a teacher? What kinds of in-school or out-of-school activities will provide some of the satisfactions which it was hoped might be gained in administration?

On the other hand, the evaluation may reveal limitations that are not sufficiently great to hinder a career in administration. If this is the case, plans may be made to overcome these limitations as far as possible through university work and experience. What kind of time schedule for the future seems appropriate? What teaching experiences are needed before applying for an administrative position? What specific administrative position seems most suitable?

And finally, plans must be carried out. We have all heard the old saying, "If wishes were horses, all beggars would ride." Wishes are neither horses nor competencies. The prospective administrator now has some indications of his potential. Whether or not this potential will be fully realized is up to him. Through careful planning, continued self-evaluation, and a program of action, the prospective administrator with potential can move forward to become an educational leader who can help realize the potential in others.

SUGGESTED ACTIVITIES

1. Think of the best school administrator you have known. Describe the competencies that he possessed that led you to judge him the "best."

2. Do you believe there are competencies that are required of good "followers"? Describe several such competencies or indicate why such competencies do not exist.

3. Describe the differences and similarities that you believe exist among the competencies required of an educational administrator, and those required of an administrator in some other type of organization.

4. It is unrealistic and unwise to assume that any one student will subject himself to all of the measuring devices mentioned in this chapter. A testing pattern that has been used with some success in basic courses in educational administration is suggested below. This pattern is suggestive in nature, and others could be developed.

   Class groups should make arrangements for group testing and for discussion of the results among themselves and with the instructor. Complete references to the instruments are found in the chapter.

   Watson-Glaser Critical Thinking Appraisal.

   Ohio State University Psychological Examination (or similar test)

   Cooperative English Test, Form C2

   Guilford-Zimmerman Personality Inventory

5. Complete the summary form presented on pages 358–62 using your best judgment and any other evidence you may have. Discuss the results with your instructor either individually or with a small group. Prepare a detailed plan for improving your competence in the area in which you seem to be most limited.

6. Develop a complete form following the pattern illustrated by Table 11.1, page 347, upon which you can record your progress in gaining professional skills and knowledge in the seven operational areas of educational administration.

SELECTED READINGS

American Association of School Administrators, *Professional Administrators for America's Schools.* 38th Yearbook. Washington, D.C.: The Association, 1960.

———, *The Professional Preparation of Superintendents of Schools.* Washington, D.C.: The Association, 1964.

ARGYRIS, CHRIS. *Executive Leadership: An Appraisal of a Manager in Action.* New York: Harper & Brothers, 1953.

CAMPBELL, R. F. and GREGG, R. T. (eds.). *Administrative Behavior in Education.* New York: Harper & Brothers, 1957. Chapters IV, IX, and XI.

GIBB, CECIL A. "Leadership," in Lindzey, Gardner (ed.). *Handbook of Social Psychology*, Vol. II. Cambridge, Mass.: Addison-Wesley Publishing Company, 1954.

HEMPHILL, JOHN, GRIFFITHS, DANIEL E. and FREDERIKSEN, NORMAN. *Administrative Performance and Personality*. New York: Bureau of Publications, Teachers College, Columbia University, 1962.

LIFTON, WALTER M. *Working with Groups*. New York: John Wiley and Sons, 1961.

STOGDILL, R. M. "Personal Factors Associated with Leadership: A Survey of the Literature," *Journal of Psychology*, 25 (January 1948), pp. 35–71.

THELEN, H. A. *The Dynamics of Groups at Work*. Chicago: University of Chicago Press, 1954.

12

Qualifying

for Educational Administration

USUALLY, WHEN A PERSON DECIDES TO DO SOMETHING, that decision is the prelude to a great deal of effort. This fact is particularly true when the decision involves the course of one's life work. We have described many aspects of educational administration and the competencies that seem to be required of those who desire to enter the profession. In this chapter, we will focus on two major ideas—the decision to become an educational administrator and the plans necessary to implement such a decision. While these ideas may seem more useful to one who decides to become an administrator, the person who has about decided that administration is not for him can also benefit from a discussion of them. The discussion might well serve as a final test of the decision to seek another type of educational position.

MAKING THE DECISION

Life is characterized by the daily necessity of making decisions. From such minor items as the choice of an entree from a menu to such major considerations as the purchase of a home, the human is blessed—or plagued —with the necessity to make up his mind.

Many fiction writers have been intrigued with the possibilities of creating heroes or heroines who could see into the future and thus base decisions on certainties about this future. In every case known to us, this power has proved to be uncomfortable for and unwanted by the fictional characters. For, actually, part of the spice of life lies in pitting our powers of decision-making against the unknown future. We must operate, to quote a para-phrase of Mark Twain's words, in the certainty only of "death, taxes, and rain on the Fourth of July." Within the framework of known facts about the past and present and intelligent consideration of the future, it is neces-sary for all of us to engage in the business of decision-making.

THE NEED FOR A DECISION

Educational administration has been characterized by some as a pro-fession whose main task is decision-making. Certainly, regardless of defini-tion, the ability to make decisions and help others do so is an important part of the job of the educational administrator. For this reason, it is paradoxical to discover an advanced graduate student or an experienced teacher who thinks that he may be interested in educational administration, but just cannot make up his mind about it. If administration and decision-making are even somewhat synonymous, the inability to make a major de-cision about one's career may be an excellent indication that that career should not be educational administration.

We do not mean to imply that this decision should not be made care-fully. A number of facts and factors will need to be considered before a person can decide that he does or does not want to pursue a career as an educational administrator. The point is, however, that these facts should be gathered, the factors should be discovered, and the decision should be made without undue procrastination.

In addition to the fact that inability to make a decision may illustrate lack of fitness for administration, what other problems can such a delay create for the potential administrator? In the first place, such a delay can hinder a person's advancement if he finally does decide to enter administra-tion. For most administrators, the road to a top-level administrative position proceeds through several positions of lesser responsibility. The older a person is before he starts in an administrative position, the fewer the opportunities he will receive to realize eventually his full potential.

Secondly, administrative positions currently require more educational background of their incumbents than was once the case. It is not at all unusual today to find vacancy notices for superintendencies and for high school principalships which state that a man with a doctor's degree will be preferred. Gaining educational background takes time. Many universities discourage students from undertaking a doctoral program after they reach the age of forty, and many men and women who have reached that age cannot well afford the cost in time or money of such a program due to family and other responsibilities. While exceptions could be pointed out, the decision to start a doctoral program in educational administration is best made before a person reaches the age of about thirty.

A third problem created by an undue delay in the decision-making process is the delay it causes in making and following a plan to implement the decision. Ordinarily, there are many steps required between making a decision and reaching the point dictated by that decision. These steps need to be planned; it is impossible to create such a plan unless the decision as to "where I am going" has been made. Whether or not a person decides to enter administration, he does have a future ahead of him and plans must be made. The longer a person takes in deciding what he wants his future to hold for him, the less future remains for him to realize his aims.

ASSESSING STRENGTHS AND WEAKNESSES

As a person approaches a decision, he should review again the data about himself gathered as we suggested in Chapter 11. How do the facts seem to add up? To what extent do strengths for administration overshadow weaknesses? A close look at one's self as related to the competencies required of an educational administrator is an important step in the decision-making process.

Much of the assessment of personal strengths and weaknesses is done in subjective terms. Both potential and conditions that will enhance or retard one's ability to reach potential need to be considered. The appraisal should be approached with neither overoptimism nor overpessimism. A careful consideration of the personal, educational, and experiential attributes, and the potential for educational administration represented by these attributes is a prerequisite to a wise decision concerning educational administration as a career.

ASSESSING GOALS

In a number of places in this volume we have described some of the factors that underlie administrative behavior. There they were presented in somewhat general terms, but as one ponders one's possible future in educational administration, personal goals must be considered. "Why do I want to become a superintendent, or principal, or supervisor?" is an important question in the decision-making process.

The prospective administrator might counter by asking, "If the question is so important, what is the right answer?" While there is undoubtedly no single "right" answer, there are indications of rightness. An important indication is whether or not the goals are realistic. If, for example, the prospective administrator has heard of some city superintendents earning yearly salaries of $40,000 or more and thus believes that he can make his fortune in educational administration, this incentive is, at best, unrealistic. If, for another example, the prospective administrator imagines that through school administration he can guarantee himself a place in the top echelon of prestige and power, he need only read such studies as that made by Hunter to realize that this ambition is likely to be unfulfilled.[1] Perhaps a more realistic goal for the school administrator centers about the opportunity to do a difficult and challenging job that is of key importance in American society.

Another indicator of the rightness of one's desire to enter administration is the test of ethics. It would not be ethical, for example, to be motivated toward a new position solely on the basis of lack of success in a present position. By the same token, in a field such as education, in which public service is a great function, it would not be ethical for motivation to come solely from the desire for personal gain or power. The ethics of education appear to dictate that motivation toward administration should include strong considerations of the possibilities for service.

A final, and perhaps not exactly co-ordinate, test in the area of goals is a test of the existence of such goals. A person finally has to ask himself if he really wants to do something, or if he is merely doing something because he is not motivated to do anything else. Many people drift into teaching and drift into administration. If one is sincerely interested in qualifying for a position at a high level of proficiency, one must do more than arrive at that position through a process of selective inertia. If administration becomes the least of a number of evils for a person, the chances that he will strive to reach competency in administration are slight. If his only motivation toward administration is a lack of motivation to teach or sell or produce, he needs to examine himself with mature judgment and develop positive motivation to do something and to do it well.

In essence, then, as a person works toward a decision to be an administrator or not to be an administrator, he must determine what his goals are and then examine these goals in the light of a clear understanding of the nature of educational administration. Only such an examination can reveal to him the "rightness" of his goals in terms of realism and of ethics.

[1] Floyd Hunter, *Community Power Structure* (Chapel Hill, N.C.: University of North Carolina Press, 1953).

ASSESSING PROFESSIONAL OPPORTUNITIES

Previous chapters of this book have indicated that in education there is a wide variety of positions that may be called administrative. In Chapter 13, the number and variety of such positions will be explored in more detail. All that need be said here is that as one attempts to make a decision about one's future in educational administration, one should contemplate the variety of positions under that heading. To consider, for example, only the city superintendency as educational administration is to restrict the scope of one's choices to unnecessarily narrow limits.

It is unfortunately true even today that many writers use the terms educational administration and superintendency as if the latter were all-inclusive of the former. Not only does such a concept produce an unnecessarily limited view of administration, but it forces unrealistic choices upon anyone who thinks that he wants to be an administrator but is certain that he does not want to be a superintendent. This desire is not only feasible but necessary if every type of administrative position is to be seen as the important position it is in its own right rather than as a mere steppingstone to "real" administration. As a person plans and decides about the future, he should consider educational administration in its full scope rather than concentrate upon only one phase within it.

THE DECISION IS MADE

That a person must commit himself—not inflexibly, but with resolve— concerning his future is obviously our belief. This commitment—and here we are speaking of the commitment to attempt to qualify or not to attempt to qualify for educational administration—should be made in terms of a careful appraisal of oneself and of the field of educational administration. Once the decision has been made and plans have been developed to implement it, an evaluative procedure must be developed also. Today's decision is made on the basis of both fact and surmise. Guesses about tomorrow can be appraised in the light of facts when tomorrow comes. The guesses and the facts sometimes agree, but even the most intelligent and informed guesses can go wrong.

The fact that a person guesses wrong need not be a serious error unless he refuses to admit that he has made an error of judgment. It should be recognized, however, that wrong guesses or errors in judgment can be fatal errors—e.g., in driving a car, or in deciding on a hunting trip that the thing moving in the thicket must be a deer and not a man. Since decisions about career choices, however, are seldom so quickly shown to be right or wrong, the person who evaluates his decision as he attempts to implement it has a much better chance to change his decision than does the hunter whose bullet has left his gun barrel. Undue procrastination cannot be excused on the basis that "I want to avoid making a mistake!"

In many cases, the only way to test the results of a decision is to make it, proceed to develop and follow a plan to implement it, and test, from time to time, the degree to which the decision seems to have been a wise one. If the attempt to follow the plan appears to cast doubts upon the wisdom of the plan, it is then time, in terms of new facts, to make a new decision. It can be seen, then, that decision-making alone is not enough. After it is made, the next problem is to create a plan to meet the requirements implied by the decision.

Creating a Plan

A classic poem reminds us that "The best laid schemes o' mice and men" often go astray. As children, we all read—but probably did not wholly comprehend—the rhyme that told of the kingdom that was lost "for want of a nail." Must we then infer that man is foolish to plan when his plans are so easily laid low? History is replete with famous men who seem to have been cast by destiny rather than self-planning into heroic or villainous roles. Careful analysis, however, indicates that planning by men is far more successful than might be assumed, and is far more prevalent among men than might be evident. History also does not reveal to us the names of potentially great men who did not make important contributions for the lack of a plan.

Without going into detailed documentation of the need for careful planning if decisions are to be carried into reality, we shall merely state that planning seems to us to be an essential step in qualifying for educational administration. It is necessary to examine the elements of a good plan and to provide some insights into planning for a specific field—educational administration.

ELEMENTS OF A GOOD PLAN

It seems to us that planning involves clarifying purposes; defining the problem; gathering, analyzing, and interpreting facts; and deciding courses of action. This is, of course, very similar to the whole process of decision-making as we defined it earlier. For our purpose here, however, it will be assumed that earlier decision-making procedures have led to a clear statement of purpose and that the problem is well defined. There will, obviously, be sub-purposes and sub-problems. It will be necessary to gather, analyze, and interpret facts and, certainly, to decide courses of action.

The plan should, then, be based on a clear understanding of the ultimate purpose and of the steps necessary to meet this purpose. Next comes a consideration of the qualifications required to make the steps. The basic elements of a good plan seem to be statements of purpose, of qualifications needed to meet purposes, and of the steps required to gain these qualifications. Thus, if one's ultimate purpose is to become a city superintendent, one's plan must include certification, university work for advanced degrees, and experience. It will undoubtedly also include a principalship as a step toward the ultimate purpose, and this step will require consideration of appropriate certification, degree work, and experience background necessary for the principalship.

Thus both short-term and long-term goals should be included in a good plan. The short-term goals should be stated in order that sequential progress toward the ultimate goal is understood and planned. The long-term goal must be stated to provide a frame of reference as one has opportunities to change positions, to go to school, or to do both. It is the long-range goal that can help a person decide if he should accept a new position or if he should stay where he is and complete, for example, the program for his master's degree.

INCLUSIVENESS OF THE PLAN

A plan such as we have been discussing cannot be too detailed, particularly as it is projected ten or even more years into the future. In addition, the plan should not be unduly specific. While, for example, it is understandable that a person might desire to be the superintendent of schools in his home town, it is not wise to restrict planning to such specific goals. The old home town can have only one superintendent at a time, and the person who clings tenaciously to this specific goal may wait in vain for an opportunity to realize it. The specifics of certification and advanced degrees are appropriate, but specifics as to geographical location of future position, exact places where nonteaching experience is to be gained, or exact salaries to be earned along the way are not.

In general, the plan should include types of positions desired, types of nonschool work or activity experiences deemed necessary, and a general picture of the economic well-being desired as the plan progresses. Just as an attractive woman may be a spinster because she waited in vain for a blond lawyer, six feet tall, earning $20,000 a year, and with a Cadillac convertible, to show up and propose, so the prospective administrator can wait in vain for a board of education in a given school district to offer him a given job at a given salary. It is far better that a plan be developed which is sufficiently inclusive of the general progress desired than that a plan be cluttered with specific and unrealistic details.

FLEXIBILITY VERSUS VACILLATION

The above discussion makes it clear that some flexibility is desirable in a plan for the future. Earlier, when the necessity of evaluation of the basic decision to pursue a specific ultimate goal was described, it was pointed out that changes in plan may be necessary and wise. How does one tell when one is being wisely flexible and when one is being foolishly vacillatory? Generally, the most simple and basic way is to test possible changes in position or in objectives against the framework of the ultimate goal and the reasons that led to the choice of that goal.

Does experience show that some of the basic reasoning which led to the choice of the ultimate goal was in error? If so, a change in goals may be wise. Does momentary fatigue or irritation seem to demand a change in the ultimate goal? If so, such a change may be extremely unwise. Does a new position fit the requirements of the next step toward the ultimate goal even though it was not a position that was envisioned earlier as a good one? If so, accepting it may be wise. Does a new position offer financial rewards but no real progress toward the ultimate goal? If so, it may prove to be unwise both professionally and financially.

A well-made, carefully considered plan, drawn up in realistically general terms, should be discarded only for major reasons related to the ultimate goal and the basis for accepting that goal. Too many "temporary" deviations from plan for reasons that are attractive but unsound can lead to permanent failure to reach an ultimate goal. This is the reason that long-range goals are necessary and should play an important role in reaching short-term decisions.

THE PLAN IS CREATED

We have now considered the making of a decision and the creation of a plan to implement it. We need now to turn our attention to a specific plan to implement a specific decision—qualifying for educational administration. The remainder of this chapter will explore some of the specific considerations to be made as one attempts to create and follow a plan that will lead to a desired position as an educational administrator.

USING TEACHING EXPERIENCE

Many would-be administrators fail to realize and to profit from the opportunities for qualification as an administrator which are inherent in a teaching position. We have already described in some detail the role of the teacher in school administration. Undoubtedly, the fulfillment of this role will lead to increased qualification as an administrator. Certain features might well be pointed out here to relate teaching experience more specifically to qualification as an administrator. Before doing this, however, we must stress that we do not view the main function of teaching to be that of a stepping-stone to administration. The teacher who holds the attitude that teaching is only a necessary evil before entering a "real" job, will probably achieve only minor success both in teaching and in the "real" job—if, indeed, the so-called real job is ever attained. While we do want to point out that teaching experience can help qualify a person for administration, we would not want to imply that this is a major purpose of teaching.

CONTINUED GROWTH AS A TEACHER

Many of the qualities of a good teacher are also qualities that are desirable in a school administrator. For example, over twenty years ago Goetting described the qualifications of a teacher in a manner similar to our discussion of the competencies required of an administrator.[2] He mentioned the importance of human relationships and the skills required to conduct human relationships effectively; he described the need for ethical conduct and presented a code of ethics; he discussed such social personality attributes as adaptability, originality, optimism, and self-confidence; he mentioned the importance of physical appearance and physical vigor; he stressed the need for a philosophy of education and a philosophy of life; he discussed academic and experience background in much the same manner as we have; and he concluded with a description of necessary professional knowledge which included much of importance in administration.

Teaching and educational administration are, then, closely related. Continued professional growth as a teacher, including growth in skill, technique, and insight, may lead to increased qualification as an administrator. Many institutions granting graduate degrees in educational administration have recognized this fact by stressing that, for many students, a master's degree program should provide emphasis in a teaching field rather than in administration, even though administration may be the ultimate goal.

Thus, until research or practice proves otherwise, we take the position that the first important step in attempting to qualify as an administrator is to become a qualified teacher. We know at least two things now: every competent teacher should not be an aspiring administrator; and an unsuccessful or incompetent teacher should not hope to be an administrator. Both of

[2] M. L. Goetting, *Teaching in the Secondary School* (Englewood Cliffs, N.J.: Prentice-Hall, Inc., 1942), pp. 23–41.

these facts indicate that every beginning teacher—be he a prospective master teacher or a prospective master administrator—should be concerned with his continued professional growth as a teacher.

This growth can be accomplished through a planned combination of university work; professional reading; participation in local, county, and state in-service growth activities; and co-operation with teachers, supervisors, principals and others who are responsible for helping teachers improve their professional competency. Travel and work experience can also be of value in the improvement of teaching ability. Yearly evaluation of teaching ability, both on a self-evaluation basis and with the help of others, is a significant aspect of continued growth as a teacher. In short, any activity that contributes to the growth of a teacher also contributes to his potential qualification as an educational administrator.

LEADERSHIP OPPORTUNITIES

The classroom teacher is, in a very real sense, a leader. The steps we have proposed as being integral parts of the administrative process— decision-making, programing, stimulating, co-ordinating, and appraising —are evident in the activities of any good classroom teacher. In many respects, the teacher can and should be a leader in his community. Organizations of teachers offer important opportunities for leadership which are, in many ways, similar to certain leadership responsibilities of a school administrator.

In qualifying for educational administration, advantage should be taken of the opportunities for leadership which come to the teacher. In the classroom, the processes of decision-making, programing, stimulating, co-ordinating, and appraising should be studied and techniques improved. Not only will this lead to future qualification as an administrator, but it will lead to increased competence as a teacher. In addition, the teacher should seek out opportunities for leadership in teacher groups and in community groups. These activities will provide insight into the required skills and techniques of leadership and will provide valuable experience in their utilization.

Many teachers, for example, find themselves involved in scouting or Sunday school activities. These are organizations which provide leadership opportunities with both children and adults. When, as often happens in such activities, the teacher is sought out by other members of the community as a leader, the experience can be used both as a means of community service and as a means of developing skills in leadership.

A number of teachers gain leadership experience in local, state, and national professional organizations. Not only is the president of a local classroom teachers' association given practice as a leader, he also is provided with opportunities to observe educational administration from a closer vantage point than is usually afforded the teacher. In working on problems of teacher welfare, professional growth programs, or matters dealing with the evaluation of teaching, the association officer gains experience both in leadership and in the more specific areas of educational administration.

SEMIADMINISTRATIVE POSITIONS

It is difficult to draw a line and declare that certain positions are administrative while others are not. In Chapter 13, we shall describe the positions we have defined as administrative. It will be noted that such positions as department heads, athletic directors, or activity fund treasurers have not been listed. For purposes of clarity, it seems best to define these and similar positions as semiadministrative positions.

There may be a number of such positions, particularly in a larger school. A high school with an enrollment of three hundred students or more might well have full-time or part-time staff members with the following semiadministrative positions: co-ordinator of instruction, director of activities, director of guidance, director of health and physical education, director of athletics, heads of departments, attendance supervisor, director of testing and research, director of cafeteria, and registrar. Certainly, in the smaller school, not all of these positions would be found, and probably none of them as full-time positions. In the larger school, most of them would be found, and many of them would be full-time positions. The fact is that regardless of the size of the school, these positions represent functions that need to be performed, and some arrangement of time and assignment will be developed to facilitate this performance of function.

Similar positions could be found in the large elementary school, although our observation leads us to believe that administrative help is more often lacking in the elementary school than in the high school. Wakefield and Lucas, for example, report that in a large school system in Ohio a high school with an enrollment of 1,279 students and a staff of 52 teachers had the following administrative and semiadministrative team (35 periods per week is full-time):

One full-time principal.

One full-time vice-principal.

Two full-time secretaries.

Athletic manager—10 periods per week.

Attendance supervisor—20 periods per week.

Book manager—10 periods per week.

Cafeteria manager—30 periods per week.

Journalism adviser—5 periods per week.

Student government adviser—10 periods per week.

Activity fund treasurer—10 periods per week.

Visual aids director—5 periods per week.

This adds up to a total of approximately seven full-time members of the administrative team, or one member for every 183 students.

An elementary school in the same system with 1,346 students and 32 teachers had the following administrative team:

One full-time principal.

One secretary—two days per week.

In this case, the team consisted of one and two-fifths members, or one for every 961 students.[3]

This is not an isolated instance nor has the situation appeared to have improved appreciably since the Lucas-Wakefield study. In terms of administration, the elementary school is generally understaffed, and opportunities for leadership, not only for the teacher but also for the administrator, are severely reduced due to the heavy load of routine and clerical duties which must be assumed by the professional staff.

Other semiadministrative positions available to the teacher include committee chairmanships of both school and school district committees, such as textbook selection committees or curriculum development groups. While the position as an adviser of a student activity may sometimes not clearly fill the role of a semiadministrative position, it is more often true than not that such a position does have administrative overtones.

The acceptance of and performance in a semiadministrative position in a school or school system can aid greatly in one's attempt to qualify for educational administration. The prospective administrator often gains through such a position the chance to try his wings under the guidance of an experienced administrator.

RELATIONSHIPS WITH ADMINISTRATORS AND BOARD

Many teachers enter university courses for the preparation of educational administrators without ever observing a board of education meeting or taking a firsthand look at the work which crosses the desk of a school principal. Curricula in teacher education rarely include any courses aimed at providing the prospective teacher with some insight into such matters

[3] Robert E. Lucas and Howard Wakefield, eds., *By Their Bootstraps* (Columbus: Ohio Education Association, 1955,), p. 11.

as school budget-making, procedures of boards of education, or administrative organization of a school district. The continued pressure from many sources for increased general education, increased subject-matter preparation, and decreased professional education courses for the prospective teacher makes it unlikely that courses or units dealing with educational administration will be added in any quantity to programs for undergraduate teacher education.

Hence even a basic familiarity with such problems must be gained on the job and in graduate courses by the in-service teacher. Many teachers ignore on-the-job opportunities to learn about educational administration and thus ignore an opportunity to begin the process of qualifying for educational administration. We have, for example, observed committees dealing with teachers' salaries both neglect and refuse to become familiar with the school budget, even though the salary program they are attempting to develop may require as much as 70 to 80 percent of this budget for its implementation. We have heard teachers complain about "secrecy" or "lack of information" when even a cursory inquiry would have revealed to them that the information they desired was a matter of public record in the central office of the school district and in the offices of the county superintendent of schools and of the state department of education. We have known teachers who did not know how many members were on their local school board, how they were selected, when or where they met, or what even one major duty of this board was.

In some cases, to be sure, inadequate or ineffective administrators make it difficult for teachers to observe the processes and details of educational administration in their school districts. For the most part, however, it is apathy rather than antagonism which leads to the teachers' lack of knowledge about administration. Certainly, the prospective administrator cannot afford such apathy. He needs to attend some board meetings, to study some budgets and other records, and to inquire about administrative problems. While course work and reading may make a real contribution to the development of an administrator, there is little doubt but that the prospective administrator should also learn through observation of and participation in administering. Careful observation of administrators in action and of administrative skills, techniques, and details in the actual school setting is one way in which the teacher who is considering administration can begin to qualify for administration.

EXPANDING EXPERIENCES

Just as teaching experience when appropriately utilized can aid in qualifying for administration, so can other experiences gained while teaching aid in the development of a school administrator. We will not repeat in detail here the various kinds of experience which increase one's potential as an educational administrator. It does seem worthwhile to point out, however, that many teachers are particularly lax in studying some of the nuances of school-community relations that can be observed by the teacher. In addition to observation, there are many forms of participation available to the teacher which aid in increasing the qualifications of a prospective administrator.

Teachers can—and administrators must—study the community forces that impinge upon the school program. Teachers can pay some attention to the extent of community understanding of school problems and can analyze some of the reasons for the presence or absence of understanding. Teachers can attend P.T.A. meetings, not as reluctant back-benchers, but as interested participants in and observers of school-community relations in action. In these and many other ways the teacher who is interested in educational administration can increase his knowledge of and his competency in the area of school-community relations.

The prospective administrator can also gain experience in the area of understanding communities while teaching. What is a community? What makes this community tick? Upon what economic base does it rest? What roles do churches, service clubs, business organizations, labor groups, or farm groups play in the community?

Every teacher lives in a community. If, as we believe, one of the important qualifications of an educational administrator is the ability to recognize and understand community forces, the teacher and prospective administrator need to utilize every opportunity to gain experience in these difficult tasks. There is no better place for the teacher to start developing this competency than in his local community.

Some examples might serve to point up the possibilities in this area. The teacher in a school district can often gain significant understanding of the influence of a community on the educational program in that district. Is science neglected while a trade and industry program flourishes? What elements in the community might have a bearing on this situation? Is a large industry the dominant force in the community? Is science important to this industry? To what extent do board members come from the personnel of the industrial firm? Answers to these and other questions can provide a great measure of community understanding.

Or, as the teacher develops a course of study, he might well consider the ways in which community resources could be used in implementing the course of study. What possibilities for field trips exist? Are there any members of the community who might discuss certain phases of a subject with the class? To what extent will service clubs or business and labor organizations provide materials or underwrite costs of special activities?

Answering questions like these will not only provide the teacher with increased understanding of his community, it can also play a major role in the improvement of the instructional program.

The social studies teacher has a particularly fine opportunity as well as an obligation to become aware of his community, and to attempt to gain understanding of its special strengths and weaknesses. In many respects, the community in which a school is located is a social studies laboratory for that school. However, whether special opportunities present themselves in the area of gaining understanding of a community or not, every teacher—prospective administrator or not—should feel an obligation to create and to take advantage of opportunities to know his community.

While the above comments emphasize experiences in the area of school-community relations, experiences in other administrative task areas are also available. The prospective administrator should be alert to such opportunities and take advantage of them as a valuable part of his preparation.

FORMAL PREPARATION

Many aspects of one's teaching experience can aid in helping one qualify for educational administration. The time must come, however, when the prospective administrator begins his formal preparation for administration, usually under the direction of an adviser from an institution accredited by the state to prepare educational administrators. The several aspects of this formal program will be considered in some detail here. It should be remembered, however, that each state has specific patterns of requirements for the administrator and that no text, article, or lecture can replace the state certification handbook as a prime source of information during the formal preparation period. By the same token, the catalog of the university or college chosen by the prospective administrator for his course work must also become a key reference book as he plans his work.

CERTIFICATION OF ADMINISTRATORS

In discussing the certification of administrators, we would stress at the outset our belief that certification requirements represent, at best, minimum requirements. Too often, an administrator-to-be gains the impression that, with certification, he is fully and perpetually prepared for any and all administrative positions. The generally low requirements for certification in most states should make it obvious that such is not the case. We believe that a master's degree is a minimum standard for administrative certification and that regular graduate work—either leading to a doctor's degree or taken as part of a post-master's nondegree program—is essential to the continuing qualification of an administrator. Certification alone is a completely inadequate criterion of the readiness of a person to assume an administrative position; a fact that has been recognized by professional associations, which have developed membership requirements more stringent than those required for certification in a number of states.

Because the certification of administrators, like that of teachers, is a responsibility and an authority held by each state, requirements for certification vary from state to state. In addition, the five regional accrediting associations for secondary schools and colleges generally create standards for administrators in accredited schools that are often higher than the minimum standards for certification.[4] For example, although many states do not require that a secondary school principal have a master's degree to be eligible for certification, three of the five accrediting associations, including all but eleven states, do require that a principal in an accredited secondary school have a master's degree or its equivalent; e.g., the Northwest Association of Secondary and Higher Schools requires the master's degree or 57 quarter hours of graduate work including 30 quarter hours in education.[5]

In the states that grant administrative certificates, a variety of kinds of certificates are issued. These include elementary principals' certificates, secondary principals' certificates, general principals' certificates, superintendents' certificates, and general administrative certificates. Without exception, one requirement for certification as an administrator is teaching experience, with three years of such experience being the usual requirement. In addition, many of the superintendents' or general administrative certificates require two or three years of administrative experience as a principal as a prerequisite. Almost all the states stipulate certain kinds of graduate courses for administrative certification. Generally, graduate credit is required in such areas as curriculum, supervision of instruction, and general administration, and in such specialized fields as school law or school finance. In addition to course work, many states require a master's degree for certification as an administrator. It is also true that, regardless of certification requirements, many school boards are including the doctorate as a

[4] The regional accrediting associations referred to are Middle States Association of Colleges and Secondary Schools, New England Association of Colleges and Secondary Schools, North Central Association of Colleges and Secondary Schools, Northwest Association of Secondary and Higher Schools, and Southern Association of Colleges and Secondary Schools.

[5] Elizabeth H. Woellner and M. Aurilla Wood, *Requirements for Certification of Teachers, Counselors, Librarians, Administrators for Elementary Schools, Secondary Schools, Junior Colleges,* 28th ed., 1963–64 (Chicago: The University of Chicago Press, 1961), pp. 1–3.

prerequisite for consideration as a superintendent in their districts and, as we have already mentioned, the American Association of School Administrators requires a two-year graduate program in an accredited institution as a prerequisite for membership in the Association. Therefore, as a prospective administrator considers the steps necessary to qualify for educational administration, he must consider requirements for both certification and a graduate degree.

As the administrator-to-be plans to qualify for educational administration, the question of certification must loom large. Many excellent opportunities are lost because a teacher or a principal has not taken the time and effort to be certificated for a higher administrative position. Either the state department of education or a university approved by the state to certificate administrators can supply complete details concerning certification requirements. These sources of information should be contacted early in the planning phase as the prospective administrator prepares to qualify for administrative positions.

ADVANCED DEGREE REQUIREMENTS

The above discussion makes it clear that the prospective administrator must consider advanced degrees as he attempts to qualify for administration. In general, there are five advanced degrees which should be included in the consideration of a long-range plan: the Master of Arts, the Master of Education, the sixth-year degree or certificate, the Doctor of Education, and the Doctor of Philosophy. In discussing these degrees or certificates, it is necessary again that we remind the prospective administrator that this discussion can be only a general one and that there is no satisfactory substitute for personal contact with the degree-granting institutions as a source of specific information about the requirements for higher degrees.

The Master's Degree

The day will undoubtedly soon be here when in every state a school administrator will be required to hold a master's degree for his initial administrative position. Usually, either a Master of Arts or a Master of Education degree will be available and will be acceptable. It is difficult to say which degree should be sought. The Master of Arts degree has, in most cases, more requirements in course work outside of the specific area of professional education than does the Master of Education degree, and the former often requires a research project or thesis which may not be required for the latter degree. Many prospective administrators earn the Master of Arts degree with emphasis on their teaching field, a procedure that has much to recommend it.

Remembering that we have stressed earlier the necessity for a broad educational background and for familiarity with both educational and other social problems, techniques, and skills, the prospective administrator should study the specific requirements in the institution of his choice and make a decision in terms of the program and his own needs and plans.

The Sixth-year Program

Many universities have instituted a degree or certificate program that comes between the master's and doctor's degrees. These programs are sometimes seen as alternatives to a doctoral program, and sometimes as steps in a graduate program leading ultimately to work for the doctor's degree. It is our belief that the former viewpoint has more to commend it than the latter. It is obvious that not every school superintendent can or should pursue a doctoral program. It is equally obvious that the completion of a master's degree program should not mark the completion of the graduate work of the school superintendent. A post-master's program developed for school administrators is needed which should be neither a trial run for the doctoral program nor a consolation award for the unsuccessful doctoral candidate.

The sixth-year program generally requires thirty semester hours of graduate work beyond the master's degree. Usually about one-half of this work is in the specialized area of educational administration, while the other half is in closely related supporting areas. Most of the programs require either a thesis or a report on a field project as one of the requirements for receiving the degree or certificate. In addition, one characteristic of most of these programs is a period of time the student spends in supervised field experiences. Often these programs require some period of residence as a full-time student.

In general, the student who definitely plans a doctoral program should not contemplate the sixth-year program. It is important, however, for all prospective administrators to realize that such programs do exist and, as their future plans are made, to include a consideration of these programs.

The Doctoral Program

There are no figures which indicate precisely the number of school administrators who possess doctors' degrees. There is evidence, however, that this number is continually increasing; and placement offices report that the possession of a doctor's degree is becoming more common as a prerequisite listed by boards of education for major administrative positions. Certainly, the prospective college professor of educational administration needs to consider the degree as a prerequisite to the attainment of his goal.

The question of whether the Ph.D. degree or the Ed.D. degree should be sought is becoming almost an academic question. At one time, the Ph.D. degree was in no way related to preparation for engaging in any highly specialized, technical occupation. This is no longer the case. In such fields as chemistry, mathematics, or engineering, where great numbers of doctoral degrees are earned, Ph.D. programs have become specialized and professional in much the same way that an Ed.D. program represents professional training in education. Actually, there are probably more differences among various programs for these degrees than there are between the two degrees. The choice of doctoral program, then, becomes much more a matter of personal preference and specific institutional programs than of the "worth" of the degrees.

Thus the major choice that faces the prospective administrator is whether or not he should include a doctoral program in his plan. Because the doctoral program is expensive in both time and money, the candidate must be willing to make a sacrifice to secure his degree, a sacrifice borne also by his wife and children. The acknowledgment often found in a dissertation in which the student expresses gratitude for the faith, support, patience, and understanding of his wife and family is much more than a mere formality. The candidate should know where he is going and how he hopes to get there if he is able to make the commitment to a doctoral program that is necessary for success.

In making this choice, the administrator must remember that many administrative positions will never require the doctor's degree as a prerequisite, that advanced graduate work can be taken without entering a doctoral program, and that the returns to him from such a program will probably be deferred ones. On the other hand, the administrator should recall that many major administrative positions do require a doctor's degree, that there is much personal satisfaction in completing a difficult intellectual task, and that the completion of a doctoral program gives a person greater flexibility in seeking advanced positions. Certainly, the majority of the educational administrators in our public schools will not complete such a program. It should be considered, however, as a part of the planning to qualify for educational administration. Intellectual ability, professional goals, research interest and ability, and personal motivations will play major roles in the decision.

Timing the Degree Programs

The decision as to when one begins to pursue an advanced degree is one based on both professional and personal factors. In general, however, a master's degree program is not started until after at least a year's teaching experience and, for most students, is completed in from one to three years, depending on whether the course work is all summer work or done during the regular academic year. If done during the summer, the student usually accumulates three or four years of teaching experience by the time the master's degree is earned and may, therefore, be ready to assume an administrative position. Care should be taken to insure that course work taken during the master's program will meet certification requirements so that the administrator-to-be is eligible to convert the "to-be" to "is."

The post-master's program should not be delayed too long after completing the master's program. We have mentioned earlier that a doctoral program is probably best begun by the time the doctoral candidate reaches the age of thirty. The doctoral program should require at least one year of full-time residence on campus. Course work plus the completion of a doctoral dissertation will usually lengthen the doctoral program to a total of from two to five years. Two full years on a doctoral program—"full" meaning that the student is not attempting concurrently to hold a position as a full-time administrator—is, for many people, a realistic estimate of the time necessary for completion.

While there are many exceptions, most doctoral students in educational administration have had fairly extensive administrative experience before completing the degree. A realistic twelve-year time table might look somewhat like this:

Year	Progress
1st	Bachelor's degree.
1st–3rd	Teaching experience (begin on-campus graduate work).
3rd	Complete master's degree.
3rd–6th	Principalship (continue part-time, on-campus graduate work).
6th–9th	Small superintendency or central office position (continue part-time, on-campus graduate work).
9th–11th	Full-time, on-campus doctoral program.
11th	Complete doctor's degree.
12th	Major administrative position (continued professional development).

A number of factors could complicate this schedule. Military service, financial problems, or other personal factors can change plans. A person should develop a fairly tight schedule for himself, however, and should observe it as closely as possible. The longer a person permits himself to delay because "he can't afford it" or because "he wants another year of experience," the more easily the whole plan can be lost.

SUPERVISED FIELD EXPERIENCE

In addition to meeting degree and certification requirements, the prospective administrator should be learning about administration and learning to administer. As we stress certificates and degrees, we must also stress that the only value of either is as they represent increased professional growth and knowledge. The mere possession of a degree or certificate does not guarantee excellence.

One aspect of the formal program for the preparation of educational administrators which has received particular attention in recent years is supervised field experience. In field experience programs, the prospective administrator has a chance to practice administration, usually under the joint sponsorship of university and school district personnel. In this way, theory and practice are related, and the qualifications of the prospective administrator can be considerably enhanced. Supervised field experience is usually gained in one or more of three ways: as a part of class activities, in a cadet program, or in an internship program.

Field Experience

There are many ways in which formal class work can be supplemented by supervised field experience. Term projects, for example, should deal with real rather than imaginary problems. Possibilities also exist during the term for field affiliations that are related to, and aid the attainment of, the objectives of a course. Students in courses that deal with school-community relations might, for example, have close relationships with local community agencies during a quarter or semester. In one such course with which we are familiar, students spent a great deal of time working on an individual basis with local Community Chest agencies on problems with educational implications. Similar possibilities exist in courses in all areas of educational administration.

Another possibility is the development of courses that revolve about field activities. One such advanced course at Ohio State University requires the students to conduct a comprehensive educational survey in a school district and to report their findings and recommendations to the board of education of the district. A similar but less extensive course at the University of California (Berkeley) required that each student assume the role of a consultant to a school district and survey an actual problem in that district. The findings of the survey were critically examined in class sessions and reported back to the school district.

Field trips are also used in many courses. School plant and school business administration courses offer a wide variety of possibilities for field trips. While such trips offer observation rather than participation opportunities, they do create another chance for the student to see theory in action.

A number of programs have been developed which include a great variety of kinds and levels of field experience. The Harvard program, for example, on the doctoral level includes a social science field research project in which the students work as members of a social science research team; usually two or more contractual studies for school systems in which students serve as policy-making as well as operating staff; and an individual administration assignment involving major responsibility in defining, planning, developing, and carrying out a significant administrative task.[6] Programs such as this provide the student with opportunities both to see theory in practice and to put his own theory to the field test.

Internship Programs

The internship program is primarily a university-sponsored program to provide a type of on-the-job training. The internship stresses the assumption of responsibility. In practice, the internship program in educational administration involves placing a student or intern in an administrative position in a school district under the joint supervision of a local school administrator and university personnel. The intern assumes responsibility for the completion of one or more administrative tasks in the district. Although in most cases he is at least partially paid by the school district, the emphasis is upon his learning and growth rather than upon service to the employing district. Such service results from the program, but it is incidental to the main purposes of the internship program.

Several dangers exist in the internship program, and several problems are present. Hooker provides an excellent cautionary statement when he indicates that:

> If the internship experience is to provide graduate students with something more than the art of being wrong with greater confidence, considerable inquiry into the professional climate of the sponsoring school district is necessary. It should be borne firmly in mind that interns are not apprentices. They are not learning the tricks of the trade nor formulae for solving problems. Under supervision they make logical deductions from basic knowledge and inference from observations.[7]

It is sometimes difficult to develop a program in which the intern assumes real rather than artificial responsibility. There is sometimes a tendency to assign interns to positions where they are familiar with practices and problems instead of utilizing the program to fill gaps in the background of the student. While this practice usually results in greater service to the school district, it does not always serve the purposes of the intern well. The internship program is costly on all sides. The

---

[6] *A Doctorate Program in Administration at the Harvard Graduate School of Education* (Cambridge: Harvard Graduate School of Education, undated).

[7] Stephen B. Hencley (ed.), *The Internship in Administrative Preparation* (Columbus, Ohio: The University Council for Educational Administration, 1963), p. 23.

intern must devote a full year to the program, usually at a low salary. Supervision, both on the part of the university and the local district, runs high in time and money. The program usually includes a seminar on campus for interns, and travel requirements between campus and school district may become burdensome both for interns and for supervisors.

A variation of the internship program is the cadet program through which a school district attempts to select, train, and promote administrative candidates within the system. Such programs usually concentrate on the training of principals, although some school districts also use the cadet program to train central office personnel.

In general, cadet programs include some class sessions under the direction of school district personnel and assignment to various semiadministrative or administrative positions in the district under the supervision of an administrator in the system. While early cadet programs did not include university affiliations, sometimes these programs do include either regular university course work or a special cadet seminar as an integral part of the plan.

The internship program is obtaining more and more recognition as a fitting climax to a program of formal preparation. In spite of the difficulties mentioned above, and others, this program appears to offer an excellent opportunity for the welding of classroom theory and field practice in the university program. The prospective administrator would do well to consider the possibility of an internship as another step in his plan to qualify for educational administration.

PLANNING THE FORMAL PROGRAM

We have now shown that the formal program for the preparation of an educational administrator will include factors involving certification, advanced degree requirements, and supervised field experiences. In any plan for a formal program, one should also consider the experience which he is gaining in teaching and plan the program to supplement and reinforce this experience. Remember too that the formal program should not result in narrow specialization. The prospective administrator should make every effort to insure that his higher education will result in his becoming a well-rounded, intellectually developed individual. It is at this point that the evaluation and planning discussed in Chapter 11 need to be reconsidered. The strengths and weaknesses of individual universities that prepare administrators should be sought out and evaluated. The kinds of programs offered, the selection procedures utilized, the kinds and scope of fellowships offered, the degrees granted, and the general reputation of higher institutions are important factors to the prospective administrator. There are certain advantages to be gained from doing graduate work in more than one university and, if this seems advisable, problems concerning the transfer of credit should be considered in advance. But, above all, as plans for the formal program are developed, the prospective administrator should remember that there are no substitutes for the written certification requirements of the state and the printed catalog of the university as authoritative and accurate sources of information concerning program requirements. And finally, the prospective administrator must always remember that his ultimate concerns are competency and professional growth. Certificates and degrees are of value only as they reflect competency in educational administration.

Seeking the First Position

Both formal training and experience finally culminate in the first administrative position for the prospective administrator. One qualification or set of qualifications which the administrator-to-be needs to consider, then, is the ability to seek and gain an administrative position.

There are several ways in which administrative positions are filled. Many principalships and assistant superintendencies and some superintendencies are filled by promotion from within a school system. When persons from outside the system are brought in, it is either by virtue of individual applications for the positions or through recommendations from commercial or university placement offices. Almost all college and university professorships are filled through placement office recommendations, while administrative positions in higher education are filled through promotion or placement office recommendation. Each of these avenues will be discussed briefly here, and then some attention will be given to selection procedures common to all of these approaches.

PROMOTION FROM WITHIN OR WITHOUT

Some large school districts fill all of their principalships by selection from the staff of the system. The assumption is made that the larger district has sufficient personnel to permit the discovery of prospective principals from within who are as well qualified as those who could be found by going outside the system.

The major danger in the process of promotion from within is "inbreeding." If all new administrators in a system are products of the same training program, new ideas and new approaches in educational administration may be scarce. This danger is not impossible to overcome, but the administrator who reaches his position by promotion from within a system should make sure that he has an open mind for ideas from outside.

One other point should be mentioned here. Sometimes those within a school system feel that it is not fair to offer administrative positions to "outsiders." The only fair policy that a board of education can follow in filling administrative positions is one which states that these positions should go to the most highly qualified applicants. The "insider" has no inherent right to such a position except as he possesses qualifications that suit him for the position better than other applicants. This implies that criteria have been developed to aid in the selection process and that these criteria are based on descriptions of the position which adequately define its duties and responsibilities.

There are two conflicting philosophies regarding the relative weight to be given an insider as opposed to an outsider. Some feel that if all other things are equal, the position should go to the insider. This feeling is based on considerations of morale of the staff, familiarity with the problems and processes of the district, and creation of an incentive for those in the system interested in administration. The other viewpoint is that if all other things are equal, the position should go to the outsider. This viewpoint is based on considerations of getting new blood and new ideas into the system, the avoidance of cliques or other human relations problems which may result from inside promotion, and the hope that more qualified people will apply for a position when this philosophy is dominant.

Each of these viewpoints has both strengths and weaknesses. The important point for the prospective administrator is that he know which of the two ideas is prevalent in his school district. Because each viewpoint can be supported on rational grounds, the prospective administrator should not feel that he is unfairly treated if the viewpoint opposite to his is the one that prevails. If he knows the situation, he can and should plan his actions accordingly.

PLACEMENT OFFICE SERVICES

A placement office is, of course, a rather dignified form of employment agency. Every university that prepares educational administrators offers placement services. These are usually free to the student, although small charges are sometimes made to cover a part of the clerical services necessary for the preparation of credentials. In addition, there are many commercial educational placement agencies. A number of these agencies are associated with the National Association of Teacher's Agencies (NATA), a voluntary organization of agencies which maintains certain minimum standards for member agencies. University placement offices also have a voluntary organization known as the National Institutional Teacher Placement Association (NITPA). Commercial agencies are probably more active in the placement of teachers than of administrators, but they do provide services in both areas. Commercial agencies have three general ways of charging for their services—a registration fee, a fee which is a percentage of the first year's income, or a combination of both. For the most part, we feel that university placement offices are more acceptable than commercial offices. The university placement personnel have a better knowledge of the candidates for positions, generally attempt to assess the position as well as the candidates in order to insure a good fit, and provide the same or better results than a commercial office, at much less cost to the candidate. It is our feeling that the profession—in this case represented by the training institutions—should provide its own placement services.

The candidate for an administrative position should take steps to see that the placement office with which he is working is aware of the types of position in which he is interested. His credentials in the placement office should be up to date and inclusive of all important data. As placement services will be utilized beyond the initial position, it is important that the administrator keep his credentials up to date while he is holding an administrative position. Many prospective and practicing administrators fail to gain new positions for which they are qualified because they have not maintained contact with a placement office. A candidate who feels that a placement agency is not serving him well may not have submitted complete records, may not have asked that recommendations for him be submitted to the agency, or may not have indicated to the agency his interest in a position. Good relations between candidate and placement office are another important part of the procedures as one attempts to qualify for and to obtain an administrative position.

INDIVIDUAL APPLICATION

The question of whether or not to apply for an administrative position on one's own in the absence of placement office or school system backing is a difficult one. The candidate, particularly for the first administrative position, must take some initiative. He must, in a real sense, be a job seeker. This fact is generally much less true as one considers administrative positions of major importance. In such cases, the job seeks the man to a much greater extent than in the case of an initial administrative position.

It is impossible to generalize about the so-called lone-wolf approach to seeking an administrative position. We do believe, however, that the approach of the position seeker to those with a position to fill is strengthened considerably if someone other than the candidate shares the candidate's confidence that he is qualified for the position. This "someone" may or may not be a placement officer, a school administrator, or a professor. In any event, the position seeker who attempts to go it alone with no recommendations of any kind will usually find the procedure a difficult one.

Thus it seems evident that the candidate for an initial administrative position should employ initiative wisely. He should be on the alert for positions in which he is interested and for which he is qualified. He should bend every effort to making his interest and his qualifications known. He should work with a placement office if possible, but he usually cannot afford to sit back and await placement. He should secure a list of people who know him and who will recommend him for a position. And—finally, but really at the head of the list—he should be sure that he is prepared for an administrative position, should one become available. The importance of being "at the right place with the right preparation at the right time" cannot be overlooked.

SELECTION PROCEDURES

Let us assume that, through a placement office or through recommendation from some other source, the prospective administrator has been invited to submit a formal application for an administrative position. What can he expect as he seeks this first position? It is difficult to specify the procedures that may be used by a given district as the candidates for an administrative position are screened for selection of the ultimate appointee. Several common procedures will be discussed here, although it is not likely that many districts will use all of these procedures.

Application Forms

While detailed application forms are common for teaching positions, less use of them is made in seeking candidates for administrative positions. The basic reason for this is probably that when administrators are sought, reliance is put upon the interview, a possible field investigation, and the credentials of the candidates. However, care should be taken to complete any required application forms promptly, accurately, neatly, and completely. Even if not interested in the position, the candidate who is asked to apply should write a letter briefly indicating that he is not presently interested and expressing some appreciation for the invitation. This practice is more than mere courtesy, for the ignored invitation can sometimes loom large in the future.

Tests

Some school boards are using one or more tests as screening devices for the selection of administrators. Such tests include written and oral English tests, essay tests over the field or fields included in the position applied for, performance tests in which candidates are appraised in situations similar to those which might be encountered in the position, physical examinations, and objective examinations organized around such areas as general administration, curriculum, guidance, methodology, and supervision. Testing procedures are found more often in city school districts than in smaller districts, but the use of tests as a part of the selection procedure is becoming more common.

The candidate for a given administrative position should ascertain if tests are given as a part of the selection procedure for that position, if examples of questions or specific descriptions of the tests are made available to candidates, and if such tests are given individually or are given to a group at a given time and place. It is likely that the tendency for school districts to give some kind of test to candidates for administrative positions will increase in the future, and the candidate should be aware of this trend.

Interviews

After the screening process, most boards of education interview the final two or three candidates for a superintendency, or the superintendent and other central administrative personnel interview the final candidates for a principalship. Although in many cases these interviews are rather vague and general in nature, a number of districts have developed a check list of specific desired qualifications about which the interviewing team plans to gain information and make evaluations during the interview. The interview is generally used to provide the prospective employer with some indication of the appearance, poise, speaking ability, and knowledge of the candidate.

The candidate should realize that the interview is a time of mutual exploration. He is being looked at, but he is also looking at the position. Thus the interview should include some time when he can become the interviewer. He should make sure that he understands the duties and responsibilities of the position, the opportunity it offers to work toward mutually satisfying goals, and the conditions of employment. He should ask some questions about the school district and the community. Often one of the factors that an employer uses in evaluating a candidate after an interview is the nature of the questions asked. For example, the young man seeking his first principalship who asks only about tenure and retirement reveals much about himself through his questions. As he prepares for his interview, then, he should be concerned with both his answers and his questions.

Field Rating

While it is not a usual procedure for the selection of a person for his first administrative position, some mention should be made of the field rating. When a list of applicants for a position is reduced to only a few, many boards of education or professional employing personnel visit the school districts in which the remaining candidates are presently employed to gain an on-the-spot evaluation. There they interview administrators, teachers, and lay citizens so that the employing officials can gain further insight into the qualifications of the candidates. There is little that a candidate can do to prepare for this procedure other than to insure that he is doing his best wherever he is. Many candidates for administrative positions have found that because they have considered their present position beneath them and have acted accordingly, they have never been able to rise to a position they consider appropriate to their ability.

THE ETHICS OF JOB-SEEKING

We have already said enough about the professional nature of educational administration to make it unnecessary to dwell at great length on the ethics of seeking an administrative position. Only a few points might be mentioned here and these but briefly. As a prospective administrator, the candidate for a position should proceed through the established channels in a district rather than trying, for example, to go directly to individual board members. The subordinate who attempts to gain an administrative position by assisting in the downfall of his administrator is unethical and is establishing a precedent that may be used by his own subordinates in the future.

A candidate for an administrative position should strive to gain that position in open, ethical competition with other qualified candidates. One cannot be proud of gaining a position by manipulation or secrecy so that the employing agency does not compare his qualifications with those of others. If he is not the best-qualified person for the position, he should not have it, and he should have additional incentive to increase his qualifications.

IN REVIEW

We have pointed out that in seeking his first administrative position, the prospective administrator should become familiar with the avenues that seem to lead to the position he desires. These may involve promotions within a system or promotions to another system. The candidate should associate himself with a university placement office and insure that his credentials are in order and up to date. He should be aware that his best chance for gaining an administrative position will usually be based on recommendations from a placement office, from administrative personnel in his district, or from both, rather than only on his individual application.

As he becomes an active candidate for a given position, the prospective administrator will find himself facing several kinds of selection procedures. These may include a review of his credentials and recommendations, the submission of a formal application, participation in a testing procedure, an interview, and a field rating. Throughout the entire process, the candidate needs to remember that he is seeking a position in a highly skilled profession and that it is important to him and to the profession that all of his acts be ethical.

Continued Professional Growth

Every administrator who assumes an administrative position is only partially prepared for that position. He will probably never be able to say realistically that he is completely prepared for the position he holds, and there will always be other administrative positions for which he is even less well prepared. Thus the effort to qualify for a position should not end upon its assumption.

CONTINUED ON-CAMPUS PREPARATION

Many major administrative positions, as we mentioned earlier in this chapter, now require that the incumbent possess a doctor's degree. The administrator will undoubtedly seek his first or his second administrative position before he earns this degree. This means that while he is serving as an administrator he will also be continuing his university work. Even if the doctor's degree does not become one of his goals, university graduate work should be a part of his continuing professional growth. Many workshops and seminars are planned particularly for the practicing administrator, and the insights gained on his job add value to any course he may take. Just as most salary policy statements in school districts require that the teacher return to a campus periodically for professional growth, it is important that the administrator consider this same requirement as it applies to him.

It should be noted also that the present trend in master's degree programs for educational administrators is to place less stress than formerly on specialization in administration and more stress on the broader areas of education in general. This means, in effect, that much of the course work in more advanced phases of administration is offered on the post-master's degree level and that such course work is planned for the person who has begun the practice of educational administration. In short, then, the master's degree represents minimum preparation for the educational administrator.

There are other possibilities for on-campus professional growth of the practicing administrator in addition to the course work we have stressed. Most universities hold conferences that offer opportunities for administrators to gain new understanding of their work. Many institutions have developed one- or two-day problem-centered clinics in which twenty or thirty administrators gather with university personnel and other consultants to deal with specific problems arising in the field. There are numerous opportunities for administrators to avail themselves of university services such as consultative service for local studies, co-operative research projects, or the development of local professional growth programs. The ideal situation is one in which the relationships between universities and administrators are continuous and mutually beneficial. Often, practicing administrators make themselves available to assist in a university's pre-service preparation program and serve in a variety of ways as co-operating university staff members. Only in this way can the two groups—the practitioners and those charged with the preparation of practitioners—provide each other with the unique and important advantages and aids which each has to offer the other.

GROWTH ON THE JOB

One of the best training grounds for the administrator is an administrative position. Every day presents him with opportunities not only to serve the schools of his school district but also to increase his own professional knowledge, skills, and competence. As we have stated much earlier here, if experience is to be educative, the educational values of experience must be actively sought. As the administrator works with teachers, with other administrators, with board members, with parents, or with community leaders, he should be increasing his qualifications as a top-level, competent administrator.

A number of activities in which administrators engage are aimed at professional growth. Included among these activities are planned programs of intervisitation, development by groups of administrators of handbooks and other materials for mutual use, and group studies of skills and techniques necessary for effective performance of various administrative tasks. Some of the most valuable activities available to administrators are sponsored by the various professional organizations to which they belong.[8]

---

[8] A detailed description of professional organizations for educational administrators is found in Chapter 13.

By working with colleagues for professional growth, the administrator can help to insure that his competence for his present position and his qualifications for other, more advanced positions will continue to grow.

Almost every high school commencement speech includes the admonition that the end of one's high school experience must not mark the end of one's learning experiences. Too often, the prospective administrator assumes the attitude that he "has it made" when he reaches an administrative position. If educational administration is to grow as a profession, its practitioners must see themselves in a continual learning situation in which the aim is both their own growth and the growth of the profession.

SUGGESTED ACTIVITIES

1. With a group of three or four other students, form a team for practice interviews. The interviewing group should prepare a prospectus of the position, including duties and responsibilities, salary, and desired characteristics of the applicant. The practice interview could take place before the entire class for critical examination by the group.

2. Prepare a prospectus outlining your background and qualifications which you would send to a board of education if you were a candidate for a principalship.

3. Outline the certification requirements for principals and superintendents in your state and one other state. Compare and evaluate the two plans in terms of your understanding of desirable qualifications for these positions.

4. Describe several leadership opportunities which you have had as a teacher. In what specific ways have these experiences aided you in developing plans for your career?

5. Describe the doctoral programs in educational administration in two universities. Compare the strengths and weaknesses of the programs in terms of your needs as a prospective educational administrator.

6. One AASA membership requirement is two years of planned graduate work in educational administration. How has this requirement been reflected in the program of your state university?

SELECTED READINGS

American Association of School Administrators, *The American School Superintendency*. Thirtieth Yearbook. Washington: AASA, 1952.

————, *Professional Administration for America's Schools.* Thirty-eighth Yearbook. Washington: AASA, 1960.

CAMPBELL, R. F. and GREGG, R. T. (eds.). *Administrative Behavior in Education.* New York: Harper & Brothers, 1957. Chapters XI–XIV.

CULBERTSON, JACK and HENCLEY, S. P. *Preparing Administrators: New Perspectives.* Columbus, Ohio: University Council for Educational Administration, 1962.

HENCLEY, S. P. (ed.). *The Internship in Administrative Preparation.* Columbus, Ohio: University Council for Educational Administration, 1963.

WOELLNER, ELIZABETH H. and WOOD, M. AURILLA. *Requirements for Certification of Teachers, Counselors, Librarians, Administrators for Elementary Schools, Secondary Schools, Junior Colleges.* Chicago: The University of Chicago Press, revised annually.

Part Three

The Profession

THE TWO CHAPTERS OF PART THREE ARE INTENDED TO ORIENT the student to the characteristics and challenges of educational administration as a profession. Chapter 13 is a realistic view of the field as it now exists—its varied and numerous types of positions, the customary promotion routes, remuneration, and tenure and security. It is recognized that in each of these areas there is considerable room for improvement. Chapter 14, on the other hand, stresses the challenges and the ideals of educational administration. The authors take the position that without adequate administrative leadership in the public schools of America our democratic way of life will be endangered. Thus educational administration, struggling to gain for itself professional status, is at the same time charged with great responsibility.

13

The Professional

Opportunities

THE PREVIOUS CHAPTERS HAVE BEEN REPLETE WITH REFERENCES to the problems of administration and to the procedures involved in becoming qualified for a position as an educational administrator. As we near the end of this discussion of educational administration, it is appropriate to spend some time exploring the opportunities and rewards available to those in the profession.

Positions Available

We have mentioned before that there once was—and still is in some places—a general feeling that school administration and the superintendency are synonymous terms, each all-inclusive of the other. Such a concept led to a separation of those preparing for a principalship and those preparing for a superintendency. Rarely, if ever, did the two groups sit together in university courses or in conferences dealing with general problems of educational administration.

More recently, it has been recognized that there are many common elements in all types of school administrative positions. It is therefore appropriate that we consider each of these administrative positions in some detail. The prospective educational administrator should not consider that he must become a school superintendent if he is to be a success. There is a great need for administrators who wish to make lifetime careers in the principalship or in other administrative positions.

The size, complexity, and diversity of the modern educational enterprise call for an administrative structure based upon the concept of teamwork rather than the outmoded, oversimplified line-staff approach. This concept requires analyzing functions—recognizing both the importance of each and the interdependence of all—and an administrative team of individuals with unique skills and the ability to work together.

The many pressures being applied to education today are causing tremendous strain upon the educational structure. Multilevel fiscal support, increasing demands for schools to participate in social action, and many other problems are most visible in complex locales such as New York City, but in only a very few semi-isolated areas is today's educational structure fully adequate to the task that confronts it.

It is beyond the scope of this volume to explore the structure of American education in detail. As we begin to describe some administrative positions, however, it seems important to indicate that the positions and functions as we describe them are under careful study and review in many quarters. The prospective administrator today finds himself at a point in time where one of his crucial tasks will be the restructuring of the administration of education. His viewpoints, then, should not be "frozen" by a description of what exists.

PRINCIPALSHIPS

Description

The principal is the chief administrative officer of an attendance unit in a school system. Such an attendance unit may be an elementary school, a junior high school, a senior high school, or some combination of these, according to the organization of the school district. In some cases, the administrative head of a junior college is referred to as a principal, but this usage is not common. The common pattern in describing the principalship is to speak of elementary school or secondary school principalships. The junior high school is usually considered to be a secondary school, although somewhat inaccurately. In some states, a junior high school principal may hold either a secondary or an elementary school principal's certificate; in others, the required certificate depends upon whether the junior high school is a departmentalized school (secondary school) or consists primarily of self-contained classrooms (elementary school); and in still others, a junior high school principal's certificate is issued.

In the larger school systems, the meaning of the term "principal" is quite clear. But in smaller school systems, usage often leads to confusion between principalships and superintendencies. It is often true that the administrator in a small school faces the difficult task of attempting to perform three roles—those of teacher, principal, and superintendent. The great difficulties of such a task are often not fully appreciated. For the purposes of this discussion, a principal is considered to be the executive officer of an attendance unit, but not the executive officer of an administrative unit. He does not, for example, have responsibilities as the professional executive officer of a board of education. In several states, the term "supervising principal" is used to describe what is essentially a superintendent. For our purpose, we would not consider this position a principalship.

Functions

The principalship is a vital position in the American public school system. In describing the influence of the principal, one writer states that the

> . . . principal is in a unique position of influence in education. He stands, as no other person does, in a pivotal relationship between the people and the school. . . .

> . . . the high school principal sets the pace for his staff and his community. He is a catalyst that initiates a process, sets it off and gets it going. He puts leadership into practice by creating the proper atmosphere for co-operative teamwork and production in order that fruitful interchange of ideas and sharing of knowledge may be established and maintained.[1]

The basic responsibility of the principal is the direction of the educational program of the school he heads. This requires that he work with teachers in the appraisal and improvement of this educational program. It requires that he work with the superintendent of schools to secure staff, material, and facilities for this program. It requires that he work with his community to determine its specific educational needs and the extent to which the school is meeting those needs.

In general, the principal works much more with teachers, central administrative officers, and lay citizens than he does with pupils.[2] Indeed, one

---

[1] J. E. Corbally, Jr., T. J. Jenson, and W. F. Staub, *Educational Administration: The Secondary School,* 2nd ed. (Boston: Allyn and Bacon, Inc., 1965), p. 140.

[2] It should be noted that, in many schools, a principal also has teaching responsibilities. Obviously, a principal in such a position will work directly with pupils to a great extent. In our opinion, however, if a position requires that one third or more of the incumbent's time be spent in teaching or other direct pupil contacts, that position cannot be correctly described as a principalship.

research study concluded that effective principals, as judged by competent observers, had far fewer direct contacts with pupils than did ineffective principals.[3]

The same will not usually be true of the assistant principal, to whom many direct pupil contact activities are delegated by the principal. In too many cases, the assistant principal becomes little more than the "chief of police" in a school. Ordinarily, his duties should include certain co-ordinating activities which will reduce the number of people directly responsible to the principal. We feel—and many others agree—that any school with over two hundred pupils should provide at least part-time assistance to the principal, and that in a school of over seven hundred pupils more than one full-time assistant to the principal is necessary.

In considering a secondary school, Edmonson, Roemer, and Bacon describe the following areas as containing typical responsibilities delegated by principals to assistants: athletic affairs, student body financial affairs, student activity programs, curriculum development, research, testing programs, homeroom programs, assembly programs, guidance and counseling programs, home visitation, attendance programs, registration procedures, public relations programs, professional growth programs, special education, health education, drives and contests, daily schedules, plant supervision, cafeteria supervision, and textbook management.[4] The same kinds of responsibilities, with the exception of those not ordinarily found in the elementary school, would be assigned to an assistant principal in an elementary school.

It becomes apparent that the principal and his assistant principals are primarily concerned with the operation of the school program in a single school. The assistant principals conduct much of the business that involves direct contact with pupils. The principal spends a major portion of his time working with teachers, with supervisors, and with central administration personnel. Much stress in recent years has also been placed on the role of the principal in his community. As the chief educational leader in a school attendance area, the principal should consider school-community relationships an important aspect of his position. This requirement makes it all the more imperative that every principal, whether in the elementary school or in the secondary school, receive sufficient administrative assistance to enable him to spend some time with community groups.

[3] Dean O. Clark, "Critical Areas in the Administrative Behavior of High School Principals" (unpublished doctoral dissertation, The Ohio State University, 1956), pp. 169–70.

[4] J. B. Edmonson, Joseph Roemer, and Francis L. Bacon, *The Administration of the Modern Secondary School*, 4th ed. (New York: The Macmillan Company, 1953), pp. 96–97.

Number of Positions

It is difficult to gather accurate data concerning the number of principal-ships available in this country. Several factors contribute to this difficulty. There being no consistent usage of the term "principal," in many cases a head teacher with no released time for administration is given that title. In other cases, actual principals are called superintendents. Furthermore, there are no agencies that gather and tabulate such data on a national scale.

We have consulted with the Department of Elementary School Prin-cipals and the National Association of Secondary School Principals—both National Education Association affiliates—in attempting to arrive at some estimate of the number of principalships available in the United States. We would stress that we can present only an estimate. It would seem in terms of our information that there are approximately 45,000 elementary school principals in charge of schools of five or more teachers and about 9,000 secondary school principals in charge of schools with fifteen or more teachers (1966).

SUPERVISORY POSITIONS

Description

In discussing administration in a school system, it is easy to get em-broiled in an argument as to whether or not supervisors are administrators. Unfortunately, those who argue that supervisors should not be considered administrators generally use the grounds that there is something about the administrative title which would reduce the efficiency of the supervisor.

Burton and Brueckner, although not speaking to this exact point, do refer to some of the problems in nomenclature faced by supervisors. They indicate that these problems grow from perhaps two basic causes: in early days, supervisors were, indeed, little more than inspectors; and the vagueness as to the functions of supervisors has led to some malpractice.[5] Certainly, if administration means only inspection, then we actually want few, if any, educational administrators. As we have pointed out, however, this is not our concept of administration, nor is it an accepted concept of supervision.

In our view a supervisor is an administrator. He is probably more a staff administrator than a line administrator, but he has certain functional responsibilities, and he must be provided with sufficient authority to meet them.[6] It is likely, however, that the supervisor will actually receive his

[5] William H. Burton and Leo J. Brueckner, *Supervision, A Social Process,* 3rd ed. (New York: Appleton-Century-Crofts, 1955), pp. 4–8.

[6] For a discussion of "functional responsibilities," see William Newman, *Adminis-trative Action* (Englewood Cliffs, N.J.: Prentice-Hall, Inc., 1951).

working authority more in terms of his ideas and group acceptance than from any position in an administrative hierarchy.

The supervisor in a local school district is usually attached to the central staff of a school system rather than assigned to a single building. Supervisors are also found as staff members in intermediate units serving a number of smaller districts, and, in many states, certain supervisors of specialized types of instruction are members of a state department of education rather than staff members in intermediate or local administrative units. Supervisors are usually classified in one of several ways. It is common to speak of elementary school or secondary school supervisors. Within these classifications are found general supervisors and special supervisors; the latter deal with special subject matter areas, while the former deal with more general questions of methods and materials. It is thus likely that a larger school system will have one or more general elementary supervisors and general secondary supervisors, as well as several special supervisors.

Functions

The supervisor plays a special role in the program for the improvement of instruction. We would emphasize here—and emphasize strongly—that the superintendent and principal cannot successfully separate themselves, through delegation, from the improvement of instruction. That is why we state that the supervisor plays a special role, but not the only role, in this program.

In describing the functions of the supervisor, it should be stressed again that he is a leader—or administrator—with special skills in the area of curriculum development and improvement. Wiles states that "supervision is a service activity that exists to help teachers do their job better." [7] In meeting this function, supervisors perform a number of activities. Included among these are individual classroom visits and teachers' conferences; evaluating and selecting books and other instructional materials which can subsequently be recommended to individual teachers or to groups of teachers for use; helping individual teachers or groups of teachers develop resource or teaching units; organizing and working with groups in curriculum development or improvement programs; organizing and directing conferences or workshops for teachers; assisting individual teachers or groups of teachers in the administration of tests and the interpretation and use of test data; preparing or assisting in the preparation of manuals and bulletins to aid teachers in instruction; assisting in the development and use of programs for the general evaluation of a school program or

[7] Kimball Wiles, *Supervision for Better Schools* (Englewood Cliffs, N.J.: Prentice-Hall, Inc., 1950), p. 3.

phases of the program; conducting demonstration teaching classes; performing as a consultant for local faculties as they study instructional problems; or assisting in the development of plans for reporting pupil progress to parents.[8] Even though this list is by no means exhaustive, it indicates the scope of the activities that may fall within the duties of the supervisor.

While we would not attempt to discuss in detail here the function of the supervisor, it is important to mention that ability in getting along with people is a vital asset. Often the supervisor must inspire teachers who are self-satisfied to strive for improvement. At times, the supervisor must overcome a teacher's opinion that he is a "central office inspector." Not only must the supervisor be knowledgeable in the field of general instruction and perhaps also in special subject matter such as art or music, but he must have the ability to work with people so that this knowledge can be put to use in the improvement of instruction. Skills in group processes, individual conferences, and general human relations are important parts of the equipment of a supervisor.

Number of Positions

Because of problems of definition and of reporting, it is impossible to give an accurate statement of the number of supervisors employed by school systems. After analyzing various statistical reports, we would estimate that there are about 40,000–50,000 supervisory positions in the schools in which the title "supervisor" is used (1966).

CENTRAL OFFICE POSITIONS

Description

In speaking of central office positions, we are referring to those positions in a school system which are concerned more with the overall operation of the system than with the operation of a single attendance unit within the system. While it is somewhat difficult to generalize on the exact titles or descriptions of these positions as found throughout the country, certain positions are common. The number of such positions and their descriptions in any given school system will, of course, vary with the size of the system and the particular form of administrative organization in use.

A comprehensive list of central office positions might be as follows:[9]

---

[8] See Burton and Brueckner, op. cit., p. 21, for a more complete list of supervisory activities.

[9] These positions have been selected from a collection of organization charts of large city school districts. The use of the terms "assistant superintendent" and "director" has been followed here although such terms as "deputy superintendent," "assistant to the superintendent," "associate superintendent," or "co-ordinator" are often used in practice.

Administrative assistant to the superintendent

Assistant superintendent for instruction

Assistant superintendent for business

Assistant superintendent for personnel (staff)

Assistant superintendent for pupil personnel services

Assistant superintendent for special services

Director of elementary education

Director of secondary education

Director of curriculum

Director of publications and information

Director of research

Director of finance

Director of buildings and grounds

Director of health services

Director of cafeteria services

Director of transportation

Director of special education

Director of adult education

Director of instructional materials

Director of audio-visual education

Purchasing agent

Attendance officer

Supervising principals

Obviously, only the largest system would have all of these positions on a full-time basis. In many cases, for example, an assistant superintendent for instruction would fulfill the roles covered by such additional positions as director of elementary education, director of secondary education, and director of curriculum. It should also be noted that there is usually a hierarchy in central office positions. A number of directors responsible for various phases of the instructional program would be under the immediate direction of the assistant superintendent for instruction.

It is beyond the scope of this discussion to describe each of these positions in detail. In almost every case, the nature of the position is self-evident from the title. The major facts we would point out are that these

are all administrative positions and that they cover a wide scope of spe-
cialities. If this list does nothing else, it should provide the prospective
administrator with an awareness of the wide field open to him and should
help emphasize once again our point that educational administration and
the superintendency are not synonymous.

Functions

The central office administrative staff is necessitated by at least two
major facts. In the first place, even a small school system is a complex
operation. One man cannot be everywhere and do everything involved in
the overall administration of such a system. For this reason, he must have
the help such a staff provides. Secondly, studies of administration have
long shown that the top administrator in an organization cannot deal
effectively on a direct and continuous basis with every other member of
the organization. We have mentioned earlier the concept of span of control
and indicated that many people feel that the chief administrator should
have a limited number of people reporting directly to him. The implementation of this concept requires a central staff through which the great
number of people in an organization can report indirectly to the chief
administrator.

One major function of central office staff members is the direction of
various parts of the school organization. In order, however, that the school
system as a whole operate as an integrated unit, this same staff must assist
in the equally important task of co-ordinating these various parts of the
organization. Often the major administrative assistants in a larger school
system form a kind of cabinet which works with the superintendent on
problems of co-ordination as well as on other aspects of administration.
In somewhat smaller school systems, this same function is performed by
the building principals.

Members of the central office staff also function as advisers to the superintendent on matters relating to their special fields of competency. Because
the staff members are dealing only with segments of the total school system,
they have opportunities to keep abreast of trends, techniques, skills, needs,
and content in their respective areas which are not possible for the superintendent. Effective superintendents must become effective generalists and
rely upon central staff members for specialized advice.

Directing, co-ordinating, and advising, then, are major functions of the
central staff. To operate effectively, these staff members need to have their
positions clearly defined; they need delegated authority commensurate with
delegated responsibility; and they need to be competent administrators in
and of themselves, fully aware of the administrative process and of the
role and function of the administrator.

SCHOOL DISTRICT SUPERINTENDENT

Description

Probably little needs to be said to define the position of school district superintendent. We find in practice, however, that there are differences in terminology even in listing this position. We define a school district superintendent as the chief administrative officer of an administrative unit that operates public schools. He is directly responsible to a local board of education, although there are some few states where he is elected by some means rather than appointed by the board of education. He is the executive officer of the local board of education. It should be noted again that many superintendents also serve as principals and as teachers. We shall be speaking here of the single role of superintendent of schools.

While the common term for such a person is "superintendent of schools," certain variations are found, particularly in rural school districts. In some cases, and in terms of our definition presented above, people with the following titles are actually superintendents:

Supervising principal

Local executive

General superintendent

Local superintendent

Superintendent of instruction

As long as the title describes a person who meets the criteria implied by our definition, we consider the position to be that of a school district superintendent, now commonly known as the superintendent of schools.

Functions

Several authors, notably Reller, have described in detail the evolution of the superintendency in the United States.[10] Such a treatment will not be attempted here. In describing the functions of a superintendent, Reeder stated:

There are hundreds of details incident to the running of an efficient school or a school system for which someone must be responsible. Plans must be made and policies adopted; the plans and policies must be properly executed;

[10] Theodore L. Reller, *The Development of the City Superintendency of Schools in the United States* (Philadelphia: published by author, 1935).

and information must be collected which will show how efficiently the plans and policies are operating, and which will also become the basis for new and better plans and policies.[11]

Perhaps the key phrase here is "for which someone must be responsible." In a real sense, the responsibility for the general planning for, operation of, and evaluation of a school system is the awesome function of a super-intendent. Too much stress, however, is usually placed on the operational aspects of administration and too little on the planning and evaluating phases. Barnard, speaking of executives in general, makes much of the point that an executive, as distinguished from a manager, must consider his major function to be in the planning area.[12] Many studies of leadership reveal that the leader must have vision and must have the time and the ability to convert vision into reality. As the chief administrative officer in a school district, the superintendent should accept this planning function.

All of the tasks of administration which we enumerated earlier come under the jurisdiction of the superintendent. It is important to note, how-ever, that his function is to see that these tasks are met—not to meet them all himself. Proper delegation is a key function in meeting tasks, and proper delegation can provide the superintendent with time and energy to perform his planning and evaluating functions.

Complete books have been written to describe the functions of the superintendent of schools. It is not our purpose here to provide such detailed information. We would conclude this description of the functions of the superintendent by repeating the obvious fact that his primary func-tion is the provision of the best possible educational program for the people of the school district of which he is the chief administrator.

Number of Positions

It is again important to recognize that a statement of the number of superintendencies available in the United States must, of necessity, be an estimate. Many administrators called superintendents should more ac-curately be called principals. While there are about 27,000 school districts in the United States, many of these exist in name only and no longer operate schools. The best estimate that we would make of the number of local district superintendents is about 15,000. This includes superin-tendents in the very small school districts as well as in the very large districts (1966).

---

[11] Ward G. Reeder, *The Fundamentals of Public School Administration,* 4th ed. (New York: Macmillan Company, 1958), p. 5.

[12] Chester Barnard, *The Functions of the Executive* (Cambridge: Harvard University Press, 1938).

POSITIONS IN INTERMEDIATE UNITS

Description

The intermediate administrative unit is between the local school district and the state educational agency. Although some exceptions may be found, the intermediate unit serves school districts rather than operates schools. While the county is generally thought of as the intermediate unit, this assumption leads to some confusion when those states which operate the county-unit system are considered. Under the county-unit plan, the county is the local school district, and a board of education and a superintendent are responsible for the operation of the public schools in that county. The states now using county units have, in fact, no intermediate units.

For clarity, then, we repeat that the intermediate unit is a service unit, which is not charged with the actual operation of schools and which lies between the state educational agency and the local school district. The administrative organization and financing of intermediate units vary a great deal from state to state and are described in detail elsewhere.[13] Ordinarily, such a unit has a separate board of education elected or appointed for the purpose of governing the intermediate unit, or it has a board of education composed of some number of members from the local boards of education within the intermediate unit.

Almost without exception, intermediate units have a chief administrative officer who is called a superintendent of schools. In those states where the county is the intermediate unit, this official is generally known as the county superintendent of schools. The number of staff members attached to an intermediate unit varies a great deal, but the kinds of positions found in such units include:[14]

General and special supervisors

Pupil personnel officer

Co-ordinator of special services

Co-ordinator of guidance

Co-ordinator of instructional materials

Specialist in finance and business management

[13] Shirley Cooper and Charles O. Fitzwater, *County School Administration* (New York: Harper & Brothers, 1954). See also *Reports* of the National Commission on the Intermediate Administrative Unit, Department of Rural Education, National Education Association, issued approximately once each month.

[14] These positions have been selected from a collection of organization charts of intermediate units. The titles listed are often not used as given here, but these titles are descriptive of the general types of positions found.

Co-ordinator of adult education

Director of purchasing

Director of data processing

Director of research

Co-ordinator of health services

Specialist in measurement and evaluation

It can be seen that certain of these positions are not general administrative positions but are, rather, administrative positions in special areas. Once again, these titles seem sufficiently descriptive to eliminate the necessity of further clarification.

Functions

The theory of the intermediate unit is that certain services can be provided more adequately and efficiently to a large number of people than to a small number. Rather than form larger operating school districts to facilitate the provision of these services, school districts have grouped together for certain service activities while remaining separate for the operation of the schools. Thus, while each of a number of small school districts could not employ several general and special supervisors, the districts as a group can economically share the services of these supervisors. A key function of the intermediate unit and of its administrative officers is, then, the provision of services to operating school districts. Inherent in this function are the equally important tasks of helping operating districts determine their needs for services and helping these districts to use effectively the services provided.

Another common function of the intermediate unit is the keeping of records. In most states, a number of reports which local districts must submit to state agencies are forwarded through the intermediate unit. As a matter of fact, this function was once the chief function of the intermediate unit and is, incidentally, too often still its major function.

Regardless of whether educational services or clerical services are emphasized in an intermediate unit—and we believe that educational services must receive major emphasis—it can be seen that co-ordination is an underlying function of all intermediate units. Administrators in the intermediate unit must be particularly adept at the co-ordinating phase of the administrative process.

Several statements of the functions of the administrator of the intermediate unit have been formulated as the result of careful studies of these units. Rinehart's summary includes the following points:

1. The intermediate unit is a means through which two or more operating school districts can share services.

2. The intermediate unit is tending to place less emphasis on clerical, regulatory, and inspectorial duties and more emphasis on professional leadership and a program of educational services.

3. Prominent among services of the intermediate unit are improvement of instruction through supervision, in-service education programs, and general curriculum leadership; development of programs and services for exceptional children; provision of pupil personnel services such as guidance, psychological services, and attendance services; provision of health services; provision of library services; development of co-operative research and study programs; and provision of special programs in vocational or other terminal education fields.[15]

Within this list of functions are implications for major educational contributions. In spite of a trend toward the creation of larger local school districts, the need for an intermediate unit to provide and to co-ordinate services will probably remain in many states. The intermediate unit administrator has functions which must be performed and performed well if every local school district is to provide a wide range of necessary services to the children in the district.

Number of Positions

In most states, the number of intermediate unit administrators can be ascertained quickly by determining the number of counties in the states. However, as was mentioned earlier, such a tabulation would not be completely accurate. According to the best estimates, there are something under 2,000 intermediate unit superintendents (1966).

STATE EDUCATIONAL AGENCIES

Description

The state, as we mentioned earlier, is the governmental unit in our country responsible for the development and general control of systems of public schools. While states do not usually operate schools, there are a number of administrative positions associated with state educational agencies.

It would be well here to describe briefly some general characteristics of state-level organization for public school purposes, although comprehensive treatments are available elsewhere.[16] State educational agencies, most

[15] John S. Rinehart, "The Function, Organization, and Operation of the County School District in Ohio" (unpublished doctoral dissertation, The Ohio State University, 1957), pp. 312–14.

[16] See particularly Lee M. Thurston and W. H. Roe, *State School Administration* (New York: Harper & Brothers, 1957).

commonly known as state departments of education, are usually under the direct administrative control of a professional educator. In general terms, this officer is known as the chief state school officer and, in most states, the incumbent is entitled the state superintendent of public instruction. A professional educator, he is usually responsible to a governing board commonly referred to as the state board of education.

Within the state departments of education, which are generally charged with specific regulatory, leadership, and research duties, are many professional educators, a number of whom perform educational administrative functions. State departments are commonly divided into divisions, each of which is headed by a director. Some typical divisions in state departments of education are these:

Vocational education

Vocational rehabilitation

Instruction

School lunch

Administration

Secondary education

Elementary education

Special education

Certification

Finance

Teacher education

Transportation

Health and physical education

Libraries

School plant

Research

Federal Programs

Each division of a state department of education often has two or more branches which are also under the direction of professional personnel. For example, an administrative division may have branches concerned with law, school district organization, statistical studies, or business management. It can be seen that there are many opportunities for service as an educational administrator in state educational agencies.

Functions

In the introductory statement to one comprehensive analysis of the functions of state departments of education, Beach explains that the broad functions of such departments may be classified under the three major categories of leadership, regulation, and operational functions.[17] In describing each of these categories, Beach points out more specifically the general functions of a state department of education.[18] Under leadership, he lists functions dealing with planning—both for its own activities and for the common school program in the state; research; advising and consulting with educators and others; co-ordinating activities both of the various local and intermediate units in the state public school system and of the various other state agencies which in one way or another have responsibilities impinging upon public education; and providing information to the legislature, the governor, and the people generally about progress and conditions of education within the state.

Under the regulatory category, the state department of education is responsible for those things which are necessary

. . . to protect the lives and health of . . . children and youth; to guarantee safety and economy in the use of educational funds; to assure efficiency in management of the educational enterprise; to provide a framework for the instructional program which would assure a basic minimum in both scope and quality; and to assure an educated citizenry.[19]

Much discretion must be exercised by a state department of education to insure that the regulatory function does not conflict with the basic American idea of local control of public education. Few would dispute, however, that state regulation is necessary; and while it is admitted that the desirable extent of such regulation is a debatable point, the legitimacy of the function itself is clearly recognized in both law and practice.

The third category—operational functions—is perhaps the area most subject to disagreement. State operation of one or more types of educational programs clashes directly with the principle of decentralized control of education. Thus, while Beach recognizes that many present-day functions of state departments of education must be considered operational in nature, he argues very strongly that these are not legitimate functions of such departments.[20] Examples include the operation of the vocational

[17] Fred F. Beach, *The Functions of State Departments of Education,* U.S. Office of Education, Miscellaneous No. 12 (Washington: U.S. Government Printing Office, 1950), p. 3.

[18] *Ibid.,* pp. 4–16.

[19] *Ibid.,* p. 10.

[20] *Ibid.,* p. 16.

rehabilitation program, the operation of normal schools or teachers colleges, or the operation of state libraries and museums. While the stimulation of such services is a legitimate part of the leadership role of a state department, the operational aspects of such services should best be performed under separate administrative organizations.

Number of Positions

There can be, at most, fifty chief state school officers. It is difficult to ascertain the number of people serving in other administrative positions in state departments of education. In general, however, we would estimate that there are over one thousand full-time educational administration positions in the fifty state departments. This number has been augmented appreciably in recent years with the need to co-ordinate and supervise various federal programs. This is an area of service for which few people specifically prepare. Yet it is an area of service with great potential and one that requires high-level competencies for educational administration.

UNITED STATES OFFICE OF EDUCATION

While considering governmental service and educational administration, it is important to devote some attention to educational administration at the federal government level. The United States Office of Education is one of several agencies in the Department of Health, Education and Welfare. It is under the leadership of the United States Commissioner of Education, who serves directly under the Secretary of Health, Education and Welfare. The United States Office of Education is organized in divisions, each one under the direction of an assistant commissioner. The divisions are organized in branches, each of which is headed by a director. Within some branches there are also bureau chiefs. The Commissioner is an appointive officer, while the remaining personnel in the Office are wholly or partially under Civil Service.

The primary function of the Office of Education is to marshal resources on a national scale for the improvement of public education in the nation. In addition, the Office provides valuable consultative service as well as conducting many statistical studies to provide insight into national educational trends. The Office has few regulatory functions, in keeping with the established doctrine that public education is a state matter.

There are, however, a variety of operational responsibilities within the functions of the Office. Beginning with the passage of the National Defense Education Act, the participation of the federal government in education has grown rapidly and extensively, culminating in the passage of the Elementary-Secondary Education Act of 1965 (PL 89-10), which represents the greatest single commitment ever made by the federal government for the support of education. This legislation, coupled with the massive Higher Education Facilities Assistance Act passed in 1964 and the Higher Education Act of 1965, has placed great responsibilities and major operational functions within the U. S. Office of Education. The staff of the Office, both in Washington, D. C., and in regional centers throughout the country, is expanding at such a rate that opportunities for service at this level are almost unlimited for qualified people.

ADMINISTRATION IN HIGHER EDUCATION

There are many educational administration positions in higher education. It should be noted, however, that administrators in higher education are not drawn only from the ranks of those we have been calling educational administrators. It is unlikely, for example, that the dean of a college of commerce would be selected from the field of educational administration, even though his position would be an administrative position in an educational undertaking. Those to whom this text has been primarily addressed might more logically aspire in higher education to one of the following positions:

Chairman, department of education

Director, school of education

Dean, college of education

Registrar, college or university

President, college or university

In addition, there are many administrative positions in junior colleges which are well within the province of educational administration. Some junior colleges are organized under the control of local boards of education and offer positions somewhat similar to those of a superintendent or of a principal. Other junior colleges are organized more in terms of college or university structure under the direction of a board of trustees. In this case, junior college administrative positions may be similar to college deanships or presidencies.

PROFESSORSHIPS

One final kind of position is available to the person interested in educational administration. This position involves the preparation of educational administrators through service as a professor in an institution conducting such a program of preparation. Although this position is not in itself an administrative position, it is a position for which administrators might aim.

The professor of educational administration has unique opportunities to engage in the three activities commonly considered a part of university teaching—instruction, research, and service. He is, first of all, a teacher. Ordinarily his students are graduate students. He is, secondly, a researcher. He is expected to be both interested and competent in research. Through his research, he may become a better teacher and he may make unique contributions to the profession of educational administration. Finally, he provides service to the field. Because of continuing opportunities in research and study which are not ordinarily available to the practicing administrator, the professor can be of assistance to practicing administrators in helping them develop new approaches to the solution of administrative problems.

A SUMMARY STATEMENT

In the preceding pages, we have described in some detail the positions that are available to educational administrators. The purposes of this discussion were twofold. First, we hoped to illustrate the fact that there is room in the profession of educational administration for many kinds of people. The wide variety of positions available should serve to make clear the difficulties we encountered in attempting, in Chapter 11, to describe the competencies required of an educational administrator.

The second purpose of this discussion was to stress our belief that one does not have to be a superintendent to be an administrator. The profession of educational administration needs people whose main aim is to be outstanding principals or competent supervisors. By presenting here an overview of the variety of positions in educational administration, it was our hope that many readers would say, "Here is the job for me!" and that they would find support for their desire to be administrators and their lack of desire to be superintendents. We estimated that in this country there are about 55,000 principalships, about 45,000 supervisory positions, about 15,000 local district superintendencies, about 2,000 intermediate unit superintendencies, and over 1,000 administrative positions in state educational agencies. These are in addition to positions as central office administrators, as higher education administrators, or as professors, for which estimates of number were not provided. It is apparent that there are about 120,000 administrative positions in all of the categories discussed in this chapter.

PROMOTION ROUTES

As one contemplates entering a profession, the question concerning ways to attain one's aim in that profession is bound to arise. Although matters of competency and on-the-job performance are important in answering this question, it is also true that certain procedural matters are involved. For example, a man who desires to be a county superintendent will want to know what series of positions seems most likely to lead there. While generalizations with regard to promotion routes are perhaps distinguished most often by the number of exceptions that can be pointed out, some attention will now be given to them.

THE STANDARD ROUTE

At one time—and no doubt many people pursue it today—the route to a city superintendency was considered to be a fixed or standard route from which one detoured only at one's peril. A person began as a high school teacher of some subject, probably social studies, and perhaps also as a coach. From here, he became a high school principal and then moved on to a small superintendency. After one or more steps through larger super-intendencies, he arrived at the city superintendency.

A teacher with patience in a large city system could perhaps hope for a high school principalship after taking these steps:

1. Junior high school vice-principal.

2. Senior high school vice-principal or junior high school principal.

3. Senior high school principal.

This route, with certain modifications, is a prevalent one today.

Although following these routes or similar ones to reach other positions has some advantages, certain key disadvantages can be noted. In the first place, it takes a long time to reach the desired position following such a procedure. Even the most able young person has to get into the "machinery," and he is often no longer young and possibly not so able when he finally reaches the desired goal. Secondly, these procedures often tend to lead to a correlation between seniority and administrative appointment. Once a person enters the promotion stages, his progress is dependent upon the amount of time he has spent in any one level rather than upon his competence for the next level.

In the third place, following these procedures often means that the administrator becomes a transient worker while seeking outside of his present school system a position where he will not be held back due to lack of seniority. But perhaps the most important disadvantage is that a whole series of administrative positions are seen as important only because they may lead to something else. The junior high school principalship, for example, is a position today which, in many cases, is taken by a person only because it may lead to a senior high school principalship.

Because of these disadvantages and others, many school systems have begun to institute new procedures for administrative promotion. It would not be realistic, however, to give the impression that the standard route has been abandoned, nor would it be fair to imply that it has no value. Certainly, experience gained in the superintendency in a small city can be valuable training for a superintendency in a large city. The following promotion routes seem to us to be the most common and standard ones. The major point to remember, however, in considering these is that each position along the way is a position with integrity in and of itself. No position should be taken only as a means to subsequent promotion. Unless a person is challenged by and competent for a position, he should not assume it.

Elementary school principal route
Elementary school teacher, both lower grades (1–4) and upper grades (4–8).
Service on school and district-wide curriculum committees.
Elementary school principal.

Junior high school principal route
Junior high school teacher.
Adviser of one or more student activities.
Some home room or counseling activities.
Semiadministrative position in junior high school.
Junior high school principal.

Senior high school principal route
Senior high school teacher.
Adviser of one or more student activities.
Semiadministrative position in high school.
Assistant principal, or principal of small high school.
Senior high school principal.

City superintendent route
Teaching on both elementary school and secondary school level. (Ideal, but seldom realized. Most commonly high school teacher.)
Follow route to principalship. (Most likely high school principalship.)
Superintendent in small school district. (Most likely under 1,000 students.)
Superintendent in small-city school district (city of under 10,000 population) or assistant superintendent in a larger district.
Superintendent in medium-sized school district (city of under 50,000 population).
Superintendent in large-city school district.

(NOTE: In many cases, an assistant superintendency in a larger school district is substituted for one or more of these steps.)

Similar suggested routes could be proposed for other administrative positions, but due to the wide variety of possible routes, it does not seem particularly fruitful. These patterns are sufficient to point out that the standard promotion route is usually long, particularly if one aspires to a position in a large organization.

SOME NEWER CONCEPTS

Is Teaching Necessary?

Although not a widely-published theory, one can often hear administrators and those preparing administrators discuss the idea that teaching experience may not be a necessary part of the promotion route for administration. This idea grows from the concept that administration and teaching are two separate things and that, although the administrator must understand teaching, it is not necessary to teach in order to gain this understanding. Those who advocate this viewpoint propose that certain students in teacher training or, as a matter of fact, in any other field be selected on the basis of administrative potential and be prepared as administrators. While it would be important that these trainees have ample opportunities to observe the teaching process in schools, it would not be necessary that they become teachers.

This concept has not been adequately tested, nor does it seem likely that it will be in the near future. Several obstacles stand in the way. Without exception, every state requires that its school administrators hold teaching certificates and that some amount of teaching experience be a prerequisite to administrative certification. The traditional concept that educational leadership cannot be exerted in a school by someone who has not taught in a similar school is too deeply imbedded to be removed readily. Many feel that certain problems now met in administrator-teacher relationships would be intensified if the administrator had never taught.

This idea may be tested in the future. It seems logical to say at this time, however, that few will enter educational administration without a teaching background or without some other previous experience in a position in a school.

The "Big Step" Route

Some administrators and professors of educational administration consider that the usual methods of reaching the top take too long. They have suggested that procedures should be developed which will aid in the early selection of high-potential, top-level administrators. When these people are found, they should be given intensive training and then major administrative responsibilities early in their careers.

Several difficulties must be overcome before we can expect widespread adoption of the "big step" idea. School boards generally seem to be somewhat reluctant to place very young administrators in major administrative positions. It is not unusual to find the age of forty, for example, specified as an acceptable age for applicants for a large city superintendency.

Another difficulty arises in the development of preparation programs which will make it possible for potential major administrators to short-cut the standard promotion routes. There can be no doubt that widespread experience in minor administrative positions can be excellent training for major administrative positions. Substitute training experiences must be developed if all or part of this experience is to be eliminated from the promotion route.

Regardless of the difficulties, it seems apparent that the future will see major efforts to move younger men and women to major administrative positions more rapidly than at present. Not only will such a step require improvements in selection procedures and preparation programs, but it will mean that prospective administrators must make the decision to become administrators earlier than they do now.

Internship and Cadet Programs

Internship and cadet programs have been described in Chapter 12. It is important to indicate here that these programs represent efforts to approach the "big step" promotion and are departures from the standard promotion routes. Districts with active programs of this nature generally have more young people in both school building and central office administrative positions than do those districts without such programs. Although they are often seen primarily as training programs, it is also true that they are promotion programs.

GENERAL COMMENTS ON PROMOTION

Educational administration is a profession with much to offer the person who has something to bring to it. We have seen the great variety of positions which may be classified as educational administration. We have just discussed the various possibilities for promotion in the profession and have emphasized the current proposals to make it possible for young people to move ahead rapidly in the profession.

A discussion of promotion should be concluded, however, with the sober reminder that, for the most part, the heights one reaches in a profession depend primarily upon one's own ability and level of preparation. The promotion routes are present, but each position along the way asks certain qualifications of its incumbent. A consideration of promotion without a corresponding consideration of aims, potential, motivations, and qualifications is almost useless. In this section, we have indicated that the right man can find good routes for promotion. The prospective administrator must now ask himself once again if he is the right man.

REMUNERATION

Although educators are often altruistic in word and in spirit, they also must feed, clothe, and house themselves and their families. Thus, the question of financial remuneration for services rendered is a pertinent one.

GENERAL SITUATION

Administrators, in general, receive higher salaries than do teachers in the same school system. This generalization must be coupled, however, with a statement that the work-year of the administrator is generally longer than that of the teacher; thus it is true in many cases that the salary of an administrator per working month is little if any higher than the salary of many teachers in his school system per working month. Also, it should be noted that the administrator in the small school system may receive a salary equal to or even less than that of a teacher in a larger school system. Certain general comparisons of salaries in large urban school districts are shown in Table 13.1.

TABLE 13.1

MEDIAN SALARIES PAID CERTAIN EMPLOYEES
IN SCHOOL DISTRICTS 1962–63

Size of District (Enrollment)	Median Salary Paid to			
	Superintendent	High School Principal	Elementary School Principal	Classroom Teacher
100,000+	$25,000	–	–	–
50,000 – 99,999	$22,500	–	–	–
25,000 – 49,999	$20,000	$11,315	$9,914	$6,114
12,000 – 24,999	$17,500	–	–	–
3,000 – 24,999	–	$ 8,569	$7,923	$5,502
300 – 2,999	–	$ 7,533	$6,580	$5,191
1 – 299	–	$ 6,091	$5,688	$4,594

Source: National Education Association, Biennial Salary Survey of Public School Employees, 1962–63, pp. 12, 14, 22.

While Table 13.1 does not report salaries in districts located in cities or localities with less than 30,000 population, the median salaries shown in the lower level are somewhat representative of those in smaller districts. A possible exception is in the area of administrators' salaries, which are often either extremely low or extremely high in small districts. Table 13.1 must be read with some caution due to the great ranges in the salaries which result in the medians shown. Superintendents' salaries, for example, range from $4,500 to about $50,000. While not quite as extreme, similar ranges exist for all of the positions shown. This fact means that generalizations about salaries of school administrators are extremely tenuous at best. In any given position in any certain kind of school district, one can find both high and low salaries. Such factors as the general wealth of the school district or state, cost of living, or the general salary picture in a community are major factors in determining the exact position in which one finds oneself in the salary range as an administrator.

State Departments of Education

It is a rare state, indeed, where the chief state school officer receives a higher salary than the highest paid city superintendent in that state. While in a few states, state educational agencies offer attractive financial compensation, the general picture is that administrators in these agencies serve in spite of the lack of financial reward.

College and University Positions

The person who contemplates becoming a professor of educational administration will find himself doing so without great financial incentive. In 1963–64, the following median salaries were paid in colleges and universities.[21]

Professors	$11,312
Associate professors	8,969
Assistant professors	7,539
Instructors	6,114
All ranks combined	8,163

It can be seen that these medians, particularly at the lower ranks, are below almost all the medians for administrators. It should be emphasized, however, that these college and university salary medians are for nine months

[21] Research Division, National Education Association, *Salaries Paid and Salary Practices in Universities, Colleges, and Junior Colleges, 1963–64.* Washington, D.C.: The Association, 1964, p. 11.

of service, while most major public school administrative positions are on an eleven- or twelve-month basis.

In considering college teaching salaries, several factors should be introduced to make the medians presented above more meaningful. For example, the kind of institution in which one teaches may make a difference in salary. Also, ranges become equally as important as medians. In addition, it should be mentioned that college professors have opportunities for research and writing which may provide extra compensation.

Median salaries for college administrative personnel in 1963–64 can be summarized as follows:[22]

Position	Median	Range
Presidents	$17,330	$4,500–$45,500+
Vice presidents	17,130	4,000– 35,499
Deans of colleges	13,644	Below 4,000– 27,000
Deans of students	10,964	Below 4,000– 24,499
Directors of admissions	9,572	Below 4,000– 22,499
Registrars	8,142	Below 4,000– 19,499

Other Positions

General salary studies of administrative personnel in intermediate units are not available. An analysis of salary practices in several states, however, indicates that such positions are probably somewhat comparable to positions in medium-size cities. Remember that median salaries do not indicate ranges and that for every kind of position there are very high and very low salaries paid.

SALARY SCHEDULES FOR ADMINISTRATORS

There is an increasing trend to develop salary schedules for educational administrative personnel, although the top administrative position in an organization is usually not on a schedule. Several kinds of salary schedules are used for administrators.

In some cases it is felt that the qualifications that a person must possess to be selected for an administrative position make it unrealistic to provide training increments in an administrative salary schedule. In such cases, a minimum salary for a given position is established, and regular service or experience increments are granted. In other cases, both training and experience increments are provided.

[22] *Ibid.,* pp. 30, 32–33.

A major salary question which often arises is whether a principal should receive a salary smaller than the salary received by any teacher in his building. While the question is subject to endless debate, practice seems to answer the question in the negative. Where administrative salary schedules exist, the minimum principal's salary is ordinarily higher than the maximum teacher's salary. This practice, however, is not without exception.

Many administrative salaries are still arrived at by the method of individual bargaining. It is our belief that administrative salaries should be paid in terms of a salary schedule; that the salary schedule should be arrived at by the same professional methods used in developing a teacher salary schedule; and that due consideration should be given in the schedule to the increased responsibilities of administrative leadership and to the increased preparation required of one who reaches an administrative position.

NONFINANCIAL COMPENSATION

The person who is interested only in financial gain will undoubtedly not find education a suitable profession. In education generally, as well as in educational administration, the profession has much to offer in addition to financial reward. Most of these additional compensations are personal in nature, varying in appeal with each individual.

The competent educational administrator receives a high degree of community respect. While we have said that he is not necessarily a community power figure, he is a respected leader. The administrator can gain much satisfaction from the key leadership role which he plays in the schools of a community, state, or nation. While it is only rarely that he can claim sole responsibility for an educational accomplishment in a school system, he can take pride in his contributions to such accomplishments.

The working conditions of the administrator are usually good, and he has an unparalleled opportunity to work with a sincere and dedicated group of professional colleagues. In almost every case, the administrator is surrounded by a group of professional friends who look upon him as an adviser and a leader rather than as a "boss." Therefore, although financial reward is important and educational administration does offer certain financial advantages, there are many other rewards available to the administrator.

TENURE AND SECURITY

In spite of laws, rules, or regulations, a man's security is dependent for the most part upon his ability and his health. Undue concern with tenure and security is not the mark of a competent administrator. However, the prospective administrator should be aware of the fact that administrators are dismissed—sometimes justly and sometimes unjustly—and that administration has a certain factor of risk.

THE RISK FACTOR

The administrator is a highly visible person. In most cases, when something seems to go astray in an organization, the top administrator is most in view as the person who "should have done something." It is also true that the administrator does, in fact, have basic responsibilities for the success of the organization that he administers. The twin facts of responsibility and visibility mean that the administrator is dependent on other members of his organization for success. Thus he is constantly in greater danger of being judged a failure than are other members of his organization.

This administrative risk is well illustrated by the following example. An able high school teacher in a small city was promoted to the principalship of the high school. This teacher was well prepared for administration, showed real promise, and was properly certified. The high school had 472 students in grades 10–12 and a staff consisting of 27 teachers, a guidance counselor, and an assistant principal who was also athletic director.

During the principal's first year of service, a biology teacher asked permission to institute a sex-education program in the required 10th grade biology course. The program seemed defensible to the principal and he approved its introduction for the following year. When the unit was introduced, however, consternation and some anger broke loose in certain quarters in the city. A controversy of major proportions ensued, during which the principal staunchly defended the teacher and the program. When contract renewal time came around, the principal was advised that he could no longer be principal and that, while he had tenure as a teacher, feeling against him ran so high that he should probably resign from the system altogether. The biology teacher was ordered to drop the controversial unit.

The principal may have exercised poor judgment and have made procedural errors. However, his visibility and his responsibility were the factors that led to his downfall in spite of the minor importance of his error. This case may be an unusual one, but it indicates clearly the fact that there is a risk factor in administration.

ADMINISTRATIVE TURNOVER

A number of studies show that administrators change positions regularly and with some degree of rapidity. This is partially attributable to the standard promotion route, which seems to require that the administrator serve in a number of positions during his climb to a major position. In addition, the turnover is partially attributable to the risk factor in administration. A third factor leading to turnover is the fact that some people prefer to move from time to time for personal reasons.

A study of the turnover rates of superintendents revealed that the average tenure of superintendents in the United States is about nine years,[23] although other studies tend to indicate a shorter tenure. Medians, of course, do not show the many administrators who have had long tenure in individual school systems. It should be recognized, however, that turnover is a problem, particularly in the superintendency.

Some authorities favor regular administrative turnover. Burton and Brueckner, for example, propose regular administrative changes for all administrators and shifting both within and without a system as a regular pattern.[24] They favor some sort of rotation plan, feeling that a plan of this nature would enhance administrative leadership. In general, however, we believe that excessive administrative turnover has many harmful effects. Rotation plans or other shifting systems seem to be based on a belief that many administrators are incompetent and that no single school or school system should be subject to the same kind of incompetence for too long a period. If incompetence is present, the rotation plan is not a good solution.

TENURE LAWS AND THE ADMINISTRATOR

Tenure laws have been developed in many states to protect the teacher from unjust dismissal. Tenure laws, of course, are not designed to eliminate dismissal, nor do they protect the right of a teacher to a specific teaching assignment.

In almost every case involving the tenure rights of administrators, the courts have held that an administrator may have tenure as a teacher, but does not have tenure as an administrator.[25] In general, it is virtually impossible to gain tenure for a specific administrative position.

Regardless of tenure legislation, the administrator who for any reason no longer has the confidence and support of his employing agency cannot

---

[23] American Association of School Administrators, *Professional Administrators for America's Schools.* Thirty-eighth Yearbook (Washington: The Association, 1960), p. 52.

[24] Burton and Brueckner, *op. cit.,* pp. 113–14.

[25] See Newton Edwards, *The Courts and the Public Schools,* rev. ed. (Chicago: University of Chicago Press, 1955), pp. 467–508 and NEA Research Division, *Trends in Teacher Tenure thru Legislation and Court Decision* (Washington: National Education Association, 1957).

function effectively in his position. While procedures need to be guaranteed which will permit the airing of charges and the presentation of all sides of a case, if these procedures result in technical tenure but continued bad relations, the administrator cannot be effective. Thus, tenure by law seems relatively unimportant for the administrator. What is important is tenure by demonstrated ability.

Civic and Professional Affiliations

The administrator, in order to exercise a leadership role both inside and outside of his school, must maintain relationships with many groups and individuals who are not professional educators. The relationships that an administrator maintains with professional and nonprofessional groups are an added feature of the administrative job. We feel that this feature is not only necessary, but a potentially enjoyable part of the professional task. We are speaking not merely of something that might be labeled public relations, but rather of contacts and relatonships which go far beyond any one phase of educational administration. Before describing some values received from professional and civic affiliations, let us examine the kinds of associations and affiliations about which we are speaking.

KINDS OF ASSOCIATIONS AND AFFILIATIONS

Community Groups

Most communities are highly organized social structures. Many of us are familiar with some which have so many organizations that it is impossible to schedule a meeting of one group which will not conflict with meetings of several other groups. Communities seem almost as prone to organize groups as educators are to form committees. The great variety and number of groups in a community require that the administrator make some choices. The superintendent, for example, cannot join every community organization. Some factors which should be considered in making such choices are set forth at a later point in this chapter.

After considering the communities we have known, the authors have made up the following example of the variety of organizations that exist in community life:

Service clubs
    Exchange
    Kiwanis

Lions
Rotary
Soroptimist
Zonta, etc.

Fraternal organizations
Elks
Moose
I.O.O.F., etc.

Business and professional groups
Chamber of Commerce
Junior Chamber of Commerce
Commercial Club
Bar Association
Medical Association
Real Estate Board
Dental Society, etc.

Special purpose clubs or organizations
Society for Prevention of Cruelty to Animals
American Legion
Veterans of Foreign Wars
Garden clubs
Women's Christian Temperance Union
Neighborhood civic associations, etc.
Athletic or musical group "booster clubs"

Welfare groups
Salvation Army
Y.M.C.A., Y.W.C.A.
Settlement house groups
Family counseling groups
Hospital boards
Boy Scouts, Girl Scouts, etc.

Cultural agencies
Library board
Symphony association
"Little Theater" group, etc.

Social groups
Bridge clubs
Others too numerous to mention

Religious groups

Labor organizations

Women's clubs

Political organizations

This list is undoubtedly far from exhaustive. The kinds of groups found
in a community are limited only by the interests, ingenuity, and organizational drives of the community. While it may well be argued that American

communities are overorganized, it seems equally safe to state that the organizational pattern will remain complex.

Professional Groups

The administrator also needs to keep in touch with professional trends and developments outside of his specific scene of operation. For this and other purposes, he will affiliate with one or more regional, state, or national professional organizations.

The largest organization for superintendents of schools is the American Association of School Administrators, an organization affiliated with the National Education Association and once known as the Department of Superintendence of the NEA. In 1965, the AASA had a membership of over 18,000.

The purpose of the organization, as stated in its constitution:

. . . shall be to maintain and elevate the professional and ethical standards of the teaching profession in general and its administrative and supervisory service in particular, and to promote activities which will look toward the accomplishment of the following objectives: to assist its members to understand the development of American culture in its relationship to education; to assist its members to develop an understanding of the fields, services, and responsibilities of education; to achieve a unified professional strength for the improvement of education; and to place before the public the facts and viewpoints which will lead to an intelligent appreciation of the work of the schools.[26]

Both elementary school and secondary school principals have national organizations which are affiliated with the National Education Association and whose purposes are similar to those stated above. The associations are known as the Department of Elementary School Principals and the National Association of Secondary School Principals.

Many supervisors and other administrators are members of another affiliate of the NEA, the Association for Supervision and Curriculum Development. The ASCD is particularly active in studying problems related to the improvement of teaching, to the development of general curriculum guides, and to the general improvement of curricular offerings in the public schools.

Administrators in all positions are members in great numbers of the National Education Association and its state and local associations. While it should not need to be mentioned, this fact is one more reminder that educational administrators are educators first and that the concerns of teachers are also the concerns of administrators.

Another organization which has made many contributions to the pro-

[26] *The Constitution and Bylaws.* The American Association of School Administrators. Article II.

fession of educational administration is the National Conference of Professors of Educational Administration. This group has little formal organization and conducts its business at an annual meeting. Although primarily composed of college professors of educational administration, NCPEA meetings are often attended by public school administrators. College professors of educational administration are also often members of the American Association of University Professors and various teacher education organizations, as well as being members of the organizations mentioned earlier in this discussion.

There are other professional organizations for administrators. These include the Association of School Business Officials, the National Council on Schoolhouse Construction, and the Council of Chief State School Officers. In addition, administrators often participate in the conferences and other activities of such organizations as the Parent-Teacher Association, National School Boards Association, and the Department of Rural Education of the National Education Association.

Almost without exception, these national organizations have state and regional affiliates. For example, each state has a state association of school administrators affiliated with the AASA. Through state and regional associations, many of the purposes of the national groups are achieved.

VALUES OF AFFILIATIONS

The prospective administrator might well say at this point, "I see that I can join a lot of groups. But why?" The "why" is not a simple thing. We believe, however, that professional and civic associations and affiliations have distinct value for the educational administrator in at least three major areas: his personal growth, his growth as an administrator, and the growth of the school system in which he is working.

Personal Growth

Through a wide variety of contacts with men in education and in other fields, the educational administrator has an unexcelled opportunity to expand his interests, to acquire general knowledge, and to gain a wide circle of acquaintances. All of these contacts, whether through formal organizations or through informal contacts, can lead to his growth as a person. One can rest assured that educational administration is a profession in which one can easily avoid personal stagnation.

Professional Growth

The many contacts which an administrator makes through his professional and his nonprofessional organizations can also lead to his growth as an administrator. Administration requires many skills, not the least of which is skill in human relations. Organizational activities requiring that one work with many kinds of people in many situations provide excellent opportunities for increasing competence in this field.

In addition, administrators often attain leadership positions in organizations and are thus presented with opportunities to gain administrative experience in various kinds of organizations. These experiences should serve to increase the educational administrator's general competence.

School System Growth

It seems worthwhile to repeat here that public schools belong to the public. The steady growth and improvement of a school system depend, to a great extent, upon the understanding and support that the system receives from the people it serves. This support depends, in turn, upon two things—the degree to which the educators understand the community in which they work and the degree to which members of the community understand their schools. One major way in which the degree of accomplishment in each of these areas can be enhanced is through having school personnel and townspeople come to know and understand each other.

The mere fact that school administrators—and, incidentally, teachers and other educators—belong to civic organizations does not guarantee excellence in school-community relations. However, if administrators look upon their community affiliations as opportunities to increase their understanding of the community and the community understanding of education, they will find in these affiliations some excellent opportunities to become educational leaders and to enhance the growth of their school system.

CHOOSING AFFILIATIONS

The school administrator, as has been mentioned earlier, cannot become a member of every community and professional organization. Choices must be made. Several factors should be considered as these decisions are faced.

School superintendents are not the only administrators in a school district. Too often, however, superintendents fail to make it possible for principals and other administrative personnel to participate in community organizations as a part of their leadership duties. Often, the superintendent finds himself "overorganized" because he is attempting to maintain community contacts by himself.

Another thing that is sometimes overlooked is that educational administrators can and should maintain contact with organizations to which they do not belong. For example, although few, if any, school administrators would be eligible to belong to a bar association or to a labor union council, this should not mean that the administrator has no contact with these organizations. He should take advantage of every possible opportunity to meet with groups or to have other members of his staff meet with groups to which he does not belong.

In contemplating the actual joining of organizations, several facts need consideration. In many cases, joining one group eliminates the possibility of joining similar groups. Often groups have conflicting times of meeting. In other cases, the school administrator is not eligible for membership. All of these factors eliminate certain choices, but do not completely eliminate all choices.

It is not realistic to propose that an educational administrator can play an active role in more than four or five organizations and still meet the other responsibilities of his job. Undoubtedly, at least one of these organizations will be a professional organization and probably one or two more will be closely related to the profession—perhaps the Parent-Teacher Association or a youth welfare group. An administrator should choose one or two other groups for active participation. These groups should not be made up primarily of the same people, and they should probably have somewhat different purposes. The major factor to remember is that the team of administrators in a school district should be active in a wide variety of groups. The superintendent should pay some attention to this and make an effort to facilitate diversified group membership.

Opportunities and Rewards

We have shown that the administrator can aim for a wide variety of positions; there are many ways in which he can serve education. In addition, although he should not expect to become a wealthy man through administration, he can expect sufficient reward, both in money and in satisfaction. To be sure, educational administration involves a certain amount of tenure risk, but it is our belief that the rewards justify the risk. And finally, we have stressed the opportunities available to the administrator for widespread association within and without the profession. All in all, we hope we have shown that the person who feels himself suited for educational administration and who proceeds to qualify for and to enter the profession, will find his choice a rewarding one.

Suggested Activities

1. Develop what would seem to you to be a good salary schedule for administrators. Suggest the criteria upon which your schedule is based.

2. Footnote 25 concerns two references which cite legal cases involving administrative tenure. Using these or other references, look up several such cases. List the general principles which seem to have guided the courts in such cases.

3. List the community organizations in your school district. Select four or five of these organizations to which it would seem important that educational administrators belong. Defend your selections.

4. List the administrative positions in an actual city school district known to you. Describe what seem to be elements common to all of these positions.

5. Read again the description of the "big step" promotion route. Describe what seem to you to be the strengths and weaknesses of such a proposal. What procedures would you suggest to implement such a proposal?

SELECTED READINGS

ALLEN, H. P. *The Federal Government and Education.* New York: McGraw-Hill, 1950.

American Association of School Administrators, *The American School Superintendency.* Thirtieth Yearbook. Washington: The American Association of School Administrators, 1952.

BEACH, FRED F. and WILL, ROBERT F. *The State and Education,* U.S. Office of Education, Miscellaneous No. 23. Washington: U. S. Government Printing Office, 1955.

COOPER, SHIRLEY and FITZWATER, CHARLES O. *County School Administration.* New York: Harper & Brothers, 1954.

CORBALLY, JOHN E., JR., JENSON, T. J., and STAUB, W. F. *Educational Administration: The Secondary School.* (2nd ed.). Boston: Allyn and Bacon, Inc., 1965.

SPAIN, C. R., DRUMMOND, H. D., and GOODLAD, J. I. *Educational Leadership and the Elementary School Principal.* New York: Holt, Rinehart and Winston, Inc., 1956.

THURSTON, LEE M., and ROE, W. H. *State School Administration.* New York: Harper & Brothers, 1957.

14

The Challenge

of Administration

AS WE REFLECT UPON WHAT WE SAID IN PART ONE about the job of administration and in Part Two about the man who is to undertake such a job, we feel some need to present and amplify the challenge or challenges inherent in educational administration. This chapter, perhaps more than any other part of the book, is our credo.

We take the position that a particular kind of educative process open to all is necessary in a society that aspires to a democratic way of life. In like manner we see a public school system characterized by certain values and practices as an essential part of the educative process; and finally, we take the position that administrative leaders who meet certain requirements occupy critical roles in the public school. We shall now amplify each of these challenges.

THE DEMOCRATIC WAY OF LIFE

We believe that the democratic way of life offers the primary challenge to educational administration. To be sure, this is a challenge to all citizens of our nation, but we think that such a challenge holds unique meaning for the school administrator.

A GREAT EXPERIMENT

The democratic way of life was and is a great experiment. When, historically, America fell heir to movements that had begun to stir Europe, one of these was the Protestant Reformation, which challenged the authority of church and state. The movement placed great stress upon the responsibility of the individual for the salvation of his own soul. John Locke in England during the seventeenth century supplied some of the intellectual foundations for popular rule. Denying that kings had any divine right to rule, he placed sovereignty in the hands of the people. The founders of our government referred to him as "the great Mr. Locke" and utilized much of his thinking in formulating our federal constitution.

As Counts has so well described it, this intellectual leadership shifted later to France:

In the eighteenth century the leadership in thought crossed the Channel to France. A galaxy of brilliant minds, with great gifts of expression, so dominated the age that it has come to be called after them and their work—the Age of Enlightenment. They proclaimed the coming victory of naturalism over supernaturalism, of science over theology, of human reason over established authority. Voltaire attacked the traditional dogmas of church and state as barriers to human advance. Montesquieu saw government, not as unchanging and sanctified by divine will, but as an expression of a people living in a particular time and place. Diderot and d'Alembert edited the great Encyclopedia which, they hoped, would bring the best of scientific and practical knowledge to many people and arouse enthusiasm for reform and improvement. Rousseau popularized the political ideas of Locke defending with the power of genius the doctrine that only the freely expressed will of the people can render any government legitimate. Condorcet, in his *Historical Sketch of the Progress of the Human Mind,* clothed with vast learning and philosophic grasp the idea of human progress and the perfectibility of man and his institutions. These men, and others like them, prepared the way for the French Revolution and other revolutions to follow in the nineteenth century.[1]

The movement to free the common man found fertile soil in America, where, in the first place, tradition was not such a binding force. Secondly, free land was available, for almost three hundred years, to any who would settle upon it and begin its cultivation. Economic opportunity appears to have had much to do with the development of social and political democracy.

But from its inception the idea of a democratic way of life was a radical one. The thought that all men could and should read and interpret the scriptures for themselves, as advocated by Luther, was in direct contra-

---

[1] George S. Counts, *Education and American Civilization* (New York: Bureau of Publications, Teachers College, Columbia University, 1952), p. 52.

diction to the established order of the Catholic Church. Locke's ideas of the sovereignty of the people ran counter to centuries of governmental practice. Yet despite the novelty of these ideas, many of them have been put into practice in America. What success they will have one cannot yet say; the experiment goes on. The impact of the idea is still being determined, for the capacity of the common man to rise to such a role is fraught with difficulties. If one is both a common man and a Negro, the difficulties appear to be somewhat greater. But the excitement of participating in a great experiment can be experienced by any who will.

OUR HISTORICAL DOCUMENTS

Despite the uneven course of the development of the democratic way of life in America, and despite times when there has been downright despair regarding the status of the movement, our historic documents attest that, in the long view, there has been steady growth in this direction. Let us make brief reference to some of those documents.

As early as 1620 the Englishmen who had set out to plant a colony in the northern "Parts of Virginia" signed what has now become famous as the Mayflower Compact. Among other things they stated that they

Do by these Presents, solemnly and mutually in the Presence of God and one another, covenant and combine ourselves together into a civil Body Politick, for our better Ordering and Preservation, and furtherance of the Ends aforesaid. . . .

This is a clear expression of the need to work together for the common good. Despite the conviction these people had that they must leave their own country and go to a new land where they could worship God according to their own conscience, they recognized that there must also be group action for the common good. This concern for the common good became one of the values of the democratic way.

More than a hundred and fifty years later, in 1776, when the Colonists felt it necessary to explain to the world their resistance to the British Crown, the Declaration of Independence was enunciated. In that document, well known to most of us, is language relevant to our purpose here:

We hold these truths to be self evident, that all men are created equal, that they are endowed by their Creator with certain unalienable Rights, that among these are Life, Liberty, and the pursuit of Happiness. That to secure these rights, Governments are instituted among Men, deriving their just powers from the consent of the governed. That, whenever any Form of Government becomes destructive of these ends, it is the Right of the People to alter or abolish it, . . .

Let us look at two of the ideas in the above excerpt. "That all men are created equal" is a powerful concept. Men, to be sure, are not equal, physically or intellectually. But before God and the law our founders contended that they are equal. With all of our fumbling regarding civil rights, this aspect of the democratic faith has persisted—persisted until the franchise was widened, until the Emancipation Proclamation was issued, until the school desegregation decision of the United States Supreme Court was handed down in 1954, and until the voting law of 1965 was passed. While general acceptance of the idea in practice has been distressingly slow, the idea itself has conquered the armies of kings and dictators and continues to be more than a match for bigotry and sophistry.

Another concept from the Declaration of Independence is that government should serve the people who create it. And when it no longer serves the purposes which the people intended in creating it, it is to be altered or abolished. Here is legal approval for revolution. Here also is the enunciation of the idea that man is of prime importance and his institutions secondary. Man's institutions, being instrumental, are to be shaped to his needs and not his needs to the institutions, as has been attempted in totalitarian regimes.

As the various states debated the federal Constitution from 1787 to 1790, it became clear that a bill of rights would have to be appended. Thus, the first ten amendments to our Constitution became effective as of 1791. The first amendment includes these significant words:

Congress shall make no law respecting the establishment of religion, or prohibiting the free exercise thereof; or abridging the freedom of speech or of the press; or the right of the people peaceably to assemble . . .

A reading of the McCollum,[2] Zorach,[3] and Schempp[4] cases will convince one that the injunction on religion is still a very live issue. And in hundreds of instances, our courts have affirmed freedom of speech, of press, and of assembly. These freedoms, despite their abridgment at times, have become part of the democratic doctrine.

Following the Civil War more specific language was necessary to insure the application of some of these freedoms to the Negroes. Thus, in 1868, the fourteenth amendment to the Constitution, part of which reads as follows, became effective:

No State shall make or enforce any law which shall abridge the privileges or immunities of citizens of the United States, . . .

[2] *McCollum v. Board of Education,* 333 U.S. 203.
[3] *Zorach v. Clauson,* 343 U.S. 306.
[4] *School District of Abington Township v. Schempp,* 374 U.S. 203.

These words definitely strengthened the hand of the federal government in protecting the rights of minorities from what had been discriminatory legislation in some of the states. More important, our national values were now to be policed by our *national* government.

In considering the extension of voting privileges, it seems rather shocking that it was not until 1920, with the addition of the nineteenth amendment to the Constitution, that women in all states of our nation were granted the franchise. Tardy as such action now seems, the event is further evidence that early pronouncements on the democratic way of life must receive later implementation.

Space does not permit us to continue this survey of our historical documents. We would, however, like to make reference to the now famous Brown case of 1954.[5] After suggesting the central place of public education in a nation such as ours, the U.S. Supreme Court said:

We conclude that in the field of public education the doctrine of "separate but equal" has no place. Separate educational facilities are inherently unequal. Therefore, we hold that the plaintiffs and others similarly situated for whom the actions have been brought are, by reason of the segregation complained of, deprived of the equal protection of the laws guaranteed by the Fourteenth Amendment. . . .

This decision by the Court and subsequent action again appear to represent movement toward full realization of democratic values.

One can quarrel with the above presentation. One could say our words as Americans are better than our deeds. They are. But we keep at it, and our deeds seem to improve. One could say that ours is essentially political democracy, and that our social democracy has not kept pace with it. Again, one might be right, but we submit that political democracy is essential if social democracy is to be achieved. Or one could say the right to vote assumes that accurate information is available to the voter, a condition which many now attempt to subvert. To be sure, this is one of our difficulties, but this very condition constitutes part of the challenge with which we are faced. In other words, what has been done and what remains to be done constitute two parts of the great experiment.

OPERATIONAL AGREEMENTS

Although our culture, as we shall show later, is far from showing unanimity on many value questions, we do seem to have reached certain operational agreements. Excerpts from *Goals for Americans,* as formulated by the President's Commission on National Goals, follow:

[5] *Brown et al. v. Board of Education of Topeka,* 347 U.S. 483.

1. THE INDIVIDUAL

The status of the individual must remain our primary concern. All our institutions—political, social, and economic—must further enhance the dignity of the citizen, promote the maximum development of his capabilities, stimulate their responsible exercise, and widen the range and effectiveness of opportunities for individual choice. . . .

2. EQUALITY

Vestiges of religious prejudice, handicaps to women, and, most important, discrimination on the basis of race must be recognized as morally wrong, economically wasteful, and in many respects dangerous. In this decade we must sharply lower these last stubborn barriers. . . .

3. THE DEMOCRATIC PROCESS

The degree of effective liberty available to its people should be the ultimate test for any nation. Democracy is the only means so far devised by which a nation can meet this test. To preserve and perfect the democratic process in the United States is therefore a primary goal in this as in every decade. . . .

4. EDUCATION

The development of the individual and the nation demands that education at every level and in every discipline be strengthened and its effectiveness enhanced. New teaching techniques must continue to be developed. The increase in population and the growing complexity of the world add urgency. Greater resources—private, corporate, municipal, state, and federal—must be mobilized. A higher proportion of the gross national product must be devoted to educational purposes. This is at once an investment in the individual, in the democratic process, in the growth of the economy, and in the stature of the United States.[6]

It seems possible to arrive at the value positions noted above from different philosophical orientations. For that reason we are stressing here our *operational* agreements rather than our philosophical differences. This we must do, in any culture as diversified as that in America, if there is to be a common ground for action.

In light of such a position, we wish to set forth a set of values which we think gives meaning to what we have been calling a democratic way of life. First, there is implied a *belief in people*. This, as we have already indicated, is much harder to live than to say. Nevertheless, our history and our action, even though the latter has at times been tardy, suggest that most of us place people above institutions. For most of us this means all people, without regard to race, color, religion, economic circumstance, or national background. In particular, we believe that educational opportunity should not be denied any person.

A second value characteristic of the democratic way of life is a belief in *co-operation for the common good*. True, some cry out against the

---

[6] Report of the President's Commission on National Goals, *Goals for Americans* (Englewood Cliffs, N.J.: Prentice-Hall, Inc., 1960), pp. 3–6.

welfare state, but when the nation has been threatened, even as early as the Mayflower Compact, we have been willing to join together, to submerge individual desires when necessary, to foster the welfare of the group. This tendency received special impetus during the era of the New Deal, but it is noteworthy that Republican administrations have repealed little of the New Deal legislation. Actually, both political parties act this way because we as people adhere to this principle.

Three, our nation believes in *freedom of the press, of speech, and of religious expression.* This was the substance of the first amendment to our federal Constitution. Again, we have abridgments and abuses of these rights, but in the end our courts and the public stand up for these freedoms. To be sure, we have had to learn that freedom is a relative matter and that it must be accompanied by responsibility. The relative nature of freedom does not mean that any one of us is free to pursue his own interests to the detriment of the group. This balance between personal freedom and the social good is the thing we are working to achieve.

Finally, our people accept *the method of intelligence* as an approach to problem-solving. In this process, some of us may exhibit a blind faith in scientism[7] or accept the intelligence of others as a substitute for utilizing our own intellectual abilities. Yet there seems to be a conviction on the part of most Americans that we can, by giving thought, solve the many problems with which we are faced. Moreover, we have a conviction that this ability to think is not the possession of just the few, but the heritage of the many.

CHALLENGES TO THE DEMOCRATIC WAY

There are both challenges *to* and challenges *of* the democratic way of life. Let us deal with the first of these. Briefly, the challenges to the democratic way might be categorized as outside and inside challenges. The chief outside challenge, as is now clear to most of us, is world communism. Communism in its Russian or Chinese expression is a far cry from what Karl Marx, its founder, visualized. To be sure, Marx advocated a militant movement, but the ends he sought seem to many to be in keeping with the Hebraic-Christian ethic to which we ourselves subscribe. He wanted an abundant life for the individual, the elimination of the exploitation of man, and the establishment of a world-wide regime of peace and brotherhood.

It has now become clear that communism in practice exalts the state above the individual, that the ruling hierarchy is straining to perpetuate autocracy, and that any challenge to the system will be quelled by force.

[7] See William H. Whyte, Jr., *The Organization Man* (New York: Simon and Schuster, 1956), Chapter 3.

It may have taken such events as the Hungarian rebellion of 1956 to convince many people, but most of us now see world communism clearly and we do not like what we see. How to keep communism from spreading is, then, a genuine challenge from without.

There is also a challenge to democracy from within. In spite of our optimism about what we believe to be long-term gains in the achievement of the democratic way, there are definite schizophrenic symptoms in our culture. Brameld has listed them as follows:

Self-interest versus social-interest.

Inequality versus equality.

Planlessness versus planning.

Nationalism versus internationalism.

Absolutism versus experimentalism.

Man-against-himself versus man-for-himself.[8]

An examination of each of these issues will convince one that at both the verbal and the operational levels of American life there are adherents of each of the contrasting approaches. Unfortunately, the perpetuation of these dichotomies obscures the point that, in many cases, it is not an either-or proposition. There may be, for instance, an enlightened self-interest that is consistent with social interest.

Seeman has also dealt with our cultural conflicts.[9] We have summarized his descriptions of these conflicts as follows:

1. The status dimension—conflict between success ideology and equality ideology.

2. The authority dimension—conflict between values of dependence and independence.

3. The institutional dimension—choice of universalist as against particular criterion for social action.

4. The means-ends dimension—conflict of getting the job done against emphasis on the process.

While these two analyses of our cultural conflicts do not correspond entirely, they have many points in common. An examination of them should make it quite clear that our society is a dynamic one, that its direction may

[8] Theodore Brameld, *Philosophies of Education in Cultural Perspective* (New York: Dryden Press, 1955), pp. 53–62.

[9] Melvin Seeman, "Role Conflict and Ambivalence in Leadership," *American Sociological Review,* 18 (August 1953), 373–80.

not always be clear, and that in the arena of ideas a good many battles are still ahead of us. This struggle is the inside challenge to the democratic way.

CHALLENGE OF THE DEMOCRATIC WAY

There is also the challenge *of* the democratic way of life. Let us examine briefly a few aspects of this part of the problem. The first of these is perhaps the challenge of accurate information. If the average citizen is to participate in his economic, social, or political destiny, he must be informed. This has always been a difficult expectation. In our early history it was a question of teaching people to read and to understand, and then of making written documents widely available.

In recent decades the process has been complicated by the tremendous development of the mass media, notably radio and television, and by the great competition for the mind of man that has evolved. As a matter of fact, the money spent annually on advertising in this country approximates that spent for the operation of all the schools and colleges in the nation. In advertising, of course, the motive is not primarily to inform but rather to sell.

The appeal of advertising to the conscious man seems serious enough, but recently, with the rise of motivation research (M-R), there is also planned, large-scale appeal to man's subconscious.[10] The application of M-R to the selling of automobiles may seem somewhat amusing, but when the same techniques are applied to presidential elections, as they were in recent campaigns, one can become cynical about the "information" made available to the average elector.

A second challenge *of* the democratic way is that of concern about public affairs. A number of studies suggest that in most communities, about 50 percent of the people are uninformed and apathetic about public questions.[11] This condition represents two potential dangers. There is first the possibility that the leadership group or power structure of a community will go unchecked. Such a course of action may mean that the leaders cease in time to represent the values and programs of their constituents. The second danger inherent in apathy is found in the possibility that citizens with no facts at hand may become prey to those who seek personal advantage and who do not hesitate to use emotional and biased approaches.

[10] See Vance Packard, *The Hidden Persuaders* (New York: David McKay Company, 1957).

[11] See Leo A. Haak, "The General Public and the Public Schools," *The Administrator's Notebook*, 4 (April 1956), 1–4.

In both of these dangers the challenge of how to create concern in people is clearly exemplified.

Along with the challenges of providing information and of creating concern, there is the challenge of action. How Americans exercise their voting privileges may serve to illustrate our point. In recent presidential elections only about two-thirds of the persons of voting age in the nation cast their ballots. In Wyoming and a few other states, over 80 percent of the potential voters cast their ballots, while in Mississippi less than 30 percent voted. This problem, particularly in the Southern states, is not merely a question of apathy, but also represents the results of a social tradition in action. One wonders why even in seemingly progressive states like California and New York only two of every three persons of voting age actually vote. If voting is indicative of other action on the part of citizens concerning the common good, and we fear it is, there is little wonder that organized efforts to thwart projects designed to foster the general welfare do succeed.

THE EDUCATIVE PROCESS

The second challenge to educational administration is the educative process. We contend, moreover, that without an educative process of the kind we shall describe, the democratic way of life is an impossibility. In other words, if the great experiment to which we have alluded is to succeed, a genuine opportunity for learning must be available to all.

MEANING OF THE EDUCATIVE PROCESS

The educative process of which we speak is much broader than schooling. Actually, much of what we have learned was not acquired in school. Our schooling seems to have relatively little to do, perhaps unfortunately, with how we vote, how we spend our leisure, and the ways by which many of us make our living. Without in any sense discrediting the school, it sharpens our discussion to recognize that education and schooling are not synonymous.

Upon reflection one soon decides that the total culture is involved in teaching and learning. Perhaps we can see this point more easily in cultures other than our own, described in the writings of the anthropologists.[12]

[12] For example, see Margaret Mead, *Coming of Age in Samoa* (New York: W. Morrow & Company, 1928), and Ruth Benedict, *Patterns of Culture* (Boston: Houghton Mifflin, 1934).

For instance, Benedict speaks of the Zuñi Indians as a ceremonious people. She says that grown men spent most of their waking hours in ceremonial observance, for which a staggering amount of word-perfect ritual had to be memorized.

The teaching-learning potential of our own culture has been dealt with in dramatic terms by Bloom.[13] After a comprehensive synthesis of the research in human development, he concludes that, with the exception of school achievement, the most rapid period of development is in the first five years of life. Thus, physical growth, intelligence, language development, and other characteristics are more than 50 percent determined by the home and its surrounding culture by the time the child enters the school.

In this educative process, or cultural adaptation, what are the important steps? As we see it, they are three in number: (1) acquiring of a feeling of being at home in one's culture, (2) learning about one's culture, and (3) contributing to one's culture. Let us look at each of these.

The first step of coming to feel at home in one's culture appears to be largely emotional in character. The affection extended to the new baby by the parents and other members of the family are part of it. The trial and error of age-mates as they learn to play together, whether in a nursery school or on the street, represent an important potential in the process. The great need for peer approval found in most adolescents and the need which all of us have for recognition on the part of other adults are also involved. Somehow we must feel that we belong.

But we must feel that we belong to the larger culture, not merely to some minority group within it. This point has particular relevance today for those who grow up in the slums of our central cities. The feelings of hopelessness and alienation of youth in slum neighborhoods has been depicted by Conant.[14] He notes that social dynamite is building up in our large cities in the form of unemployed out-of-school youth, particularly in the Negro slums.

But the educative process cannot stop with belonging; there is also the necessity for understanding. This places great demands upon all of us. How can we learn about the social and physical world in which we live? Much can be gained from observation, but we soon find a need for trained observation, and observation, without reference to some conceptual scheme, may be relatively pointless. Regardless of the field of study, we soon learn that we need to consider the observations, the feelings, and the reflections of others. This process would seem to constitute the beginning of scholarship, whether in or out of an organized school.

[13] Benjamin S. Bloom, *Stability and Change in Human Characteristics* (New York: John Wiley & Sons, Inc., 1964).

[14] James B. Conant, *Slums and Suburbs* (New York: McGraw-Hill Book Co., 1961).

But there is still another aspect of the educative process. Feeling at home in and knowing about one's culture ought to lead one to contribute to that culture. Contributions, to be sure, will vary greatly in nature and in quality; and ways of improving the culture will be apparent only to those who have the capacity to examine critically the cultural practices now extant.

The challenge of the educative process to equip people to reflect critically about the conditions of life around them and to project possible improvements is, we believe, the aspect of the educative process most important to the survival of the democratic idea. Unfortunately, those who attempt to examine our way of life critically, in an attempt to make improvements, are often misunderstood and sometimes even called subversive. Many people fail to recognize the value and importance of this critical examination, and ignorantly use words of abuse to describe people who, through their criticisms, are contributing toward the improvement of our way of life.

MANY INSTITUTIONS CONTRIBUTE

Many institutions make contributions to the educative process. The home, despite the suggestion of some that it has reached a point of declining influence, still seems to be the most important educative agency we have. Our basic personality characteristics, including such simple matters as friendliness or distrust, are in large part a product of the home. Our attitudes toward religion, government, sex, and learning itself reflect the home environment. To be sure, the home also tends to reflect the biases of the culture of which it is a part. In other words, a middle-class home has different standards with respect to cleanliness and schooling, for instance, than a lower-class home has. The home, as any social worker or psychiatrist can testify, is a significant influence in whatever a person learns.

For most people the church, too, is an important agency in the educative process. That segment of our population that affiliates with a church and participates in church activities is subject to an educative influence of considerable magnitude. For instance, the attitudes of these people toward marriage, toward childbearing, toward authority, and toward social behavior are greatly influenced by the church. For those people who belong to no church, the influence of the church may be less direct, but it is nonetheless significant. The nonchurchgoer as well as the churchgoer is affected by the Hebraic-Christian tradition as it has found expression in our ethics and in our law.

Also important is the street corner or the play group of one's peers. Beginning at about age eight or ten and continuing through adolescence, most young people feel great need for acceptance by their peers. Often it takes expression in the clothes that are worn. If cashmere sweaters are the thing, then cashmere sweaters there must be. Woe to any parent who has the temerity to suggest that there is a satisfactory substitute. Many times status with one's fellows is acquired by doing those things which the gang has decided to do. Drag-racing with souped-up cars, for instance, in some communities among certain youngsters has become a prestige activity. Anyone not joining in the activity is labeled "chicken." Clearly, then, these peer groups have great influence with young people and are thus potent educative influences.

Nor should we stop with young people. Riesman has made the point that our culture is becoming more and more other-directed.[15] In other words, the sanctions one feels, which influence one's behavior, have their origins in the group to which one belongs rather than in one's upbringing as reflected in one's conscience. Whyte makes a similar point when he speaks of the organization man.[16] For all of us, the group or groups with which we affiliate, particularly in our work, seem to be decisive forces in determining our family life, our goals for educating our children, our dress, our leisure, and our values in general.

All of this has caused Hart to point out that "education goes on whether school keeps or not." [17] Having made this point, however, we should not overlook the fact that the school has a unique role in the educative process, as we shall soon see. May we conclude this section by emphasizing the point that an educative process that is comprehensive, tolerant, and permissive is essential to the democratic way of life. This means that the educative role of many institutions in our society should be recognized. It means, too, that each institution should exercise its role with some recognition that other influences and agencies are and must be at work in our kind of society. Finally, it means that class barriers should be sufficiently flexible so that one's place and position in society can be altered through the educative process.

THE PUBLIC SCHOOL

The third challenge to educational administration is found in the public school itself. Despite the breadth of the educative process, as suggested

[15] David Riesman et al., The Lonely Crowd (New Haven: Yale University Press, 1950).

[16] William H. Whyte, Jr., op. cit.

[17] Joseph K. Hart, Education in the Humane Community (New York: Harper & Brothers, 1951), p. 4.

above, we hold that the public school has a unique, indeed an indispensable, part to play in that process. Let us examine such an idea.

CHARACTERISTICS

Most of the children and youth in this country attend public schools. Indeed, recent reports indicate that 85 percent of the elementary school pupils and 89 percent of the high school pupils of the nation attend such schools.[18] Without in any sense deprecating the role of the private school in American education, it seems clear that a great part of the task of providing formal schooling is placed squarely upon the public school.

The significance of the percentage of total school enrollment found in the public school is not entirely a matter of numbers. The pupil populations of the public schools tend, by and large, to be more heterogeneous than the pupil populations of the private schools. Although this circumstance has its problems, it is just here that the public schools find one of their real opportunities, for the public school becomes a prototype of our society itself. The diversity of our nation socially, economically, politically, religiously, racially, and academically is well reflected in the public school.

We do not wish to overdo this matter. We are well aware of the fact that many individual public schools, particularly in urban and suburban areas, have pupil populations with relatively less diversity than suggested above. Indeed, some suburban communities have segregated exclusive schools and central cities tend to have segregated slum schools. Programs of slum clearance, urban redevelopment, and enlargement of small school districts may alleviate segregation of both social class and race. It now seems clear, however, that there must be deliberate social planning of both housing and school attendance areas if most youngsters in the public schools are going to have the opportunity to find out how the other half lives.

In this diversity, once common and now harder to attain, the public school pupil has an opportunity to acquire a sense of realism as to what people are like; he can note the variety of contributions that its various members make to the group; and he can learn much about relating himself to many kinds of people. These skills are essential in our kind of culture.

The public school has still another opportunity. More than any other nonschool community agency, and possibly more than most private schools, the public school can be the most impartial institution in our culture. Business, labor, and farm organizations have great difficulty in viewing all sides of a controversial issue, particularly if the issue affects them in any

[18] *Statistical Abstract of the United States, 1964* (Washington, D.C.: U.S. Government Printing Office, 1964).

way. Most churches must approach problems within a particular framework. Thus, useful as these organizations are for some purposes, they alone cannot nurture adequately the person with an inquiring mind who wishes to weigh the evidence on all sides of a tough problem and come to his own decision.

We recognize that some teachers in the public schools are not adequately prepared to guide objective inquiry, but we still maintain that the opportunity for objective inquiry is present in the public school and that it is being admirably exploited in some instances. Moreover, we have found that thoughtful members of special interest groups such as business, labor, and agriculture are expecting the public school to exercise its role of impartiality.

THE SCHOOL'S UNIQUE ROLE

With this brief consideration of what the public school is like, actually and potentially, we shall next turn to the unique role of the public school. This is a difficult task, for over the years public schools have gradually taken on more and more functions, usually as a result of public demand. Moral education on one hand, and driver training on the other, are two cases in point. Sometimes it seems that relatively little examination of the appropriateness of the new functions being placed in the public school has been made either by the public or by the school people. Perhaps, in some cases, other agencies in society are better equipped to meet these new demands than is the school. We believe that the transfer of certain child-rearing functions from the home to the school is a case in point.

Another reason it is difficult to delimit the public school's role is the concomitant character of learning. As a child learns to read and write he is also learning many other things. He may be learning to like or dislike school. He may be learning to like or dislike teachers. He may find in his acquiring of skill with words that the doors to ideas have been unlocked, or he may find reading a wearisome task, never to be pursued except under duress. We cannot ignore or be unconcerned about these concomitants.

Despite the difficulties inherent in depicting the unique role of the school, we shall attempt such a task. Our concern is that the public school recognize some sort of priority in what it does, so that those things which are essential to the democratic way of life and to the educative process shall not be left undone. We are not offering objection to the fact that other functions can and in many cases should be performed. We do hope, however, that as the demands placed upon the public school increase, the financial resources to meet such demands will be proportionately increased.

The first task we would place upon the public school is teaching for literacy. To read, to write, and to figure are old, old expectations of what the school is to do. We recognize that with the advent of mass media reading has come to seem relatively unimportant to some people. Moreover, literacy alone may simply make people prey to those who control what is to be read. However, this is an unlikely result of literacy in a free country, and it is clear that all citizens of a nation such as ours need skills in reading, writing, and numbers.

The fact that literacy is a matter of acquiring certain skills—skills that are helpful in developing certain understandings and appreciations—might cause some to suggest that those understandings and appreciations were the *sine qua non* of education, and that the skills were only instrumental to their achievement. Much as we recognize the logic of this position, we still think there are practical reasons for the public school to consider its first indispensable task that of teaching for literacy.

If the public school does not do the job of teaching for literacy, it will not be done. For most people the private school cannot do it. Relatively few parents are equipped to do it. Other agencies in society are even less able to step into such a role. Literacy on the part of most citizens is indispensable to our way of life, and the public school is indispensable to providing this literacy.

The teaching of critical thinking is, we think, the second unique task of the public school. This is really the purpose that the founders of our public schools had in mind when they spoke of the need of intelligence on the part of all people. Note a part of what Caleb Mills had to say to the legislature of Indiana in 1846:

The true glory of a people consists in the intelligence and virtue of its individual members, and no more important duty can devolve upon its representatives in their legislative capacity than the devising and perfecting of a wise, liberal, and efficient system of popular education. . . . It is, indeed, a favorable circumstance that appropriate and efficient action on this subject will awaken no sectional jealousies, alarm no religious prejudices, subserve the interests of no political party. It is emphatically a topic which, ably discussed and wisely disposed of, will benefit every part of the State, improve every class in the community, give permanence to our civil and religious institutions, increase the social and literary capital of our citizens, and add materially to the real and substantial happiness of everyone. Such a system of improvement ought surely to require no logrolling to secure its adoption by the representatives of an intelligent people, nor will the burden its operation may occasion be reluctantly borne by a community that scorns the repudiation of a debt incurred for the construction of railroads and canals.[19]

Mills and others may not have appreciated fully what it takes to get people to behave intelligently, but there was no question in their minds

[19] Quoted in Ellwood P. Cubberley, *Readings in Public Education in the United States* (Boston: Houghton Mifflin, 1934), 192.

about the need for such behavior. Nor did those early champions of the public school foresee the age of propaganda, the rise of mass media, and the intensity of the struggle for the mind of man. Yet the objective they had for public education still stands, even though its achievement has been beset with new difficulties.

What do we mean by critical thinking? We mean simply the ability to define a problem, to seek the relevant facts having to do with it, to weigh the evidence, and to make decisions based upon the evidence. In short, we are talking of problem-solving or the scientific method. Literacy, as we have discussed it above, is a necessary tool to most problem-solving, but literacy alone is not enough. Also necessary are the ability to suspend judgment until the evidence is in, and the ability to analyze the evidence so as to detect when personal bias or privileged position has obscured, slanted, or selected the facts, There is, finally, the courage to accept the position supported by the evidence even in face of preconceived notions.

This is a big order. The capacity of people to learn critical thinking, even with the best of tutelage, varies just as it does with other kinds of learning. The public school must provide opportunity and encouragement for such learning. We have already indicated that the public school can be the most objective institution in our society. Such objectivity must be exploited by teachers if children are to learn critical thinking.

Perhaps Thelen has given us a cue as to how critical thinking is to be fostered when he says:

. . . inquiry involves firsthand activity in real situations. In most cases, the inquiring student is aided by working close to some adult with whom he can identify—some adult he would like to be like, perhaps, but at the least an adult he can easily trust. This adult must be without ulterior motives in dealing with the students. He has a job to do; he helps define the role of the student on the job, and the demands the student has to meet come either from the nature of the task or from the nature of the social conditions obviously required to get the work done. In other words, I want the student to transact his business directly with the work and the work environment; I want him to discover that there are realities outside of his own personal desires or those of "authorities," for it is only within such a stable framework of action that his own behavior can be assessed unequivocally by himself. It is only thus that he can discover and learn to depend on his abilities and that he can face up to weaknesses, because they cannot be blamed on other persons.[20]

The White House Conference on Education in 1956 highlighted the third unique task we shall suggest for the public school, the facilitation of social mobility. A part of the Report reads:

[20] Herbert A. Thelen, *Education and the Human Quest* (New York: Harper & Brothers, 1960), p. 107.

The schools have become a major tool for creating a Nation without rigid class barriers. *It is primarily the schools which allow no man's failure to prevent the success of his son.*[21]

To be sure, other institutions in our society contribute to social mobility. For some the ladder is supplied by business, for others by the military, and for others by the church. But the schools seem to be the chief agency in society that can and should accept as one of its prime tasks the providing of opportunity for the upward (or downward) mobility of its students. Again, the relative inclusiveness of public school enrollments is a pertinent matter. For most of our people the public school can discover and encourage ability. When the school accepts this as one of its major functions, those who live "across the tracks" have an opportunity to rise in the world.

To suggest that the school should contribute to social mobility opens up a larger question. While we believe that the primary purpose of the school is educative in nature, the school is also an instrument of social policy. Havighurst[22] maintained that the program of the school was the most powerful factor contributing to the decision of middle-income people to live in the central city or the suburbs, or to live in one section of the city or another. In a very real sense one can say that as go the schools so goes the city. Boards of education and school workers fail, at times, to recognize the social import of their decisions; indeed, they occasionally rebel at the social role they are required to play. We see no alternative. Education has become a powerful social factor and those who are charged with its governance cannot escape their social role.

This whole matter of the need for social mobility and the part the public school might play in such a process has taken on new urgency in our present manpower shortage. In practically every skilled and professional occupation the shortage of workers is serious. Overall, the only source of supply to meet this deficit is to be found in the unskilled workers and the children of unskilled workers. If these children are to enter new jobs and acquire new social status, they must have more schooling. For most people the extent of upward mobility in a single generation is probably limited, but the need for such mobility and the role of the school in the process should be clear.

To summarize, if the public school is to fulfill its unique role in the educative process necessary to our way of life, it must teach literacy, stimulate critical thinking, and provide opportunity for those with ability to rise

---

[21] The Committee for the White House Conference on Education, *A Report to the President* (Washington: U.S. Government Printing Office, 1956), p. 9. (Italics in original.)

[22] Robert J. Havighurst, *The Public Schools of Chicago* (Chicago: Board of Education, 1964), p. 28.

occupationally and socially. We need to recognize that as the school performs these functions it also serves as a powerful instrument of social
policy.

ADMINISTRATIVE LEADERSHIP

The fourth challenge that we see, perhaps the pivotal one as far as this
book is concerned, is the challenge confronting administrative leaders in the
public schools. Or, to put it differently, an indispensable condition necessary
for the public school to perform adequately its unique role is the type of
administrative leadership we shall now describe. When we speak of administrative leaders, we refer to appointed or official leaders in the school system,
such as principals, supervisors, directors, and superintendents. It is the
challenge confronting them as official or status leaders with which we are
concerned.

We do not wish to minimize the roles played by classroom teachers as
the public schools attempt to meet their obligations. Teaching and learning go on only through the teachers. At the same time, teachers and researchers alike have repeatedly indicated that a good part of what any
school does is dependent upon the administrative leadership given to that
school. The principal, for instance, has a key role in setting the tone,
establishing the conditions, and providing stimulation for the kind of living
and learning in his school. It is the challenge inherent in such a role that
we wish to discuss here.

As suggested in Chapter 7, each administrator finds himself related to
certain major reference groups. In each of these relationships there is a
challenge to administrative leadership. We shall, therefore, examine the
nature of that challenge with respect to the community, the board of
education, the teaching staff, and the pupils.

THE COMMUNITY CHALLENGE

Since we are speaking of administration in the public schools, obviously
the public or the community is a major reference group with which
any school administrator must work. Most people see this clearly as it applies to the superintendent of schools. For the school principal, however,
such recognition is not as general. As a matter of fact, some of the studies
suggest that principals have almost no relationships with the citizens of
their respective attendance areas or school communities.[23] This condition

[23] For example see Odean L. Hess, "Critical Areas of Administrative Behavior of
Elementary School Principals" (unpublished doctoral dissertation, The Ohio State
University, 1955).

seems most undesirable to us. We think every superintendent and every principal in the public schools must deal extensively with the public. While supervisors and directors may deal somewhat less with the public, we are convinced that they, too, must be involved in some public relationships.

The public, as we indicated in Chapter 7, is not monolithic in nature. Actually, there are many publics. Shipton proposed the idea that the school administrator stands alone among other administrators in the great number of publics to whom he feels responsible.[24] Moreover, let us point out that these publics are more than local in nature. Often decisions affecting local school districts are made at county, state, and national levels. This very condition suggests one aspect of the challenge. It is necessary that the administrator ascertain for his school or school district who these publics are and how they believe and act with respect to school matters.

Thus it is necessary that communication with the many publics of a school community be a two-way process. The old business of selling, or telling, or interpreting the schools just will not suffice. Just as the problems, the achievements, and the shortcomings of the public schools must be explained, the feelings, the beliefs, and the aspirations of the people who make up the various publics must also be ascertained. There is, then, the need for listening as well as telling; the need for assessment as well as projection.

But the real challenge to the administrative leader in dealing with the many publics of the school community comes in what he does with the feelings, beliefs, and aspirations of the people. Ordinarily, he cannot accept these data alone as providing the basis for charting courses of action, any more than he can impose his own professional values on a community without consideration of the factors existing in the particular situation. In other words, the administrator finds out what people think, what they value, and what they want in order to determine where to begin or to determine what are the reasonable limits beyond which action cannot go.

The excitement comes in finding and helping arrange ways by which people get new ideas, gradually come to accept new values, and come to have more realistic expectations of the public school. Or it may be that in the diversity of ideas and aspirations among the publics of a school community, ways can be found by which a greater degree of agreement can be reached so that the course of school operation can go forward at a higher level.

We are not suggesting that the administrator can be all-wise in this situation, nor that his task is simply one of ingenious manipulation. Actually, the administrator may be no wiser than other leaders in his school com-

[24] James M. Shipton, "Who Are the Critics of the Public Schools?" Harvard Graduate School of Education, Harvard University Staff Research Memorandum, No. 3 (September 1954).

munity. He would do well to relate himself to people in such a way that he might learn from them as well as influence them. We do suggest, however, that the administrator needs professional knowledge, and values that include a conviction that the democratic way of life is important and that the public school has a significant role to play in the realization of that way of life. With that as his prime motivation, he can keep a focus without offending by insisting upon patterned behavior.

In the end the community must take action for public education. This may involve the selection of wise school board members, the passing of bond issues, and the approval of operating levies. Important and necessary as these separate acts are, the continuous voice of the community as it gives expression to what schools ought to be, and as it reacts both favorably and unfavorably to what schools are, may be even more indicative as to how well the community challenge is being met.

THE BOARD CHALLENGE

Public schools in America are controlled through legally constituted boards of education. These boards have been given broad grants of power by the respective state legislatures. In most states the board members are publicly elected to their offices, and while they are assumed to be representative of the people of the school district, the courts have actually declared them to be state officers.

School board members are usually selected from the professional and managerial groups of society, though in rural areas they are often farm owners. This fact has caused some to conclude that boards would be strong defenders of the status quo. Studies of board performance indicate that that interpretation is too simple an explanation and in many cases not warranted. Actually, most board members are seriously concerned with their responsibility and welcome professional help in interpreting and implementing this responsibility.

Clearly, the board of education is the major reference group with which the administrator must deal. In most school districts the superintendent of schools, as the chief school administrator, will be most directly concerned with the board of education. On occasions, however, superintendents will ordinarily involve other administrators in the board relationship, and board opinions, board action, and board policies are always significant to administrators.

The superintendent of schools has two major roles to play if he is to meet the challenge of working with the board of education. First, he is the chief executive of the board. This may involve helping a board decide what its legislative and judicial functions are, and what the executive functions of the superintendent are. Even after such definition there may be the continuing necessity of clarifying the board-superintendent relationship. This clarification may be even more necessary as new members come on the board.

Assuming that reasonable agreement concerning the board-superintendent relationship can be reached, the superintendent still has the challenge of the executive function. Can he and his staff develop an adequate instructional program? Can he and his staff secure competent personnel? Can he and his staff develop a satisfactory building program? Can he and his staff project accurately the financial needs of the district? Can he and his staff expend efficiently the available funds, and account accurately for them? These represent some of the major expectations most boards of education hold for their superintendents.

In addition to being the chief executive officer of the board of education, the superintendent has a second role as chief educational adviser to the board. In this role the superintendent helps the board form basic policy for school district operation. It is in this role that he brings professional knowledge to board deliberation, and that he broadens the understanding of board members so that they function with greater intelligence as the chief policy-makers for a school district. Allison,[25] as noted earlier, found that most board members not only expect their superintendents to implement board decisions, they also rely heavily on them to help in establishing policy.

For the superintendent to serve as chief educational adviser to the board, certain conditions are necessary. As in the case of the community, the superintendent must bring to his task professional understanding and convictions. Moreover, he will find it necessary to work closely with his staff so as to reflect the best possible insights to the board of education at a particular time and place. Meeting these conditions may help the superintendent become, in a very real sense, the teacher of the board of education. In few places is teaching a more critical occupation.

THE STAFF CHALLENGE

Another major reference group for any school administrator is the school staff. We use the word "staff," at this point, to designate all certificated personnel within a school system, including teachers, pupil personnel workers, and administrators. Much of what we shall say about the certificated personnel also applies, of course, to the noncertificated personnel of a school system. The staff represents another challenge to administrative leadership, the nature of which we need to examine.

[25] Howard C. Allison, "Professional and Lay Influences on School Board Decision-Making" (unpublished Ph.D. dissertation, Department of Education, University of Chicago, 1965).

The first challenge is that of building and maintaining a staff that is thoroughly equipped to do the job of the public schools. If the district is a sizable one, there must be a staff for the central office. For any school district there is the problem of building the staff for each school building, whether there is one or a hundred. These circumstances make it clear that building a staff is the obligation of the chief administrator assisted by his entire administrative staff, including each of the building principals.

There are also other aspects to the staff challenge. The manpower shortage, which affects the supply of school personnel as it does personnel in many other areas, makes the building of a staff in many schools and school districts a most difficult task. The appropriate involvement of staff members already in a school or school system in the selection of new staff members is also a part of the challenge being suggested here. For instance, some superintendents have not yet learned how to use their building principals in getting teachers well suited for the positions that are open.

There is also the challenge of evaluating the work of staff members. Ascertaining the competence of teachers or administrators is a very difficult matter. Establishing criteria of competence is essentially a valuing procedure and may vary from district to district. The collection of evidence on teaching or administrative performance is difficult when criteria are clear and practically useless when criteria are nonexistent or confusing. Thus, it is understandable that superintendents and principals are, at times, a little hazy on the matter, and no wonder at all that the problem is even more dimly perceived by the lay mind. Despite these difficulties, there are ways of checking the performance of any prospective teacher and administrator in order to get at least a rough measure of how well he fits the job description. By employing these ways and keeping a record of his batting average, any practicing administrator can increase his power of discrimination regarding personnel selection.

May we emphasize the critical nature of each staff selection! The school system may actually work years with a relatively incompetent teacher in order to help him reach a better level of performance. A better selection in the first place would have saved hundreds of hours of effort on the part of the principal and the supervisors. Or the selection of an inadequate principal may mean that for years the program and atmosphere of an entire building, often with hundreds of youngsters involved, may be seriously handicapped. To secure for each position the most competent available person is a continuing challenge to administrative leadership.

Assuming the administrators of a school system have been able to build a competent staff, there is still the challenge of keeping the staff productive. In too many school systems one can find teachers and even administrators and supervisory personnel who, once vigorous, stimulating, and effective people, have now settled into a dull routine of doing what has to be done but with no zest for the task as it now exists or as it might be altered. The factors contributing to such a situation are undoubtedly complex. They may include low salaries, which force many teachers to take a second job and thus become part-time teachers. They may include a seeming lack of opportunities for promotion, particularly within the teaching ranks. But we suspect that other factors of importance lie within the control of administrators and thus constitute a part of the challenge to their leadership.

Perhaps the crux of this matter has been suggested by some of the recent studies on administrative behavior. Halpin found that staff members preferred their superintendents to be strong both in consideration and in the initiating of structure in group interaction.[26] Research clearly supports the concept that organizations have both a normative and a personal dimension, and that both of these must be taken into account to explain organization behavior.[27] In fact, no proposition in administration has been as well documented as the one that effective administrators perform above the mean in *two* major areas of behavior. The first is consideration or adequate human relations. The second is the initiation of structure or the development of understanding concerning roles and responsibilities of people within an organization.

The evidence suggests clearly that it is not enough for an administrator to be concerned with human relations only. Personal concern on the part of the administrator for each member of his staff is necessary and appropriate. In addition, the administrator must be able to help a staff develop goals and a plan of action, he must be able to help each staff member see where he can make his particular contribution to the total effort, and he must stimulate each staff member to make his contribution the best of which he is capable. Thus, with staff as with the board of education, the administrator is required to become a teacher of high order.

THE PUPIL CHALLENGE

Another major reference group with which administrators must deal is composed of the pupils—the children and youth who are enrolled in school. In a sense all challenges to administrative leadership have their focus here, because the pupils are the immediate consumers of the school program. School–community agreements, school board action, and staff efforts culminate in what happens to youngsters. These more remote and instrumental programs, no matter how pretty they appear on paper, are of no avail unless

[26] Andrew W. Halpin, *The Leadership Behavior of School Superintendents,* 2nd ed. (Chicago: Midwest Administration Center, University of Chicago, 1959).

[27] Jacob W. Getzels, James M. Lipham, and Roald F. Campbell, *Administration as a Social Process: Theory, Research and Practice.* Forthcoming.

they make a difference in the programs of instruction and services to pupils. This is the whole purpose of educational administration, as was suggested in Chapter 3.

Of all administrators and supervisors within a school system, the building principal is nearest to the teaching–learning situation. His influence in that situation is a strategic one. As a matter of fact, what central office people can do to influence instruction must, for the most part, be expressed through the building principal. In better schools the principal, more than any other person, can see that teacher assignments are appropriate, that necessary pupil personnel services are made available, and that extra-class activities are made significant experiences for youngsters.

The principals of most school buildings will wish some direct contact with pupils, but research is tending to suggest that there are appropriate limitations to such activity. Effective principals recognize that their chief work group is the faculty and that most of their influence with pupils will be expressed through the faculty and through the programs of the school.

In working with his staff to build and to implement a school program the principal must recognize three aspects of such a program: the classroom instruction, the pupil personnel services, and the extra-class activities. There is always the question of how each of these parts should fit into the total offering. Continually, there is the need to keep classroom instruction stimulating and challenging. Often with the extra-class activities, particularly at the secondary level, there is the problem of keeping them educative and not exploitative or simply commercial. With respect to pupil services, there is the need of providing those services, whether in health, guidance, or some other area, which will contribute to the total development of each youngster or permit his learning to go on more effectively. Trying to provide the best possible program for each pupil enrolled is the tremendous challenge to public education. As the principal deals with instruction, with services, and with extra-class activities, he, like other school workers, needs to be aware of the social role the school is playing.

A FINAL WORD

We began this chapter by presenting challenges to educational administration. We said that our first challenge, the democratic way of life, is dependent upon an educative process open to all, in which the contributions of many agencies are recognized. While we noted that the educative process is much broader than that provided by the public schools, we maintained that the public schools of this nation perform a role that is an indispensable part of that process. Finally, we took the position that the public schools cannot perform adequately except as administrative leaders in those schools give appropriate direction to the enterprise.

Now let us reverse the process. If the administrative leaders of the public schools of this nation can visualize the crucial place of the public schools, and if they can bring adequate understanding and skill to their task, the public schools can contribute substantially to the development of the people's capacity to do critical thinking. People with such capacity can, and we think will, take steps to preserve that which should be preserved in our culture and to change that which needs to be improved. These people will function through numerous community agencies, and thus the programs of those agencies will reinforce and complement the efforts of the public schools. This effort will perpetuate and extend the democratic way of life. To the educational administrator is given the privilege of participating significantly in this whole endeavor.

Index

A

R

S